AF478511

RAYNAL PELLICER

PHOTOBOOTH

THE ART OF THE AUTOMATIC PORTRAIT

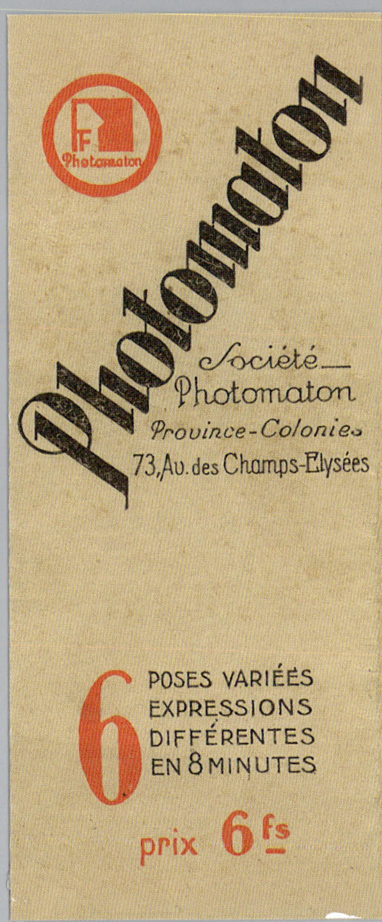

Translated from the French
by Antony Shugaar

Abrams, New York

CONTENTS

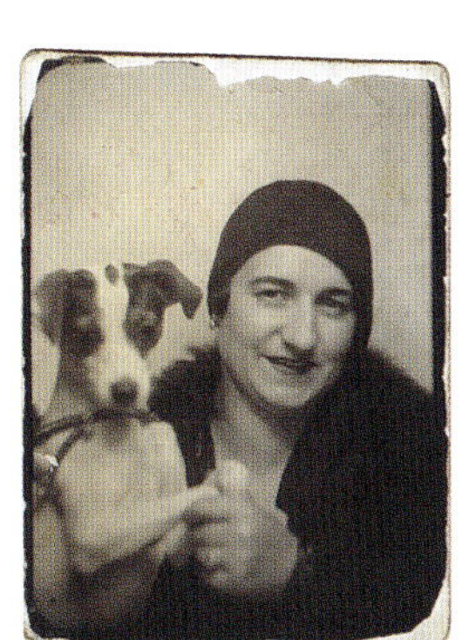

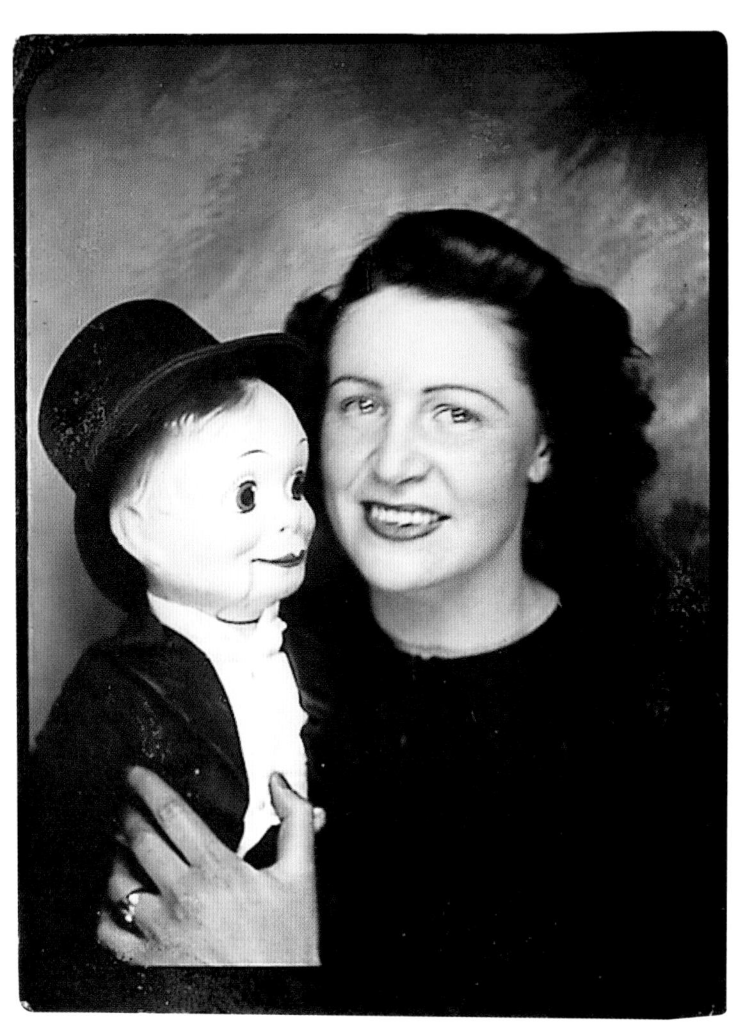

PREFACE

The photobooth is almost a century old. Patented in 1925 by a Russian-born American inventor named Anatol Josepho, it was not the first instant and automatic photographic process. Still, it enjoyed immediate, lasting, worldwide success. Long before it became one of the standard forms of identity imagery, the photobooth snapshot carved out a place for itself in our way of life and our collective memories. What were the reasons for its success?

At first, the booths were set up in fairs, amusement parks, and department stores. Advertising for them emphasized how much fun it could be: having your picture taken was "no longer a chore—now it's a game." Available to everybody, free of aesthetic ambition, and cheap, the automatic photobooth quickly replaced the formal photo studio, and therefore also eliminated the eye of the photographer. For the first time, the idea of intimacy was paramount. The subject was free to turn his or her back on the lens, invent various characters, pose with a friend, a dog, a cigarette, a glass in one's hand, or—as Raymond Queneau or Jacques Prévert chose to do—indulge in all sorts of expressions, mimicry, playacting, and face-making.

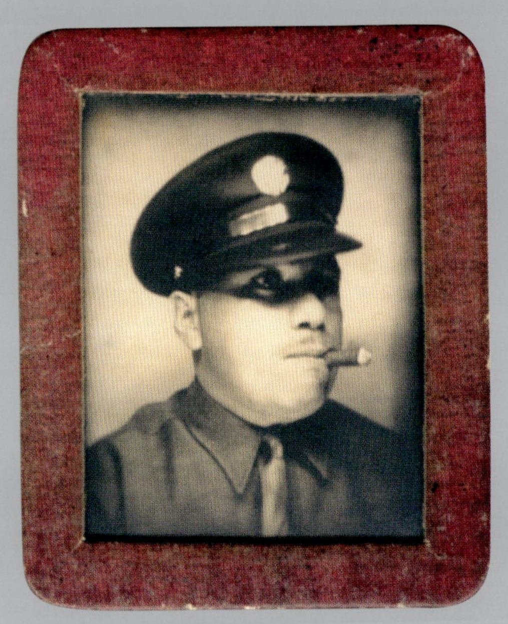

Until the middle of the nineties, and the advent of digital photography, a single ritual seemed destined to persist unaltered.

Alone or in company, you stepped into the narrow automatic photobooth. In order to ward off unwanted observers, you pulled the curtain, which shielded from outside view only the upper half of your body, the part being photographed. (Were you protecting yourselves from the view of others, or were you concealing from others your most intimate facial expressions?)

You adjusted the uncomfortable revolving stool, you stared into a sheet of mirrored glass, able to see your own reflection and guess that behind it was a camera lens. One last check of your appearance, a quick brushing or combing of your hair; a collar to straighten or a button to fasten. Then you slipped coins into the slot. The automatic photographic process was triggered, and it was as if time stood still for a few moments. The first flash always seemed to catch you by surprise, as did the other three, even though they popped off at regular intervals. Then you waited. Out of the four snapshots, how many would match your expectations of the image you have of yourself? The strip of photographic paper inched through the developing process. A few minutes later, the booth spat out the series of self-portraits into a special slot. You would impatiently grab the strip of paper, still damp, taking care not to touch the surface of the newly developed pictures. And you would start blowing on your portrait, to hasten the drying process, which brought the acrid odor of the chemical developers to your nostrils.

Blurry, eyes closed, vacant expression, face out of the frame, stupid expression, or look of surprise . . . these are just some of the unexpected products of the photobooth snapshot. Disappointed customers would rip up their strips of photographs and discard them as defective, lost forever, in almost all cases. As for the other snapshots, they would generally wind up at the bottom of a drawer, in a photo album or wallet, or, most often, a box of memorabilia. No one saw them for years and years. And then came exclamations at how young you were, what a ridiculous haircut or hairdo; the winged shirt collars, a pair of old-fashioned glasses; and sometimes you were found sitting next to a relative long dead, or a lost first love.

Whether anonymous individuals or world-famous celebrities, it matters little. In fact, the absence of any décor in the background and the constraint of a single, narrow frame combined to eliminate

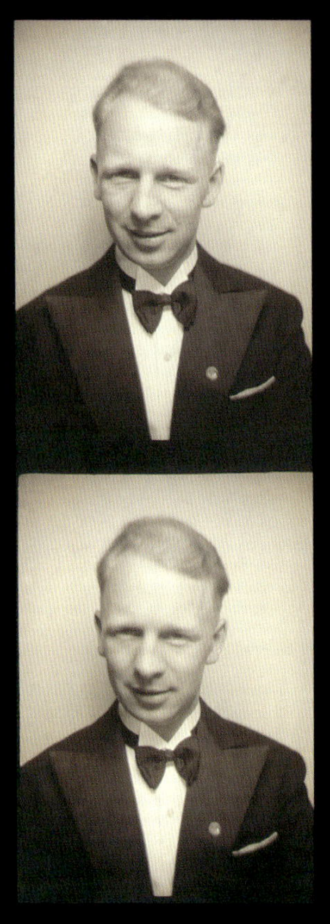

almost entirely the social dimension from the photostrip. All that remains is the portrait in its simplest representation. Thus stripped of all aesthetic ambition, the photobooth snapshot became the standard identity portrait, with a single purpose: a rapid identification of the individual.

The extremely stiff form of the photobooth snapshot, apparently objective, has certainly helped to arouse the interest of numerous artists since its invention. In fact, as early as 1929, the Surrealists hijacked the "automatic photo" from its mass-market or identity-related functions. In the sixties, Andy Warhol played with the mechanism and the repetitive nature of the process, while Roland Topor and Al Hansen produced short "stories without words," in four successive snapshots, and Francis Bacon, fascinated by the reproduction of movement, did numerous portraits and self-portraits based on photobooth strips.

This book looks back to the origins of the photobooth and the identity photograph. In particular, it devotes considerable space to the artists who worked around the technical limitations imposed by the automatic photobooth, whether it used film or digital photography, endowing the self-portrait and the identity photograph with a meaning and a point of view that transcend the functional aspect of the four snapshots developed on a single strip of paper. Through a personal selection of unique artworks and short interviews, this book illustrates the degree to which the photobooth, since its invention, has also—and perhaps, above all—been a unique field of photographic experimentation and an artistic tool in its own right.

THE ORIGINS OF AUTOMATIC PHOTOGRAPHY

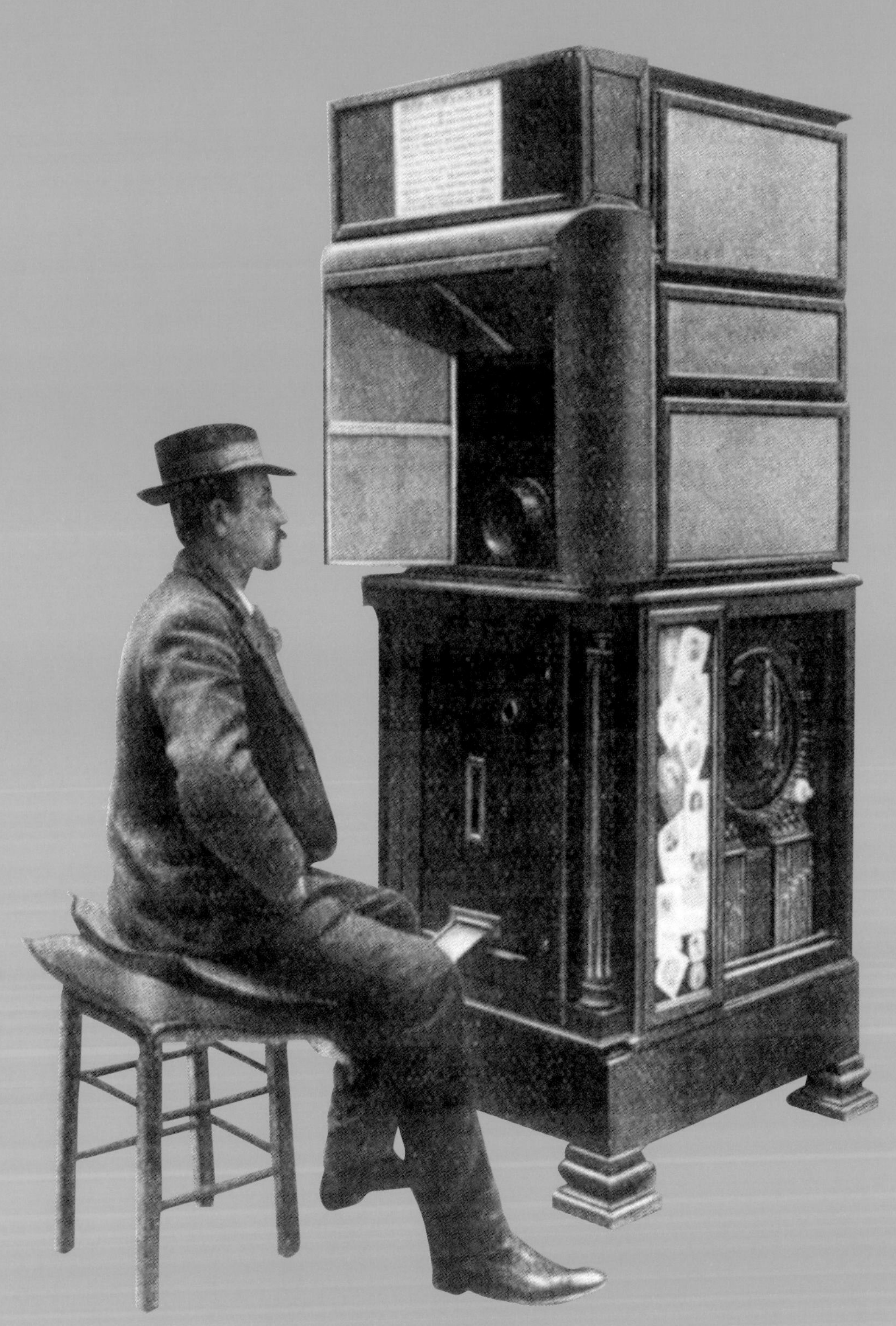

PHOTOGRAPH YOURSELF ! EIGHT POSES IN EIGHT MINUTES.

I n the years between the late nineteenth century and the early twentieth century, numerous patents were granted for inventions concerning "automatic photographic processes." These devices, genuine precursors of the Photomaton, or photobooth, for the most part operated through the insertion of a coin, and were intended, according to their inventors, to automatically photograph "people and objects." They developed and distributed photographic impressions through what is known as the ferrotype process. This photographic technique, first used in 1852, resulted in the direct creation of a positive proof on a metal plate painted black. A photographer was therefore able to deliver a portrait to the client just minutes after the picture was taken.

Containing as many as four hundred prepared metal plates, "these devices for instant photography could be installed and left to operate on their own in public places, squares, parks, theaters, etc." Among the numerous patents issued for such items, three in particular enjoyed a certain degree of success: the Bosco Automat, invented by Conrad Bernitt, and the automatic photo devices of Ernest Enjalbert and Ashton-Wolff.

At the Exposition Universelle in Paris in 1889, Ernest Enjalbert, who had previously invented the Photo-Revolver, displayed his process for automatic photography, described in Walter E. Woodbury's *Encyclopedic Dictionary of Photography*: "designed to perform all the photographic operations necessary to obtain by the ferrotype process the portrait of an individual who sits in front of it, and who has previously dropped a sufficient number of coins into the cash box." The actual exposure lasted from three to six seconds, and the device delivered a framed ferrotype photograph after five minutes. The resulting photograph was a wet collodion proof on a thin metal plate "covered with a perfectly black glossy lacquer." The first devices were installed in Paris at the Jardin d'Acclimatation. But the pictures that were delivered were often mediocre in quality, the machines frequently broke down, and the price was too high. The Enjalbert process quickly vanished. The magazine *La Nature* recalled in 1895 the failure "of an automatic device that delivered for 50 centimes a tiny plate upon which a portrait could barely be seen, and was often unrecognizable."

ERNEST ENJALBERT, ENGINEER AND BUILDER IN PARIS

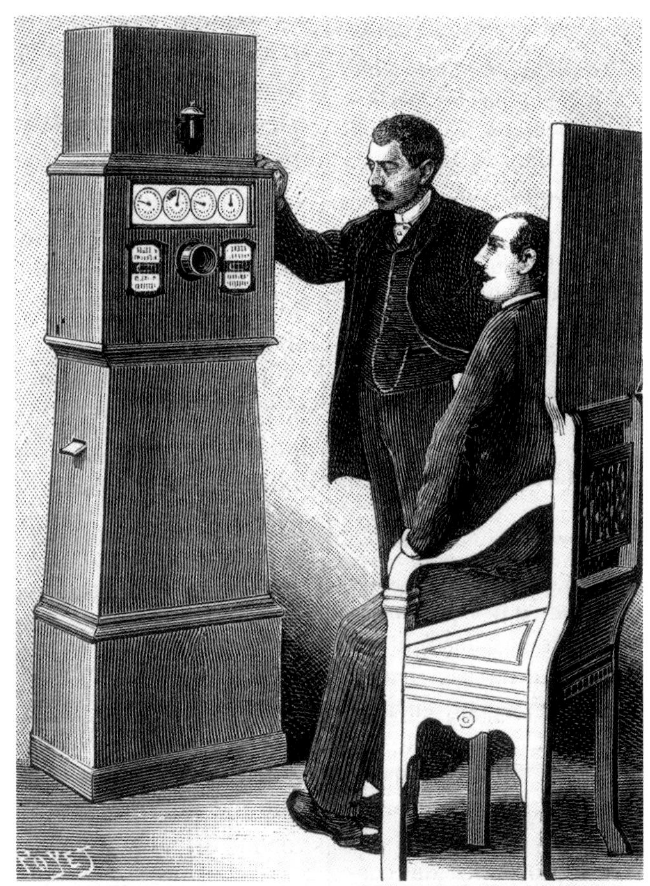

Fig. 1. — Appareil de photographie automatique de M. Enjalbert.
(Vue extérieure.)

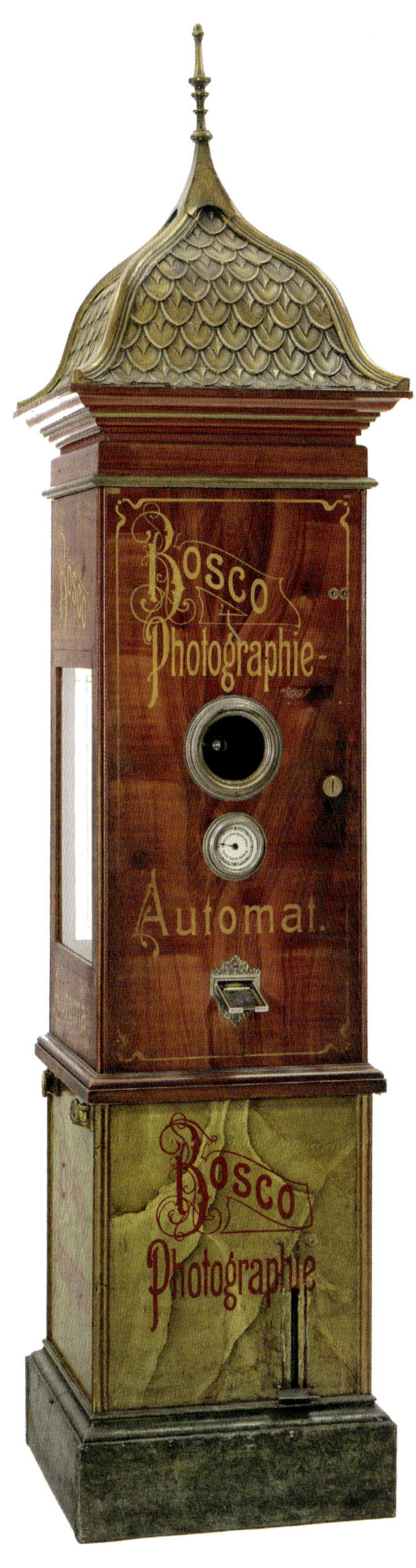

THE BOSCO, A FUN FAIR DESTINY

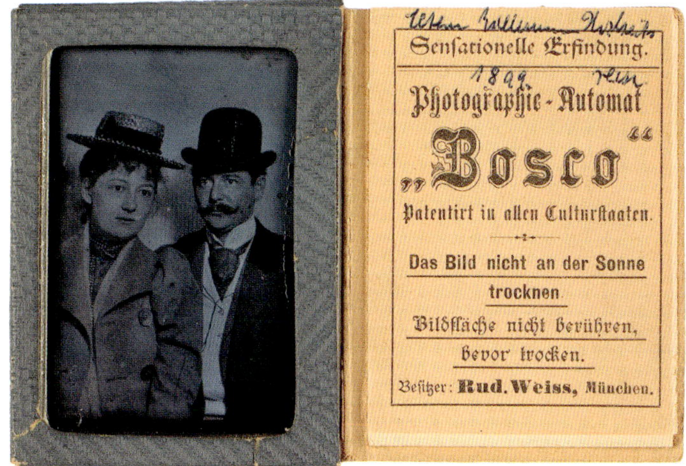

During the first international exposition of amateur photography at the Hamburg Kunsthalle in 1893, the German inventor Conrad Bernitt presented his Bosco, which utilized an automatic photographic process that was quite similar to Enjalbert's, but cheaper and easier to use. The Bosco Automat, which delivered a ferrotype photograph in three minutes, enjoyed enormous success at fairs, amusement parks, and *cafés-concerts* at the turn of the twentieth century.

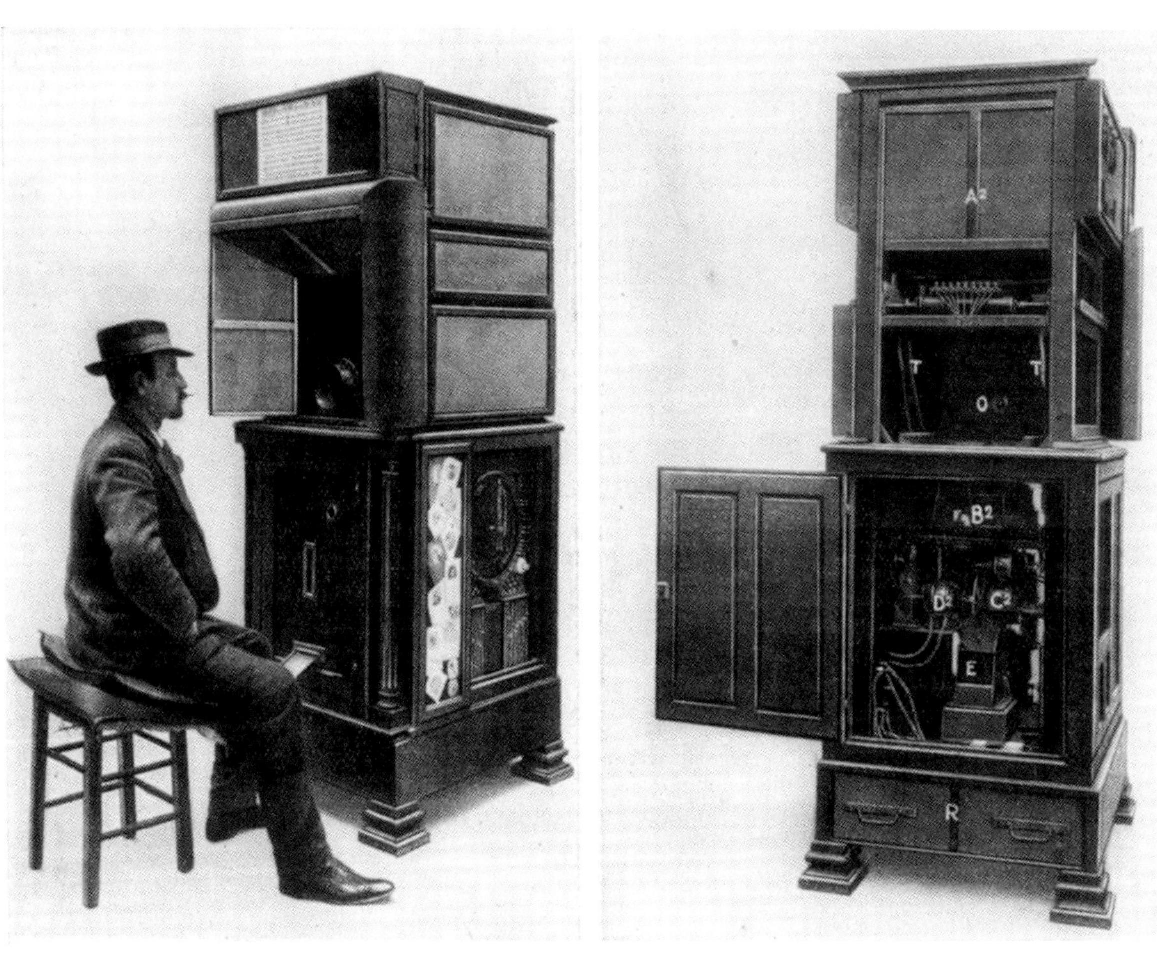

1   2

Fig. 1. *Le client posant devant l'appareil automatique Ashton-Wolff.* — Fig. 2. *Vue arrière de l'appareil, portes ouvertes et panneaux enlevés pour montrer le mécanisme.* (A₂, *bacs à solutions*; B₂, *cuvette de développement*; C₂, *moteur du distributeur*; D₂, *moteur électrique*; E, *essoreuse*; O, *objectif*; R, *réservoir de vidange*; T, *tuyaux d'écoulement des solutions*).

THE ASHTON-WOLFF AUTOMATIC PHOTOGRAPHIC DEVICE

On January 11, 1913, the weekly magazine *La Nature* introduced the Ashton-Wolff automatic photographic device with the following words: "This is a photographic device that 'operates itself.' Instead of an operator, a simple coin does the job. The customer inserts the coin into a special aperture, he sits upon a revolving stool facing the lens housed in a cone, and looks into a small convex mirror that resembles the viewfinder of a box camera. In turn, the coin falls behind a small window where it remains visible during the entire procedure, completing the electric circuit that activates the device. A bell rings immediately; then, a small sign set right in front of the eyes of the person posing lights up, announcing: 'Attention! Turn your head to the right, look at the cross above the mirror…and smile!' and an artificial light, prompted by an arc lamp with a certain number of incandescent bulbs concealed on the left wall of the rectangular booth turns on. At that instant, a second bell is heard and just below the red cross a slot slides open, revealing the traditional phrase: 'Sit still and don't move.' Then the shutter is released, the impression is made instantly on the light-sensitive paper, and the lighting is turned off, while the phrase lights up: 'Thank you, the photograph has been taken, you may stand up. In four minutes your portrait will come out of the bottom of the device.' And in fact, after four minutes, the subject of the photograph can pick up his portrait, on a postcard, developed, rinsed, and dried."

These different photographic processes illustrate that the principle of automation had already been more or less successfully mastered around the turn of the twentieth century. Following the insertion of a coin, the photograph was taken, the chemical development process was completed inside the machine itself without human intervention, and the self-portraits were delivered in a matter of minutes. There was no longer any need for a negative or for a glass plate.

One other patent, which primarily involves the photographic substrate, rather than the process of taking the picture, deserves mention in this context. In 1911, Spiridione Grossi, a photographer with a shop in Brighton, England, developed a photographic device that would "deliver a certain number of photographs on a single strip of paper." Six portraits fit on a narrow photographic strip (measuring 2 by 1½ inches [5 × 3.8 centimeters]), with an adhesive gum spread on its back. Once the gum was moistened, the photographs could be glued to any paper backing. It was this feature that gave the process its name: "Sticky Backs." On each shot, there appeared a serial number along with the name and address of the studio. Even though this was a manual photographic process that required the intervention of a photographer, "Sticky Backs" can be considered a forerunner of the photobooth strips.

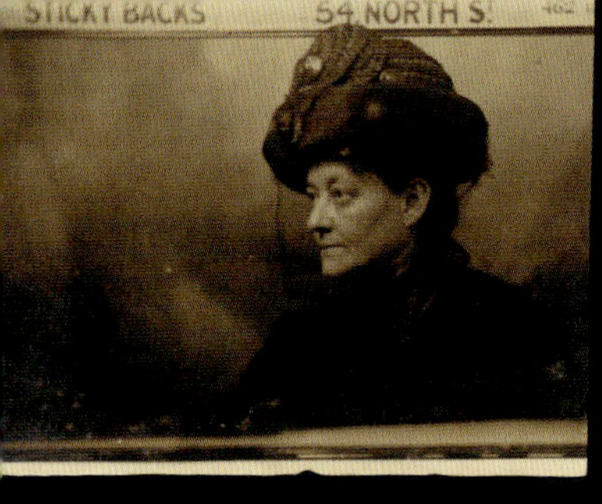

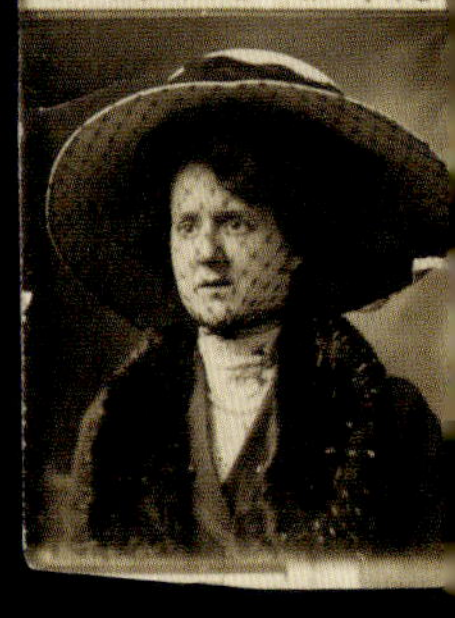

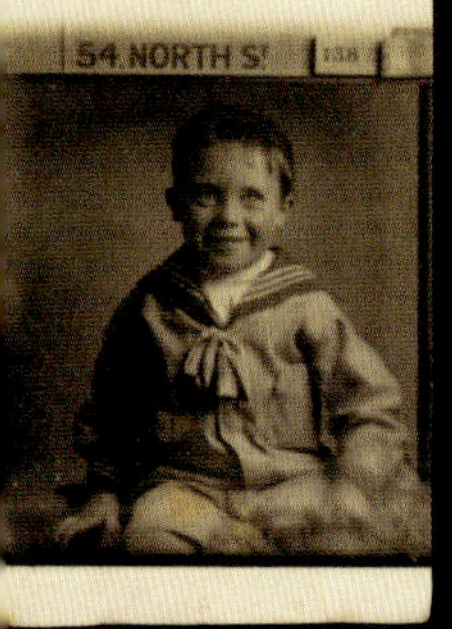

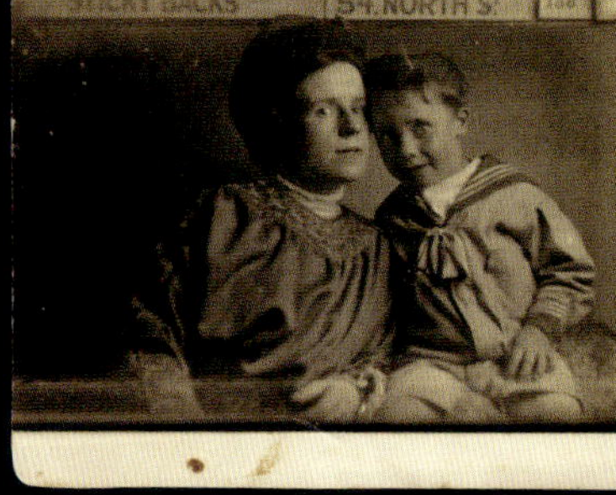

Above and opposite: Photographs done at the Grossi's
Sticky Back & Post Cart Studio, 54 North Street, Brighton

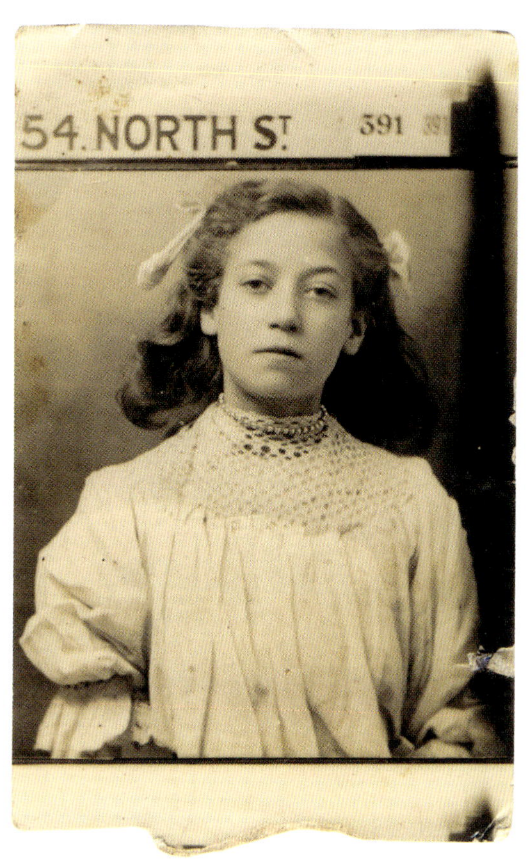

54. NORTH ST.
391

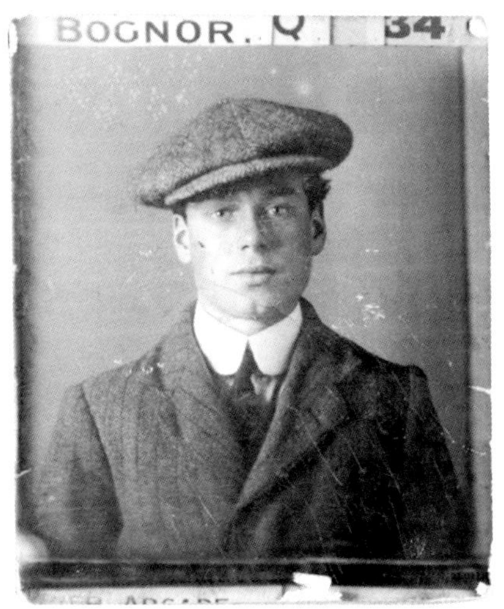

Until the twenties, many photographic devices delivered photostrips consisting of a number of identical portraits. The top of the print provided the address of the studio as well as a serial number, and in some cases, the name of the process used: Photo-Mécanique or Photo-Automatique in the examples shown here. (The term "Photo-Automatique" refers to the automatic nature of the actual photography, not a device available to the public for direct use.)

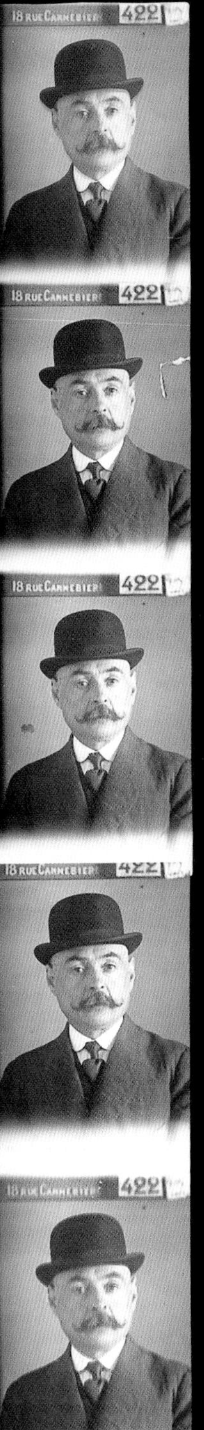

A series of photographs, in a format identical to the "Sticky Backs," but featuring a Paris address: 18 Rue Cannebière (which was once spelled with a double "n"), in the 12th arrondissement.

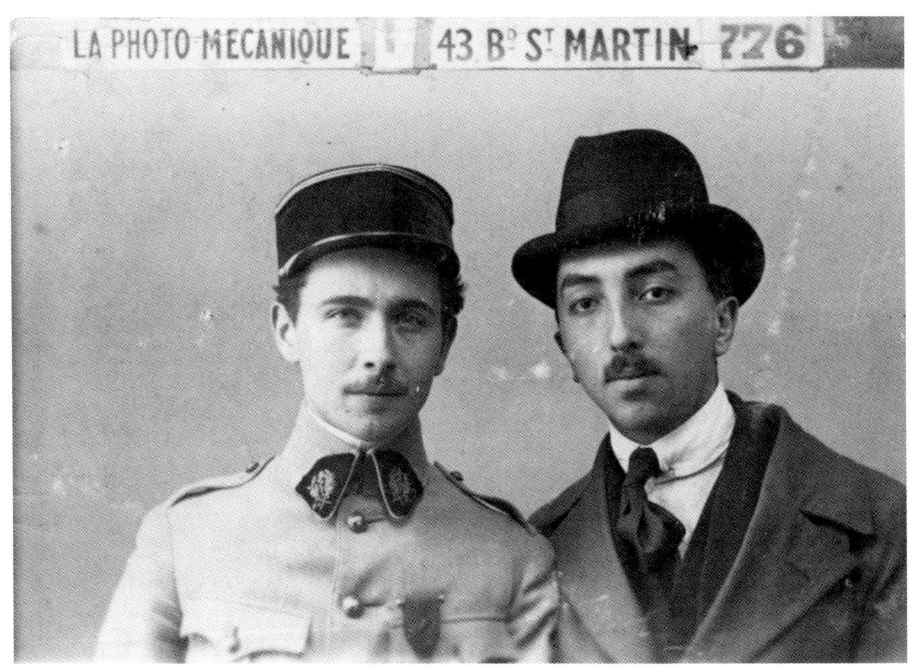

Surrealists Louis Aragon and Théodore Fraenkel. "La Photo-Mécanique"
43 Boulevard Saint-Martin, Paris. After enlisting in the French army on September 3,
1917, Aragon met Fraenkel in 1918, which is likely when this photograph was taken.

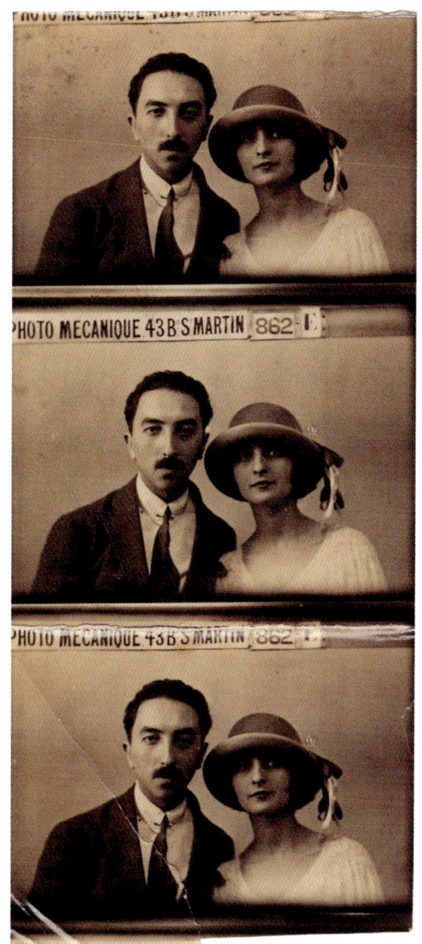

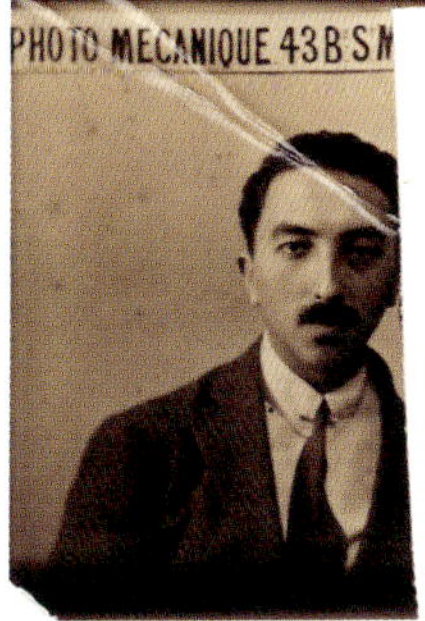

Théodore Fraenkel and his wife, the actress
Bianca Maklès, known as Lucienne Morand, from
c. 1918–1920. "La Photo-Mécanique," 43 Boulevard
Saint-Martin, Paris.

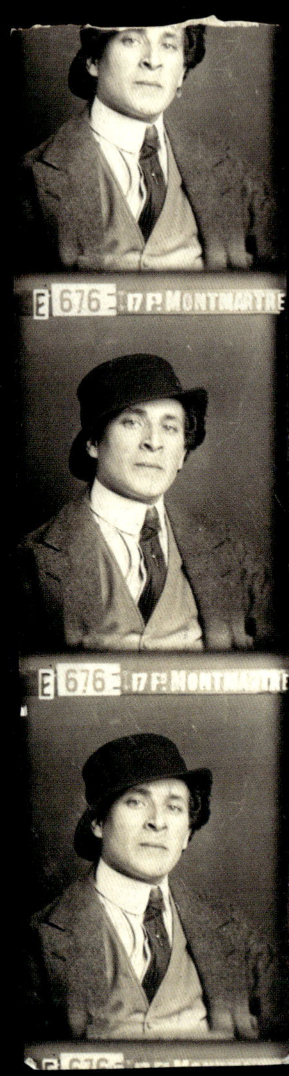

Marc Chagall.
17 Faubourg Montmartre,
c. 1915–1920.

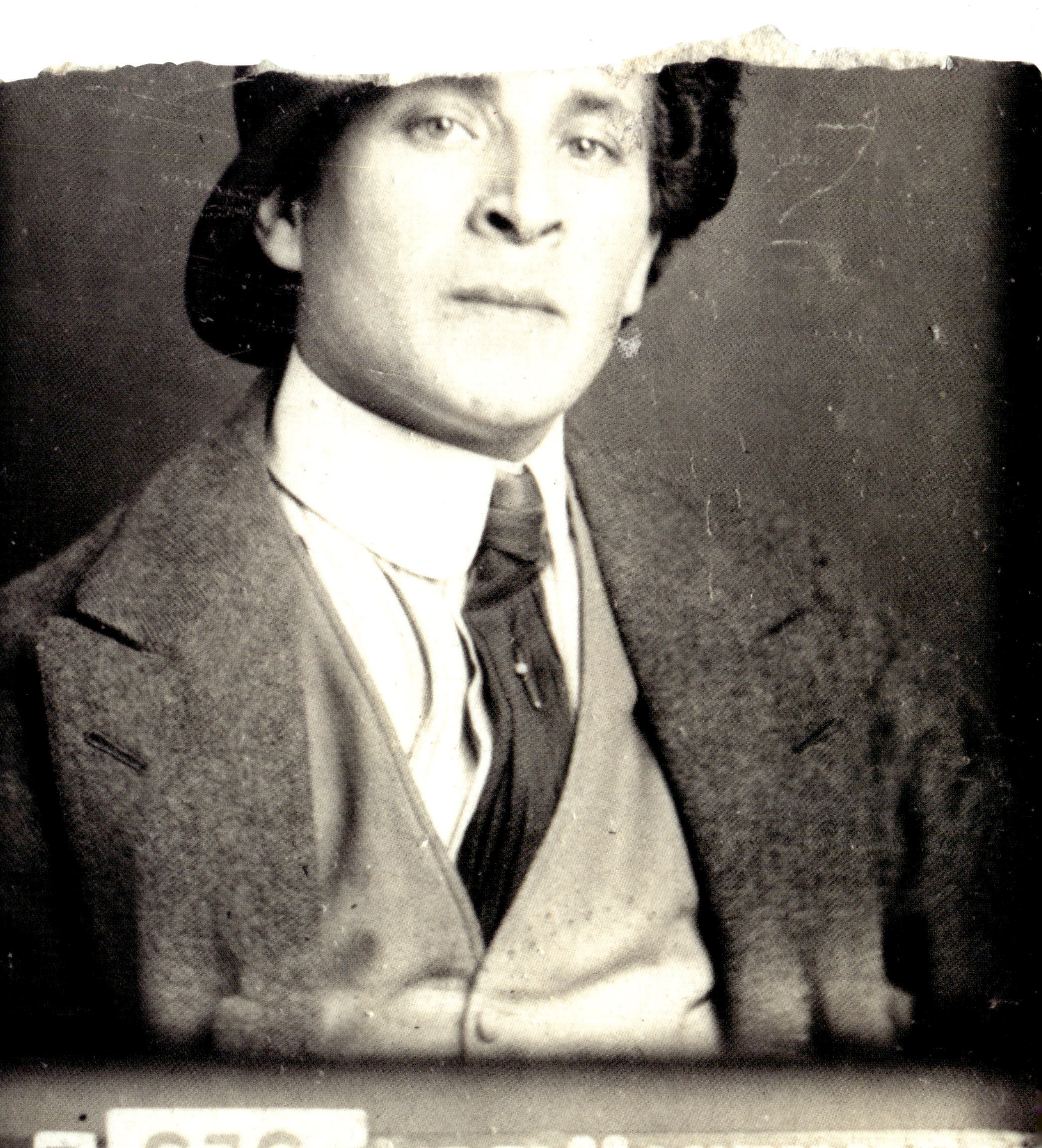
F 676 17 P. MONTMARTRE

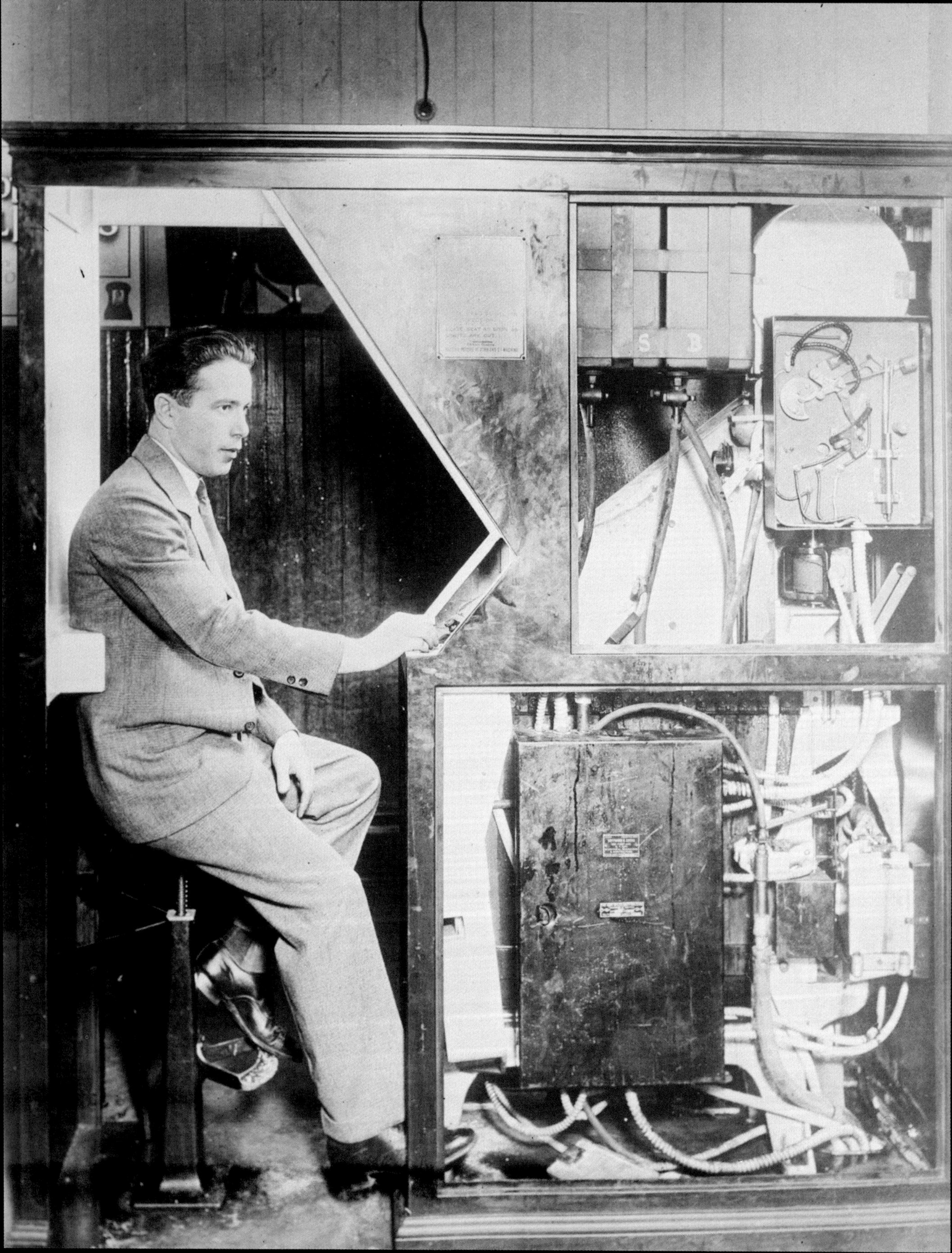

P_hotograph yourself! Eight poses in eight minutes._ In September 1926, in New York City, on Broadway between West Fifty-first and Fifty-second streets, a thirty-two-year-old Russian inventor named Anatol Josepho set up the first entirely automatic photo studio: a small booth where in a matter of minutes it was possible to obtain eight different identity portraits in a sepia tint on a single strip of paper without a photographer. The shutter snapped automatically after the insertion of a quarter—and the Photomaton was born.

The process was simple, reliable, devoid of aesthetic pretense, and cheap. Success was immediate. Lines stretched out, and soon the queue was no longer for one booth—it was for five different booths. In the issue dated April 4, 1927, _Time_ magazine estimated that 280,000 customers had patronized the studio during its first six months. Al Smith, governor of New York, and his wife, Catherine, contributed to the Photomaton's popularity by taking a number of pictures there.

In early 1927, Josepho sold the United States rights to his invention to a group of investors for the cool sum of $1 million (more than $12 million by today's standards). The news made the front page of the _New York Times_ on March 28, 1927: "Slot Photo Device Brings $1,000,000 to Young Inventor."

THE FIRST PHOTOMATON: EIGHT PHOTOS IN EIGHT MINUTES FOR 25 CENTS

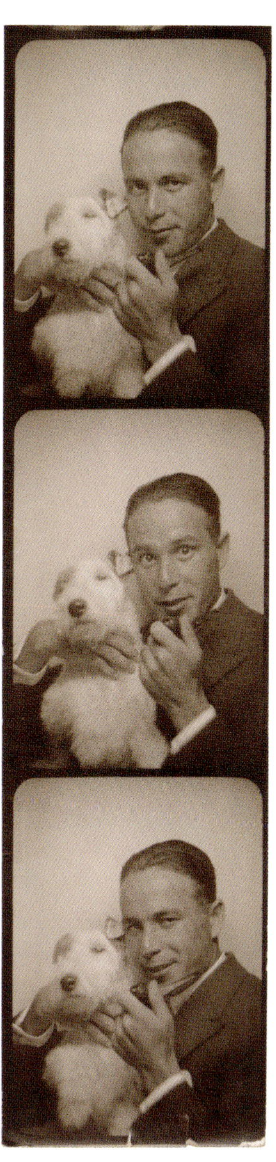

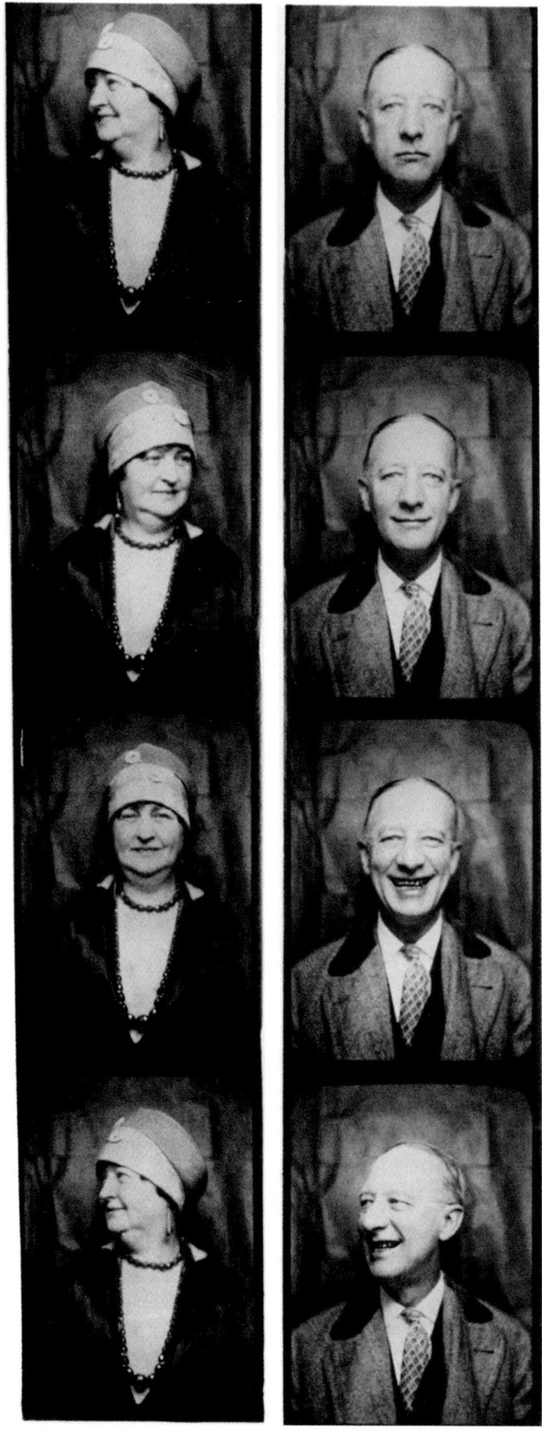

Governor Al Smith and his wife, née Catherine A. Dunn, on April 16, 1927.

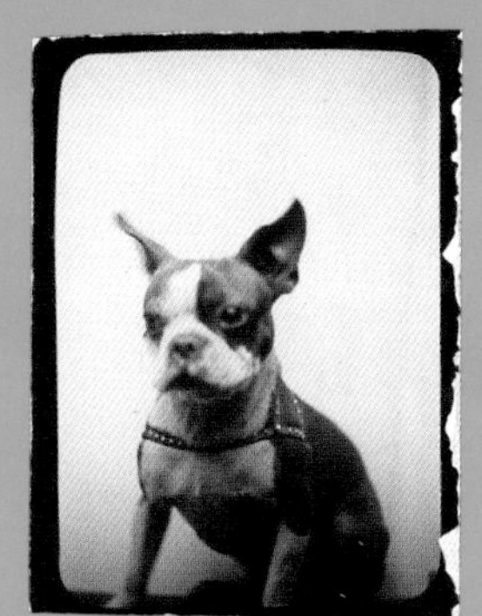

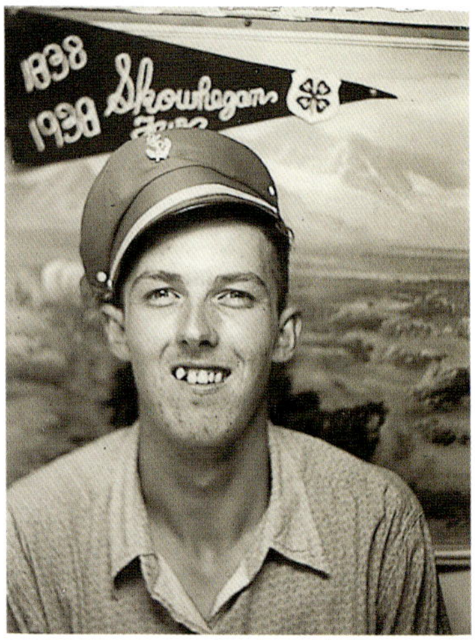

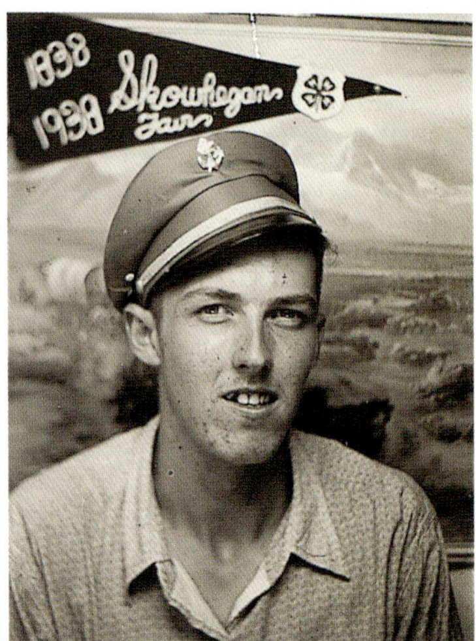

Souvenir from the Skowhegan Fair, Maine, 1938.

Pages 33–37: Photomaton photographs taken during the Chicago World's Fair, from 1933 to 1934.

Henry Morgenthau Sr., former American ambassador to Turkey and the head of the new consortium, Photomaton, Inc., announced, "We will begin to dot strategic points in this country with studios at a rate slightly more rapid than one a week." At the end of April 1927, Franklin Delano Roosevelt—the future president of the United States—was appointed director of the consortium, and the group of investors established the objective of installing 220 Photomaton studios throughout the country before the end of 1928. The first booths were installed in train stations, subway stations, penny arcades, and many other public places.

Throughout the early years of their commercialization, Photomaton booth backgrounds could be composed of painted, interchangeable decorative sheets, which in some cases revealed invaluable information for determining the origin of images: an event, the year of the photograph, the location of the studio. In certain booths, the revolving stools rested on scales and the sitter's weight was inscribed on the shots. Certain Photomaton studios offered other services such as framing or wallet-size formats, the creation of photo albums, cutting the strips into individual photographs, or hand-coloring of the portraits.

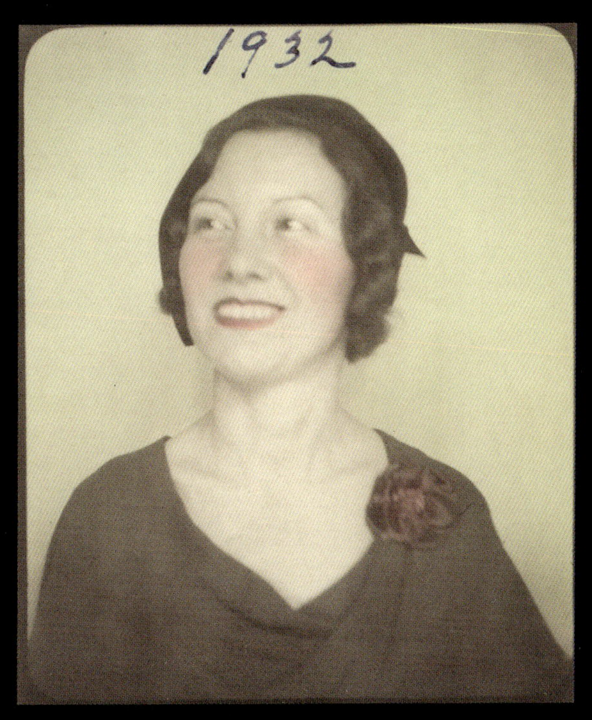
1932

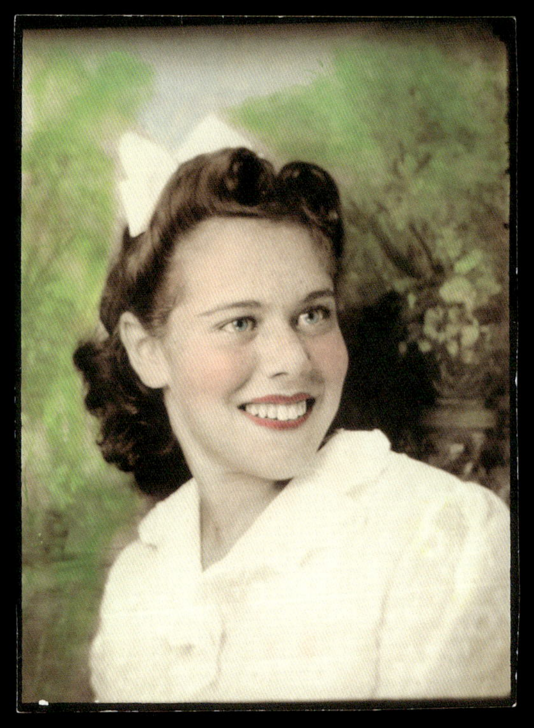

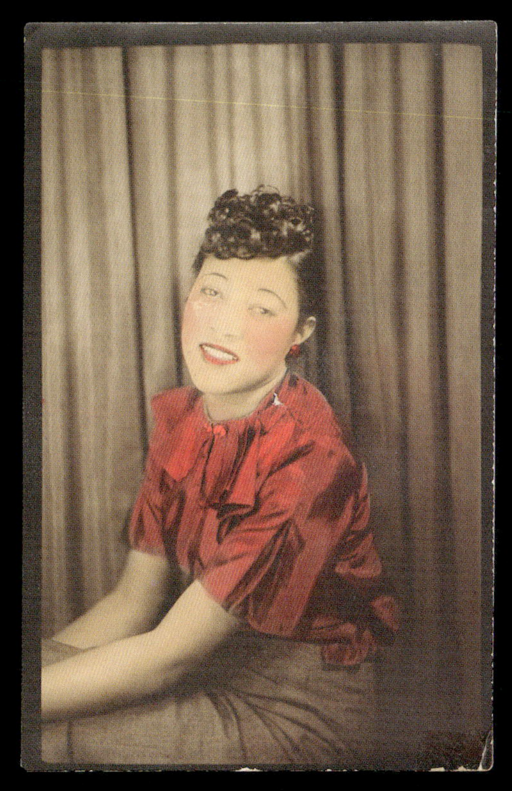

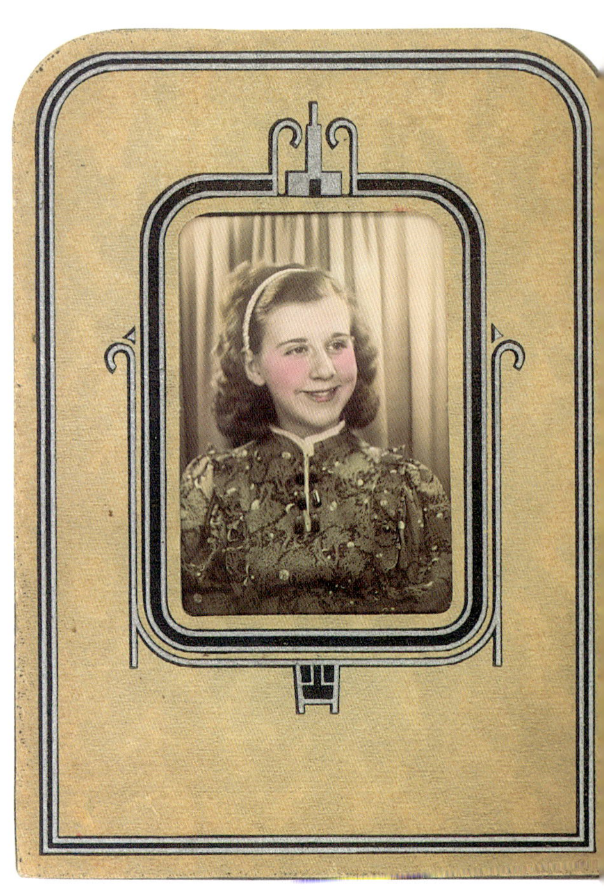

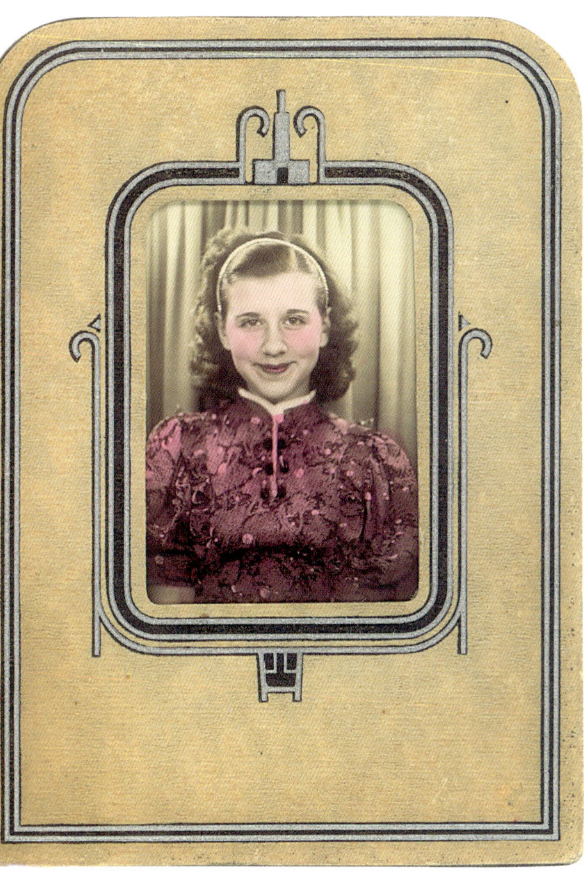

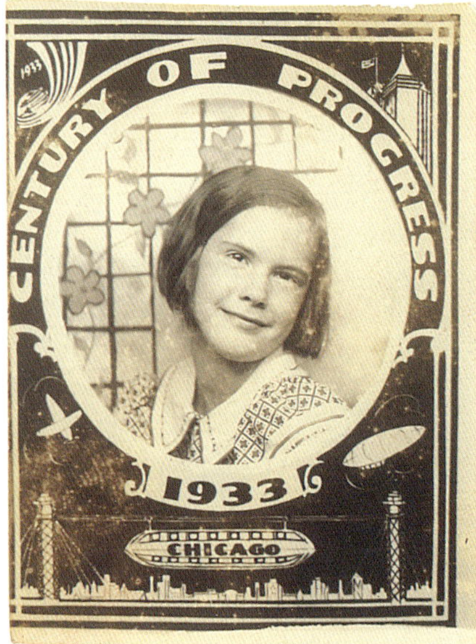

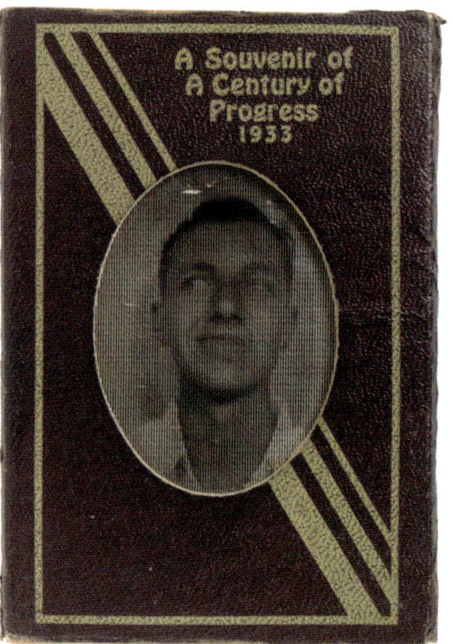

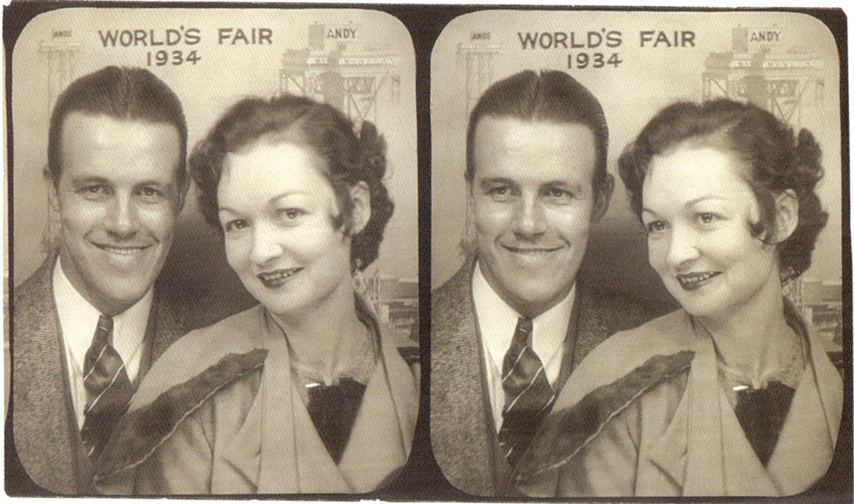

Above: Photomaton photographs taken during the Chicago World's Fair: lenticular process. Depending on the viewing angle, three different Photomaton images appear, creating the illusion of movement.

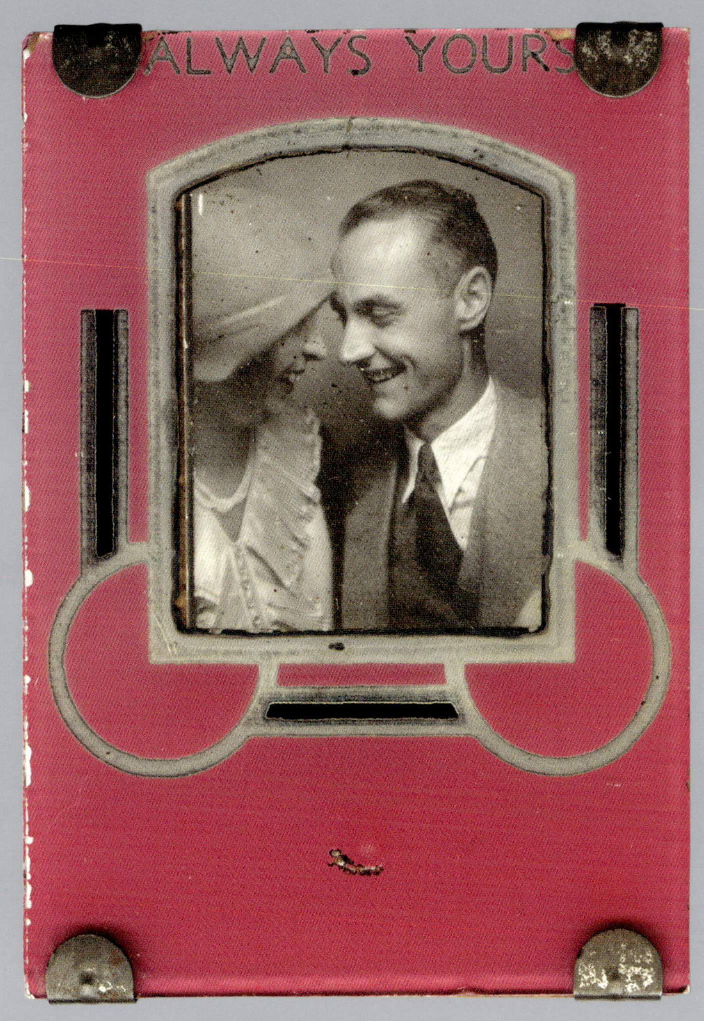
ALWAYS YOURS

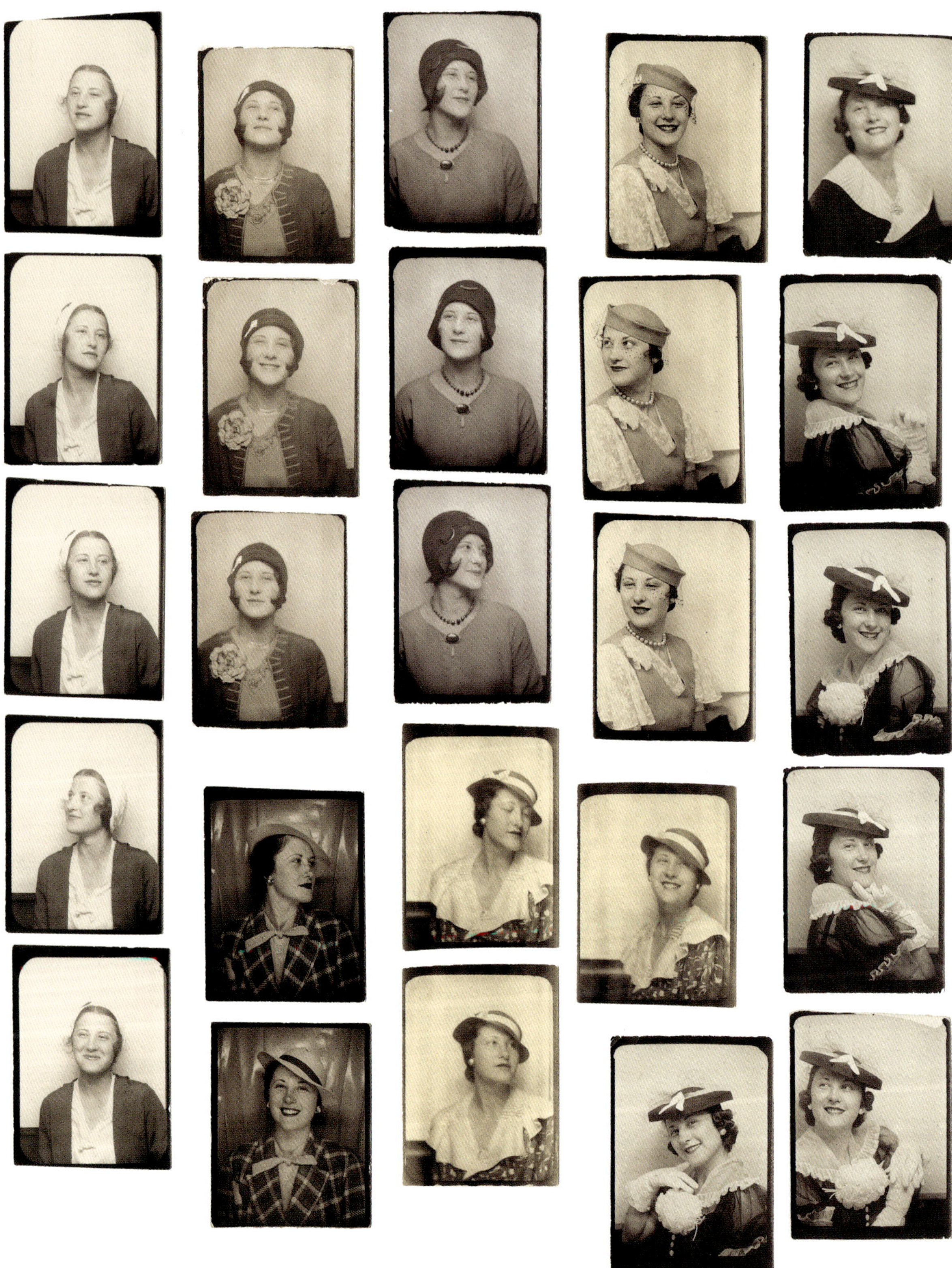

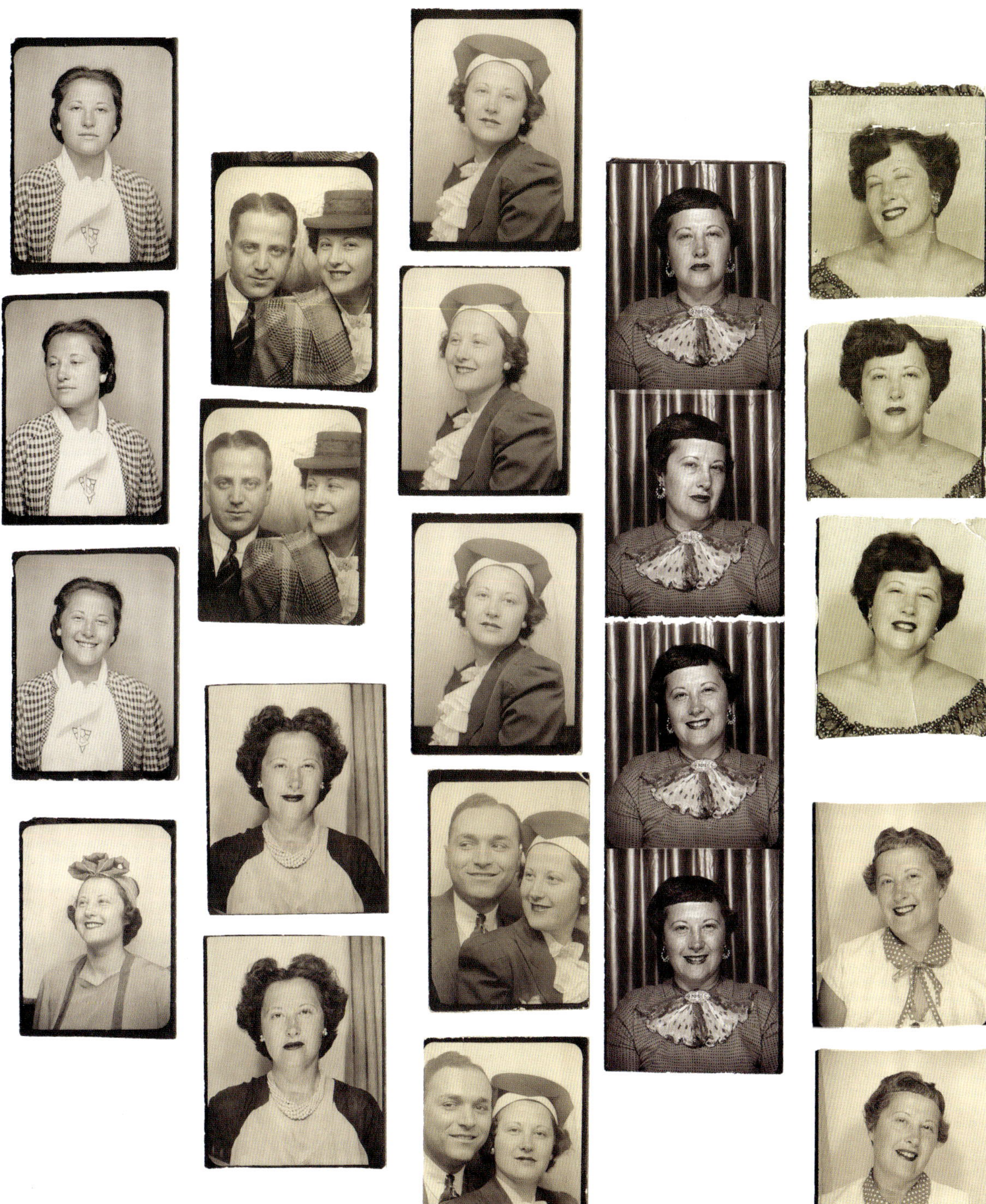

Series of photobooth portraits of the
same woman, dated between 1928 and
1948. Hollywood, California.

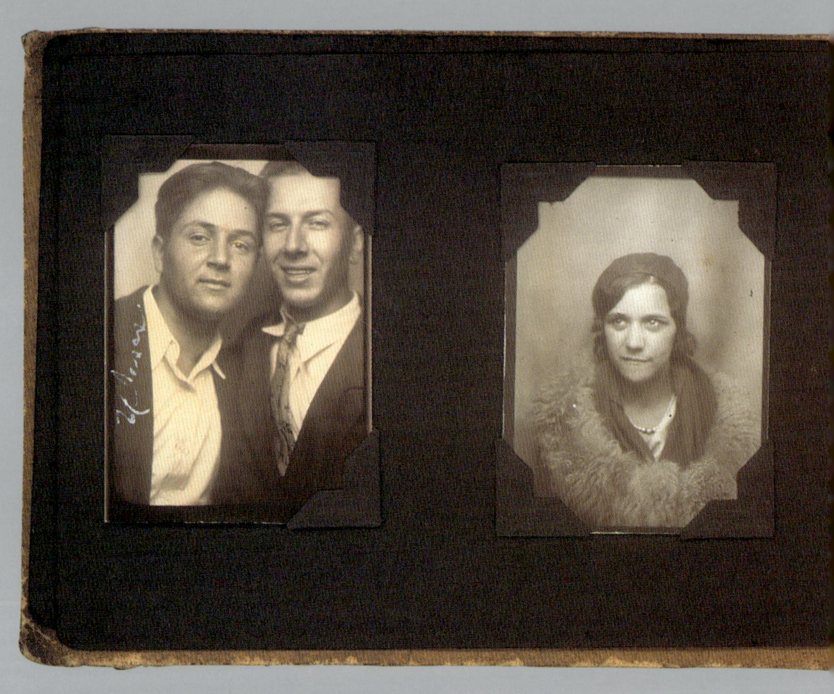

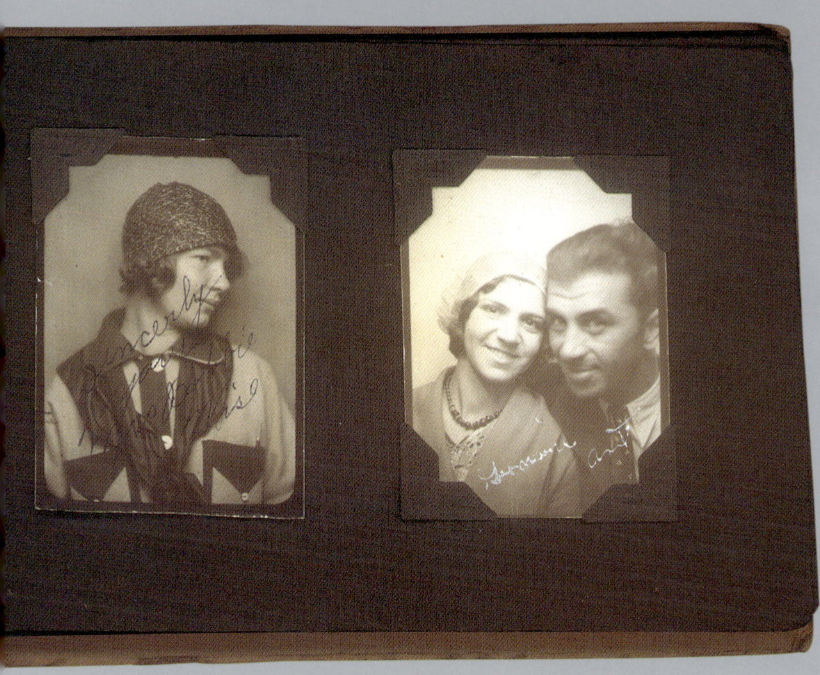

"Souvenir of Old Orchard Beach, Maine." Photobooth album, c. 1930.

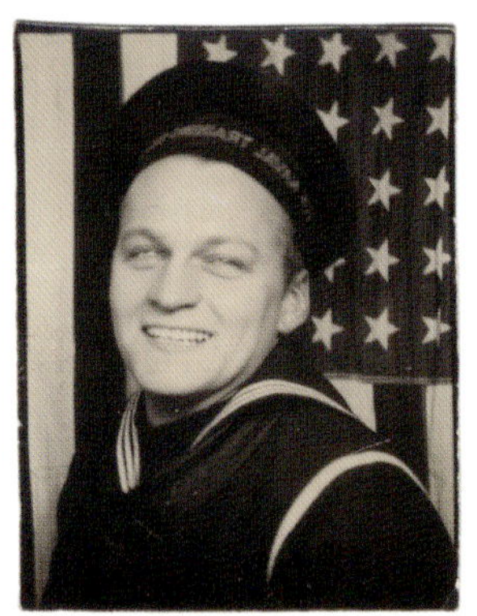

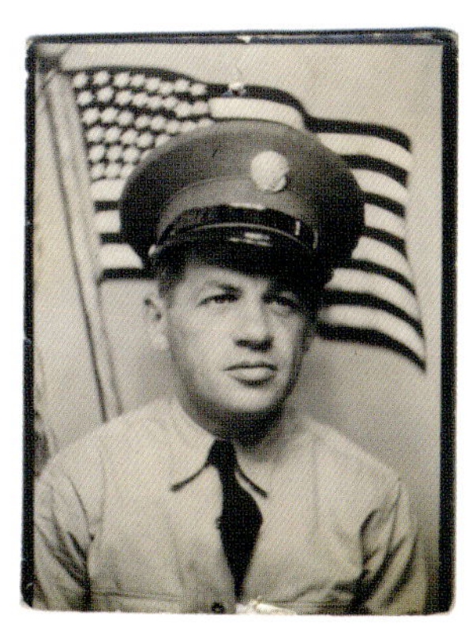

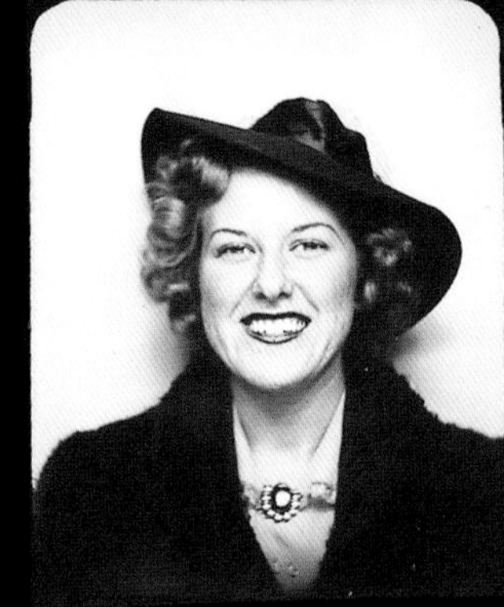

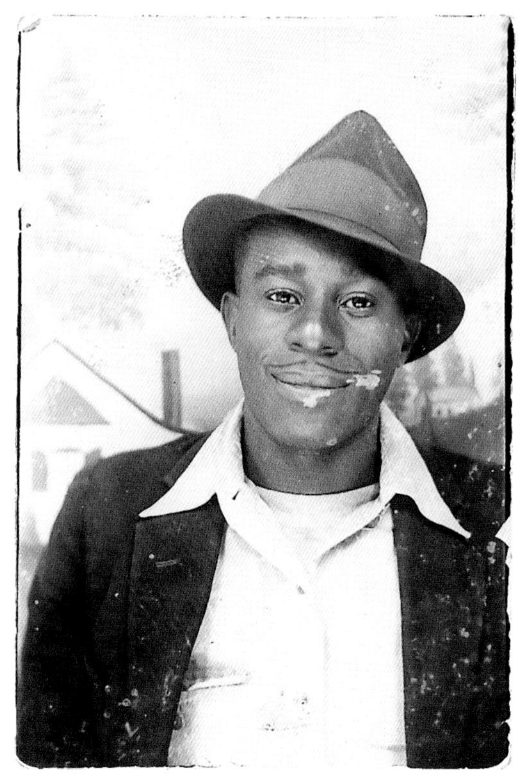

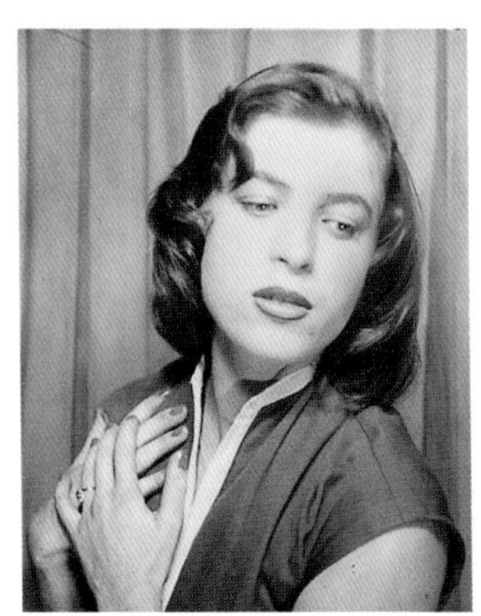

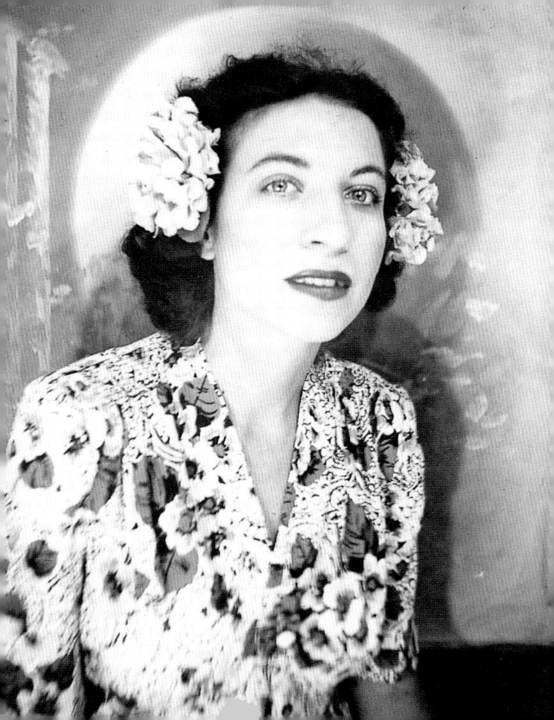

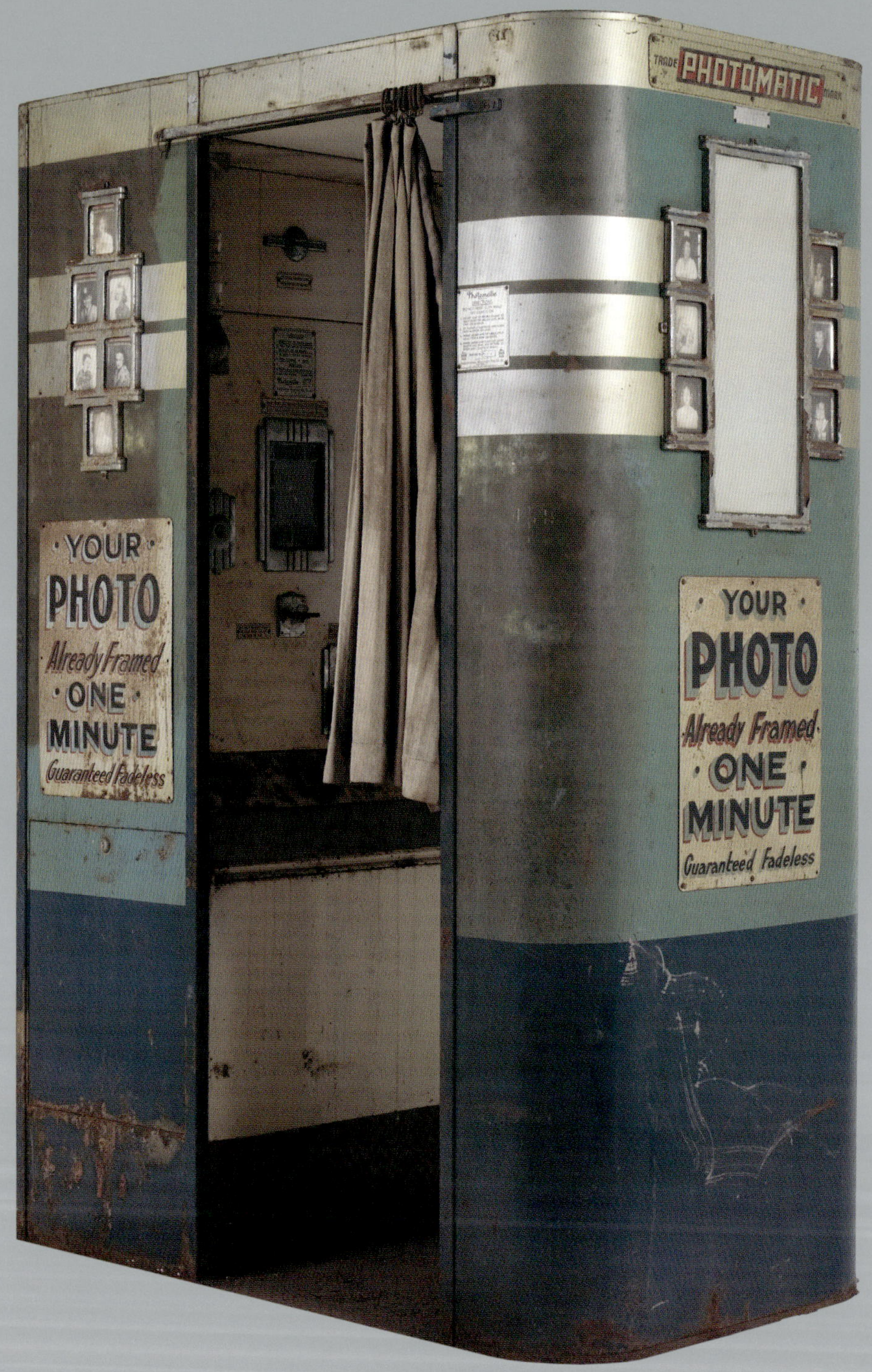

Photomatic booth from the International
Mutoscope Reel Company of New York.

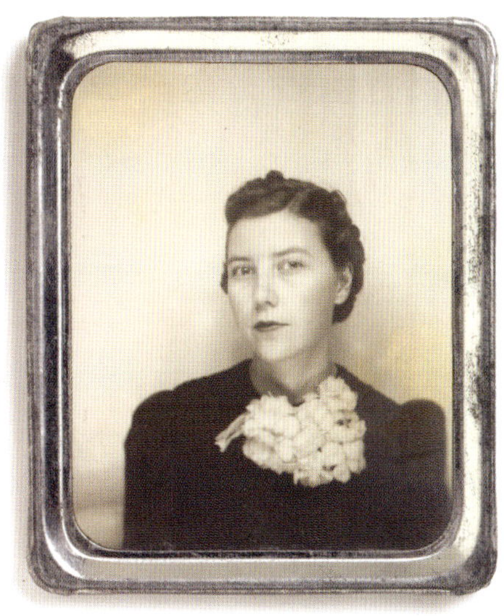

IN TERMS OF THE COMPETITION: PHOTOMATIC AND PHOTOTERIA

In the wake of the Photomaton's success, numerous rival processes appeared at the beginning of the thirties, among them the Photomatic and a Canadian system called the Phototeria.

The International Mutoscope Reel Company of New York, which manufactured projection equipment (the Mutoscope), games, and carnival attractions, also marketed the Photomatic. What was the principle? A single photo, developed in less than a minute, for 15 cents. With a larger format than that of the Photomaton (3 × 2½ inches [7.7 × 6.6 centimeters]), the snap was "guaranteed fadeless" and delivered in a metal or cardboard frame. A folding tab on the back made it possible to stand the picture upright. Advertisements and other references included on the prints allow us to establish the location of the booths and to date the portraits. The first Photomatic booths were installed in the Grand Central Terminal in New York and in the train station of New Haven.

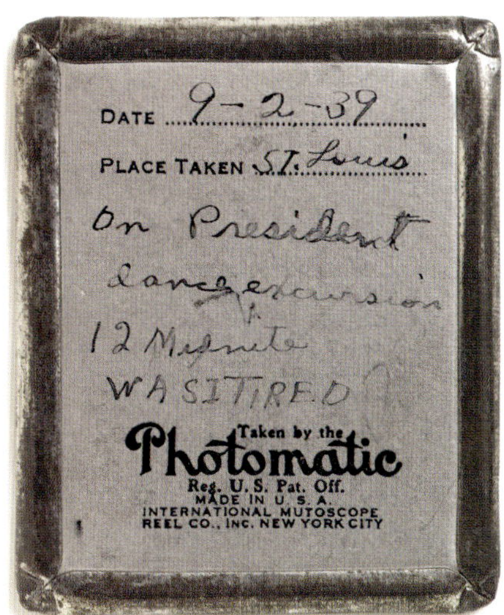

"9-2-39. St. Louis, on President dance excursion, 12 Midnite, WAS I TIRED."

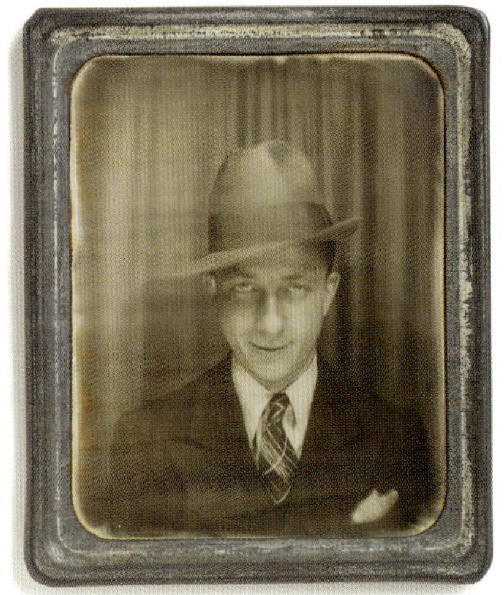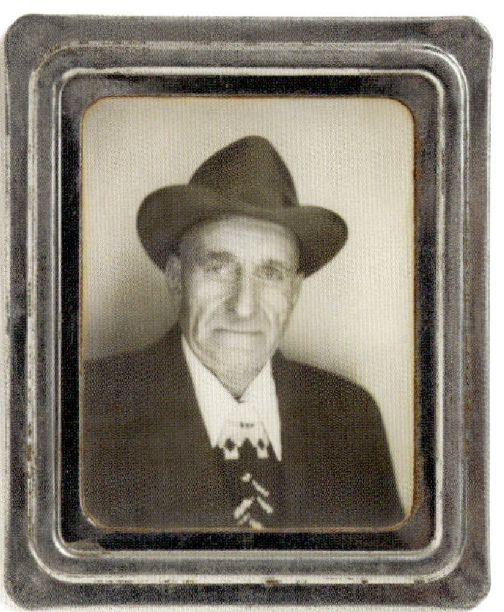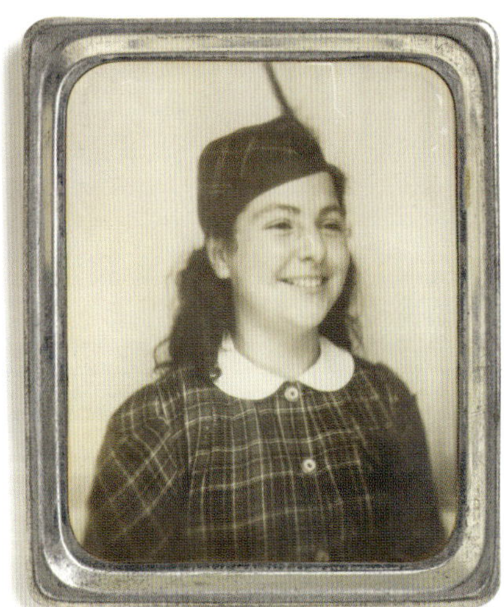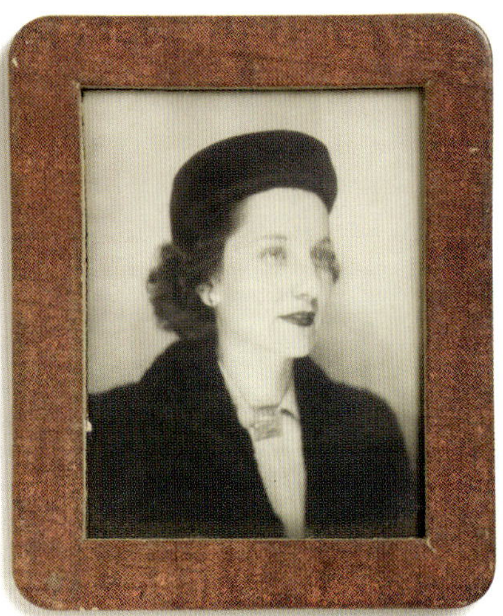

Photomatic snapshots, mid-twentieth century.
Bottom, from left: New York, October 21, 1939; Penn Station, New York, June 1944.

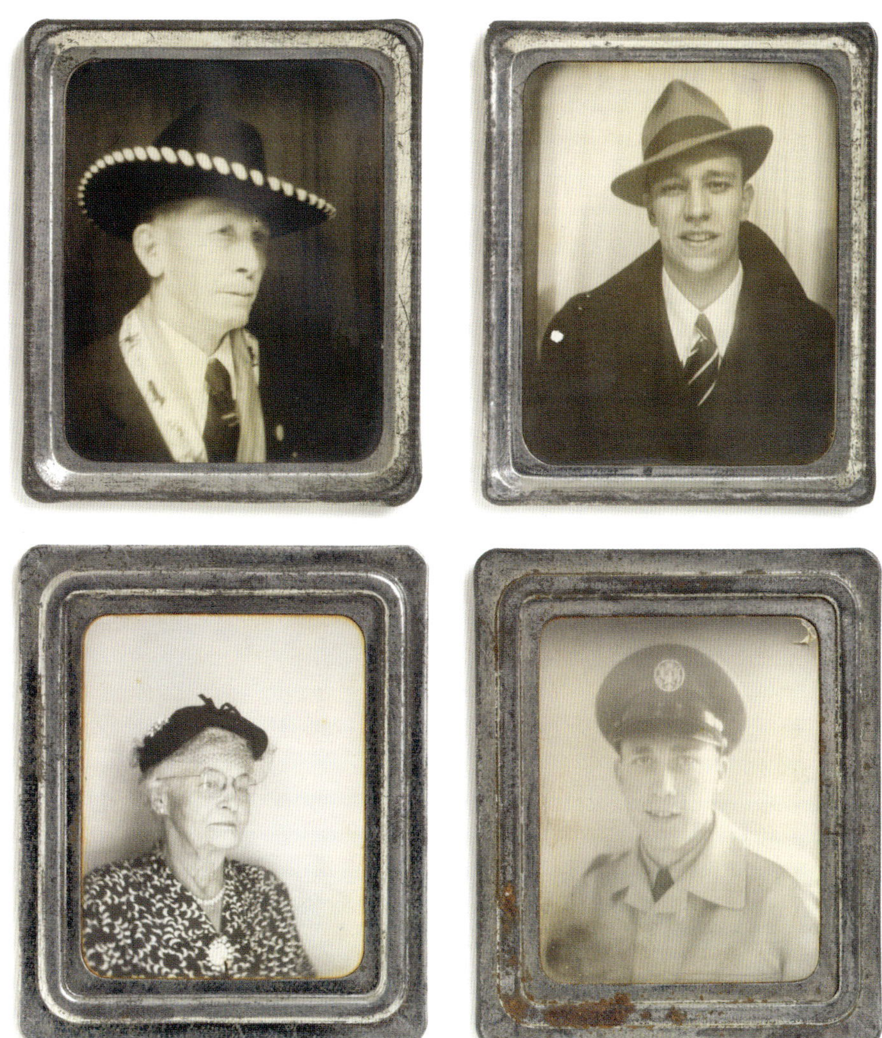

Photomatic snapshots, mid-twentieth century.
Top left: Angel Island, San Francisco, February 14, 1934.
Bottom left: Chicago, 1953.

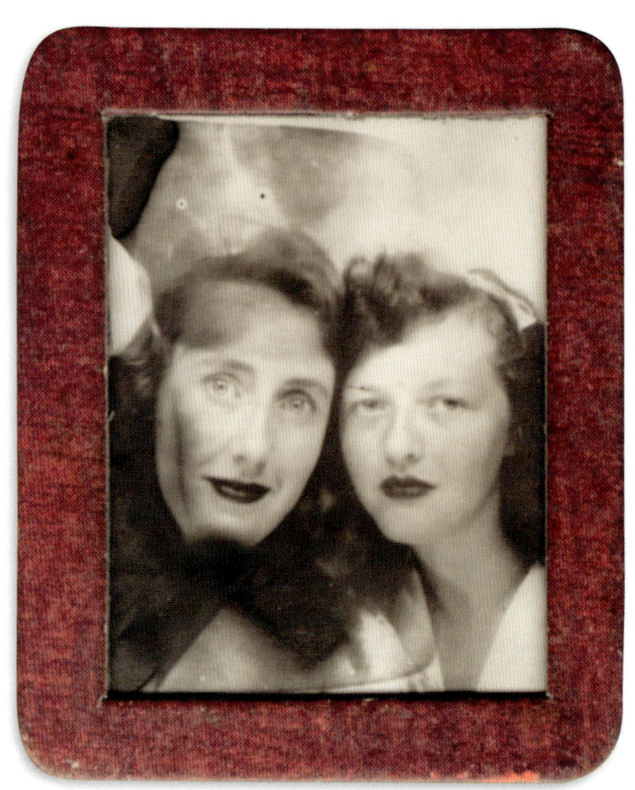

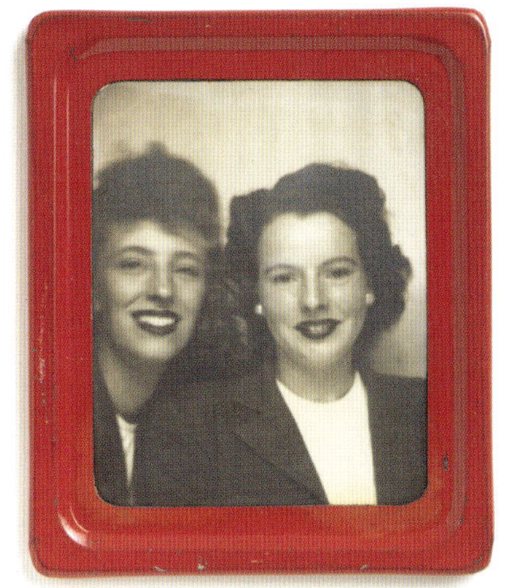
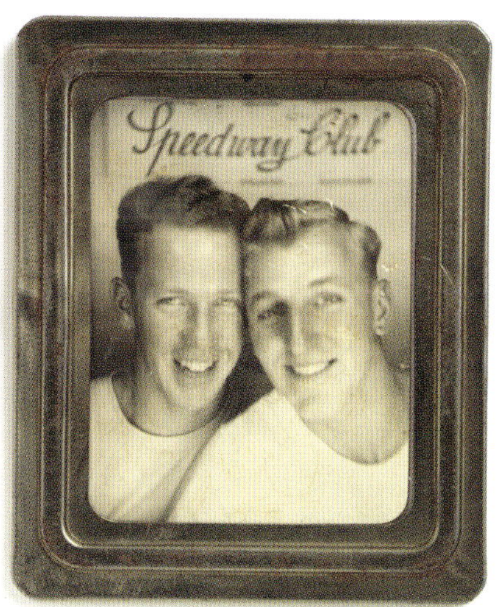

Speedway Club

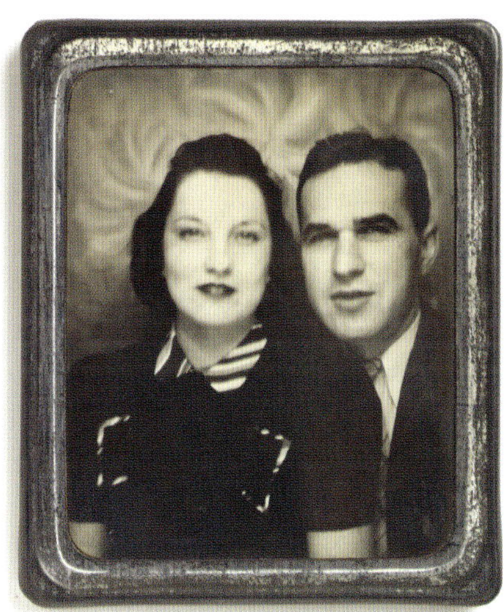
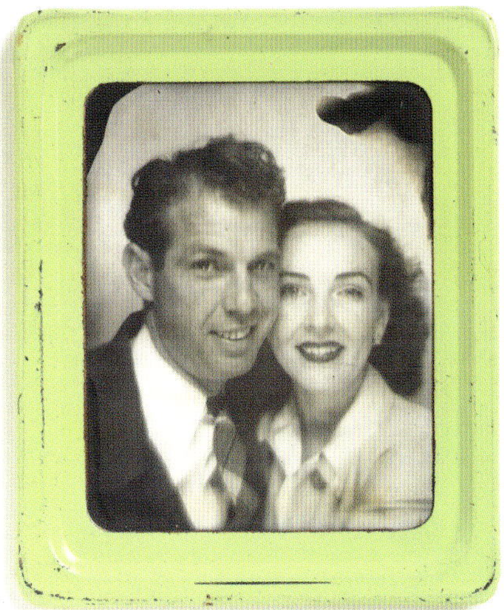

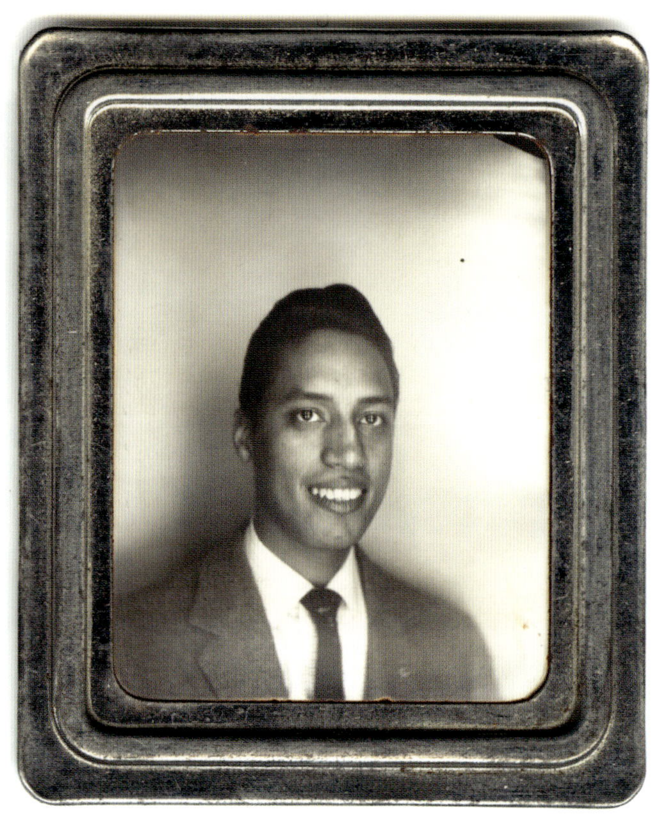

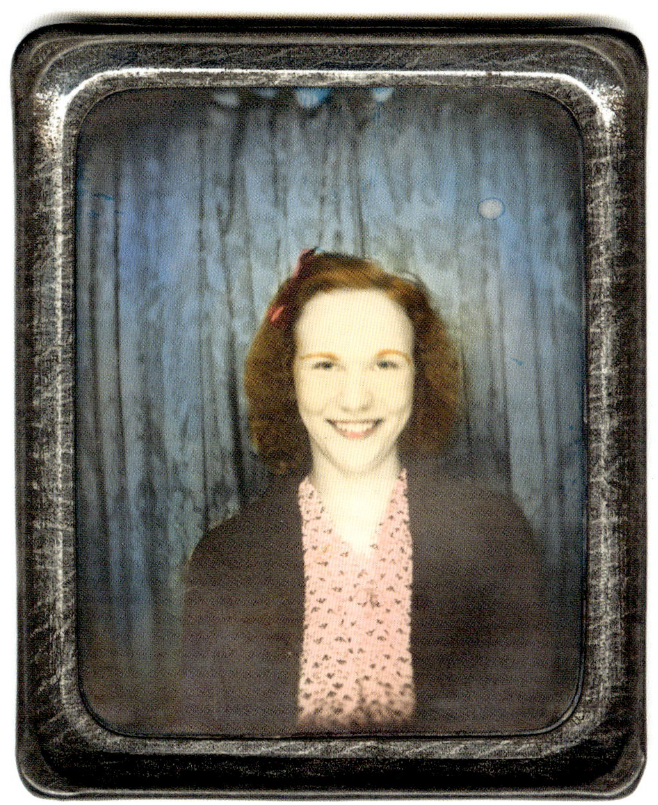

Colorized Photomatic portrait, c. 1940.

IDENTIFICATION
NAME
ADDRESS
EMPLOYED BY:
Taken by the
Photomatic
T. M. REG. U. S. PAT. OFF.
SEE PATENTS LISTED ON
OUR DAYLIGHT LOADING MAGAZINE
MADE IN U.S.A.
INTERNATIONAL MUTOSCOPE
CORPORATION—NEW YORK CITY

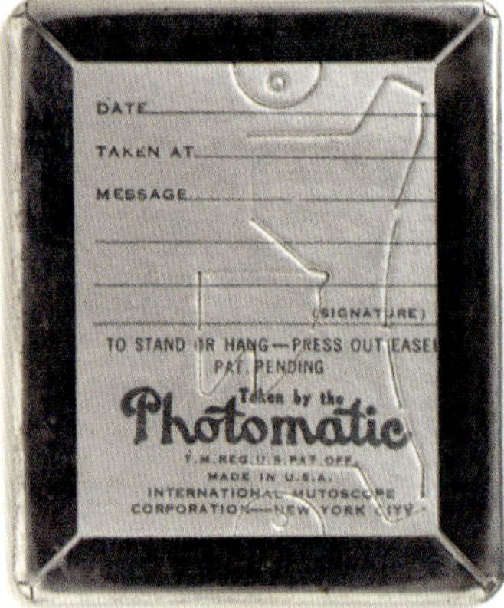
DATE
TAKEN AT
MESSAGE
(SIGNATURE)
TO STAND OR HANG—PRESS OUT EASEL
PAT. PENDING
Taken by the
Photomatic
T. M. REG. U. S. PAT. OFF.
MADE IN U.S.A.
INTERNATIONAL MUTOSCOPE
CORPORATION—NEW YORK CITY

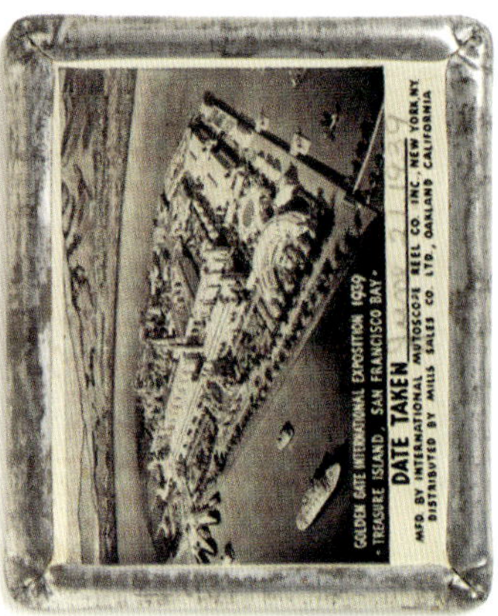
GOLDEN GATE INTERNATIONAL EXPOSITION 1939
TREASURE ISLAND SAN FRANCISCO BAY
DATE TAKEN
MFD BY INTERNATIONAL MUTOSCOPE REEL CO. INC. NEW YORK, N.Y.
DISTRIBUTED BY MILLS SALES CO. LTD, OAKLAND CALIFORNIA

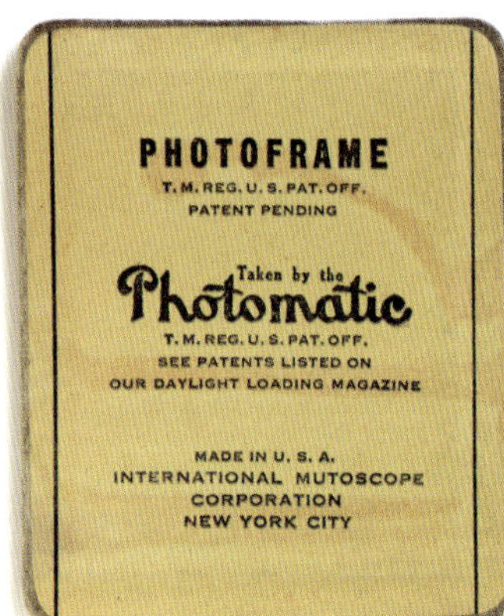
PHOTOFRAME
T. M. REG. U. S. PAT. OFF.
PATENT PENDING
Taken by the
Photomatic
T. M. REG. U. S. PAT. OFF.
SEE PATENTS LISTED ON
OUR DAYLIGHT LOADING MAGAZINE
MADE IN U. S. A.
INTERNATIONAL MUTOSCOPE
CORPORATION
NEW YORK CITY

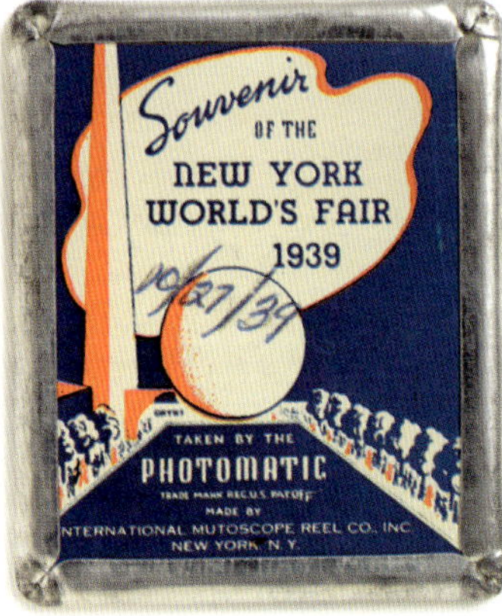
Souvenir
OF THE
NEW YORK
WORLD'S FAIR
1939
TAKEN BY THE
PHOTOMATIC
TRADE MARK REG. U.S. PAT. OFF.
MADE BY
INTERNATIONAL MUTOSCOPE REEL CO. INC
NEW YORK, N. Y.

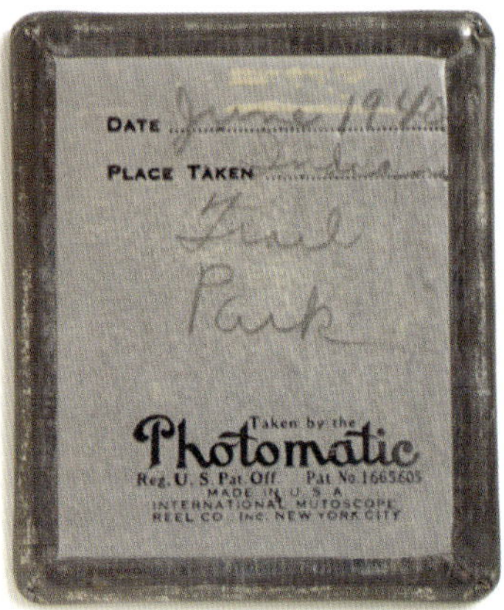
DATE
PLACE TAKEN
Taken by the
Photomatic
Reg. U. S. Pat. Off.   Pat No. 1665605
MADE IN U. S. A.
INTERNATIONAL MUTOSCOPE
REEL CO. INC. NEW YORK CITY

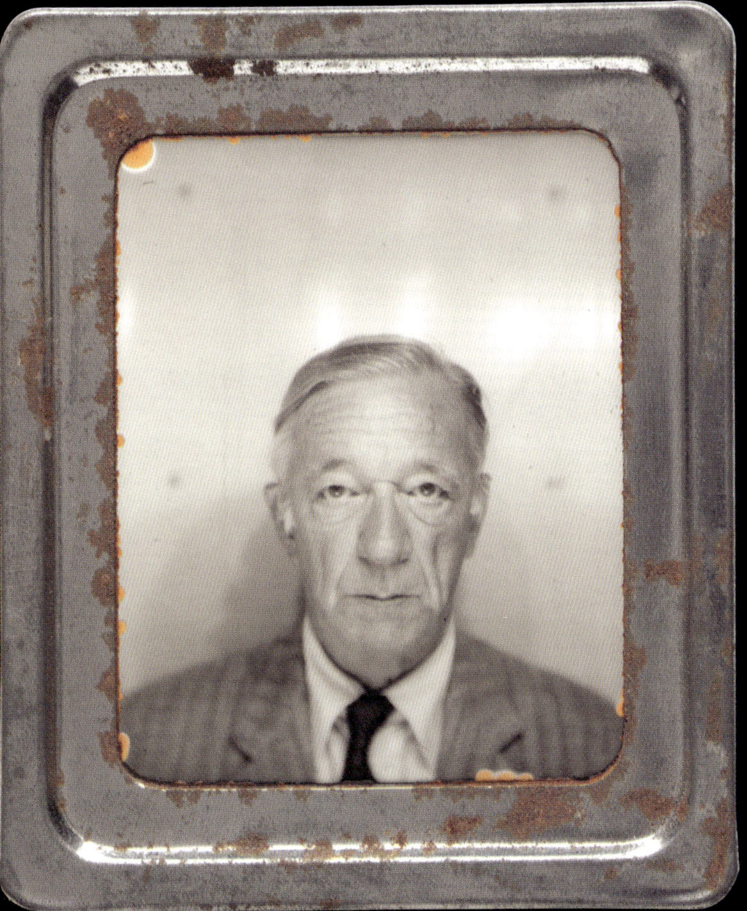

Walker Evans. Photomatic portrait dated on the back by the
photographer, June 23, 1970.

P H O T O M A T I C

TRADE MARK REG. U. S. PAT. OFF.

PARTS CATALOGUE

"DE LUXE MODEL"

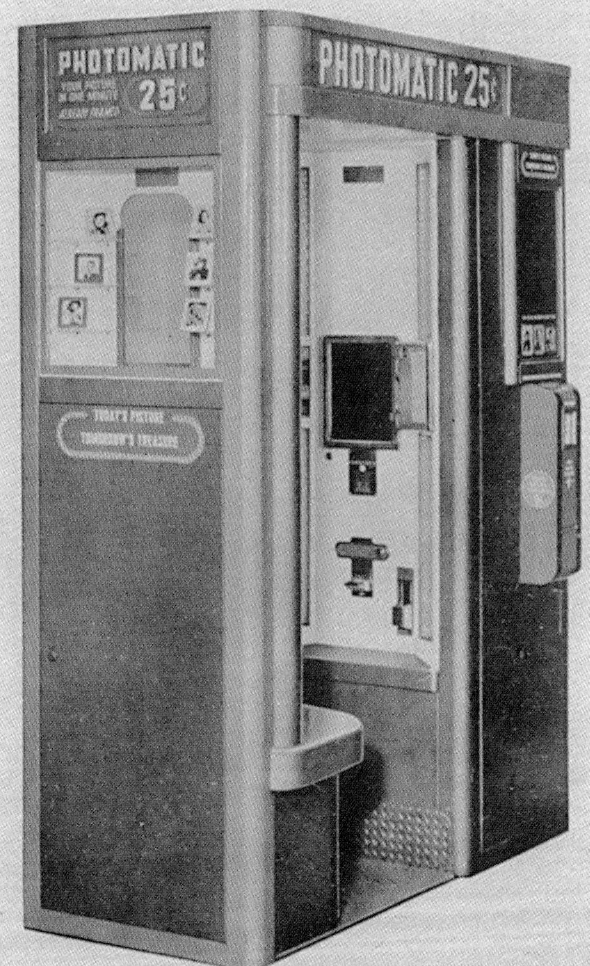

MANUFACTURED BY

INTERNATIONAL MUTOSCOPE CORPORATION

MUTOSCOPE BUILDING

LONG ISLAND CITY 1, NEW YORK, U.S.A.

Printed in U. S. A.

SECTION 1 - CABINET, EXTERIOR FIXTURES, SIGNS. (See illustrations 1 and 2.)

PART NO.	DESCRIPTION	QTY. per MACHINE
09-251	Side Mirror Frame	2
09-384	Opening Window for Lens	1
09-385	Ribbed Wire Glass for left lower fluorescents	2
09-386	Ribbed Wire Glass for left upper fluorescents	2
09-387	Ribbed Wire Glass for right lower fluorescents	1
09-388	Ribbed Wire Glass for right upper fluorescents	1
09-416	Etched Plate, Coin Return Button	1
09-417	Etched Plate, Picture Delivery	1
09-418	Height Meter Mirror	1
09-419	Etched Plate, Height Meter	1
09-420	Window & Mirror Frame	1
09-421	Picture Receiver	1
09-422	Coin Return Pocket	1
09-425	Etched Plate, Coin Insert 15¢	1
09-426	Etched Plate, Coin Insert 25¢	1
09-520	Instruction Panel	1
09-522	Sign, Side Glass, price included on new glass, specify requirements	2
09-523	Sign, Front Glass, price included on new glass, specify requirements	1
* 09-524	Frosted Glass Partition above Show Case	1
09-525	Show Glass Window	1
09-526	Show Case Mirror	1
09-527	Side Mirror	2
09-528	Show Case Shelf	6
* 09-533	Decal for Cabinet Back Door	1
09-535	Decal for Side Mirror top and bottom	2
* 09-537	Price Sign, Side 25¢	2
* 09-538	Front Price Sign 25¢	1
09-540	Price Sign, Side 15¢	2
* 09-541	Price Sign, Side 20¢	2
09-543	Front Price Sign 15¢	1
* 09-544	Front Price Sign 20¢	1
09-546	Photomatic Trade Mark Sign (Etched Plate)	2
09-548	Side Mirror Assembly, including frame, mirror and sample pictures	2
09-549	Decal for Front Door	1
09-552	Etched Plate, Coin Insert 20¢	1
09-553	Display Mutosnaps, sold in sets	12 per set
09-556	Top Side Decals "Take Your Own Photo -- Now"	2
* 09-646	Single Rotating Lock for fluorescent lamps	10
* 09-647	Combination Rotating Lock for fluorescent	10
* 09-648	Fluorescent Lamp Starter, for 15 Watt	3

* Part not shown on illustration.

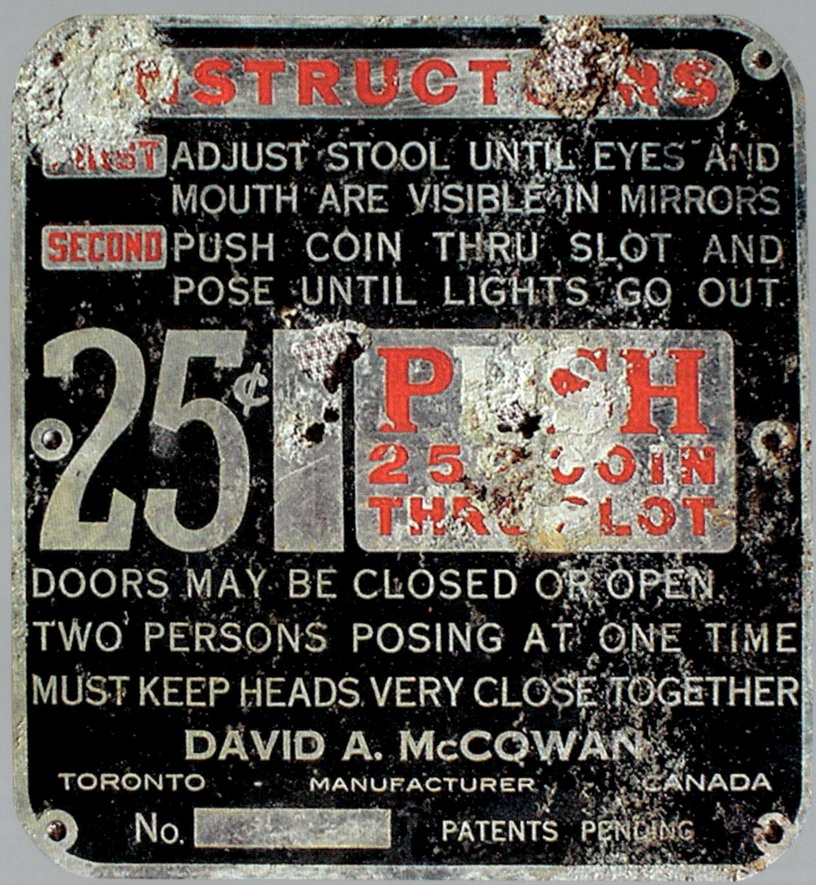
INSTRUCTIONS
FIRST ADJUST STOOL UNTIL EYES AND
MOUTH ARE VISIBLE IN MIRRORS
SECOND PUSH COIN THRU SLOT AND
POSE UNTIL LIGHTS GO OUT.
25¢
PUSH
25¢ COIN
THRU SLOT
DOORS MAY BE CLOSED OR OPEN.
TWO PERSONS POSING AT ONE TIME
MUST KEEP HEADS VERY CLOSE TOGETHER
DAVID A. McCOWAN
TORONTO - MANUFACTURER - CANADA
No. PATENTS PENDING

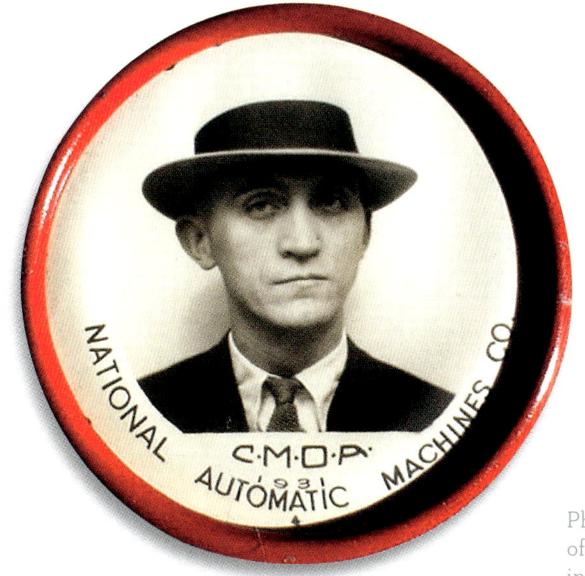

Phototeria self-portrait of David A. McCowan, inventor of the process.

Invented in March 1928 by the Canadian David A. McCowan and presented for the first time in Toronto during the Canadian National Exhibition, the Phototeria delivered a black-and-white photograph in a circular format, not unlike a badge, with a diameter of 2 inches (5.1 centimeters).

On April 14, 1928, the *Toronto Star Weekly* devoted a full-page article to McCowan and his invention: "Here at first sight is a booth that is like a telephone booth. You enter and sit on a stool which you may adjust to your height. You focus your face with the aid of a couple of mirrors which give your eyes, nose, and mouth the correct alignment. All the time you are looking pleasant, please, into a hollow white reflector designed with curves that will flood your face with light. Then you drop a quarter in the slot and watch for the dickey bird to come out. There is a whirr as the electrical mechanism starts. Powerful lights flash on that are like the Klieg lights of a moving-picture set. Eight seconds pass—and the camera clicks. You are taken. Stroll out to the back of the booth and wait. Within a minute your mirror-photo drops out of a slot into a waiting cup."

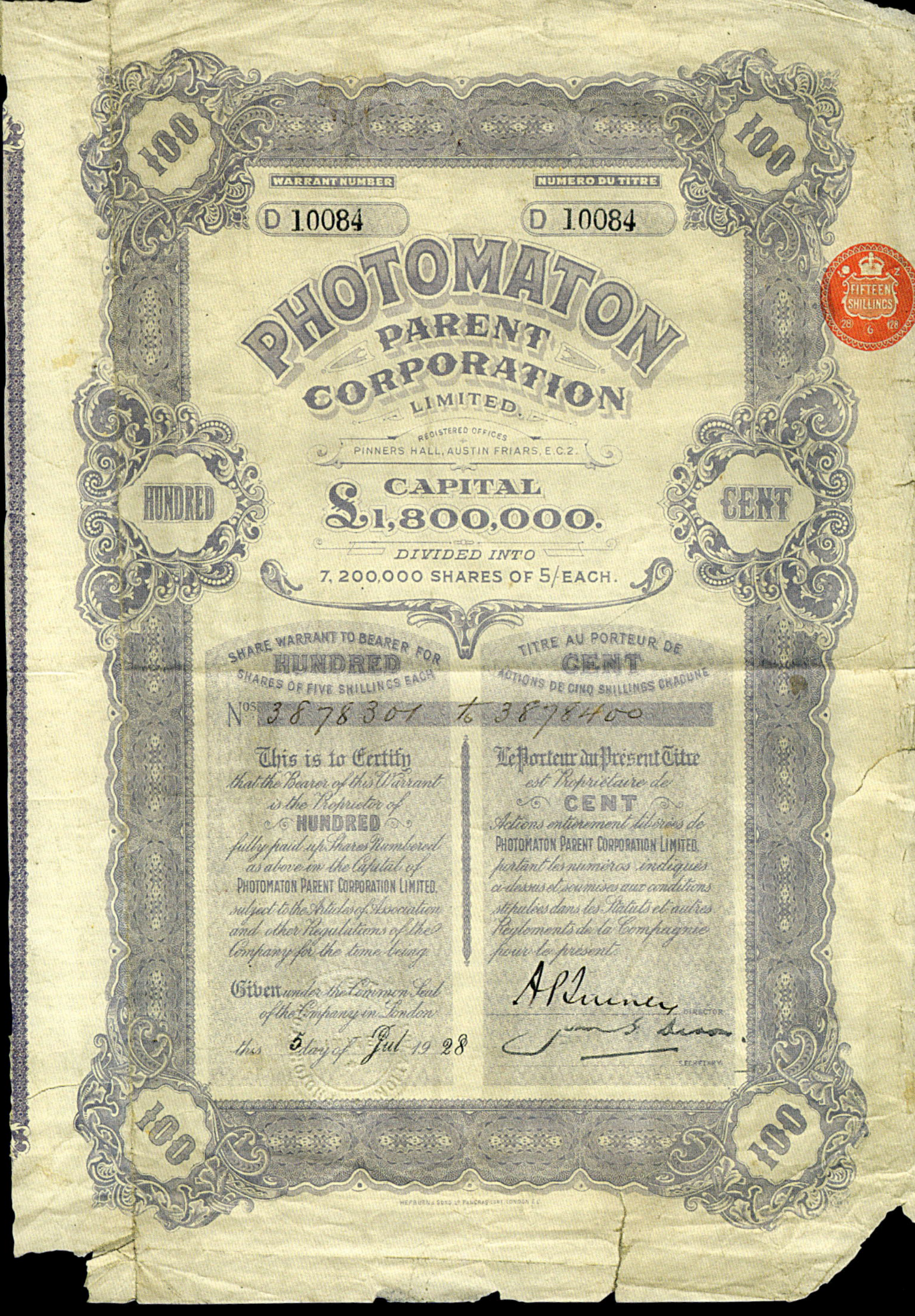

Share in the British Photomaton Parent Corporation valued at £1.8 million, London, 1928.

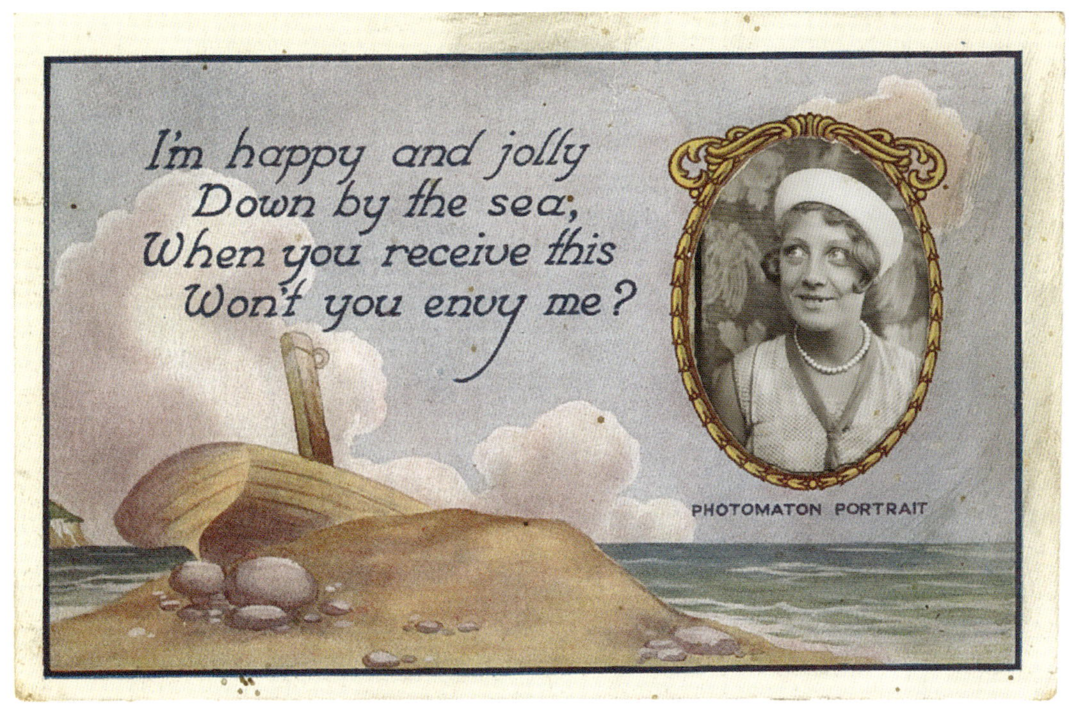

Foldout postcard for a Photomaton portrait. London, c. 1930.

THE PHOTOMATON CONQUERS THE WORLD

In December 1927, the Photomaton became an export. A group of British investors purchased the rights to distribute the machine in England, France, Germany, Italy, and Canada. The machine's success spread over the globe, and the financiers were overjoyed.

In London, the businessman Clarence Charles Hatry was the head of the British Photomaton Parent Corporation and the Far Eastern Photomaton Corporation. In September 1929, his holdings were entangled in an enormous case of fraud and bankruptcy that triggered a plunge in the London stock exchange in September 1929, a prelude to New York's notorious Black Thursday stock market crash on October 24 of that year. The Photomaton Parent Corporation became emblematic of a sharply overvalued company. Hatry, sentenced to fourteen years in prison for fraud, was freed after serving nine years.

Beginning in 1928, Major Keith Trevor, a British millionaire and a representative of the Photomaton Parent Corporation, enjoyed exclusive rights to market the Photomaton name and trademark "in France, in the colonies and the protectorates." To ensure the greatest publicity, the first "automatic photography" booths run by the Société Continentale Photomaton were installed at the Galeries Lafayette, in the headquarters of the *Petit Journal*, in Luna Park, at the Bon Marché, and in the Jardin d'Acclimatation, a children's amusement

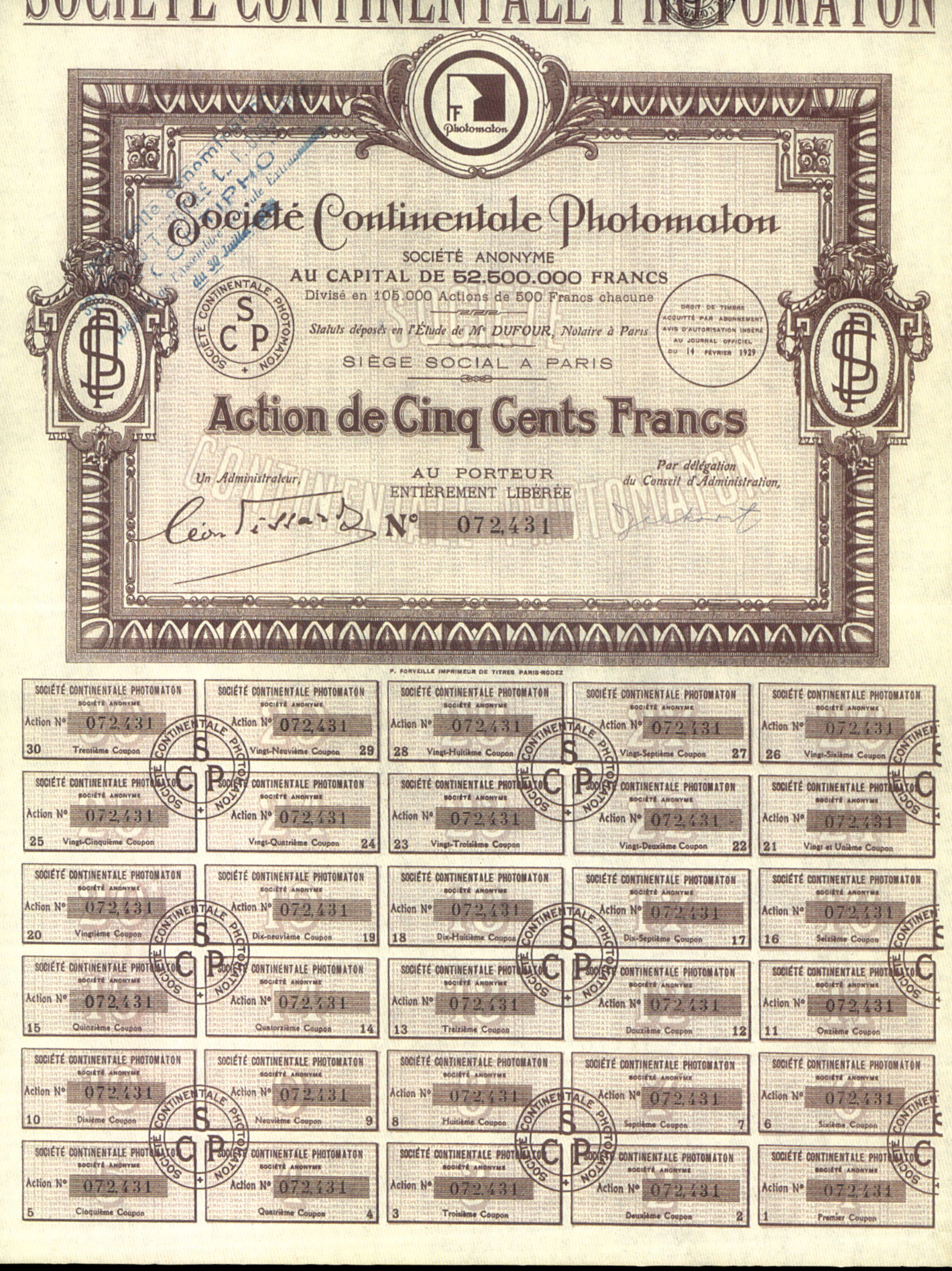

Five-hundred-franc share in the Société Continentale Photomaton, Paris, 1929.

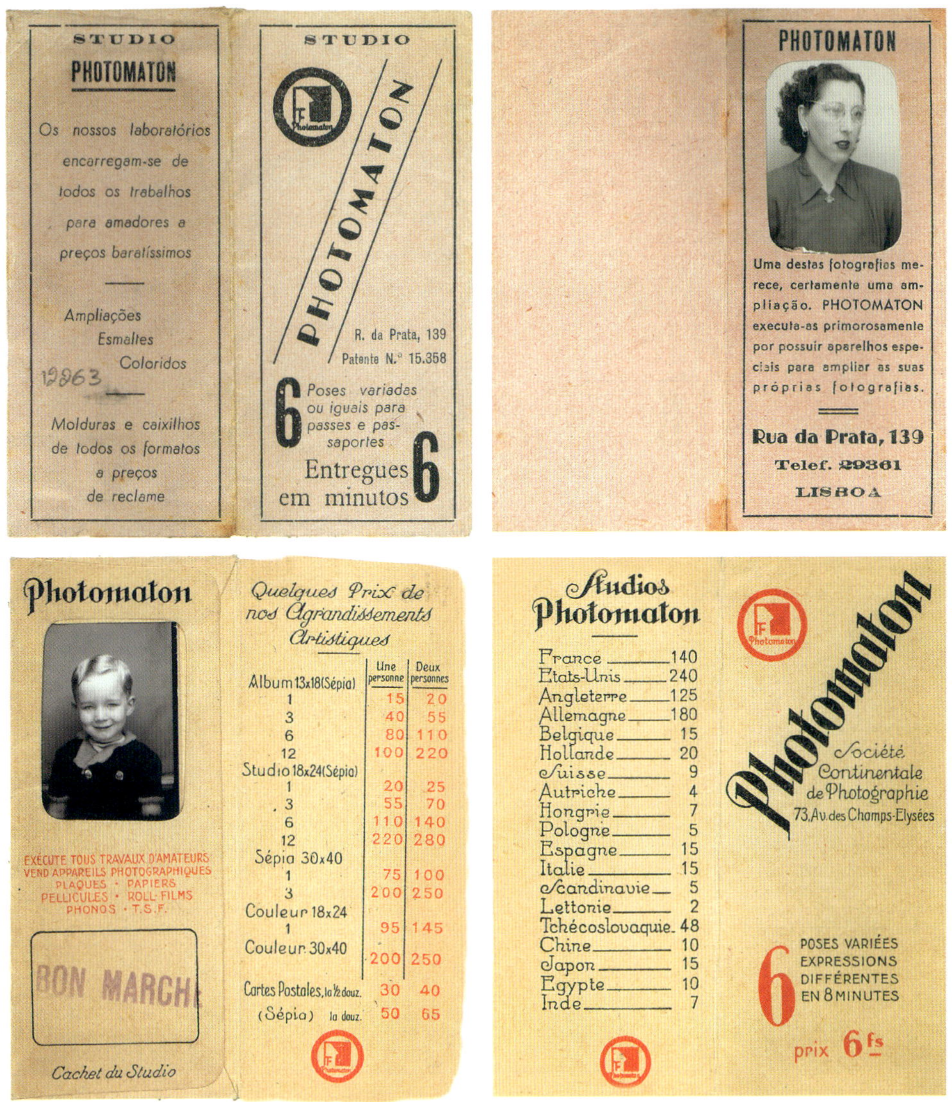

Top: Photobooth booklet, Lisbon, Portugal, c. 1950.
Bottom: Photobooth booklet, Bon Marché department store, Paris, c. 1930–1940.

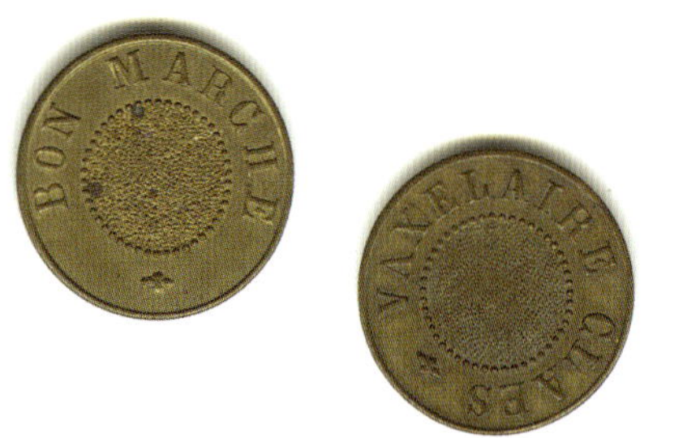

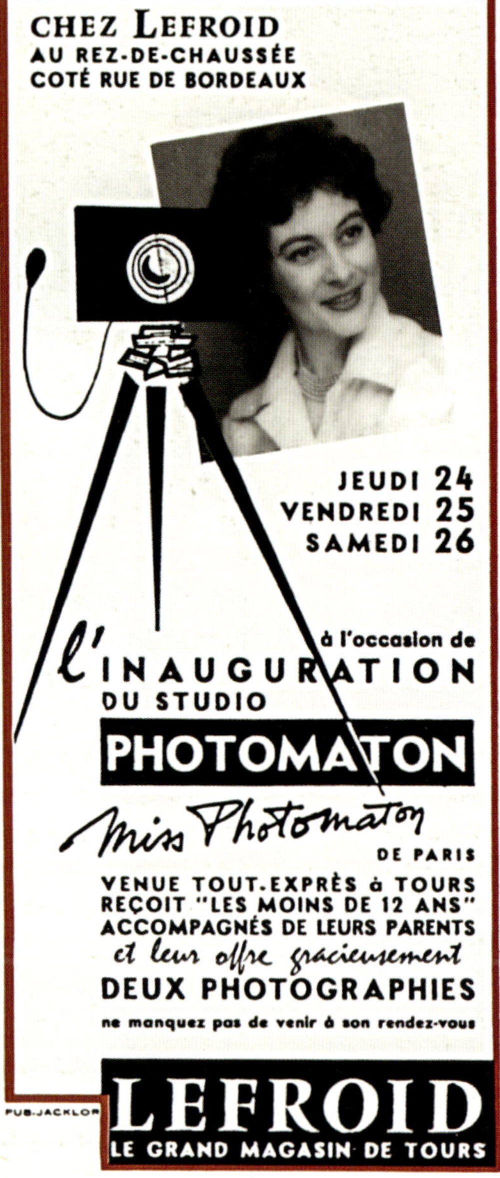

park in the Bois de Boulogne. For five francs, which were exchanged for a token, "you pose for 16 seconds, moving, turning, and assuming a variety of poses and expressions; 8 minutes later, you will automatically receive six perfect photos, each one different from the rest. You can pose whenever you like, when you feel you are looking your best; you will waste no time, and it's no longer an ordeal, now it's a game."

Imported directly from the United States, the first Photomaton booths in Europe were equipped with coin slots calibrated for the insertion of a 25-cent piece. In France and in Belgium, the camera would only snap the picture after receiving a token with a diameter of 1 inch (2.35 centimeters), the size of the American quarter.

While the terms of the patent registered in New York by Josepho on March 27, 1925, suggest an entirely automated photographic process, the Photomaton booths installed in France still required the intervention of an operator. A Miss Photomaton, dressed in a blue uniform, suggested poses and adjusted the diaphragm before taking the picture. It was not until 1968 that photobooths were finally operated simply by the introduction of a coin, and the customer was left completely alone in front of the lens— that is to say, more than forty years after the invention of the "quarter-in-the-slot" machine.

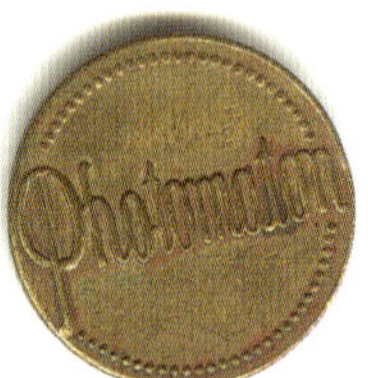

Top and above: Photomaton tokens, "Bon Marché–Vaxelaire Claes," Brussels.

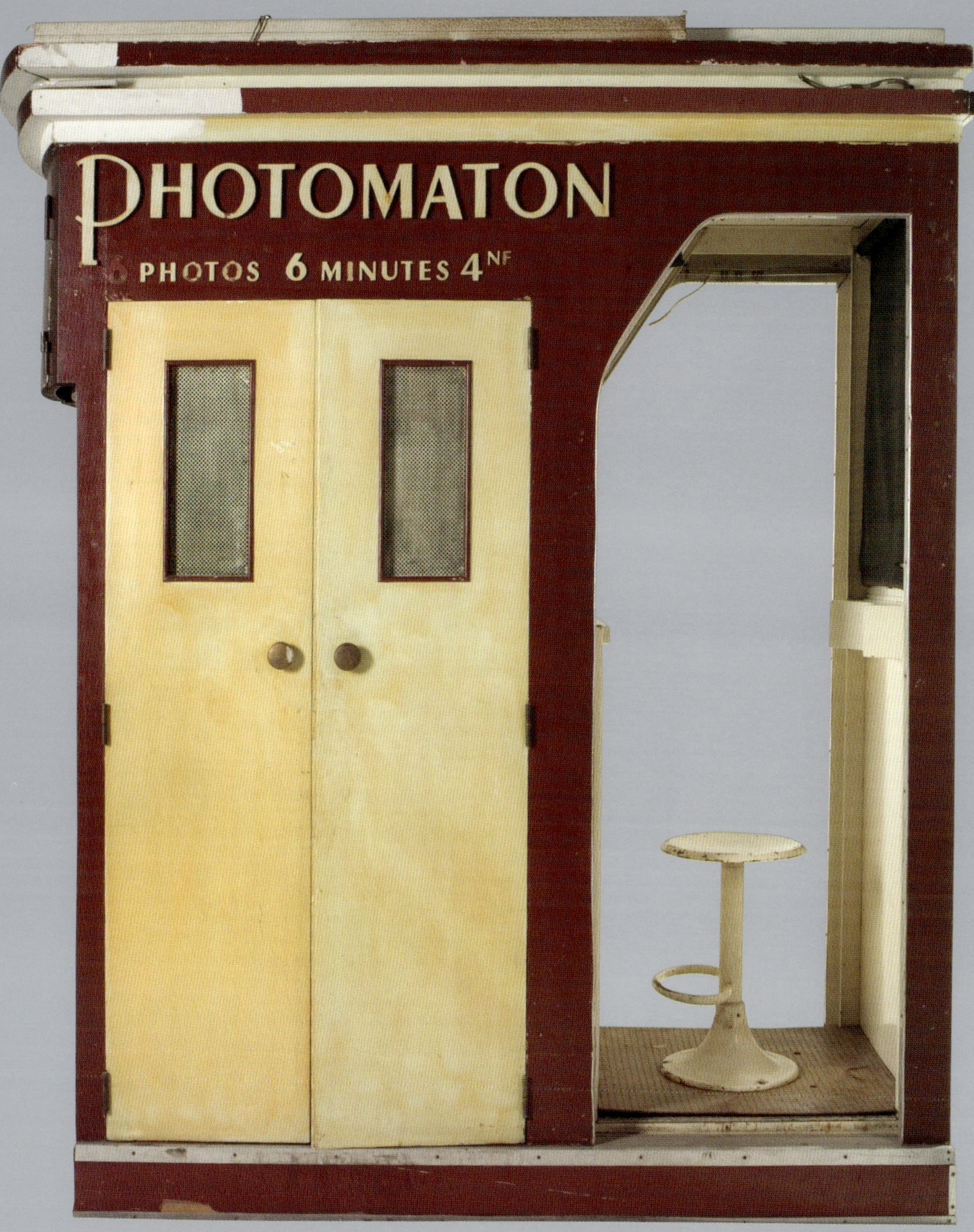

The first Photomaton booths in Europe used tokens that were the same size as American quarters.

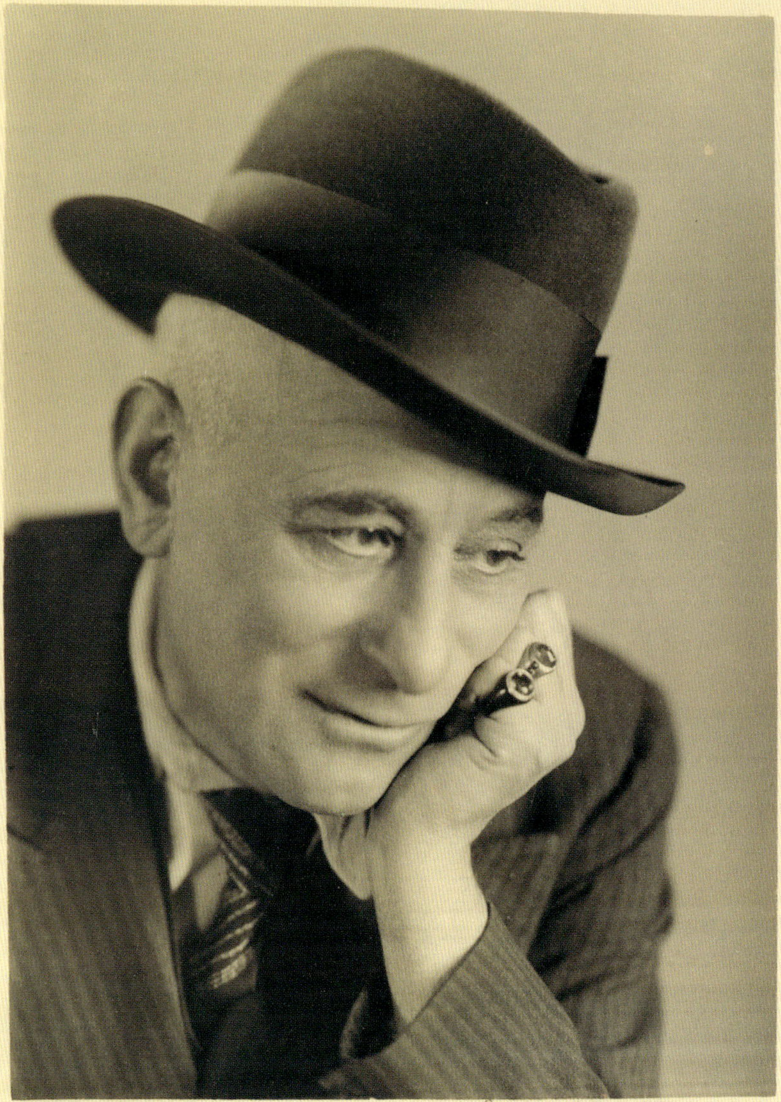

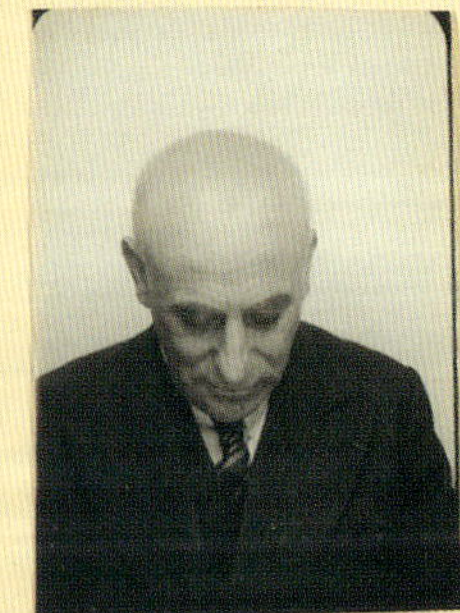

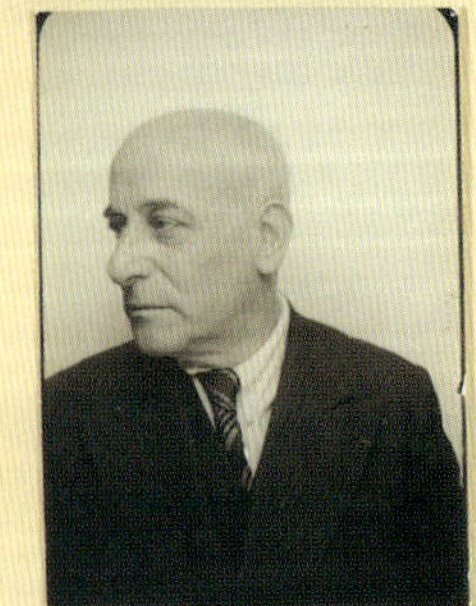

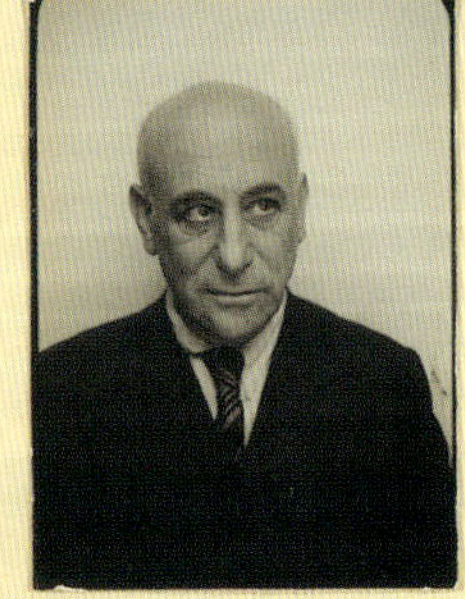

à mon ami Willy michel

le photographe des rois

le roi des photographes.

Max Jacob

avril 36.

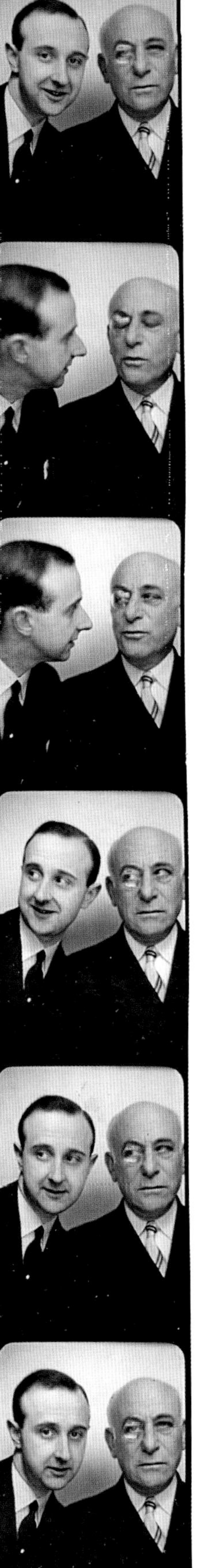

WILLY MICHEL AND HIS STUDIO D'ART PHOTOMATON

Because the intervention of a Photomaton operator was necessary in the earliest European versions of the photobooth, the machines were frequently installed in photographers' studios. In June 1928, at 26 Boulevard des Italiens in Paris, Willy Michel, a twenty-four-year-old photographer, opened his own "Studio d'Art Photomaton." Working until the mid-1950s, he created an incredible series of portraits of celebrities, including the actors Charles Boyer, Bing Crosby, Errol Flynn, Erich von Stroheim, Michel Simon, Maria Casarès, and Maurice Chevalier; the boxers Marcel Thil and Georges Carpentier; the pianist Arthur Rubinstein; and even the Infante Jaime de Borbón of Spain. Actors, singers, dancers, American movie stars, and the celebrities of bygone days all took a seat in the strangely public space of the photobooth, while Michel systematically clicked off a series of photographs.

On April 20, 1936, Max Jacob wrote the following to the young poet Jean Fraysse: "Willy Michel, the photographer of the Photomaton in the Boulevard des Italiens, asks great men to have their pictures taken free of charge, he invites them out to enjoy lavish dinners, he buys books, etc."

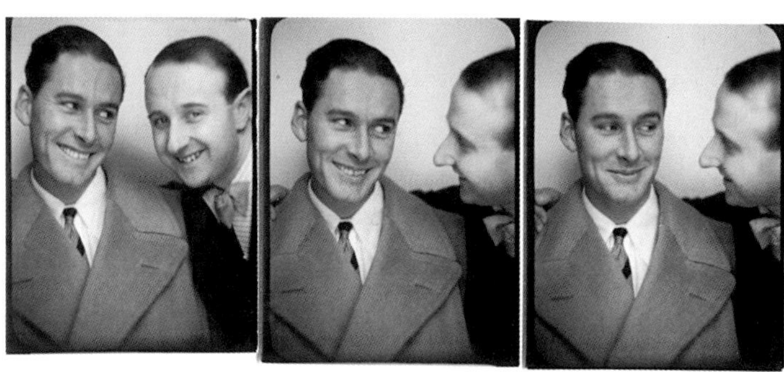

Errol Flynn.

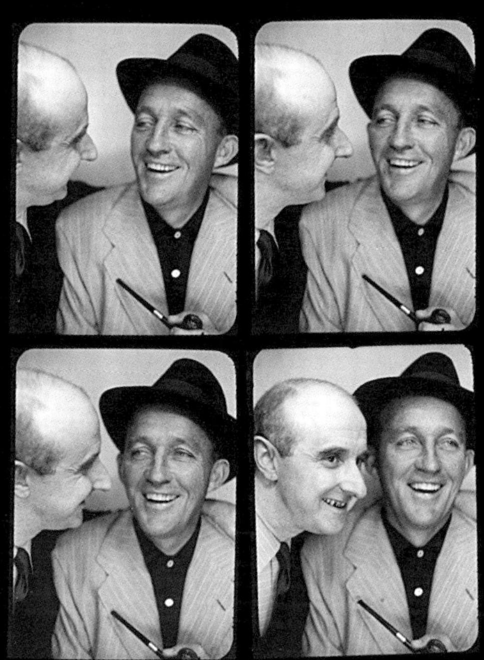

Singer Bing Crosby: May 19, 1953, the day of his performance at the Moulin Rouge for the twenty-fifth Bal des Petits Lits Blancs (Ball of the Little White Beds).

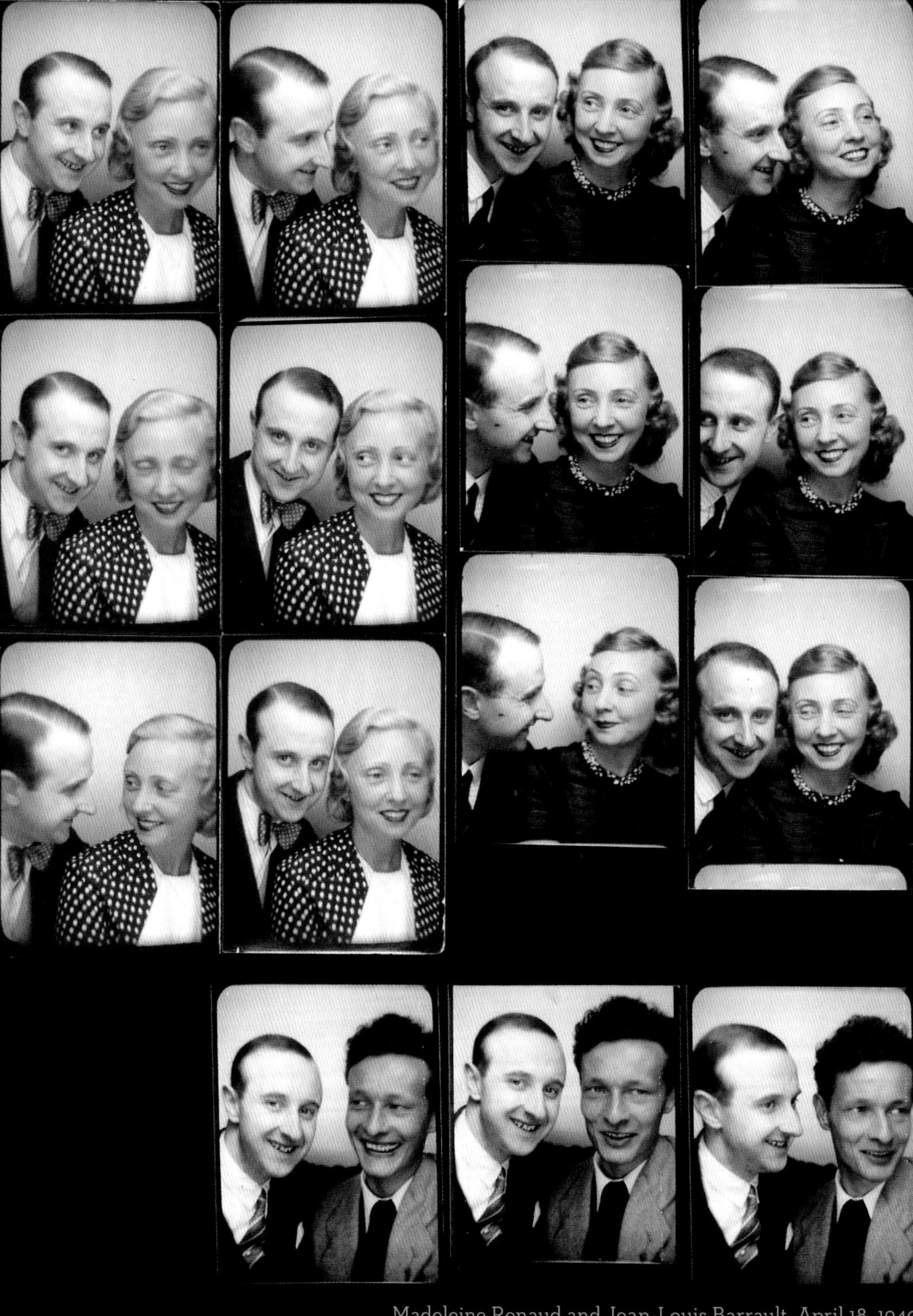

Madeleine Renaud and Jean-Louis Barrault, April 18, 1940

Michel Simon
and companions:
December 12, 1938;
April 24, 1944; and
December 4, 1944.

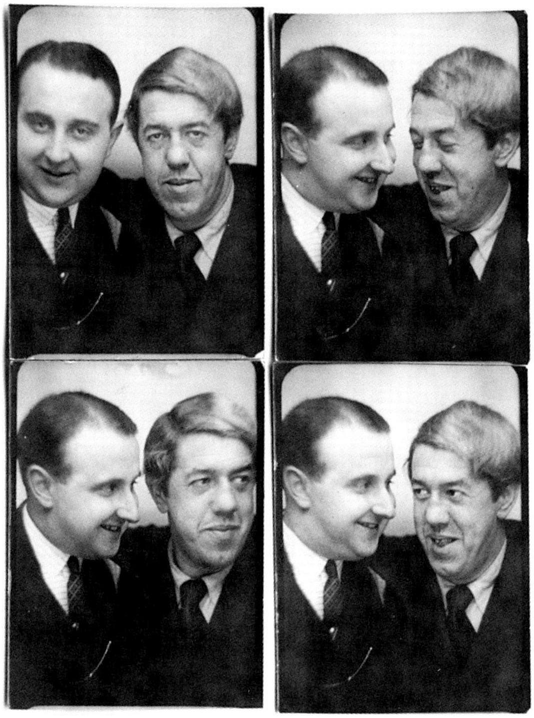

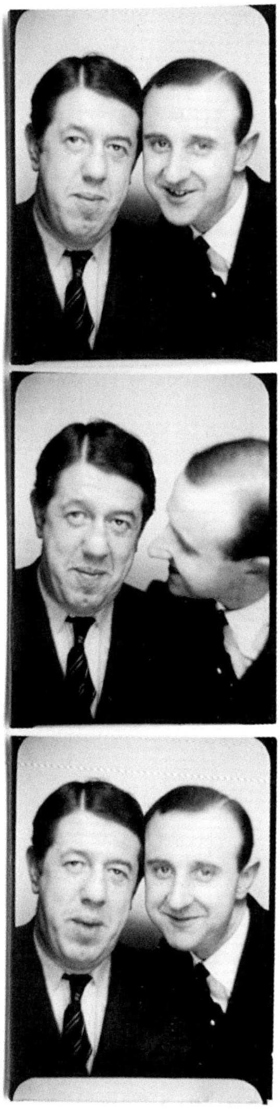

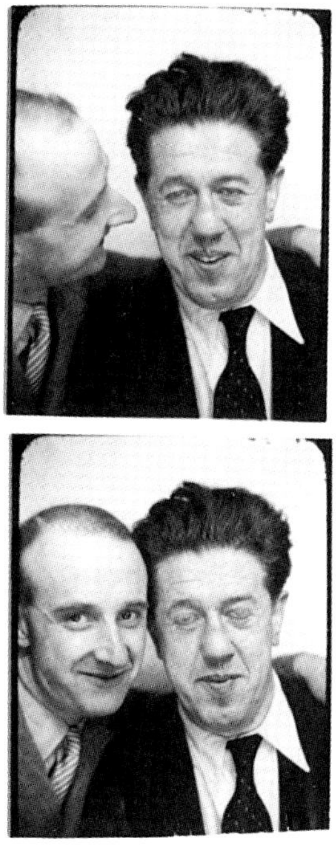

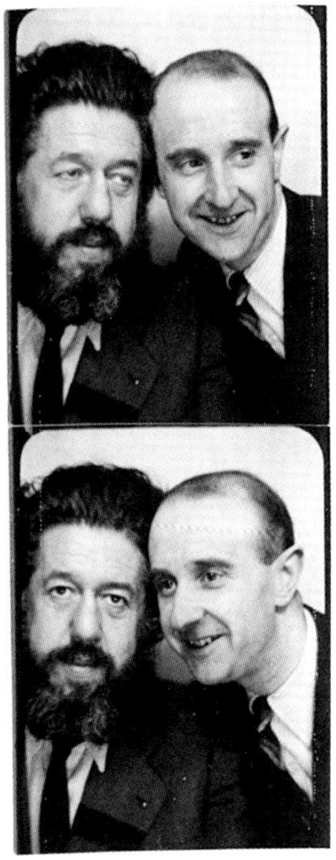

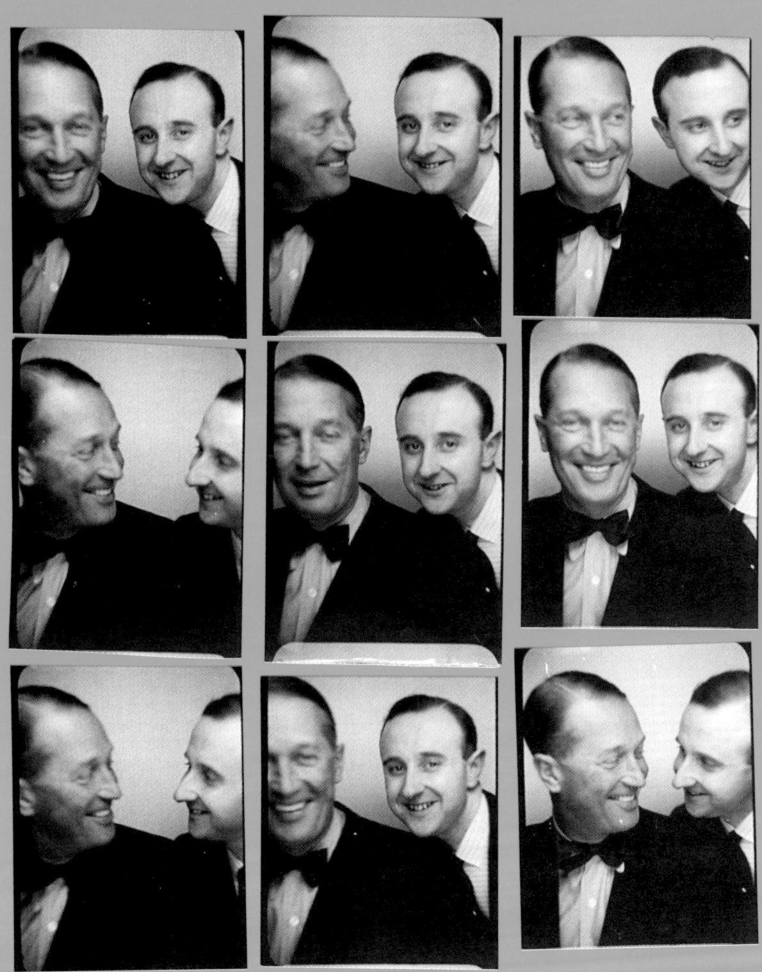

Actor Maurice Chevalier, September 1938.

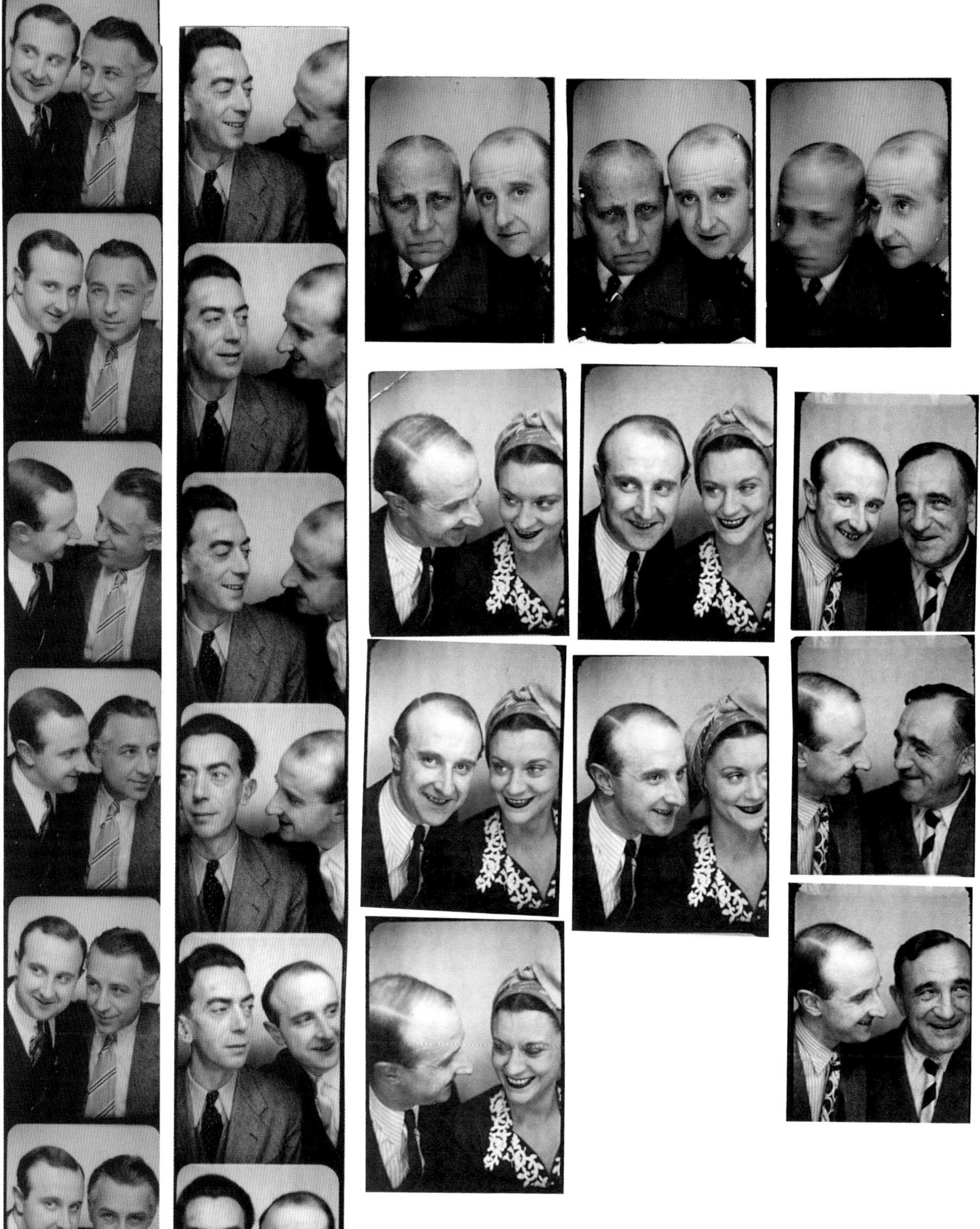

From left: Abel Gance, Marcel Aymé, actor Erich von Stroheim, 1949; Maria Casarès, April 8, 1946; director Charles Vanel, September 14, 1942.

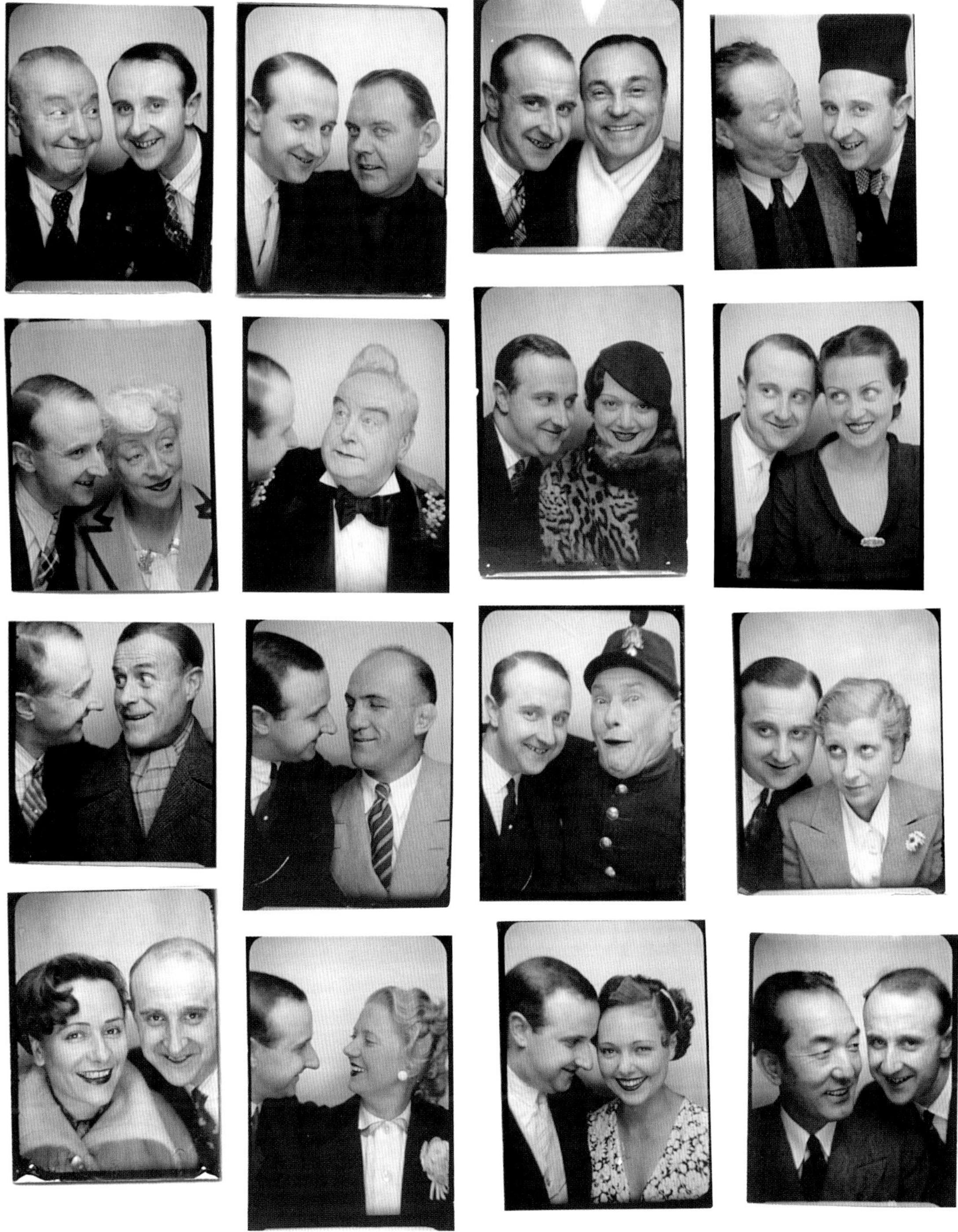

From left to right and top to bottom: François Fratellini, Fernand Ledoux, Andrex, Bach, Françoise Rosay, Felix Mayol, Edwige Feuillère, Lise Delamare, Gaston Modot, Marcel Thill, Luar, Mireille, Denise Vernac, Denise Grey, Paulette Dubost, Sesshu Hayakawa.

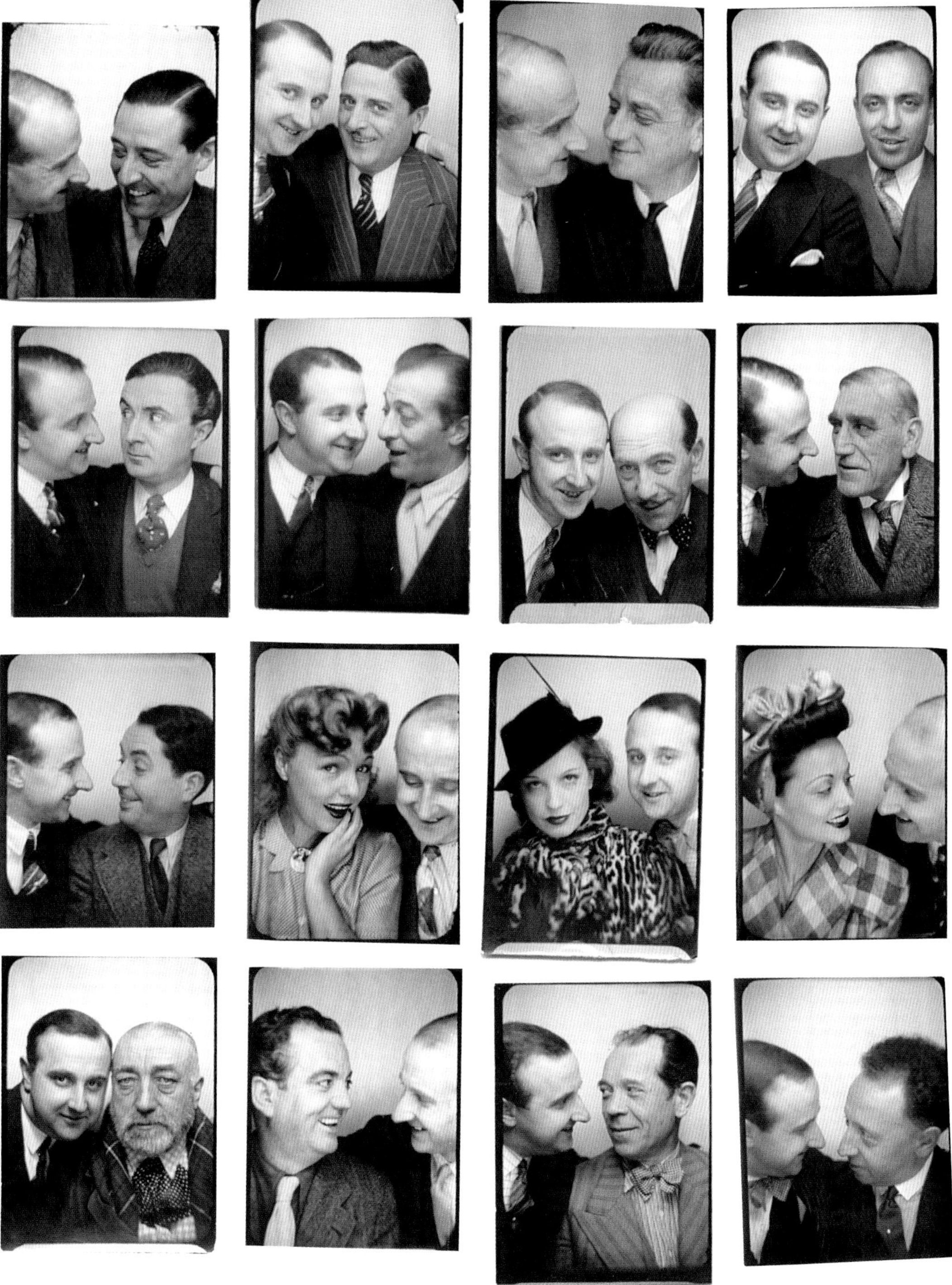

From left to right and top to bottom: George Thill, Henri Bosc, Claude Dauphin, Ray Ventura, Noël Noël, Jules Berry, Charles Deschamps, José Davert, Carette, Paulette Dubost, Lili Damita, Louise Carletti, Paul Poiret, Raymond Cordy, Larquey, Arthur Rubinstein.

14. Angabe, aus welchen Einkünften der Unterhalt bestritten wird .... State from what income the maintenance is provided for Indicazione di quali rendite il mantenimento si paga Indication de quelles revenues les frais de maintien seront payés	**LOHN**
15. Beschäftigt bei? (Firma, Sitz, Ort, Straße Nr.) .... Employed at? (Firm, place, street, Nr.) Impiegato da? (Casa, sede, luogo, strada, no.) Employé chez? (Maison, siège, lieu, rue, no.)	**BRUNO KOSCHMIDER** **BETRIEBE GROSSE FREHEIT HAMBURG**
16. Ist ein gültiger Befreiungsschein — Arbeitserlaubnis — vorhanden? (Behörde, Geltungsdauer, Nr.). Is there a valid permit of liberation — working permit? (Office, duration, number) C'è un attestato di disimpegno — permesso di lavoro? (Autorità, validità, no.) Existe-t-il une attestation de libération — un permis de travail? (Autorité, durée de validité, no.)	
17. Voraussichtliche Dauer und Zweck des Aufenthalts? .... Probable duration and purpose of stay Durata probabile e scopo del soggiorno? Durée probable et but du séjour?	**ZWEI MONATE**

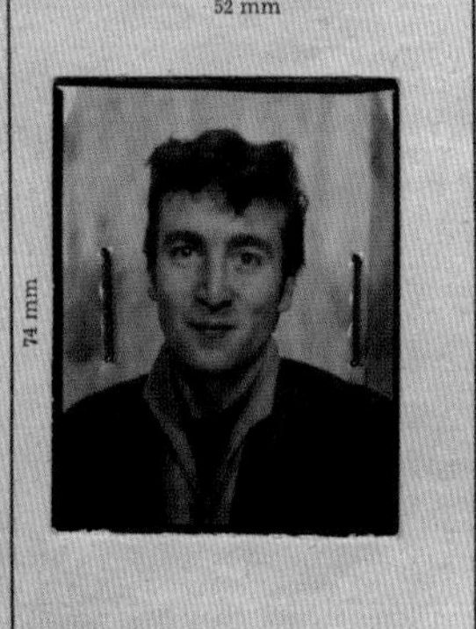

52 mm

74 mm

Ich versichere, daß ich die vorstehenden Angaben nach bestem Wissen und Gewissen gemacht habe. Mir ist bekannt, daß unrichtige Angaben behördliche Maßnahmen zur Folge haben.
I herewith assure to have made the preceding statements most conscientiously. I know that any false statement will be persecuted.
Io asserisco aver fatto le dichiarazioni presenti secondo della mia miglior conoscenza. Io sò che le dichiarazioni falsi saranno la cagione di misure ufficiali.
Je déclare avoir fait les indications précédentes consciencieusement. Je sais que les indications inexactes ou fausses seront poursuivies.

HAMBURG   **25/8/60**

(Ort)   (Datum)
(Place)   (Date)
(Luogo)   (Data)
(Lieu)   (Date)

(Unterschrift des Ausländers, Ruf- und Familienname)
(Signature of the foreigner, family name and Christian name)
(Firma dello straniero, nome di famiglia e cognome)
(Signature de l'étranger, nom de famille et prénom)

1. Abgemeldet am _______ 6.1.61

    nach _______

2. Mitteilung an „AZR."

3. Karte zur B-Kartei

4. Zu den Sammelakten _______ 6-1-62

10

THE IDENTITY PORTRAIT

At the end of the nineteenth century, the Paris Prefecture of Police under Alphonse Bertillon (1853-1914) codified the processes for criminal suspects and recidivists. The files listed measurements, fingerprints, distinguishing features, and photographs, one facing front and one in profile. Before long, the use of photographs was extended to the production of identity papers. By the early thirties, the Photomaton portrait became a standard of identification photography.

In May 1941, the Société Continentale Photomaton offered its services to the German authorities: "We imagine that the assembly of certain categories of individuals of the Jewish race in concentration camps will necessarily result in the administrative need to create dossiers, files, and identity cards, etc.

"We are specialists in matters concerning identification, and so we venture to bring to your attention in particular how useful our automatic Photomaton machines would be. They are capable of photographing a thousand people in six different poses, in just one routine day of work. In cases where it is necessary to photograph significant numbers of workers, we bring machines, with an operator, out to the site. We have done this when it was necessary to execute identification photographs, in the plant buildings themselves, of the staffs of the leading French factories. We have also undertaken identification photo campaigns in work camps and prison camps. (*Conversations secrètes des Français sous l'Occupation*, Antoine Lefébure).

Though the German forces declined this ignoble (to put it mildly) offer, the Photomaton

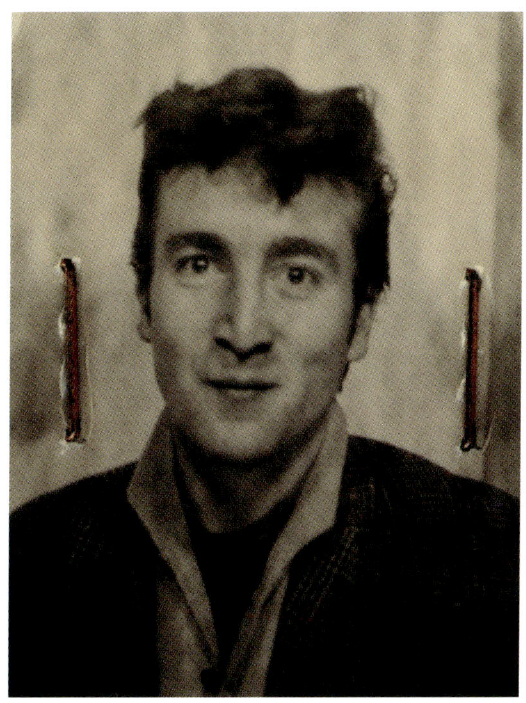

Opposite and above: Work permit and identity photo issued to John Lennon, then nineteen years old, for a series of Beatles concerts in Hamburg, Germany, starting in August 1960.

booth was put to use after the Allied liberation for the production of identification photos. Practically nothing changed until 1968, when color photographs began to compete with black-and-white ones, and the French Minister of the Interior declared that color photographs could be used as long as they were in the 1.4 × 1.6-in. (3.5 × 4-cm) format. The photos had to be "good likenesses, without any retouching, facing forward, bareheaded."

The development of digital photography in the early nineties changed everything. Photobooths could now produce four identical photographs, in a single pose, for the sole purpose of identification.

"Don't fool around with your identification photographs!" warns a sign that now appears on all the Photomaton booths in France. In

Nom : _de Chirico_ **Nationalité :** _Italienne_

(s'il s'agit d'une femme mariée, indiquer le nom patronymique comme suit : X... *née* Y...)

Mode d'acquisition de cette nationalité :
Filiation - Mariage - Naturalisation
(Rayer les mentions inutiles.)

Prénoms : _Giorgio_

Age _____ ans; né le (date) _10 7 à 1888_ _Volo (Volo_

	PÈRE	**MÈRE**
Noms et prénoms :	_Evariste_	_Gemma Cervetto_
Date de naissance :	_d o d_	_d o d_
Lieu de naissance :	_Ital_	_Ital_
Nationalité :	_Ital_ de naissance, par naturalisation.	_Ital_ de naissance par mariage par naturalisation

Né de

Célibataire — Marié — Veuf *(veuve)* — Divorcé — Biffer les mentions inutiles

Renseignements sur le conjoint.

Nom : __________ Prénoms : __________
né le _____ à présent à __________
Nationalité avant mariage __________
Si le conjoint est en France, N° de la carte d'identité __________ ; si non, où réside-t-il? __________
Date et lieu du mariage : __________

Enfants

	NOMS	PRÉNOMS	SEXE	DATE ET LIEU DE NAISSANCE	EST-IL EN FRANCE (oui ou non); si non, où réside-t-il?
1°					
2°					
3°					
4°					
5°					
6°					
7°					
8°					

Adresse actuelle { Rue _Square Léon Guillot_ N° _2_ à __________

Dernier domicile à l'Étranger { __________

Profession habituelle { _Arts_

Loi du 8 août 1893 { Numéro : __________ Date : __________

Pièces d'Identité produites { _1er déclaré Du Pass.t Ital 618835 délin le 21.12.29 à Paris Vu à l'entré en France Modane le 10.12.1933._

Giorgio de Chirico, application for a residence permit, Paris, December 10, 1933.

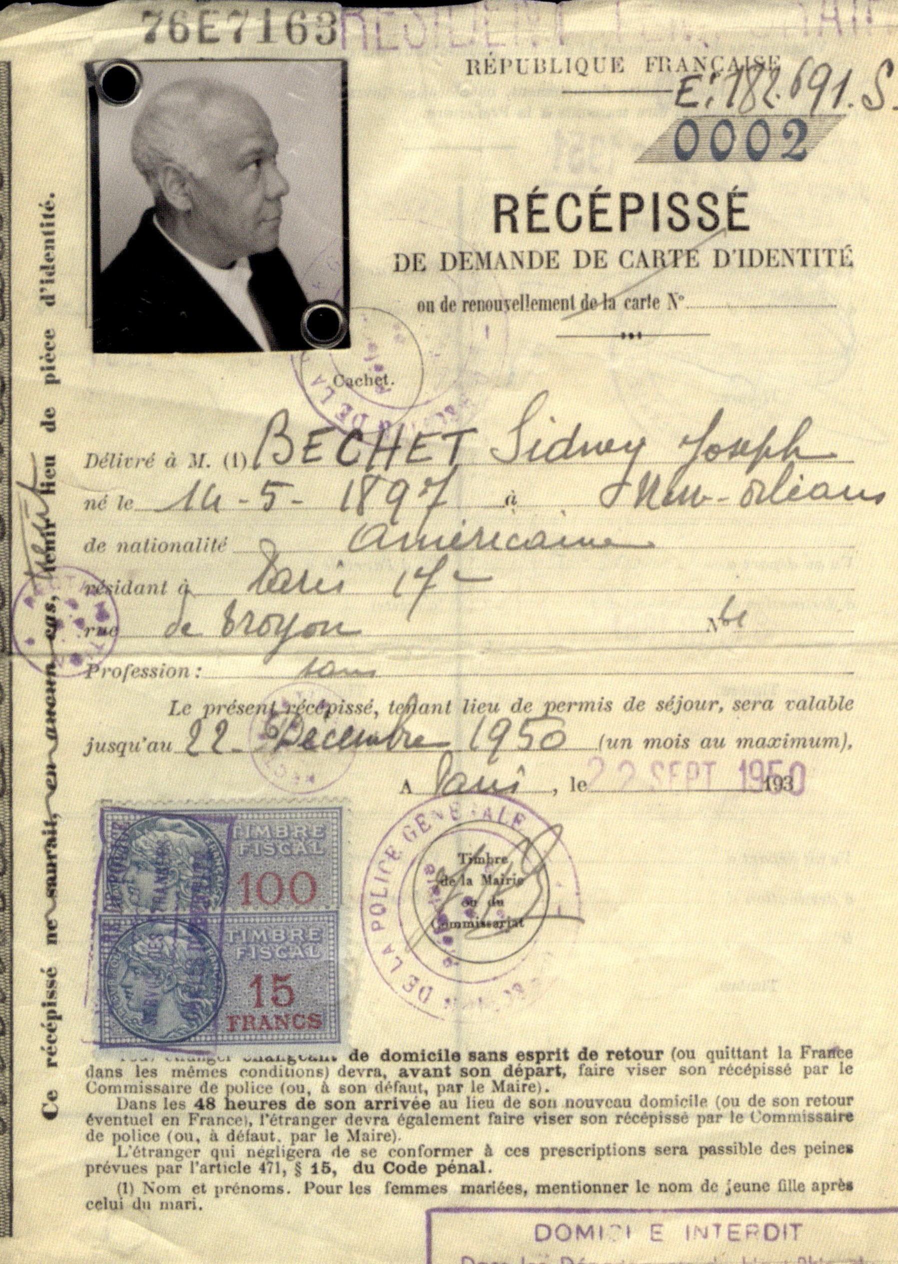

Sidney Bechet, receipt for a residence permit application, Paris, 1950.

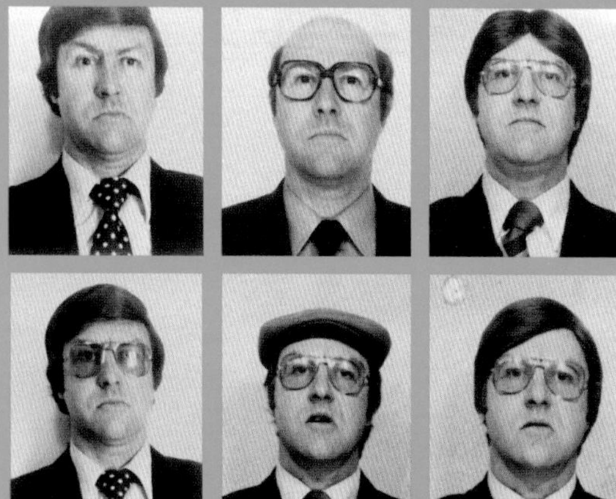

Jacques Mesrine. Wanted by the French national police in the seventies, he was Public Enemy Number One, and was also known as "the man with a hundred faces."

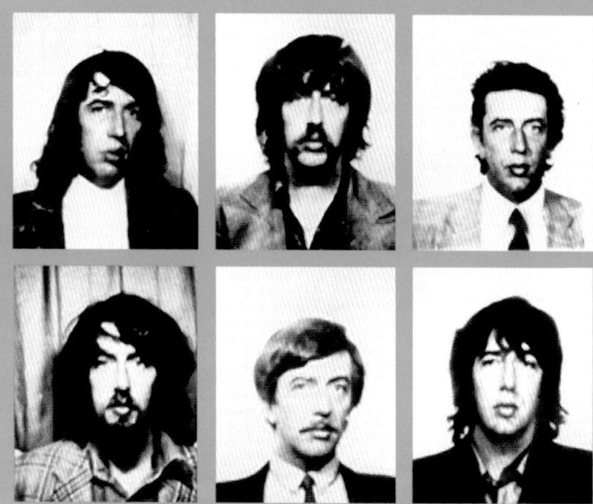

Howard Marks, also known as Mr. Nice. Between 1970 and 1987, Marks was a major hash dealer, wanted by the British and United States police. He operated under forty-three different identities. Mr. Nice was finally arrested in the United States in 1988. Sentenced to twenty-five years in prison, he was released on parole after serving seven years.

England, the warning is even more explicit: "*Smiling is not accepted by passport authorities.*" The September 11, 2001, terrorist attacks in the United States helped to accelerate the introduction of computer science to border identity checks. The introduction of the biometric passport—"very difficult to falsify or counterfeit," according to the French Ministry of the Interior—only served to further codify the norms governing the photographs.

From now on the size of the face should be between $1^1/4$ to $1^1/2$ in. (3.2 to 3.6 cm), measuring from the tip of the chin to the top of the skull (excluding hair), and the photo must be clear, without scratches or folds. A color photo is strongly recommended. The head must be uncovered; head coverings, scarves, and other hair bands are forbidden. The subject must face the lens, head held straight, looking into the lens, with a neutral expression and mouth closed. The face must be unobstructed, the eyes perfectly visible and open (eyeglasses are discouraged). It is practically the Bertillon method all over again.

In order to comply with the new demands, computerized photobooths are now equipped with software that automatically adjusts the orientation and position of the head, reframing and cropping identity photos to ensure they respect the geometric criteria of the vertical position of the line separating the eyes and distances between the various facial features and the edges of the photograph. Detection and reframing are followed by a verification process that eliminates any photos that do not meet these standards. As early as 1979, the writer Roland Barthes wrote in *Camera Lucida*, "For it is not indifference which erases the weight of the image—the Photomat always turns you into a criminal type, wanted by the police."

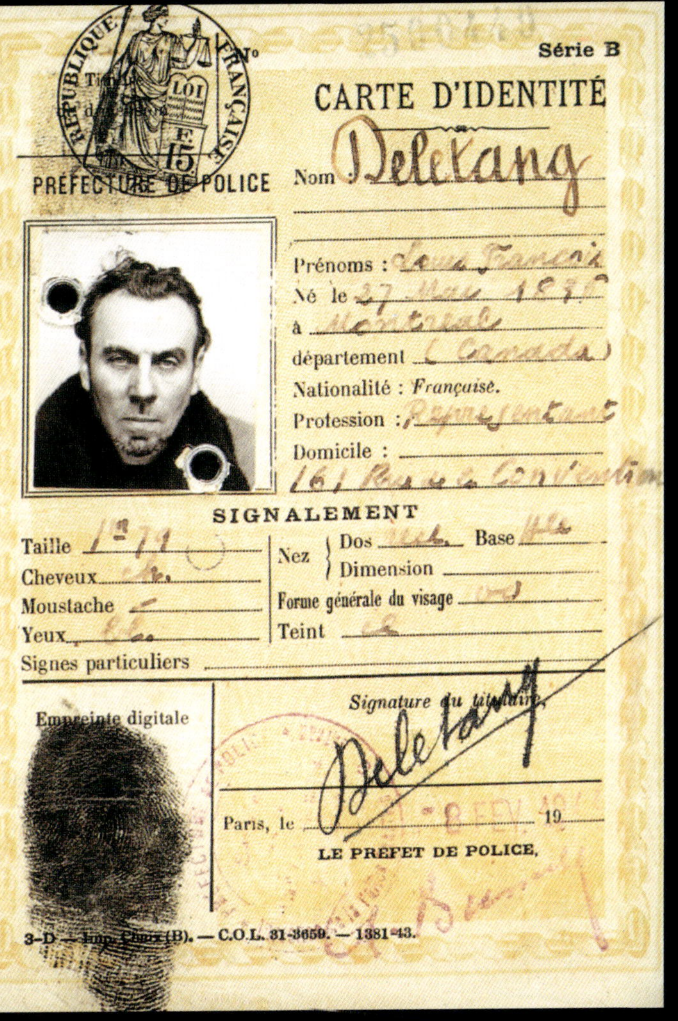

Louis-Ferdinand Céline. In June 1944, following the American landings in Normandy, Céline, the author of three anti-Semitic pamphlets published between 1937 and 1941, and responsible for providing "literary" support for the collaborationist Vichy government, left France first for Germany, and then Denmark.
False identity cards for Céline and his wife Lucette. Louis-Ferdinand Céline, born Louis-Ferdinand-Auguste Destouches on May 27, 1894, became Louis-François Deletang, salesman. His wife, Lucette Destouches, née Almanzor, on July 20, 1912, in Paris, became Lucette Alcante, a physical fitness instructor. In 1950, Céline was sentenced to one year in prison, a 50,000-franc fine, and the confiscation of half his property, and was declared a national disgrace.

THE ARTIST
IN THE
PHOTOBOOTH

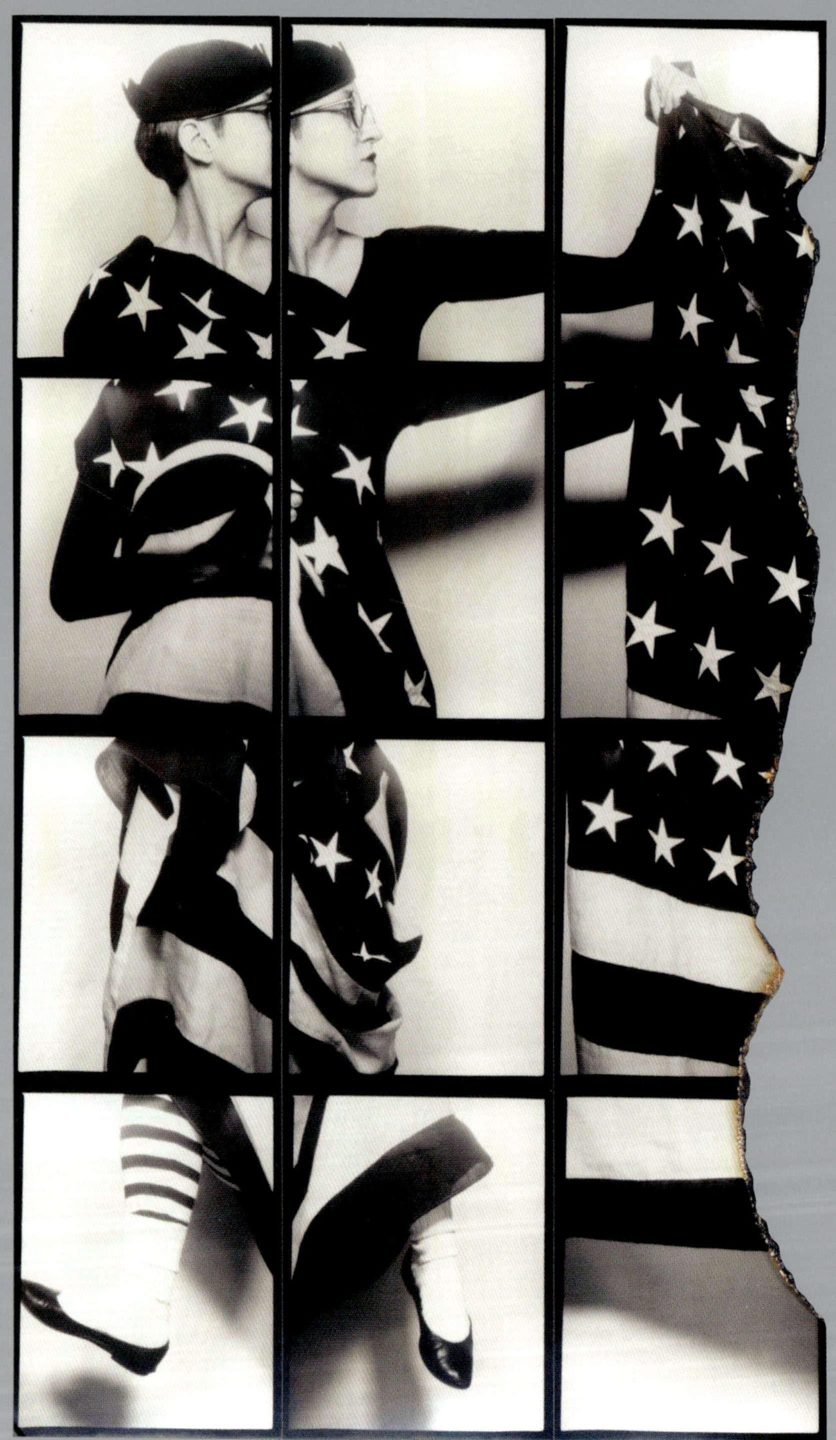

Herman Costa, *The Patriot*, 1992.

Variétés, December 15, 1928

It took less than three years for the photobooth to be hijacked from its purely commercial use. In 1929 the final issue of the magazine *La Révolution Surréaliste* published sixteen self-portraits of the principal members of the Surrealist movement. For the first time, the photobooth portrait was identified with something beyond identity pictures or cheap keepsake photos offered at fairs and amusement parks. It became a full-fledged artistic medium. Up to the mid-nineties, a period that corresponds to the progressive disappearance of silver-emulsion photobooths, many artists found liberation within the technical constraints imposed by the photobooth. The narrow space, the single frame, the frontal lighting, the fixed lens, the very short pose times, and the frequent malfunctions would contribute, paradoxically, to making the photobooth portrait and self-portrait a source of continuous inspiration and a major photographic and artistic challenge.

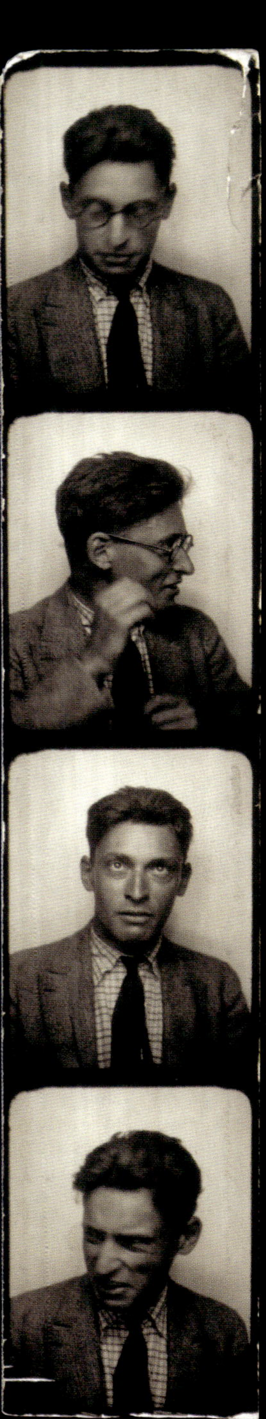

Raymond Queneau.

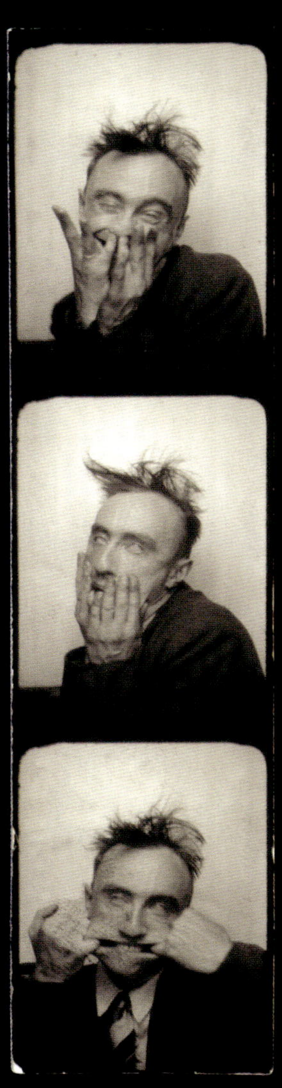

Yves Tanguy.

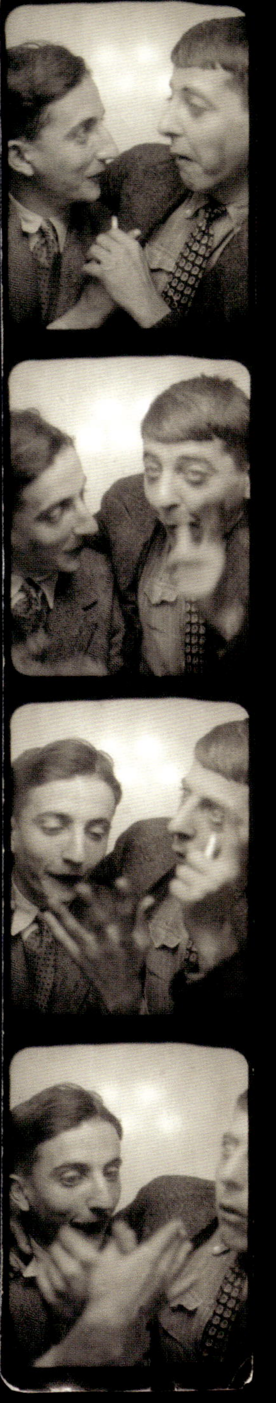

Pierre and Jacques
Prévert.

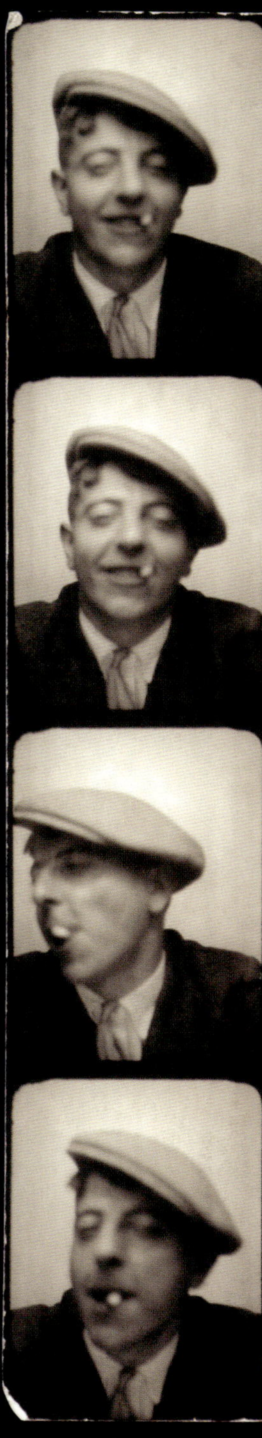

Jacques Prévert.

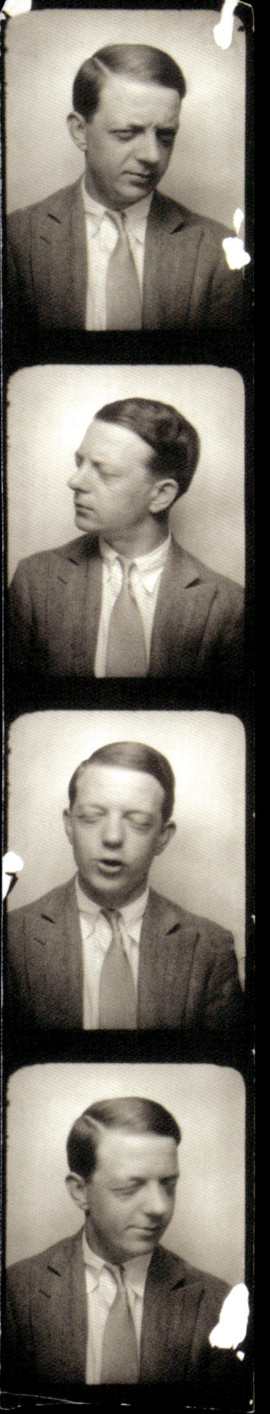

Marcel Duhamel.

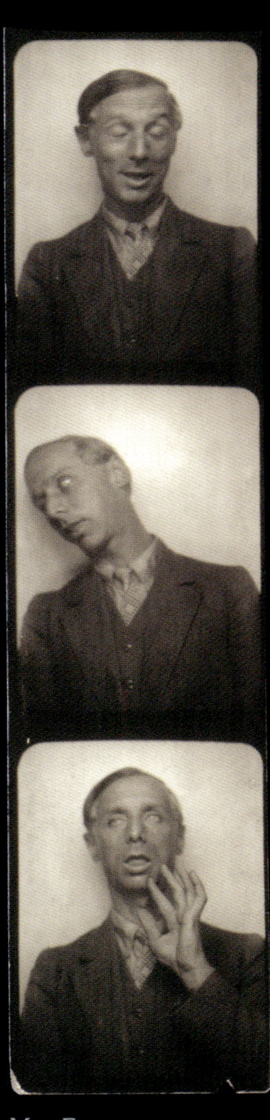

Max Ernst.

THE SURREALISTS

In April 2003, during an auction at the Hôtel Drouot in Paris, the André Breton collection was scattered to various museums and private collectors. Among the countless books, manuscripts, paintings, drawings, and photographs, there were dozens of photobooth snaps of Breton himself as well as Max Ernst, Paul Eluard, Suzanne Muzard, the Préverts, and Yves Tanguy.

These self-portraits, preserved by Breton in his studio at 42 Rue Fontaine, Paris, show the excitement that the Surrealists felt about the Photomaton in the wake of its arrival in France. While the principle of automatic photography was the perfect extension of the idea of automatic writing as defined in the First Surrealist Manifesto in 1924, it would appear that in the very earliest period the photobooth was seen as an object of play. In March 1928, Eluard in fact wrote to his wife, Gala, about "automatic photos": "5 francs a strip. If you grimace, it's funny." The Surrealists frequently went to the photobooths of Luna Park (an amusement park located at Porte Maillot in Paris) where, between grimaces and tomfoolery, they had fun with a vast number of self-portraits.

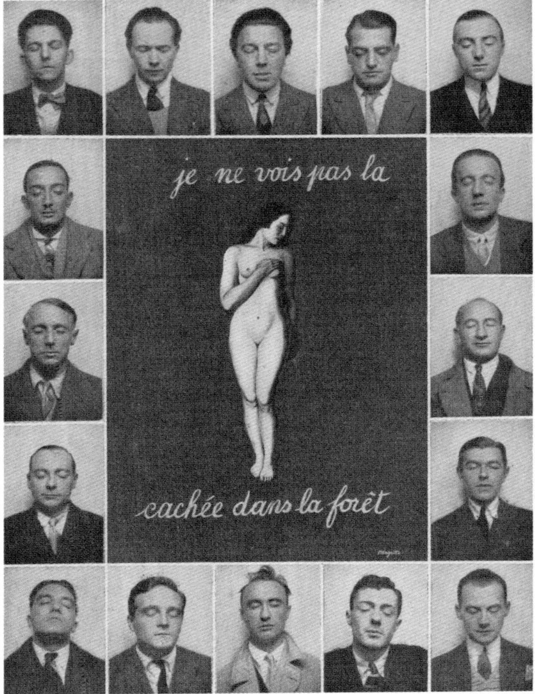

Photomontage published in the magazine *La Révolution Surréaliste* (no. 12), December 15, 1929. Clockwise, from top left: Maxime Alexandre, Louis Aragon, André Breton, Luis Buñuel, Jean Caupenne, Paul Eluard, Marcel Fourrier, René Magritte, Albert Valentin, André Thirion, Yves Tanguy, Georges Sadoul, Paul Nougé, Camille Goemans, Max Ernst, and Salvador Dalí.

Opposite: Original photobooth portraits for the montage.

On December 15, 1928, the Belgian magazine *Variétés* (subtitled *Revue Mensuelle Illustrée de l'Esprit Contemporain*), to which many members of the movement contributed, provided the following definition of the photobooth: "The Photomaton is an automatic device that provides you, in exchange for a five-franc token, with a strip of eight attitudes caught in photographs. Photomaton, I've been seen, you've seen me, I've often seen myself. There are fanatics who collect hundreds of their 'expressions.' It is a system of psychoanalysis via image. The first strip surprises you as you struggle to find the individual you always believed yourself to be. After the second strip, and throughout all the many strips that follow, while you may do your best to play the superior individual, the original type, the dark fascinating one, or the monkey, none of the resulting visions will fully correspond to what you want to see in yourself."

A month later, the same publication first reproduced Photomaton shots of Max Ernst. That year, in the twelfth and final issue of *La Révolution Surréaliste* (dated December 15, 1929), Photomaton self-portraits of Paul Eluard, Max Ernst, André Breton, Salvador Dalí, Louis Aragon, Luis Buñuel, and others framed a reproduction of René Magritte's *Je ne vois pas la [femme] cachée dans la forêt*. This collective portrait thus brought together sixteen members of the Surrealist movement; they posed with their eyes closed. According to Clément Chéroux, curator of the Centre Pompidou exhibition "La subversion des images," this photomontage illustrates the concept of the interior model: "It displays what the Surrealists see when they close their eyes, whether sleeping or dreaming: a feminine presence. This artwork this refers to the importance of the feminine in the Surrealist movement."

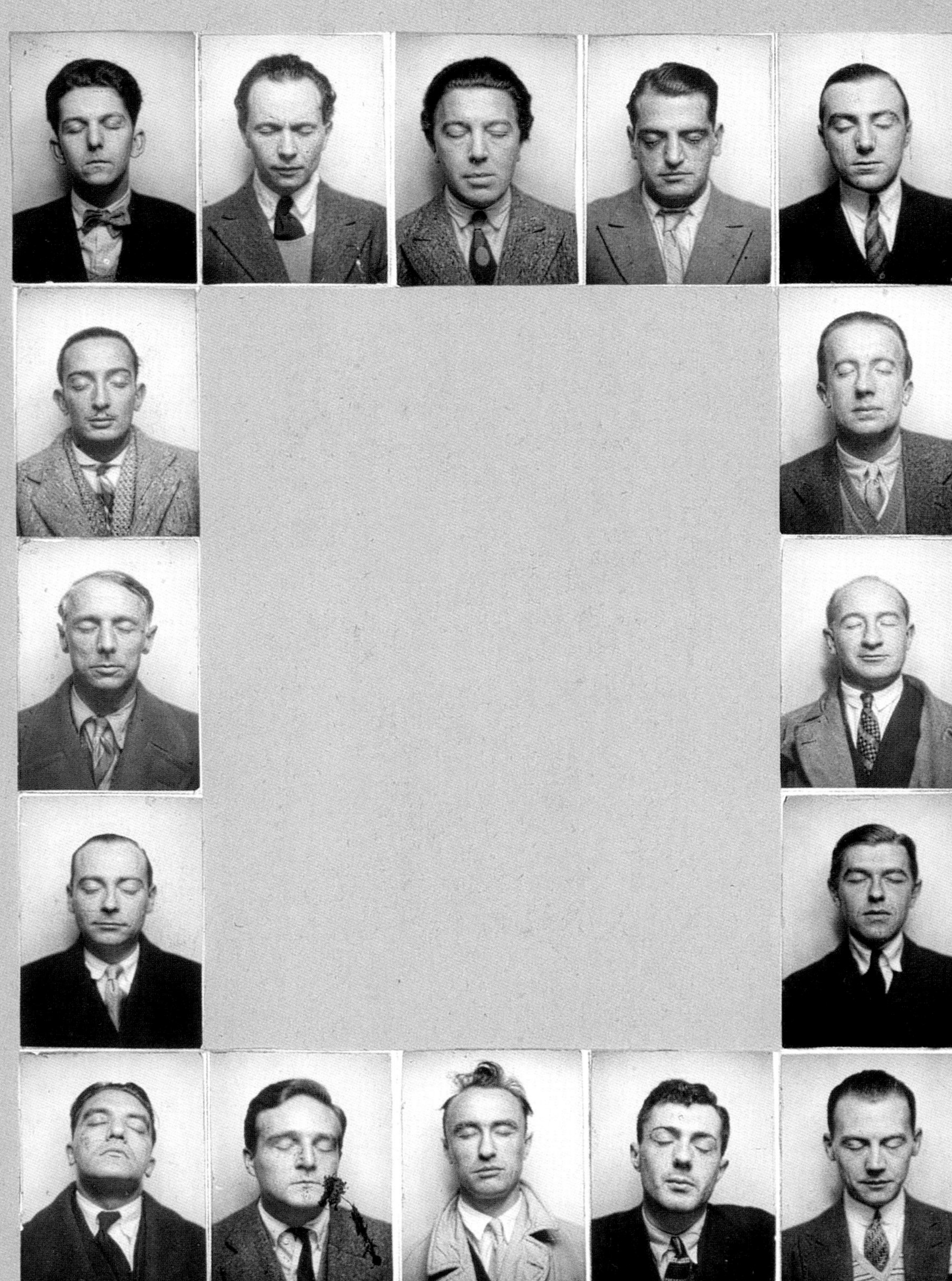

UN CADAVRE

Il ne faut plus que mort cet homme fasse de la poussière.

André BRETON *(Un Cadavre, 1924.)*

PAPOLOGIE D'ANDRÉ BRETON

Le deuxième manifeste du Surréalisme n'est pas une révélation, mais c'est une réussite.

On ne fait pas mieux dans le genre hypocrite, faux-frère, pelotard, sacristain, et pour tout dire : flic et curé.

Car en somme : on vous dit que l'acte surréaliste le plux simple consiste, revolvers aux poings, à descendre dans la rue et à tirer au hasard, tant qu'on peut, dans la foule.

Mais l'inspecteur Breton serait sans doute déjà arrêté s'il n'avait pas tout de l'agent provocateur, tandis que chacun de ses petits amis se garde bien d'accomplir l'acte surréaliste le plus simple.

Cette impunité prouve également le mépris dans lequel un Etat, quel qu'il soit, tient justement les intellectuels. Principalement ceux qui, comme l'inspecteur Breton, mènent la petite vie sordide de l'intellectuel professionnel.

Les *révélations* touchant par exemple Naville ou Masson ont le caractère des chantages quotidiens exercés par les journaux vendus à la police. La méthode et le ton sont absolument les mêmes. Pour les autres appréciations sur d'anciens amis, chers parce que l'inspecteur Breton espérant qu'ignorant sa qualité ils le nommeraient président d'un Soviet local des Grands Hommes, elles ne dépassent pas les ignominies ordinaires des habitués de commissariat, ni les coups de pied en vache. A cette heure où sont maîtresses de la rue ces deux ordures : la littérature et la police, il ne faut s'étonner de rien. Aux deux extrêmes, comme Dieu et Diable, il y a Chiappe et Breton.

Que Dada ait abouti à ça, c'est une grande consolation pour l'humanité qui retourne à sa colique. — Mais dira-t-on, n'avez-vous pas aimé le surréalisme ? Mais oui : amours de jeunesse, amours ancillaires. D'ailleurs une récente enquête donne aux petits jeunes gens l'autorisation d'aimer même la femme d'un gendarme.

Ou la femme d'un curé. Car on pense bien que dans l'affaire le flic rejoint le curé : le frère Breton qui fait accommoder le prêtre à la sauce moutarde ne parle plus qu'en chaire. Il est plein de mandarin curaçao, sait ce qu'on peut tirer des femmes, mais il impose

G. RIBEMONT-DESSAIGNES.

(Voir la suite page 2)

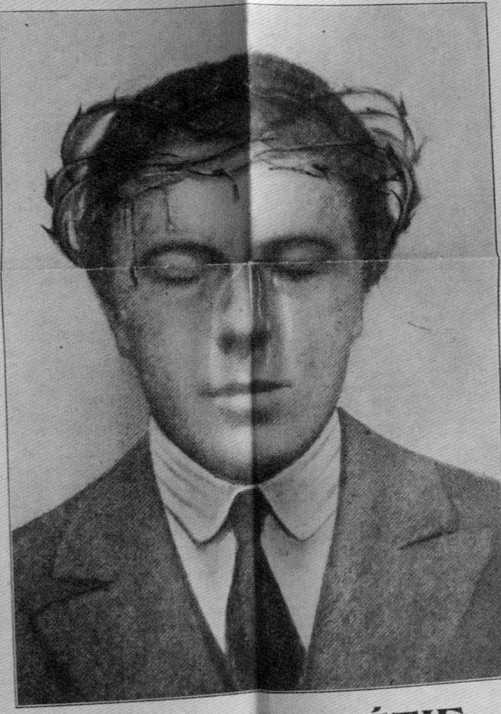

AUTO-PROPHÉTIE

Ce monde dans lequel je subis ce que je subis (n'y allez pas voir), ce monde moderne, enfin, diable ! que voulez-vous que j'y fasse ? La voix surréaliste se taira peut-être, je n'en suis plus à compter mes disparitions. Je n'entrerai plus, si peu que ce soit, dans le décompte merveilleux de mes années et de mes jours. Je serai comme Nijinsky, qu'on conduisit l'an dernier aux Ballets russes et qui ne comprit pas à quel spectacle il assistait.

ANDRÉ BRETON, *Manifeste du Surréalisme.*

MORT D'UN MONSIEUR

Hélas, je ne reverrai plus l'illustre Palotin du Monde Occidental, celui qui me faisait rire !

De son vivant, il écrivait, pour abréger le temps, disait-il, pour trouver des hommes et, lorsque par hasard il en trouvait, il avait atrocement peur et, leur faisant le coup de l'amitié bouleversante, il guettait le moment où il pourrait les salir.

Un jour il crut voir passer en rêve un Vaisseau-Fantôme et sentit les galons du capitaine Bordure lui pousser sur la tête, il se regarda sérieusement dans la glace et se trouva beau.

Ce fut la fin, il devint bègue du cœur et confondit tout, le désespoir et le mal de foie, la Bible et les chants de Maldoror, Dieu et Dieu, l'encre et le foutre, les barricades et le divan de Mme Sabatier, le marquis de Sade et Jean Lorrain, la Révolution Russe et la révolution surréaliste (1).

Pion lyrique il distribua des diplômes aux grands amoureux, des jours d'indulgences aux débutants en désespoir et se lamenta sur la grande pitié des poètes de France.

« Est-il vrai, écrivait-il, que les Patries veulent le plus tôt possible le sang de leurs grands hommes ? »

Excellent musicien il joua pendant un certain temps du luth de classe sous les fenêtres du Parti communiste, reçut des briques sur la tête, et repartit déçu, aigri, maîtrechanter dans les cours d'amour.

Il ne pouvait pas jouer sans tricher, il trichait d'ailleurs très mal et cachait des boules de billard dans ses manches ; quand elles tombaient par terre avec un bruit désagréable devant ses fidèles très gênés il disait que c'était de l'humour.

C'était un grand honnête homme, il mettait parfois sa toque de juge par dessus son képi, et faisait de la Morale ou de la critique d'art, mais il cachait difficilement les cicatrices que lui avaient laissées le croc à phynances de la peinture moderne.

Un jour il criait contre les prêtres, le lendemain il se croyait évêque ou pape en Avignon, prenait un billet pour aller voir et revenait quelques jours après plus révolutionnaire que jamais et pleurait bientôt de grosses larmes de rage le 1er mai parce qu'il n'avait pas trouvé

Jacques PRÉVERT,

(Voir la suite page 2)

Un Cadavre, January 15, 1930.

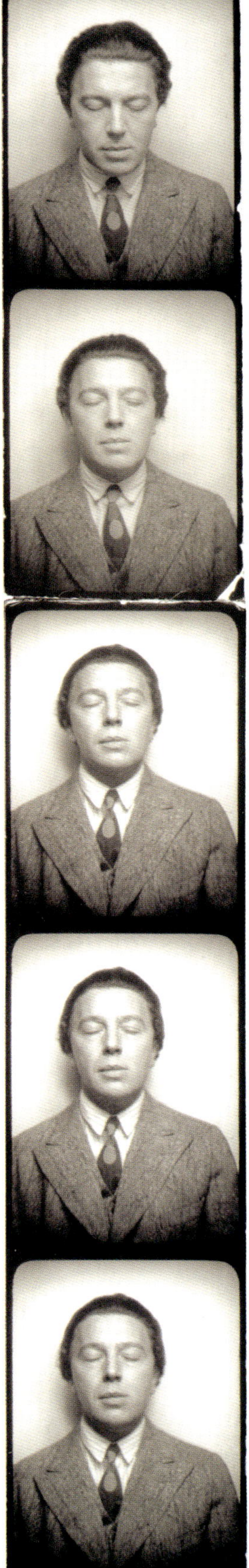

André Breton.

On January 15, 1930, in response to the *Second Surrealist Manifesto*, Georges Bataille, Michel Leiris, Robert Desnos, Raymond Queneau, Jacques Prévert, and others published a tract entitled *Un Cadavre*. In this pamphlet they denounced André Breton's "papal dogmatism" and his "moralistic principles." Jacques-André Boiffard, with the assistance of Eli Lotar, created a photomontage that transformed a Photomaton portrait of Breton, then aged 33, into Christ wearing a crown of thorns. (Bataille said that the original press run was 500 copies and that he had destroyed about 200 copies.)

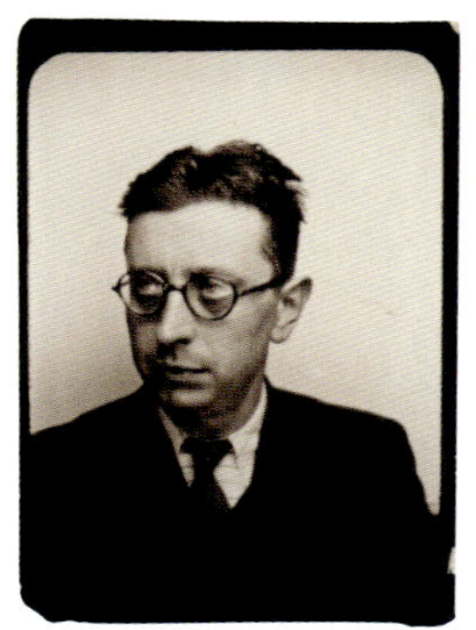

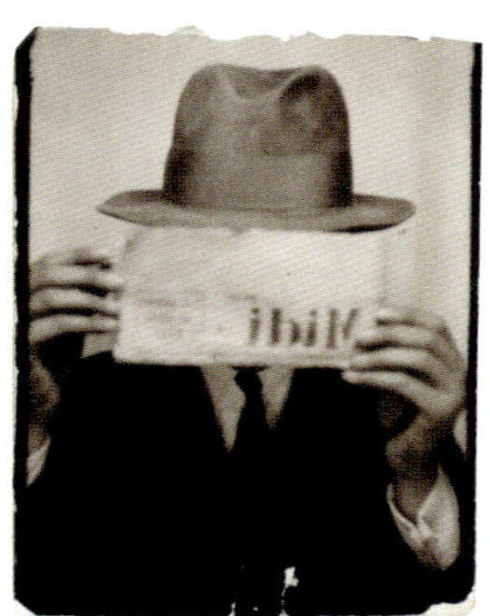

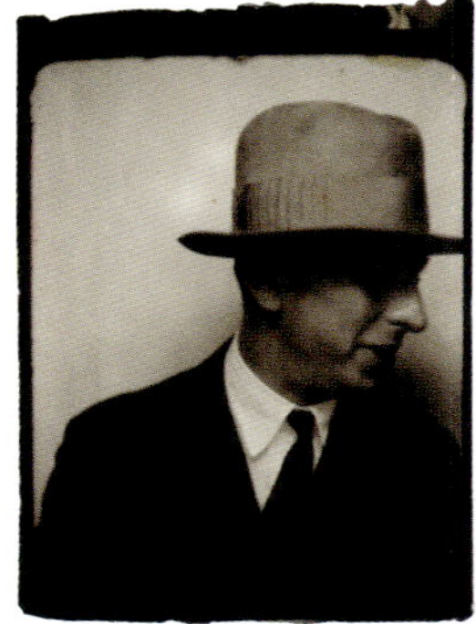

Robert Desnos.

Opposite: Paul Eluard.

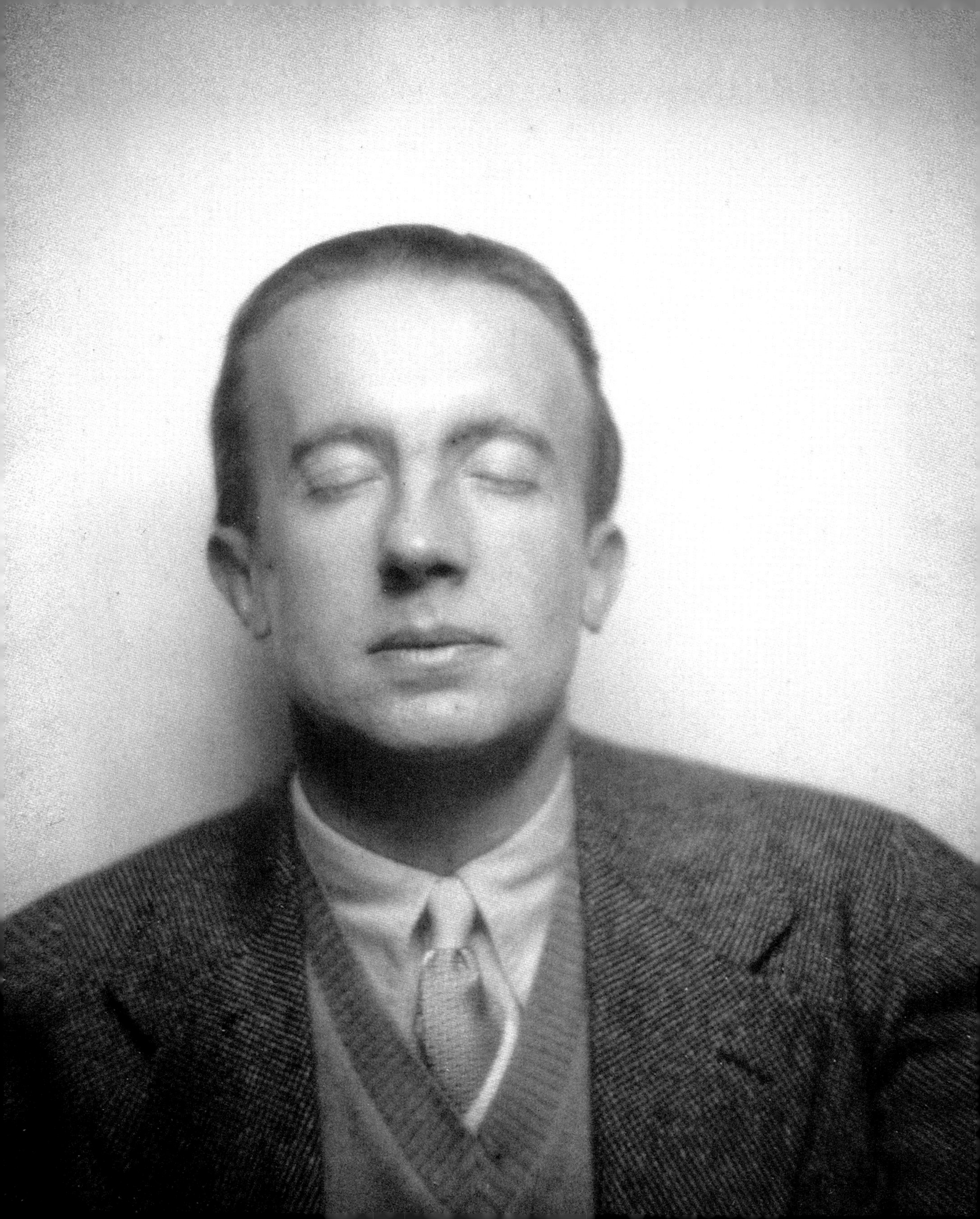

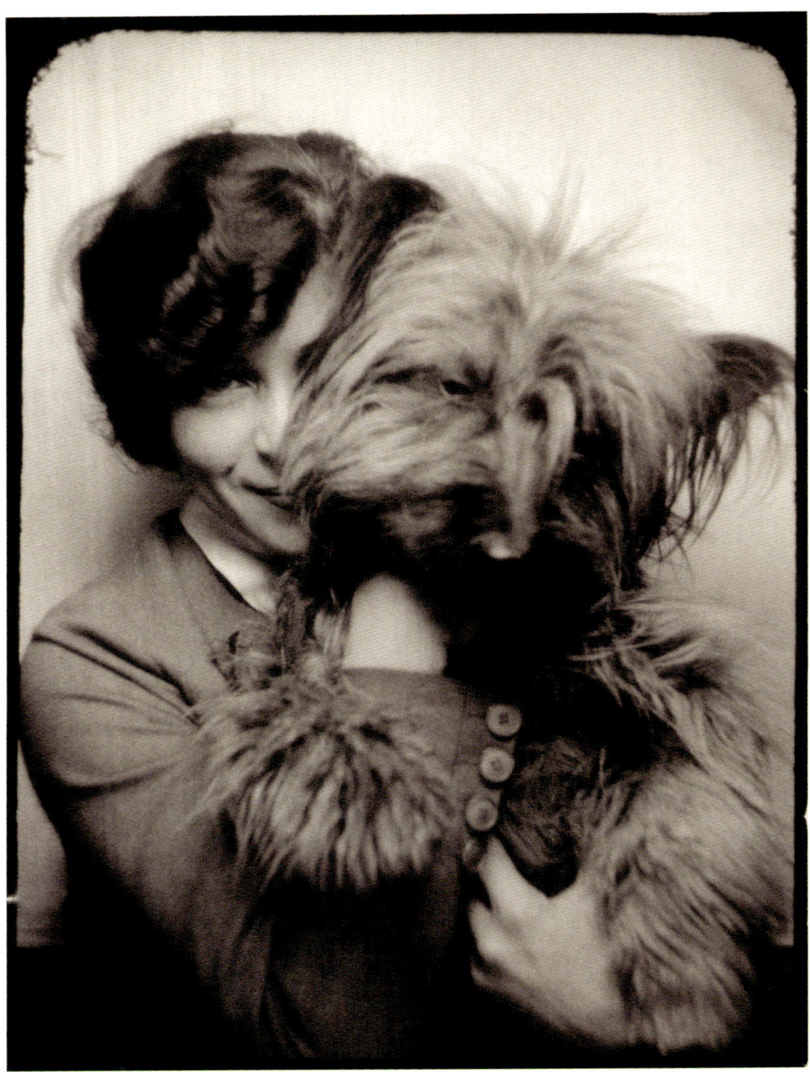

Suzanne Muzard. From the fall of 1927 until the spring of 1931, Muzard was Breton's mistress. In the words of the historian and writer Georges Sebbag, "Suzanne Muzard was a Surrealist in the Photomaton. We see her in the photo booth doing her hair, hugging her dog Melmoth, or mothering a suffering Jacques Prévert" (André Breton, *L'amour-folie*).

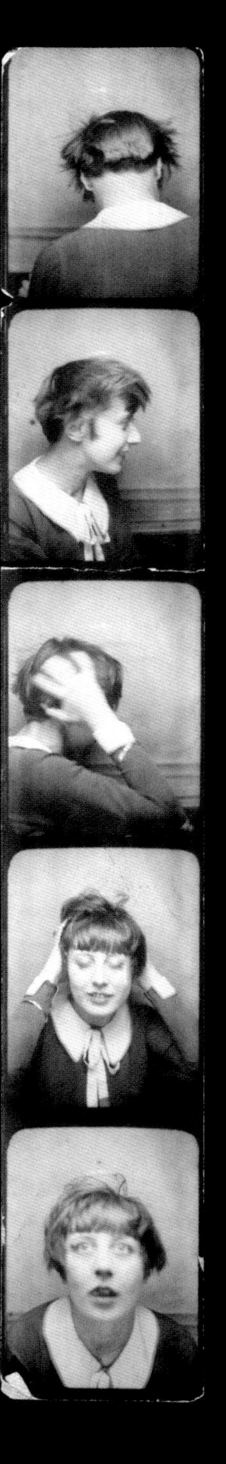
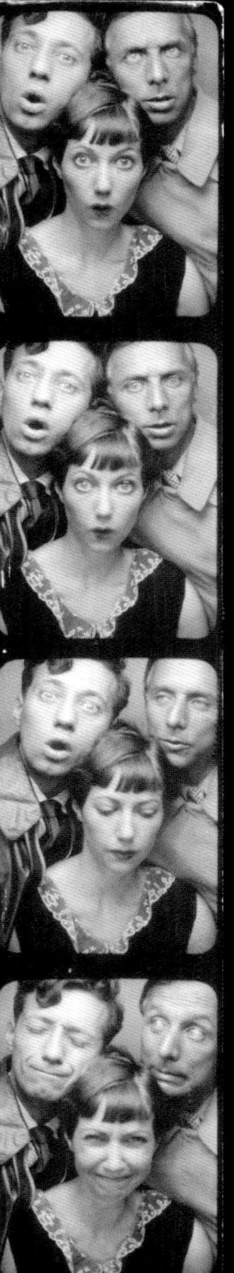

Marie-Berthe Aurenche. At right with her brother Jean and and Max Ernst.

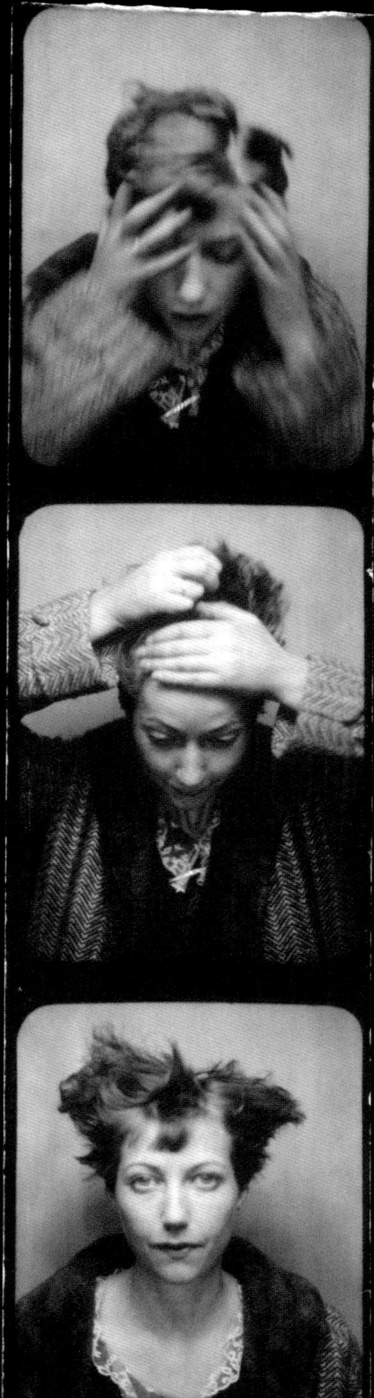

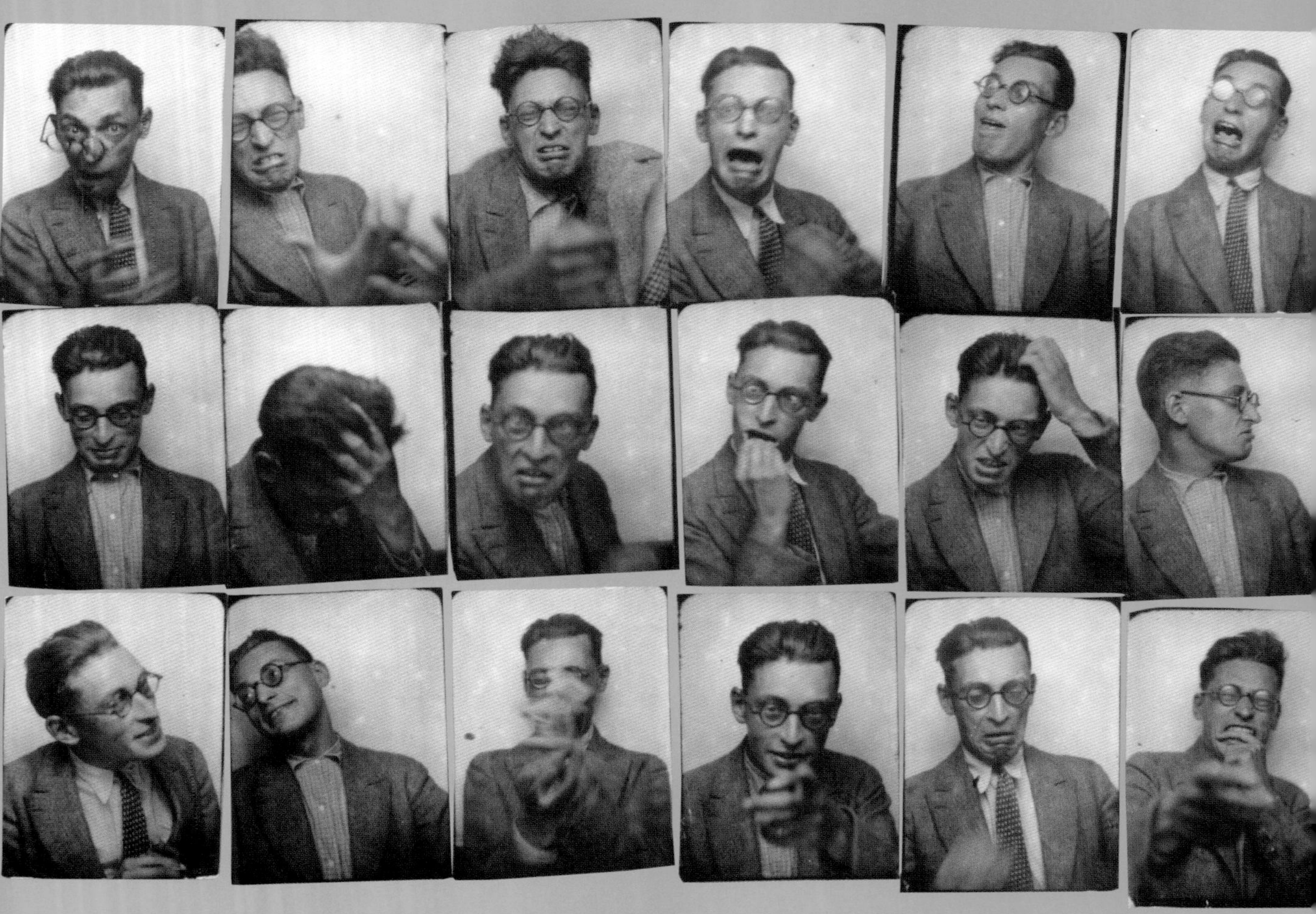

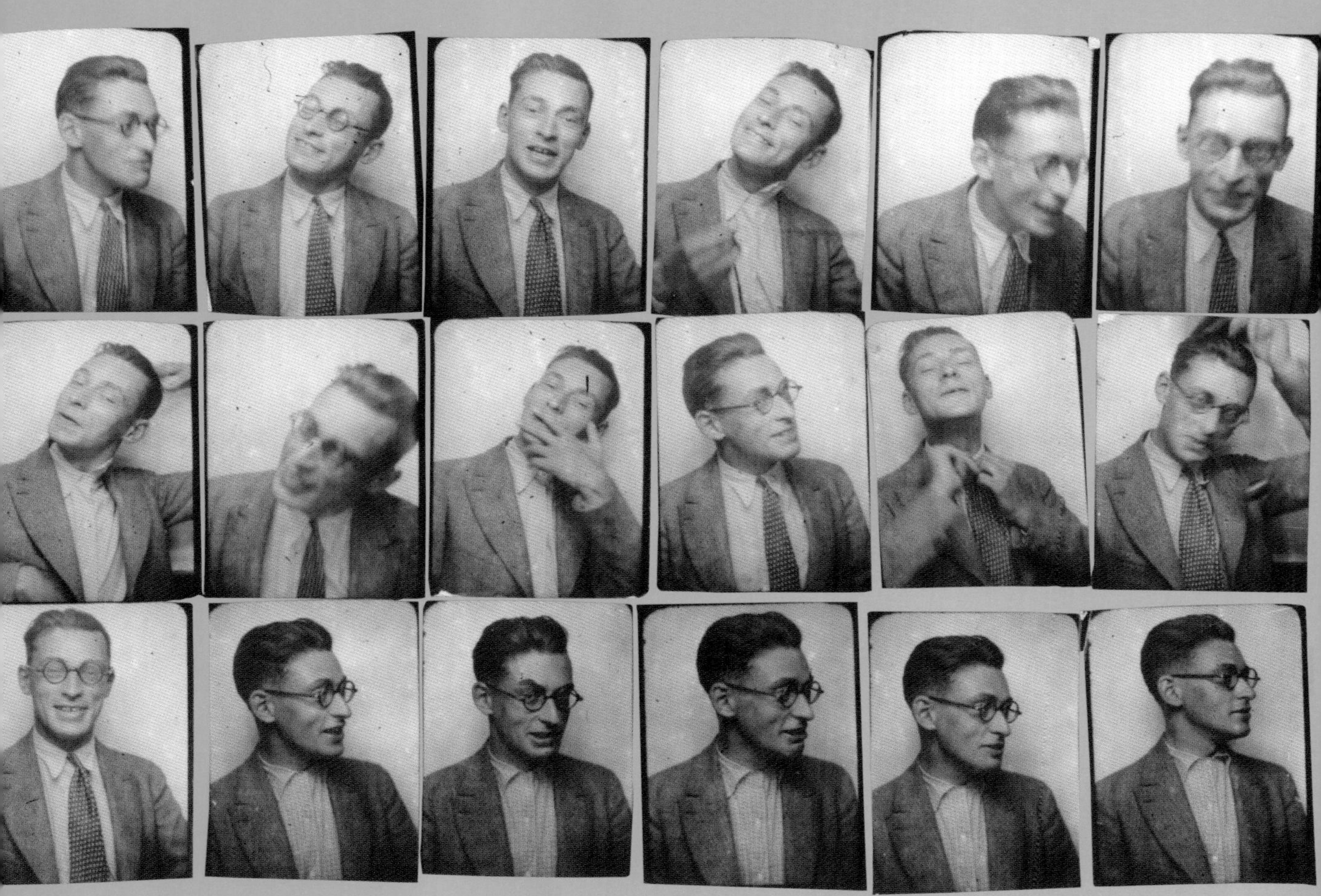

Raymond Queneau, 1929.

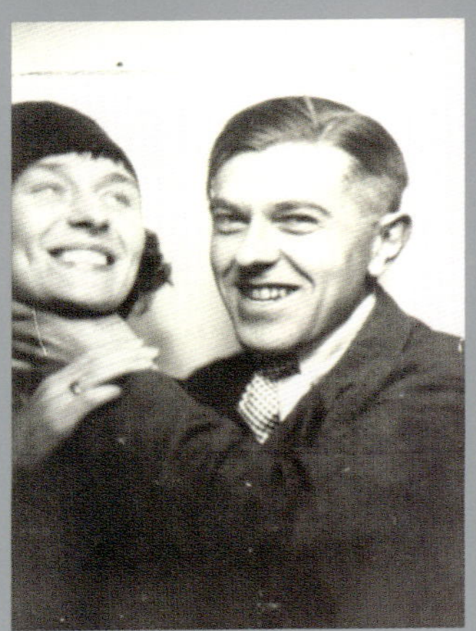

Georgette and René Magritte.

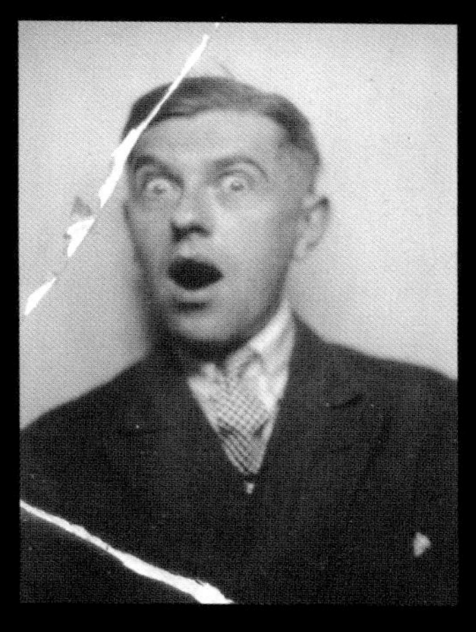

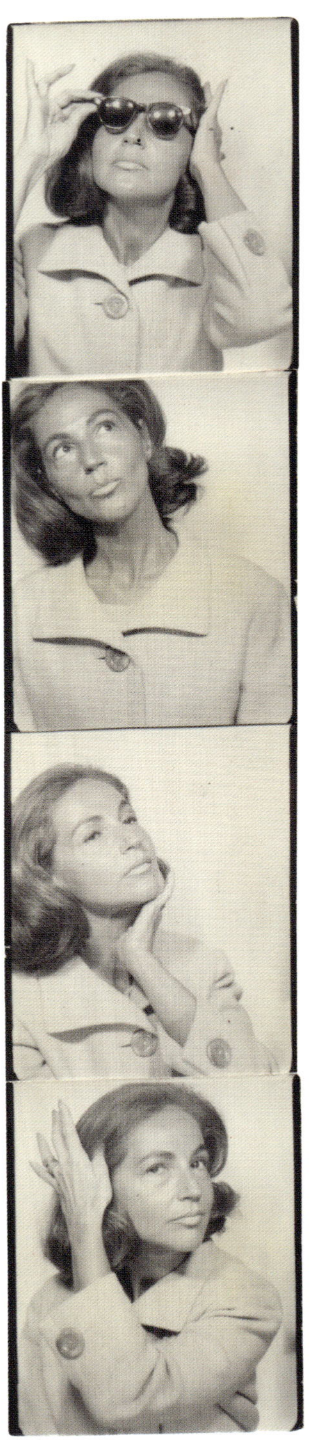

Ethel Scull.

ANDY WARHOL

(1928–1987)

In June 1963, at the request of New York art collector Ethel Scull, Andy Warhol undertook the first of a long series of commissioned portraits. The photo shoot took place in a photobooth at the corner of West Fifty-second Street and Broadway, and dozens of four-shot strips were exposed. Knowing that Scull was very self-critical, Warhol carefully selected the best portraits, clipping them with a pair of scissors. Twenty-four strips were transformed into a silk-screened mosaic consisting of thirty-six frames, each frame painted a different dominant color (certain portraits, used repeatedly, were subjected to recropping or a symmetrical horizontal rotation when they were printed on the canvas). *Ethel Scull 36 Times* (actual size: 79³/₄ × 143 in. [202 × 363 cm]) is now considered a major Pop Art piece.

Between 1963 and 1965, Andy Warhol did numerous series of self-portraits and photobooth portraits of such models as Gerard Malanga, Judith Green, Edie Sedgwick, Edward Villella, and Judith Raskin—most of which are now in the Andy Warhol Museum in Pittsburgh.

Up until his death in 1987, Warhol did more than one thousand commissioned portraits. Celebrities, intellectuals, and fortunate anonymous individuals paid $25,000 to have the privilege of coming face-to-face with the camera lens of the "pope of Pop Art."

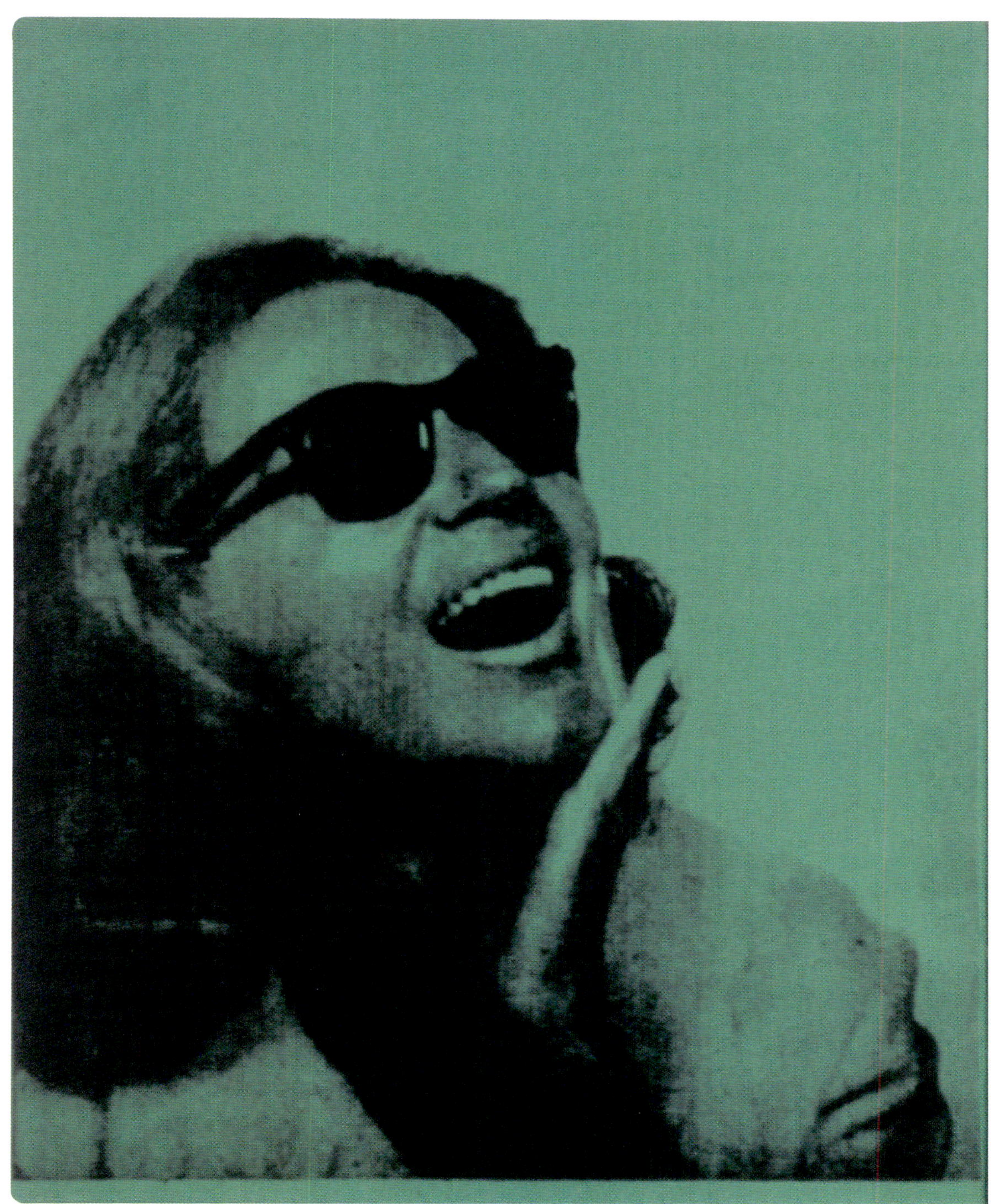

Ethel Scull 36 Times, 1963 (detail).

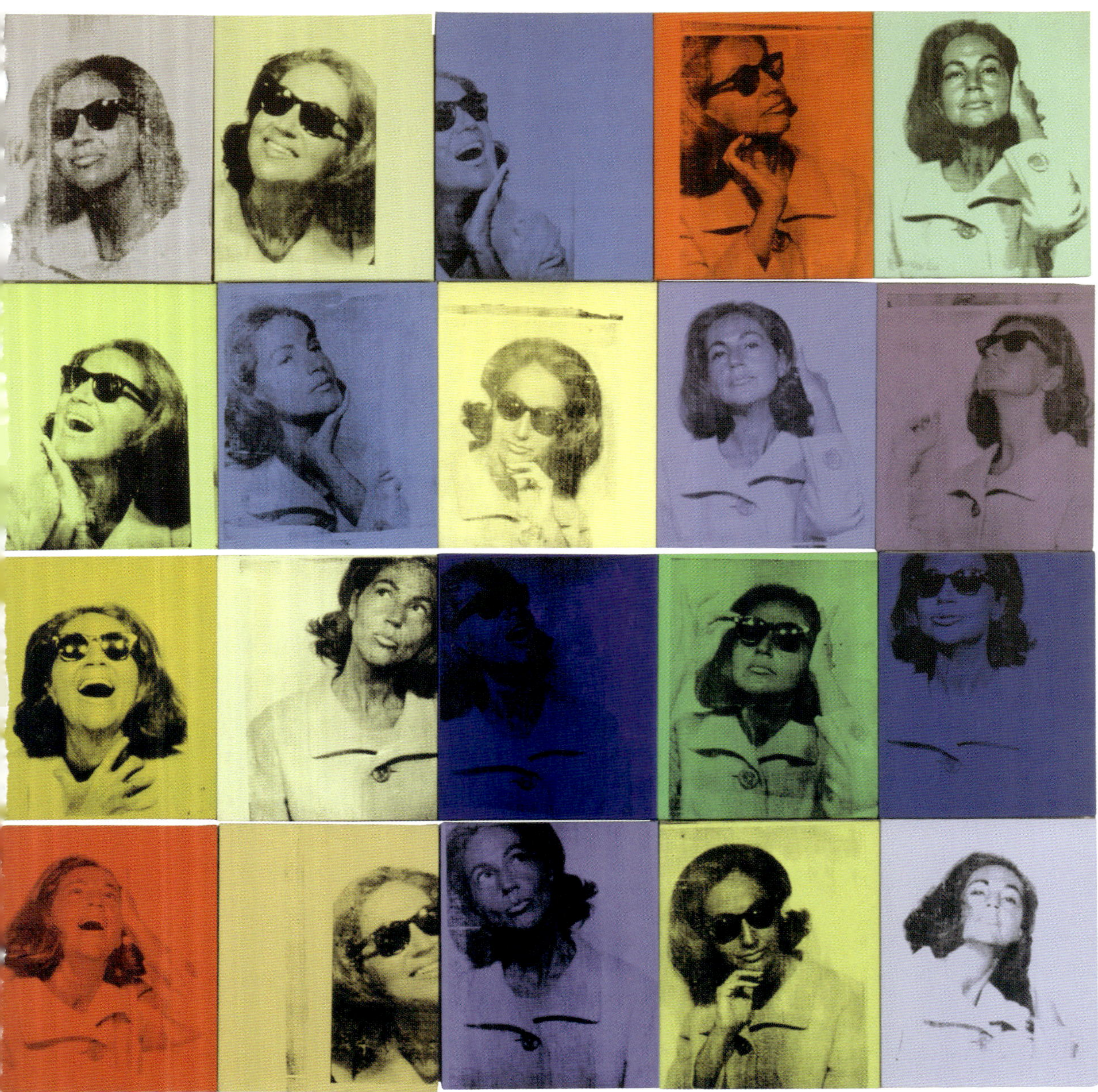

Andy Warhol, *Ethel Scull 36 times*, 1963.
Acrylic and silkscreen on canvas.
80 × 144 in. (202.6 × 363.2 cm)
Jointly owned by the Whitney Museum of American Art
and The Metropolitan Museum of Art;
Gift of Ethel Redner Scull, 2001.

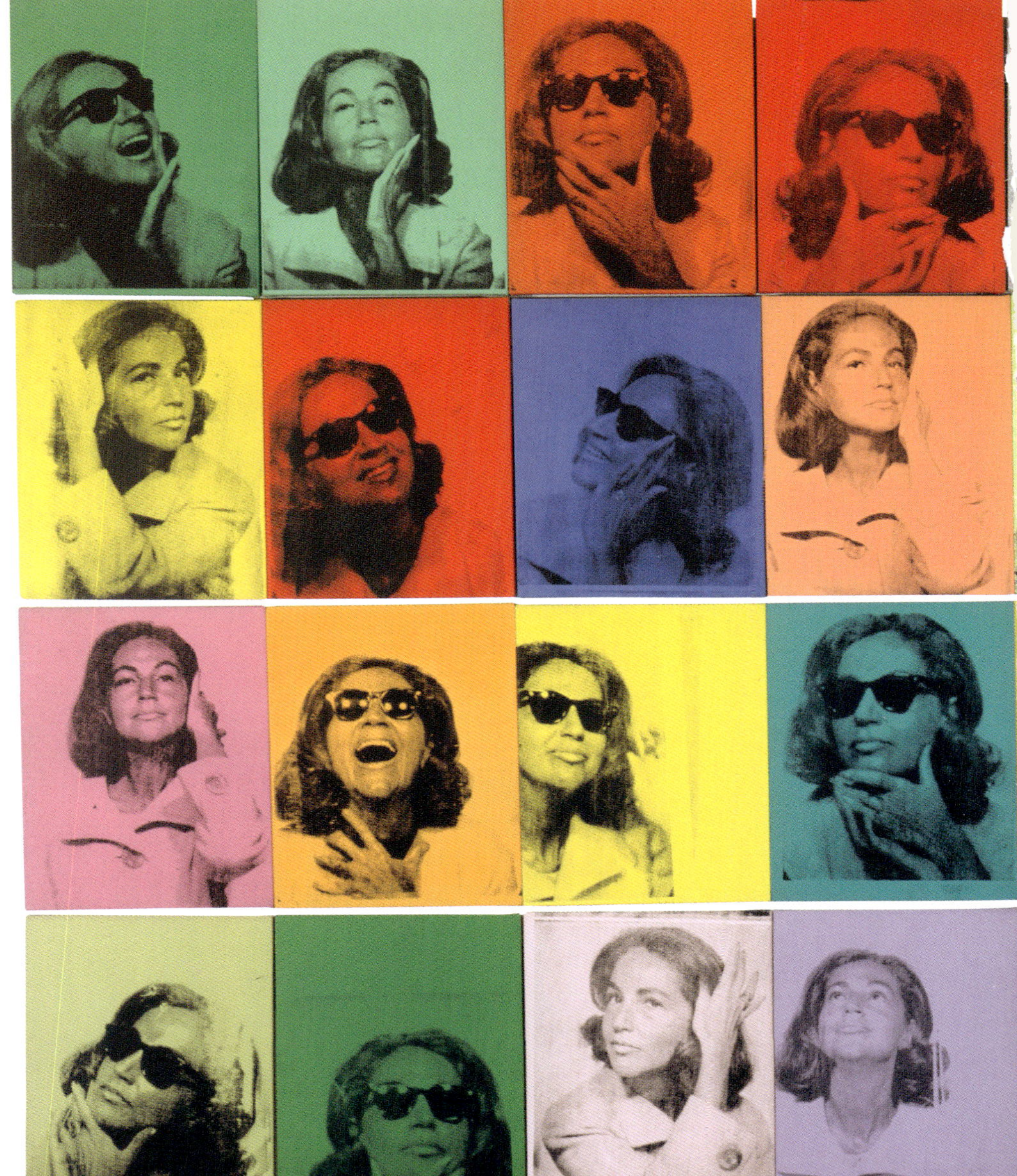

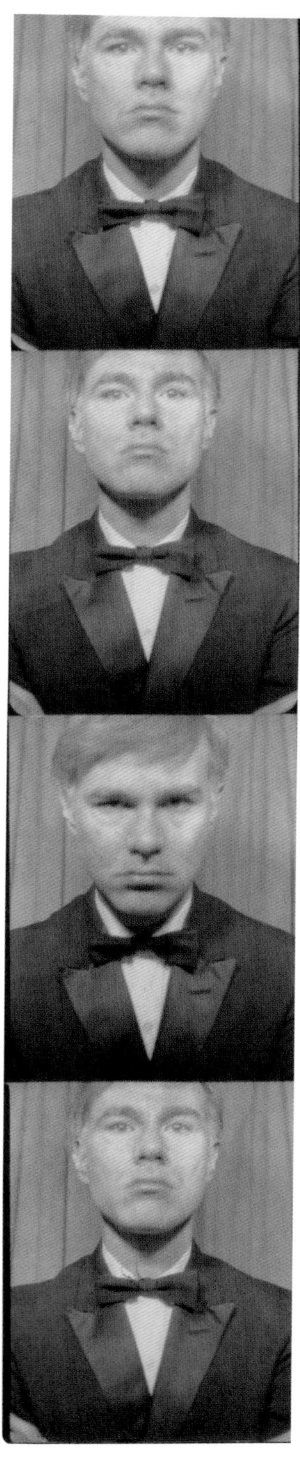

Self-portrait (Tuxedo), 1964.

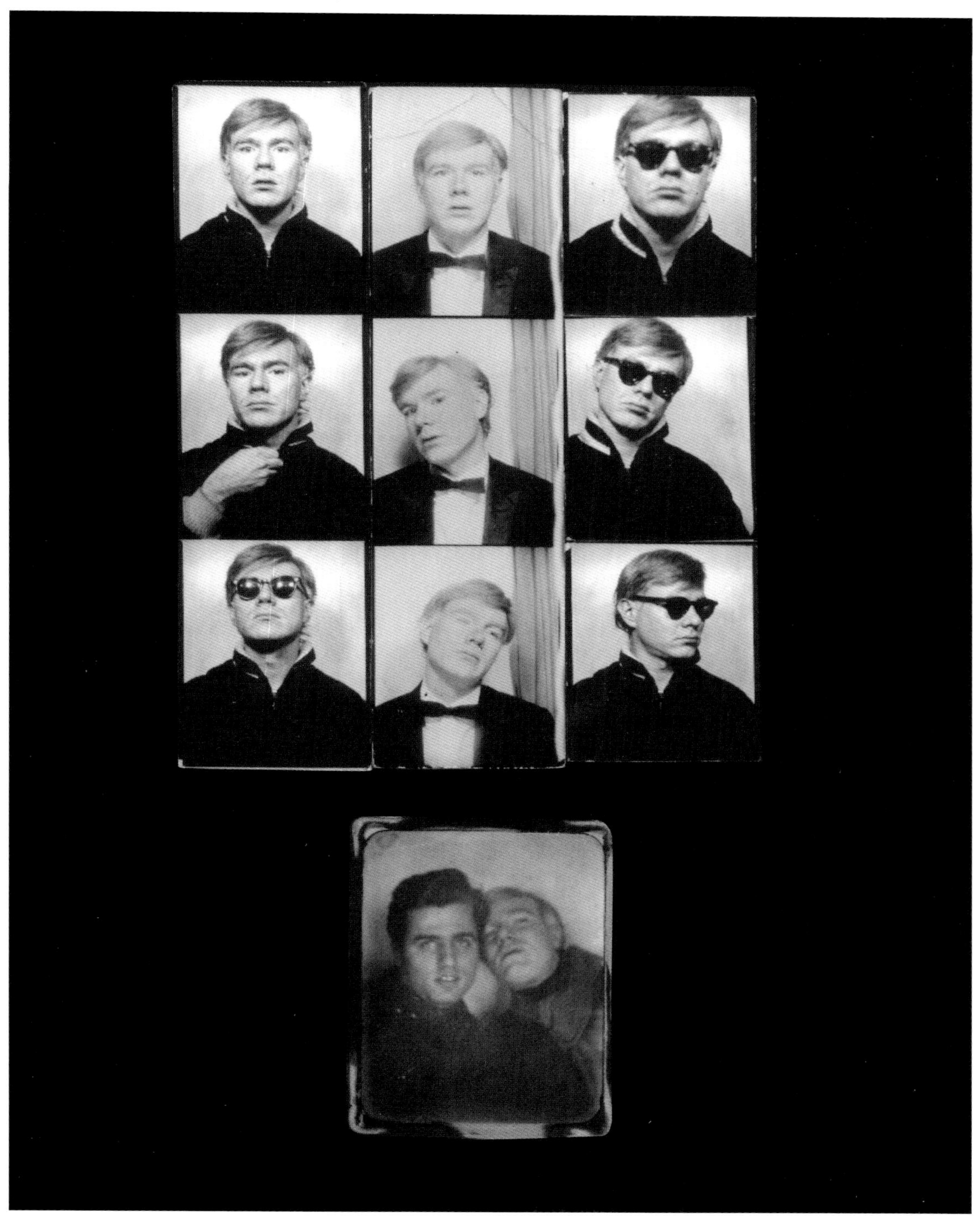

Andy Warhol Photobooth Assemblage, 1964.

GERARD MALANGA

(1943–)

An American poet, photographer, and film-maker, Gerard Malanga was, according to the *New York Times*, "Warhol's most important associate" between 1963 and 1970. Over the course of those years, he collaborated with the master of Pop Art on the series *Screen Tests*—silent film portraits each lasting three minutes, and created the magazine *Interview*. After his 1970 departure from The Factory, where he had been one of its emblematic figures, he photographed numerous personalities from the literary, artistic, and musical worlds, including Allen Ginsberg, Mick Jagger, William S. Burroughs, and Iggy Pop.

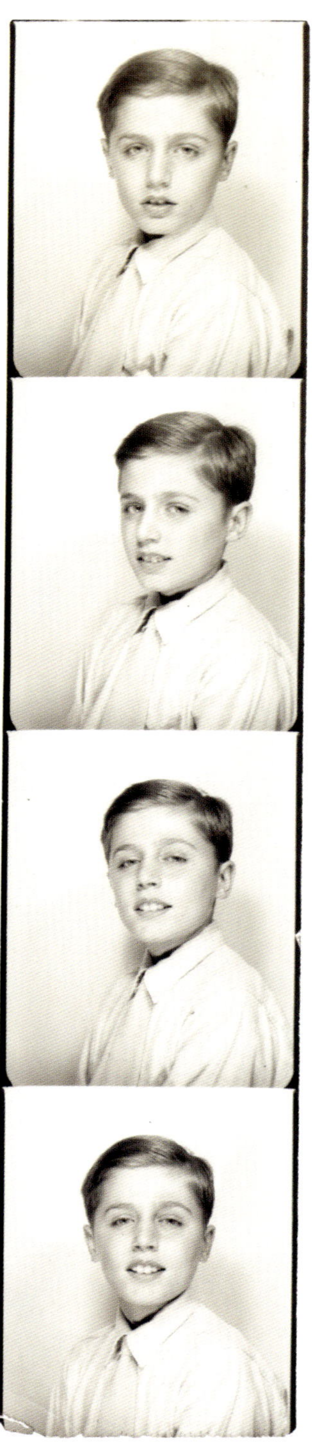

RAYNAL PELLICER: Tell me why you decided to use a photobooth.

GERARD MALANGA: I was always fascinated with photography ever since I can remember. Every Sunday my mom would bring home the Sunday edition of the *Daily News*, which included a Sunday supplement called *Coloroto* magazine. In it was a vertical column called "New York's Changing Scene" (which I found out decades later was edited by a very important New York preservationist named Margot Gayle). Anyway, the column consisted of two black-and-white photographs of a New York street scene. The top photo was of the earliest vintage, say 1890 or 1910, and the bottom picture would be a present-day shot, which was 1953 or '54. The two pictures were nearly identical from the camera angle, or at least that was part of the plan. I would cut the columns out of the newspaper and paste them into scrapbooks, and I must've amassed three or four along the way. One Sunday, to my joyful surprise, my neighborhood was depicted! So what you have here is a sense of visual transformation, and that's how I related to photography at an early age.

At least four times a year my dad would take me to see a first-run movie of my choice at a fancy Broadway theater in the Times Square area. After the movie let out we would have an early supper at the Horn & Hardart Automat, and afterwards we'd head over to this establishment called Playland, which had all kinds of games and amusements. It also had a photobooth where for a quarter you could step into the booth and have your picture taken. It was on one of these occasions that I decided I wanted to make a self-portrait of myself. I must've been nine or ten at the time, but I distinctly remember that it was a conscious effort on my part to wanna make a portrait of myself in the booth. I even posed my head a certain way and made eye contact with the camera hidden behind a glass panel. Now, there weren't any photobooths in the vicinity of where we lived in the Bronx, so it was only on these excursions downtown that I had opportunity to wanna do this. So what we have illustrated here is the very first and only surviving specimen of those many visits. Of course, it was years later I would start experimenting with the photobooth once again, both as subject and as director.

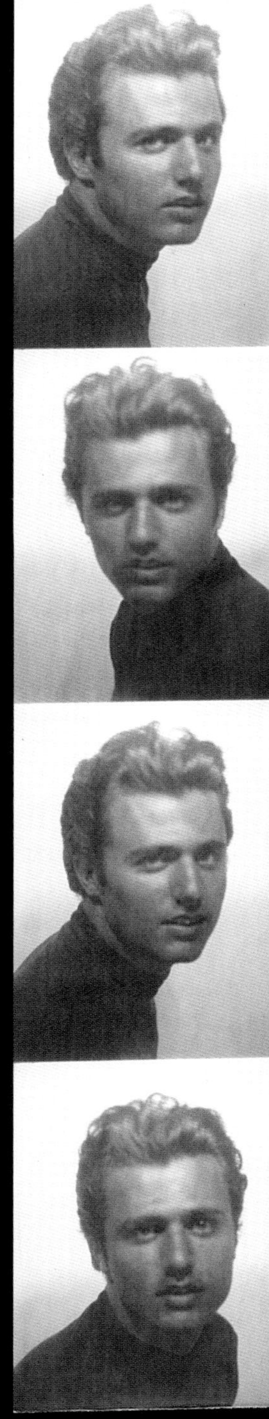

RP: Don't you think there was a paradox here to use the photobooth, a place where you couldn't interfere with the light, the focus, or the aperture and shutter speed?

GM: You pose a very interesting dynamic. As I came to appreciate the photobooth, in the mid-fifties of my childhood and again in the sixties, I had this sense that the photobooth's allure made you feel that you became your own self-portrait by the decision to want to step into the booth.

If you recall, back at the turn of the nineteenth century when the Eastman Kodak Company made photography popular among the masses, their catchphrase slogan was "You take the picture. We do the rest." In other words, they were saying, here's our camera. You snap the pictures and return the camera to us and we'll send you back the processed pictures and then the cycle repeats itself, and that's how the company profited from this give-and-take exchange.

Well, the photobooth operates under a similar kind of consumerism. You put your quarter in the slot (by the end of the sixties it became four quarters!) and you waited three minutes and the slot on the outside of the booth would roll out four square-formatted unique pictures, all on one strip of paper, and the paper is wet! So the spontaneity of this machine's mechanics even predates the Polaroid camera. So the photostrip is yours. You take it home, and it ends up in a shoebox or photo album or you give it to your girlfriend. That was the fun of it.

You see, you made the decision to step into the booth and sit and have your portrait made, but since there was no one behind the camera except for your own mirrored reflection on the paneled glass, you became the author of your own image.

Obviously you couldn't hold the photobooth to take the picture, but by allowing yourself to be encompassed by the booth, it was akin to stepping into a camera. I find this quite spiritual.

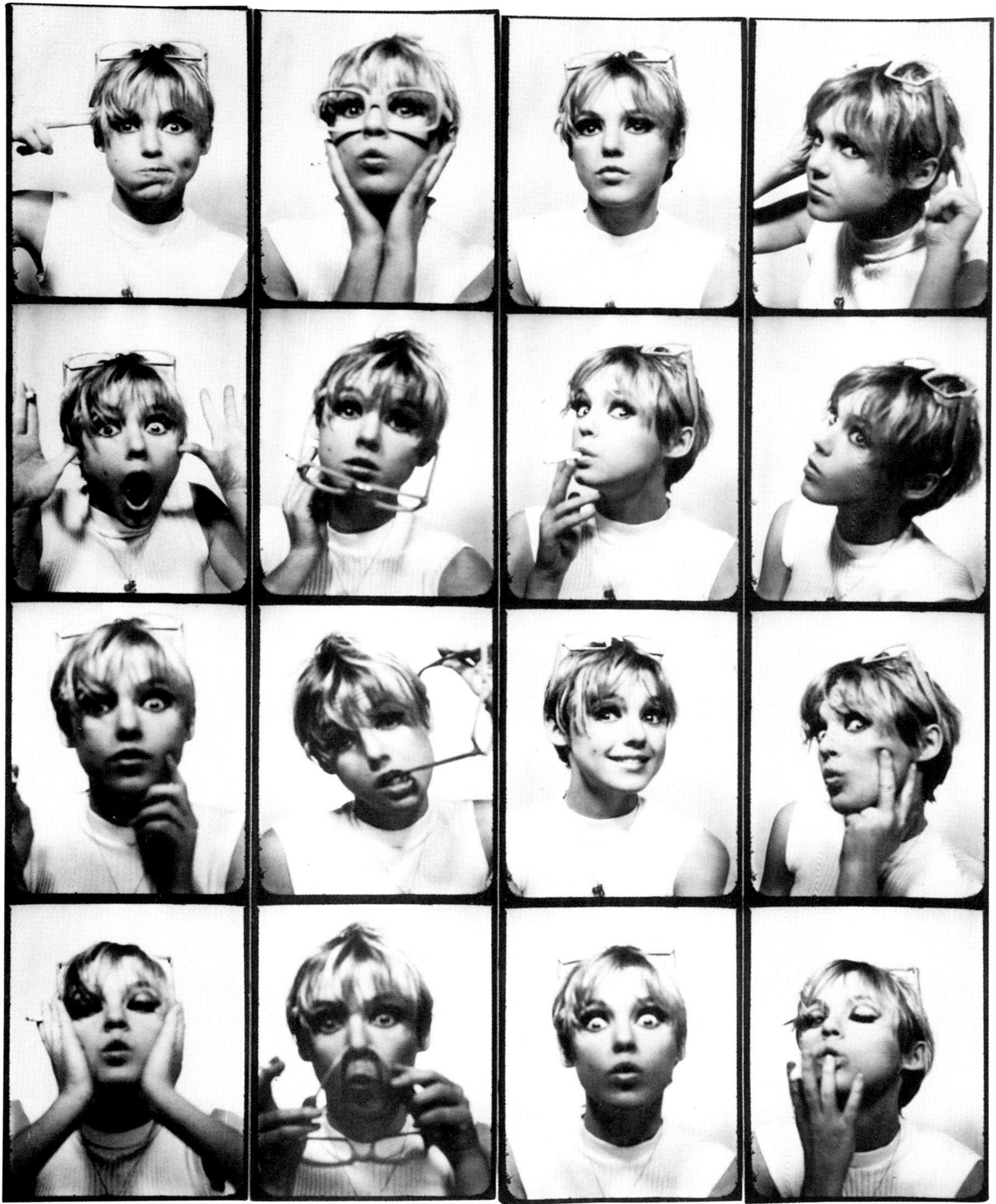

Gerard Malanga, *Edie Sedgwick Photobooth Portrait*, 1966.

RP: The photobooth strips are made of a succession of images that have been taken at short and regular times. That's very cinematographic. Should we see this as a prefiguration of your *Screen Tests*?

GM: Let me first say that the three intervals between each picture—that is, if we're talking about four pictures here—were usually five seconds. That would've given you enough time to turn your head or fix your hair or change your expression. So all told we're looking at here not more than twenty seconds, and then it took about three minutes' developing time before the photobooth would spit out the photo strip—and mind you, it was still wet! You'd have to blow on it with your breath so it would dry faster.

Now I can claim to be one of the few users of these booths to have actually seen its inner workings. It's pretty amazing. Nothing high-tech. It was almost primitive. There's a scene in the movie *The Wizard of Oz* where Toto the little dog pulls the curtain aside where the Wizard is performing his magic and is thus revealed as not performing any magic at all. It was all illusion.

Well, when I saw the inner mechanics of the photobooth, I was stunned. It reminded me of that scene in the movie. Once the photo strip was exposed to the light-flash four times, the strip of paper was then carried along on a primitive sort of conveyor belt made up of guy-wires, which were pulled by a gearwheel that would stop and then dunk the paper strip into a tin can of developer and washing chemicals you'd normally have in a darkroom printing from negatives. So with each dunking the paper strip would move along to the next tin can, and the process would be repeated until it was washed in a can of fresh water to remove any lingering chemicals. So this is the waiting process that took three minutes. The photo strip would then reach the mouth or opening, where it was gently pushed through and emerged into the real world. Presto!

I don't know if I would attach any kind of cinematographic significance to this. It was more of a kind of primitive process that allowed you to sit and pose for your picture in four intervals. There was no negative involved. No film. Everything was pretty much static. The only thing that really did move was the paper strip inside the guts of the booth.

A dear friend and colleague, Peter Wehrli, in an essay he wrote about my work published in the prestigious Swiss magazine *Camera* back in '80 or '81, made the astute observation that my silkscreening work with Warhol led me "to an intensive preoccupation with the medium of photography, its function and its possibilities, to practical work even before he ever held a camera in his hand." That's about as good as it gets, I would say. In fact, it's the best assessment that I can recall.

The same can easily be said for my photobooth series, which certainly prefigured the development of taking pictures with a still camera, and this can be carried over to the *Screen Tests* as well. The irony here is that Andy and I were making still portraits not by using a standard still camera but by shooting with a movie camera, and this long before either of us used a still camera in a professional way. Thus, in a very real sense, we were what you would call proto-photographers.

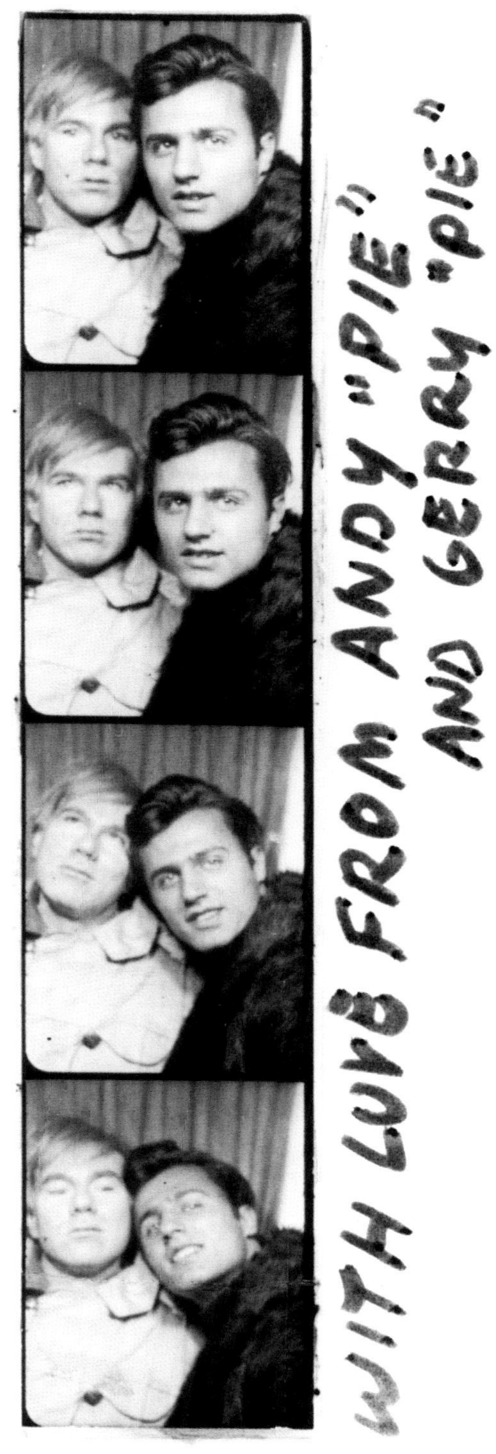

Love from Gerry Pie & Andy Pie, 1963.

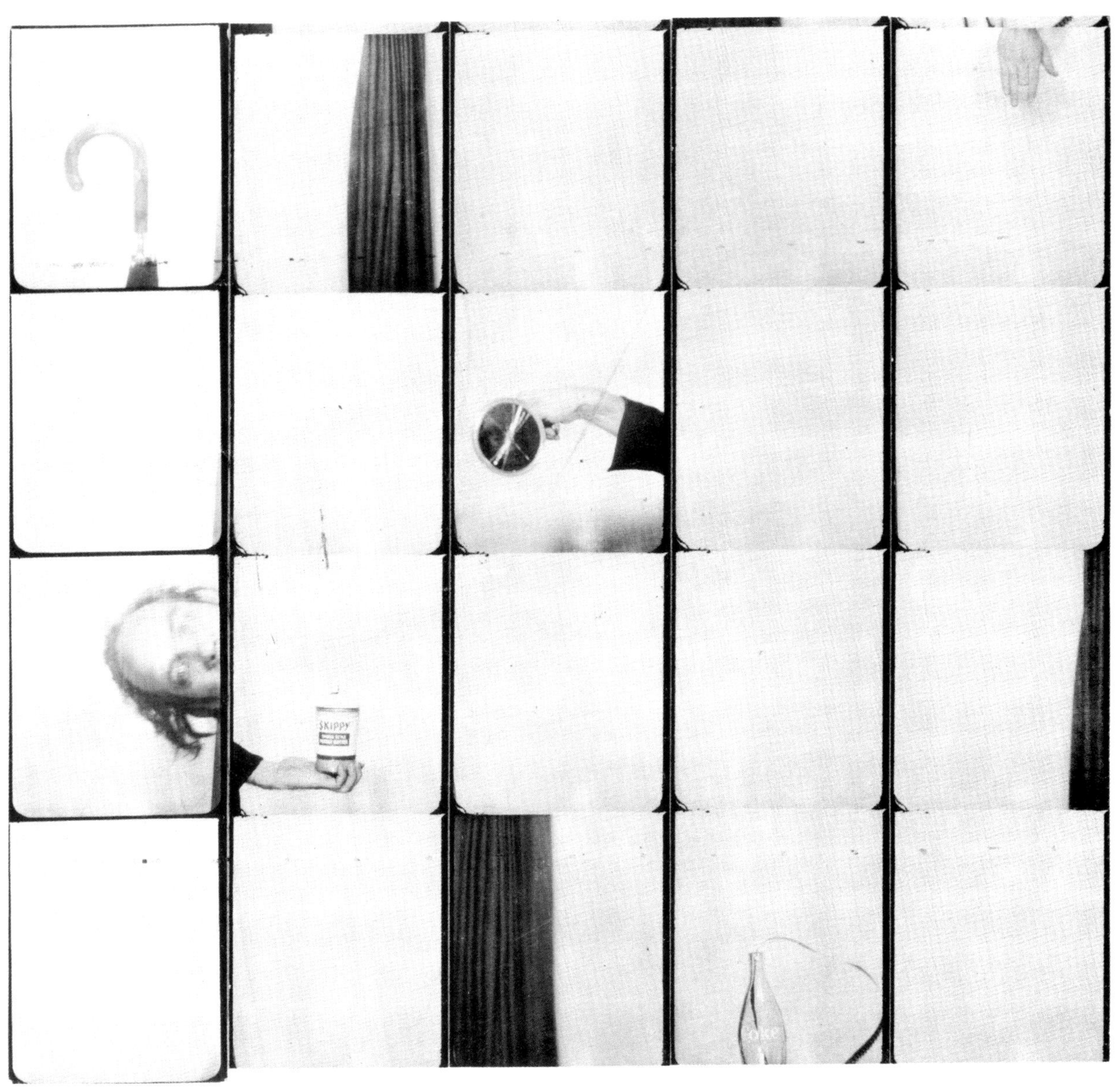

SKIPPY

AL HANSEN

(1927–1995)
American artist, one of the leading figures
in Fluxus, the contemporary art movement
founded in the sixties

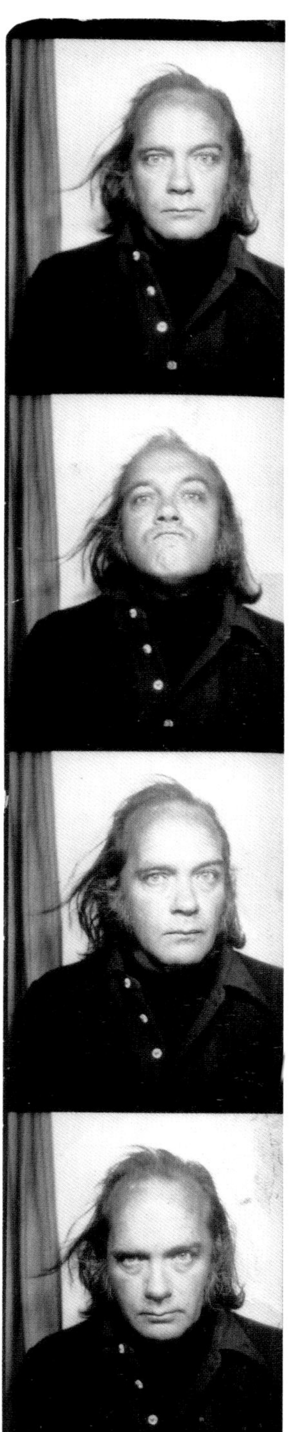

Al Hansen explored the use of photo-booth pictures in the same way he immersed himself in his signature Venus images, thoroughly and throughout his lifetime. Evidence suggests he began using the photo-booth strips in the early sixties while living in and around Greenwich Village in Manhattan.

"As a working-class artist, living and creating on an economic high-wire, he tirelessly quested after affordable art resources and ingenious solutions to overcome his lack of access to traditional materials, space, and equipment. He made collage from castoffs and detritus like candy wrappers, matchsticks, and cigarette butts, and he made performance art in cold-water lofts, on street corners, and in 'four for a quarter' photobooths.

"We can see in the artist's photobooth pieces, the influence of his childhood fascination and delight with both comic strips and film, as well as the reflection of his more serious adult inquiry into the gestalt of the picture frame. When he died in 1995 in Cologne, Germany, among the artworks he left behind were many based on the photobooth strip, offering us an enchanting glimpse into Hansen's life and unique art process."

—Bibbe Hansen

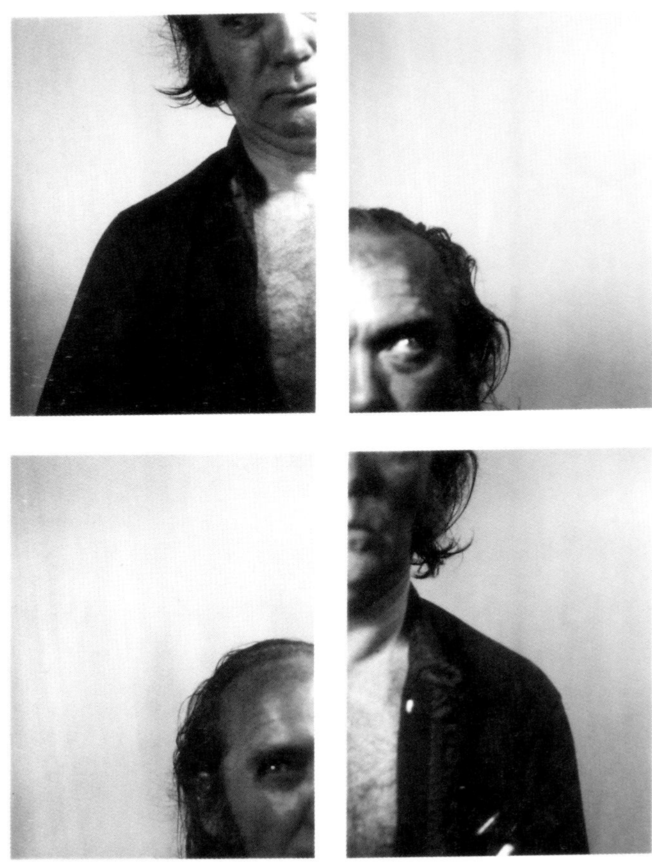

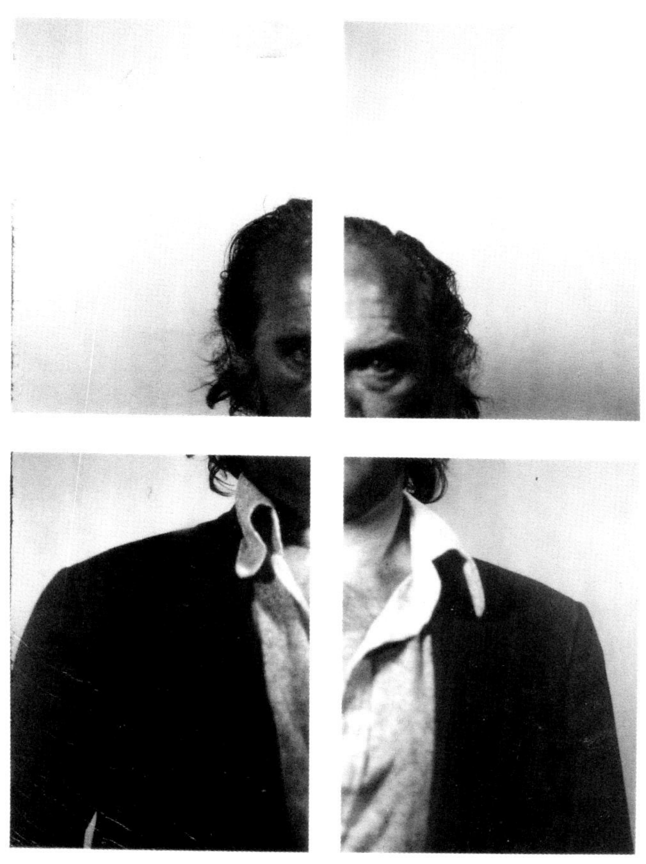

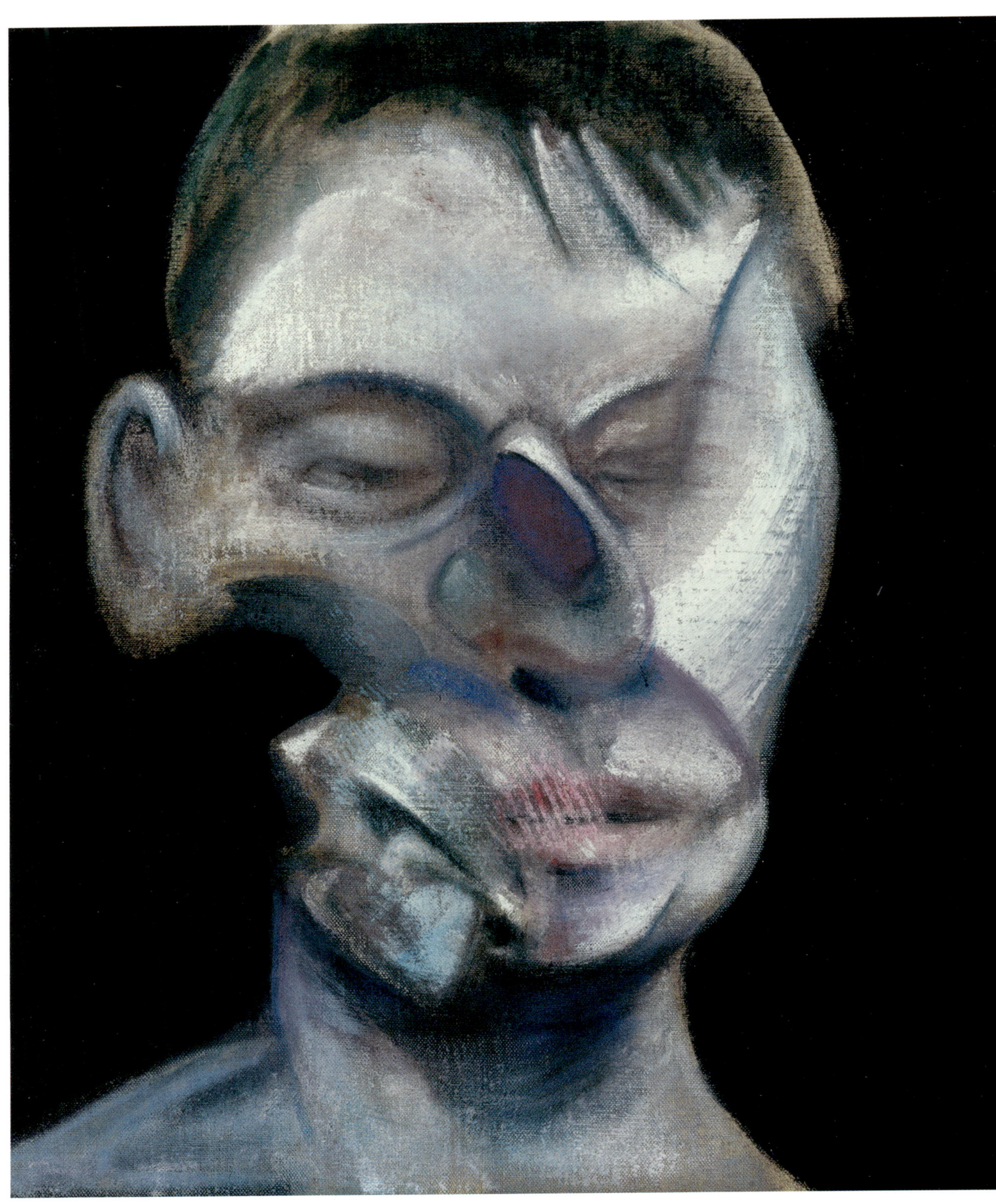

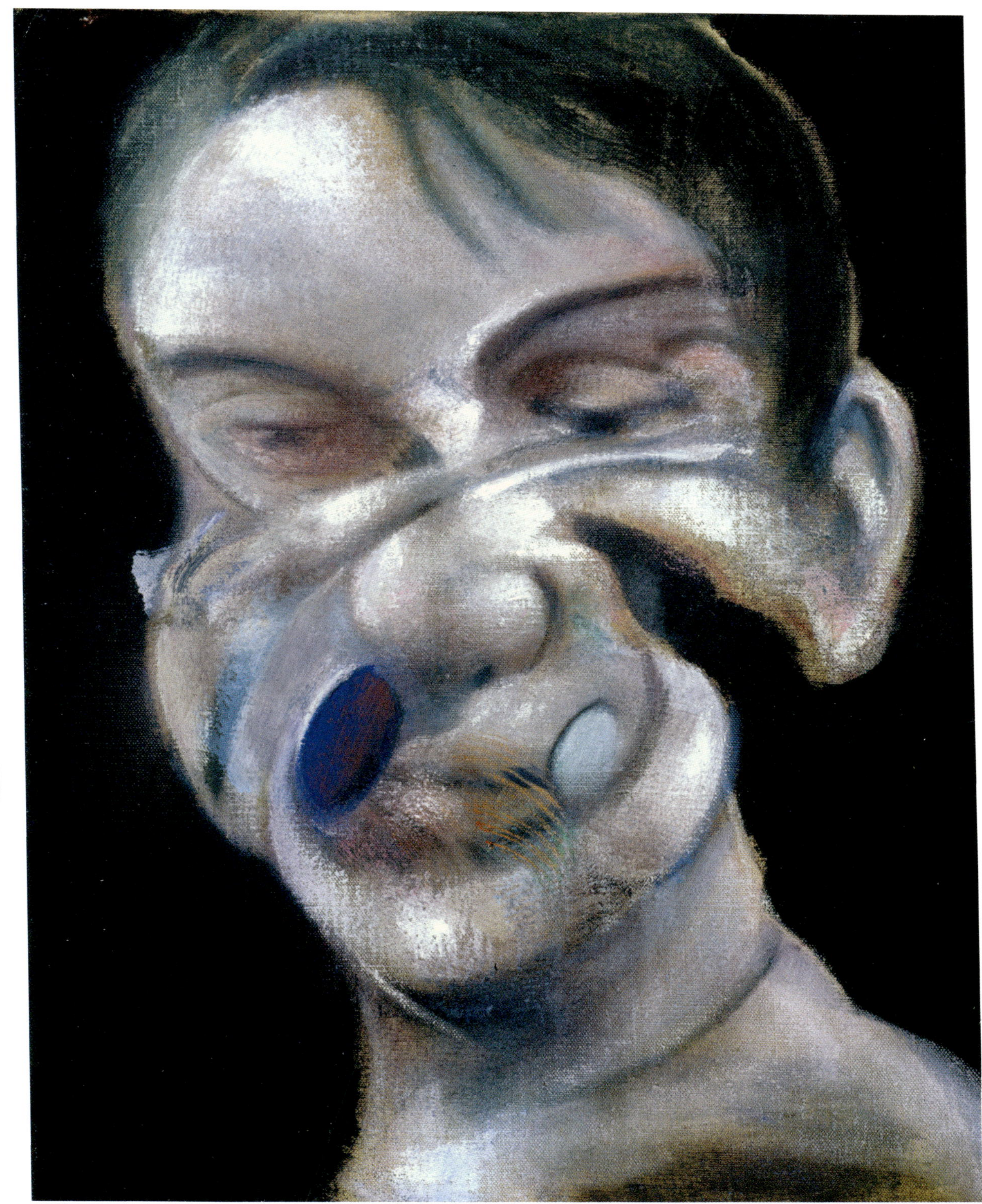

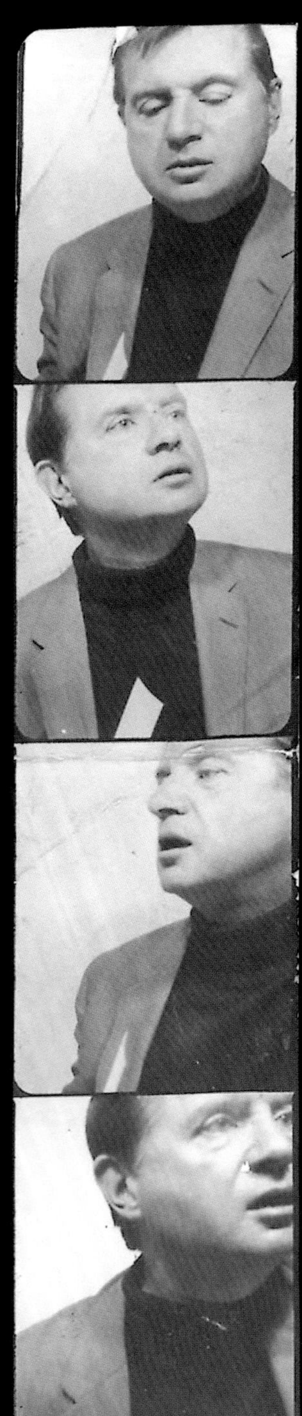

FRANCIS BACON

(1909–1992)

At the end of the sixties, Francis Bacon did a number of self-portraits, occasionally using photobooth photographs as his model. He was very interested in the different points of view obtained in each shot and reproduced this strip principle in his *Four Studies for a Self-Portrait* in 1967 and in *Three Studies for a Self-Portrait* in 1972. Bacon had already extensively analyzed the principle of the succession of images and the attempt to record human movement in the photographic work of Eadweard Muybridge.

During private interviews with the British writer and art critic David Sylvester, done between 1971 and 1973, Bacon talks about painting portraits from photographs: "Even in the case of friends who will come and pose, I've had photographs taken for portraits because I very much prefer working from the photographs than from them." During the course of the same interview, Bacon explained why he preferred being alone with those photographic portraits than in the presence of his models: "They inhibit me. They inhibit me because, if I like them, I don't want to practice before them the injury that I do to them in my work. I would rather practice the injury in private by which I think I can record the fact of them more clearly."

A number of photobooth strips, of himself but also of certain of his models, were found in his studio after his death.

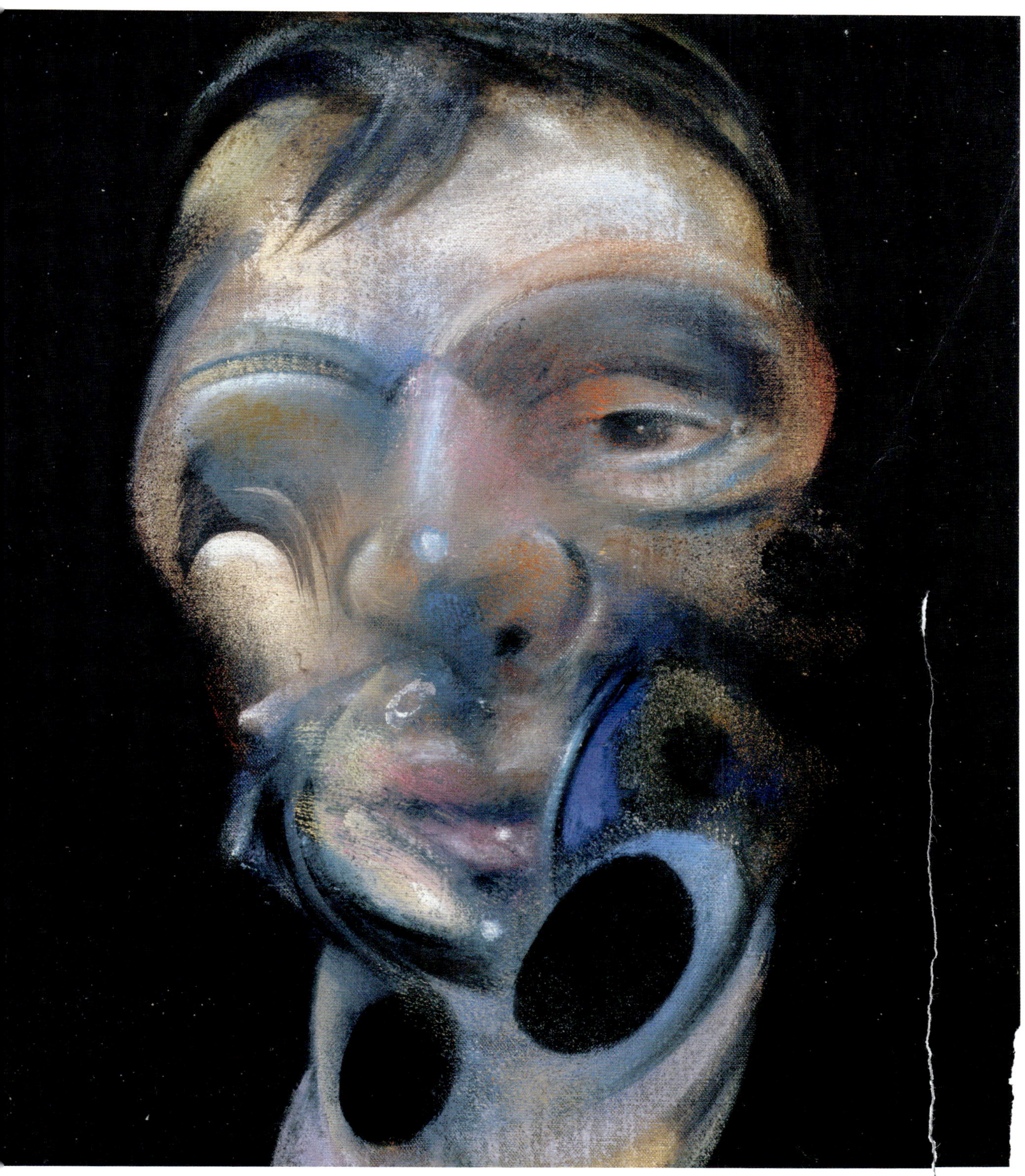

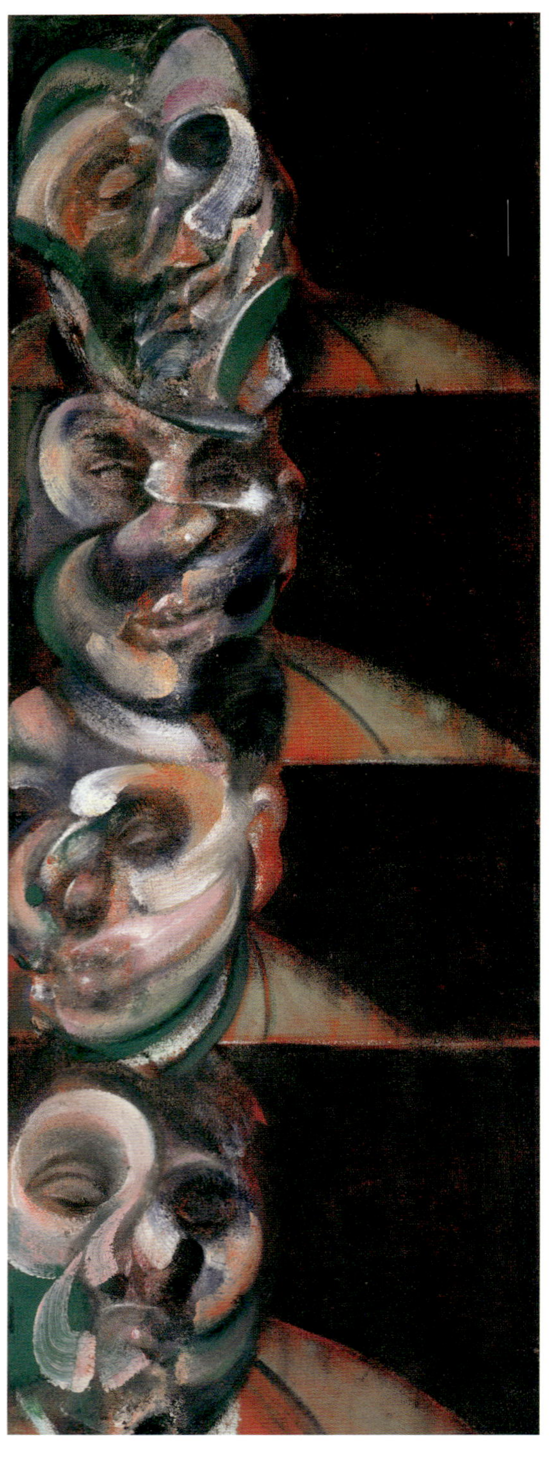

Four Studies for a Self-Portrait, 196

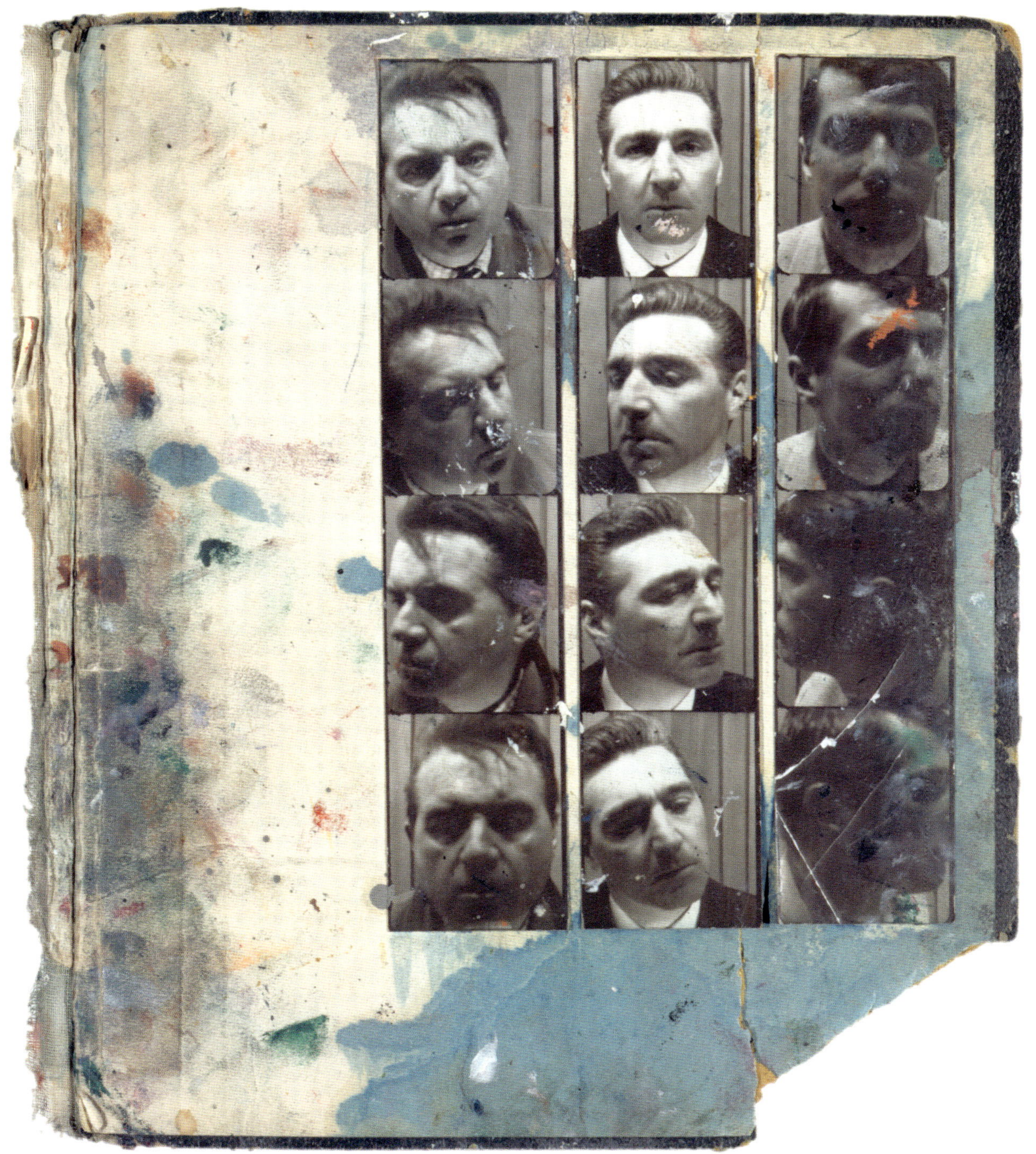

Photobooth portraits of Francis Bacon, George Dyer, and David Plante in
Aix-en-Provence, 1966–1967, glued to the inside cover of a book.

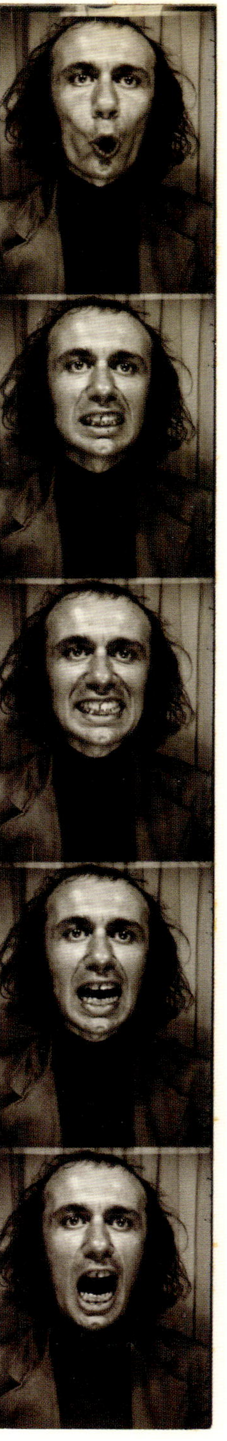

VITO ACCONCI

(1940–)
American artist, performer, architect, film-maker, and photographer

• Sitting in a *Photomatic* booth, which provides 5 photographs for 50 cents (the machine automatically photographs continuously, with a brief pause between each picture).

• While the photographs are being taken, enunciating clearly and broadly each syllable in the first line of Cole Porter's "Anything Goes" ("In-old-en-days-a-glimpse-of-stock-ing-was-looked-on-as-some-thing-shock-ing").

• What is recorded on the photographs are my facial gestures for the syllables that I happened to be enunciating while each photograph was taken.

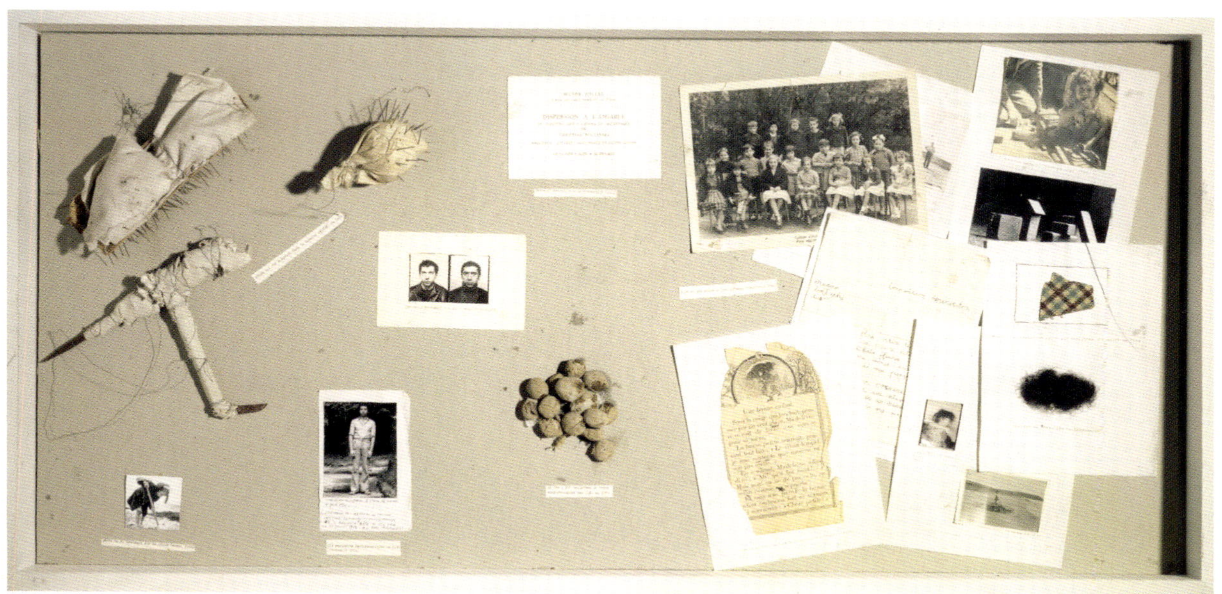

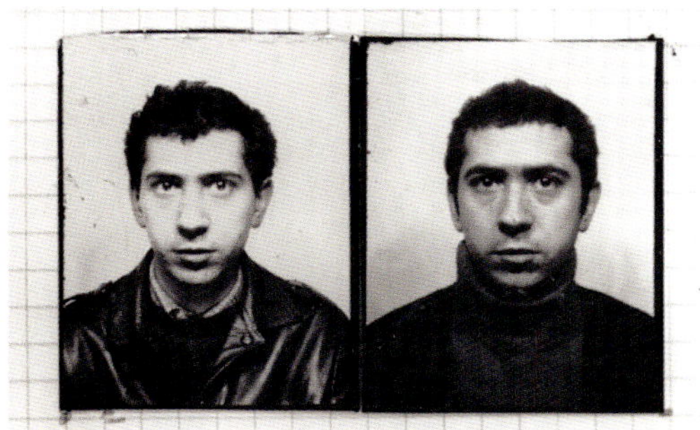

Photobooth photos of Christian Boltanski "at a distance in time of 5 years, 3 months."

Top: *Vitrine of Reference* containing photos, locks of hair, scraps of clothing, a writing sample, a page from a notebook, 14 balls of earth, and three snared objects, all belonging to the artist, 1971, 23½ × 47¼ × 4.9 in. (59.6 × 120 × 12.4 cm). Musée National d'Art Moderne, Centre Georges Pompidou, Paris.

CHRISTIAN BOLTANSKI

(1944–)
French artist

These two identity portraits are found, beginning in 1970, in numerous installations called *Vitrines of Reference*. The *Vitrines of Reference* are composed of a diverse array of elements such as photographs, hair, scraps of fabric, paper, clods of earth.... Through his artworks, Boltanski attempts to present a reconstruction of his own past, in a blend of fiction and reality, as he sets out found objects alongside other objects that really belonged to him. The artist thus offers an ongoing meditation on memory, heritage, and time.

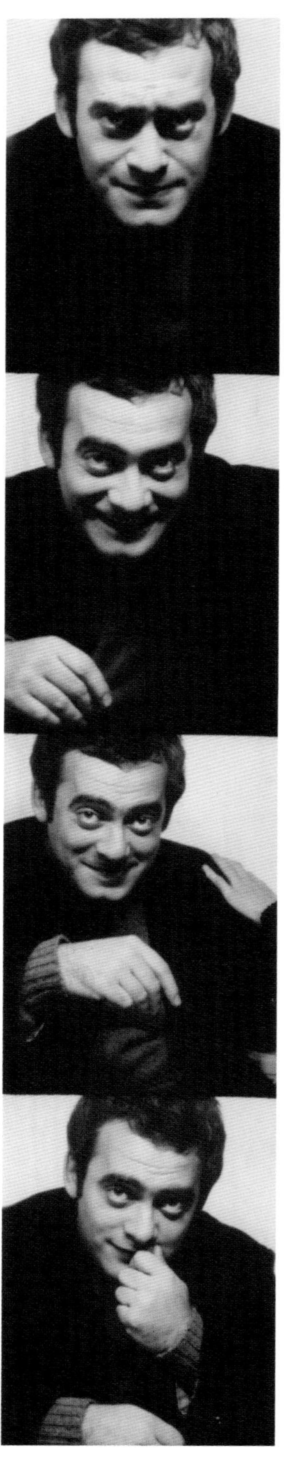

ROLAND TOPOR

One of the very first articles about the Photomaton, published in the *New York Times* on April 27, 1928, ran under the headline "Make Your Own Movies for a Quarter!" At the end of the sixties, the artist Roland Topor did make his own movies, serving as screenwriter, actor, and director all at once. He called these "Topor-matons." Topor conceived of these short stories in four panels as genuine comic strips: a succession of self-portraits with varied expressions and attitudes, often exaggerated, and accompanied by short typed texts. The continuity of those Photomaton strips show that these odd wordless stories, probably written in advance, were produced in a single "sitting," that is, in less than twenty seconds. In their arrangement, the Topor-matons were similar to the animation techniques used in the late nineteenth century for the removable strips of the Praxinoscope or the Mutoscope.

"'I am allergic to reality,' Roland liked to say. To cure that allergy, he would seize at random concrete aspects of his days and transform them into illusion, bursts of laughter, black champagne, and other subversive fantasies, his daily oxygen. After newspaper photographs, shafts of light, and rain on his balcony, one day he was captivated by a photobooth and turned it into a short novel, the falsely naïve hero of which was him."

—Jean-Michel Ribes
Playwright, theatrical director, and filmmaker

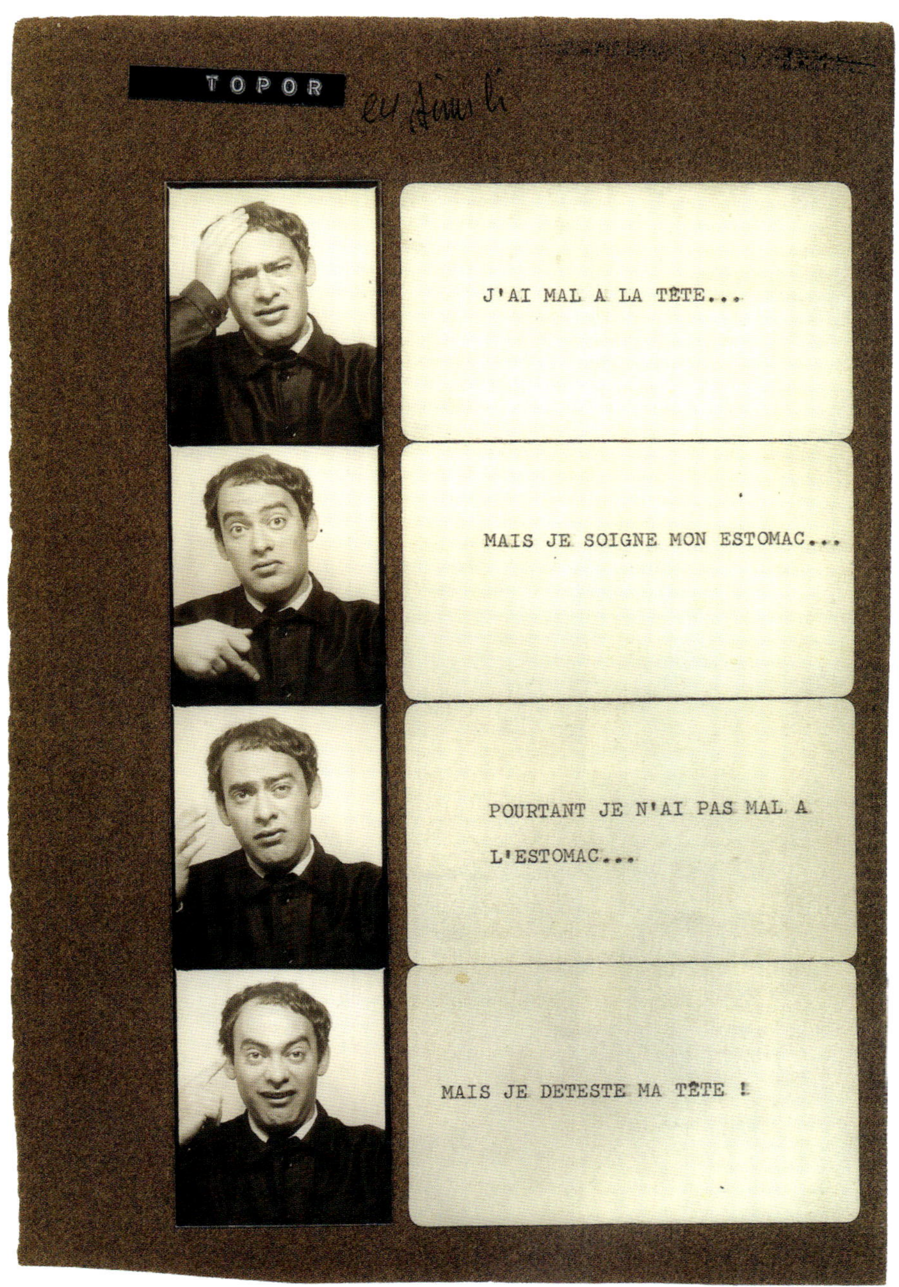

Above and pages 126–127: Topor-matons were published in the magazines *Action* and *Charlie Hebdo* between 1967 and 1970.

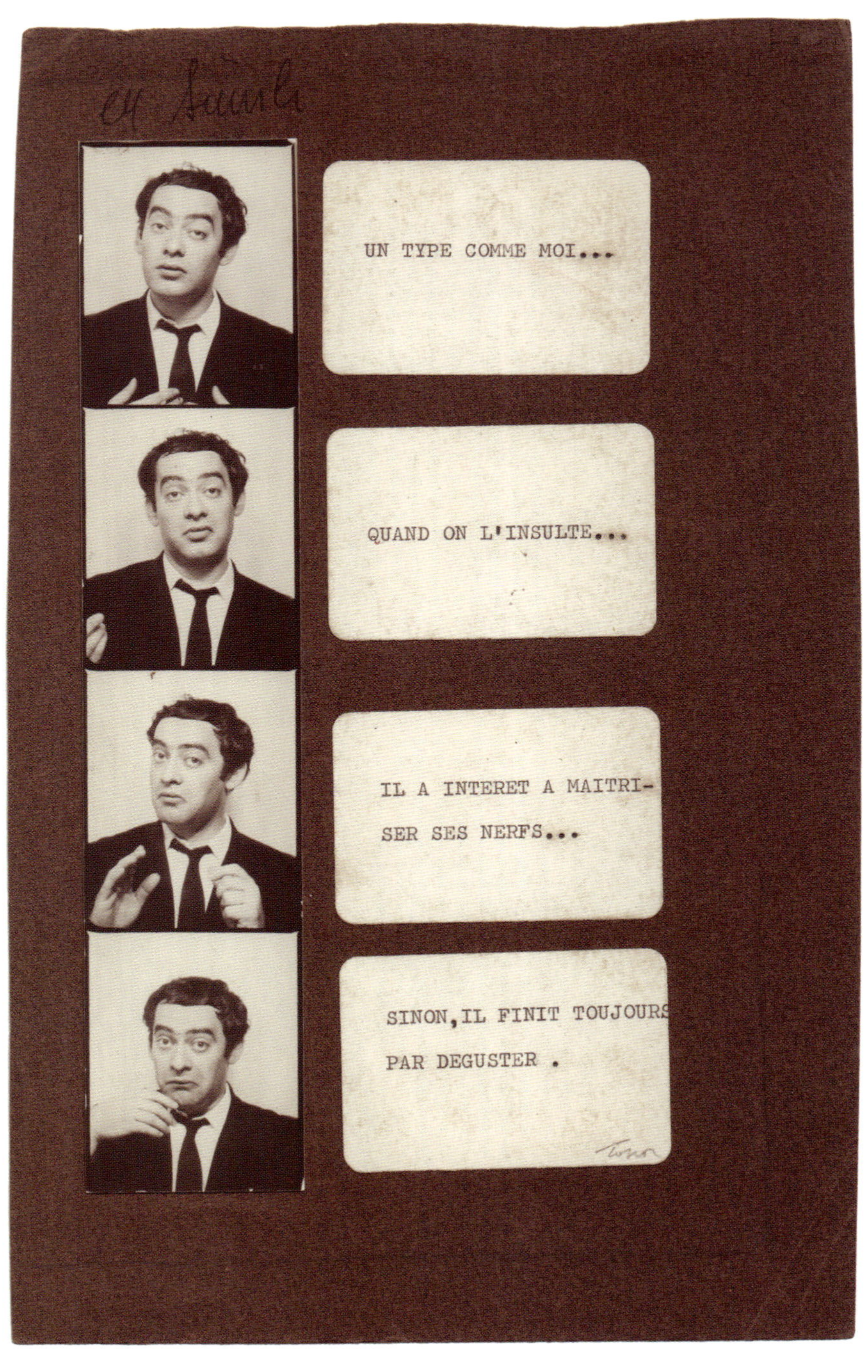

UN TYPE COMME MOI...

QUAND ON L'INSULTE...

IL A INTERET A MAITRI-
SER SES NERFS...

SINON,IL FINIT TOUJOURS
PAR DEGUSTER .

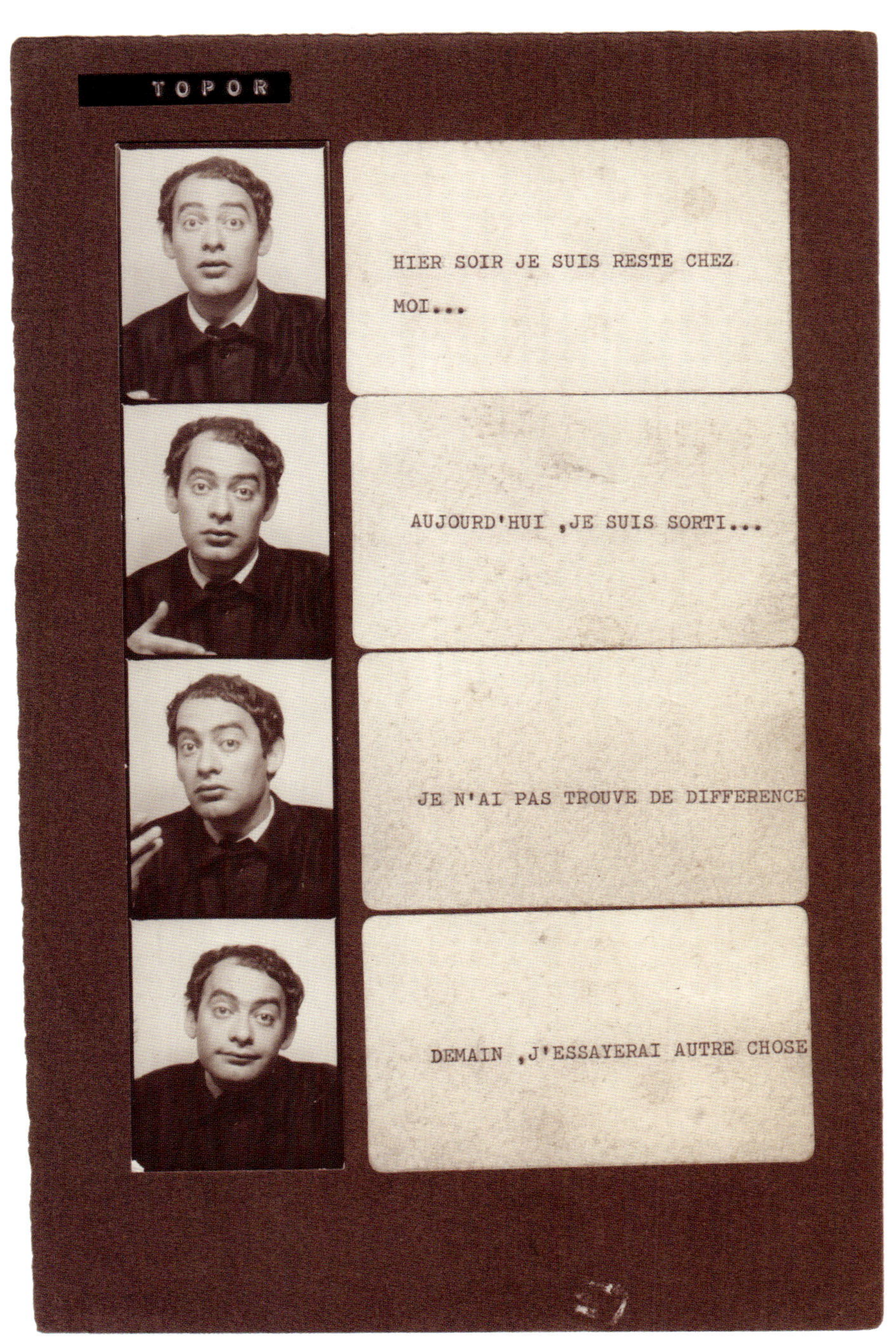

TOPOR
HIER SOIR JE SUIS RESTE CHEZ
MOI...
AUJOURD'HUI ,JE SUIS SORTI...
JE N'AI PAS TROUVE DE DIFFERENCE
DEMAIN ,J'ESSAYERAI AUTRE CHOSE

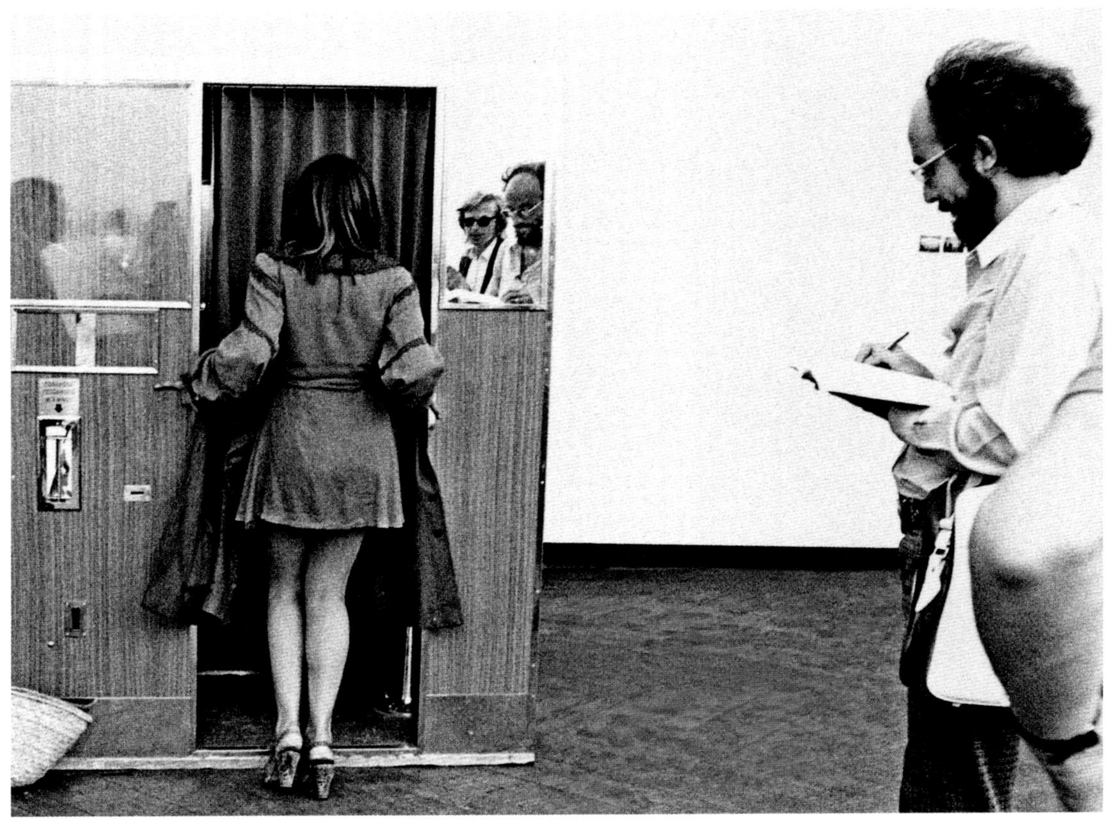

FRANCO VACCARI

(1936–)
Italian experimental photographer

"In the sixties and seventies, the interest focused on artworks shifted from perception as an object toward the mental dimension. I was, for my part, interested in a form of artistic production in which the work of the artist would be minimized. In 1972, I was invited to the Venice Biennale, which featured the theme 'Work or Behavior?' Since I was given a hall for my own use, I had a photobooth installed, and I proposed an *Esposizione in tempo reale* (an 'exhibition/exposure in real time') in which every visitor could leave a trace of his or her passage. More than five thousand paying spectators ultimately impressed on these walls their photobooth portraits. In 1973, I decided to further explore this experience through an initiative entitled 'Photomatic d'Italia.' Seven hundred photobooths were installed throughout Italy, for one year [a similar undertaking was extended to Prague and then to Tokyo]."

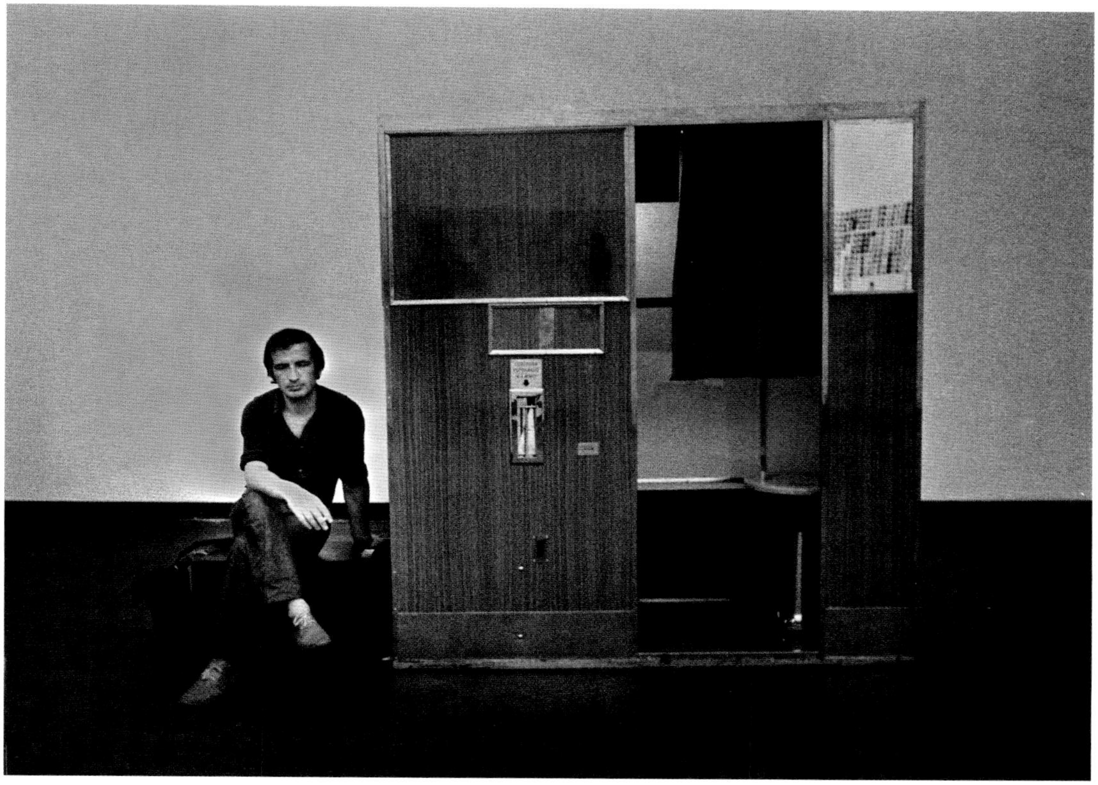

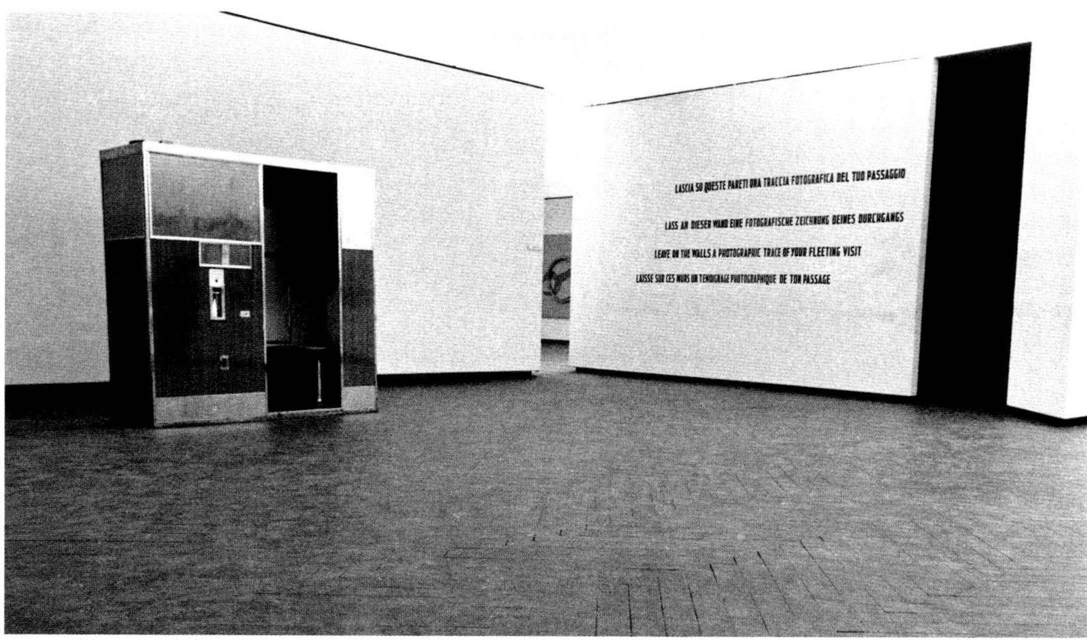

LASCIA SU QUESTE PARETI UNA TRACCIA FOTOGRAFICA DEL TUO PASSAGGIO

LASS AN DIESER WAND EINE FOTOGRAFISCHE ZEICHNUNG DEINES DURCHGANGS

LEAVE ON THE WALLS A PHOTOGRAPHIC TRACE OF YOUR FLEETING VISIT

LAISSE SUR CES MURS UN TEMOIGNAGE PHOTOGRAPHIQUE DE TON PASSAGE

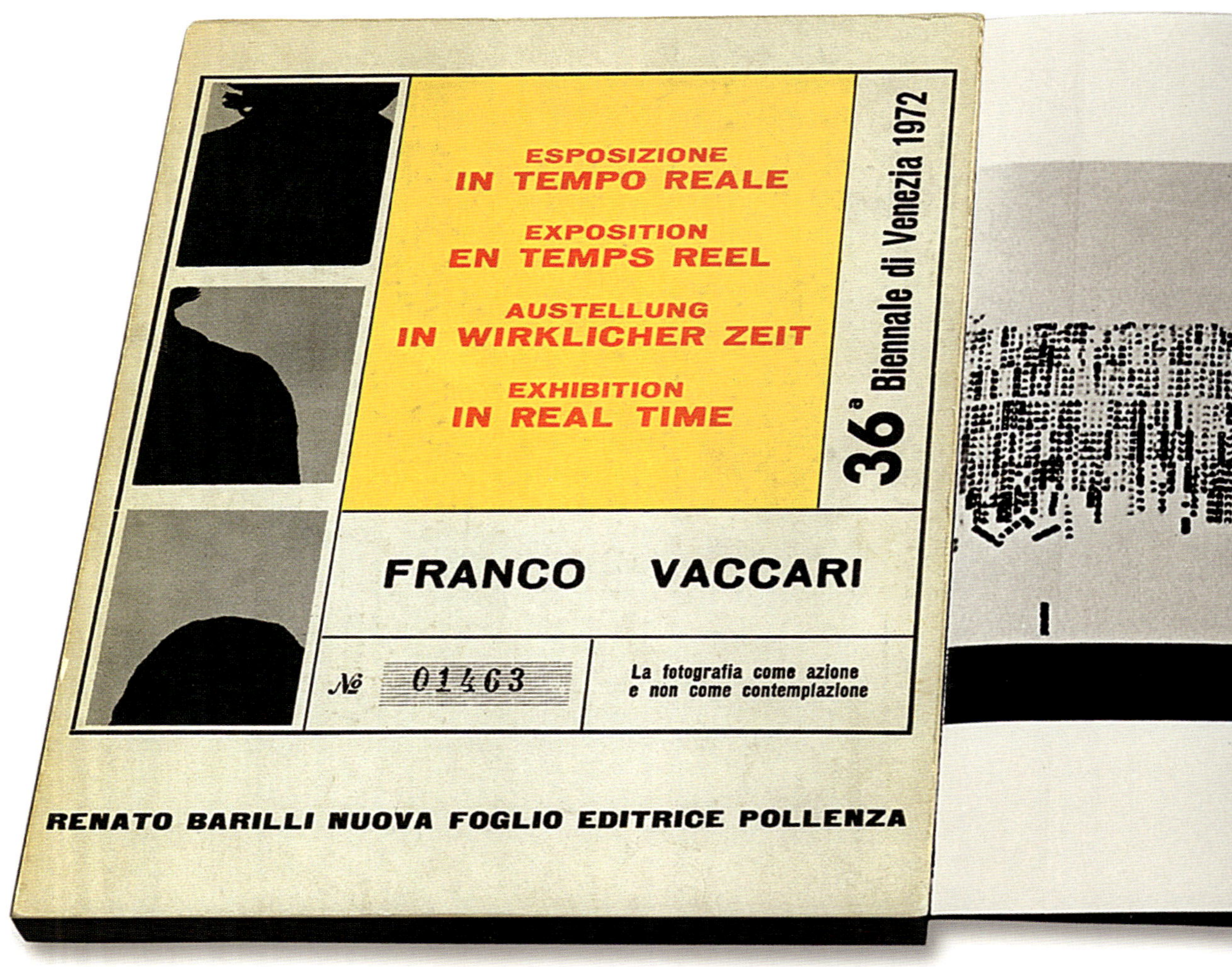

Franco Vaccari, *Exhibition in Real Time*, Venice Biennale, 1972.

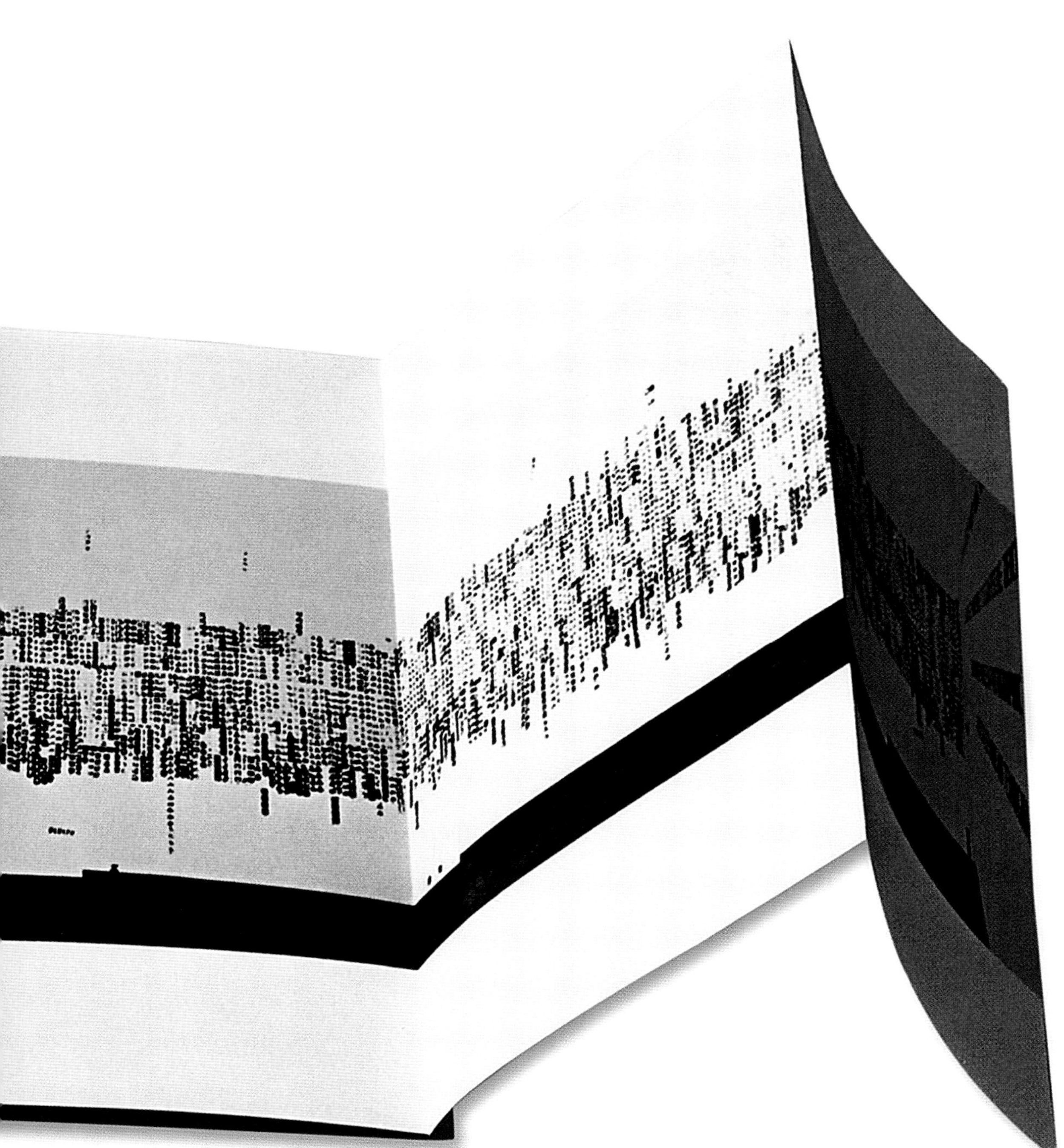

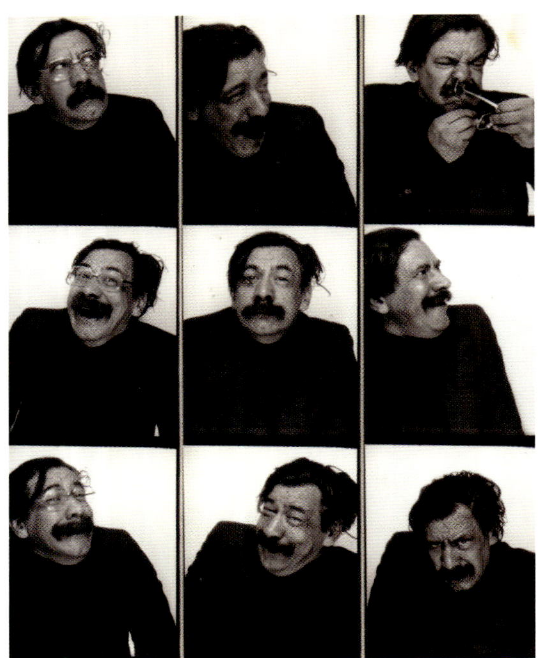

CHRISTIAN DOTREMONT

(1922–1979)

This Belgian poet and author was the cofounder of the Surrealist group *La Main à Plume* and the instigator of revolutionary Surrealism in Brussels in 1947 and, in 1948, of the international experimental art movement Cobra (an acronym of Copenhagen, *Brussels*, and *Amsterdam*). In 1962, his logograms were "one of the great poetic inventions of the twentieth century, to no less a degree than Apollinaire's *calligrammes*," according to Pierre Caizergues.

"My brother, Christian Dotremont, loved to take photographs, have himself photographed at regular intervals of time, in the same locations and in similar poses. He also enjoyed having his photo taken in Photomaton booths, creating 'scenes' like the one in which you see him devouring a copy of the magazine *Strates*, which he published from 1963 to 1966. He was intensely interested in photography, and in 1950, he wrote a fundamental text on the subject, *Les buts de l'œil*. 'In the final analysis,' he wrote in that book, 'photography has no objective but to decorate walls, it has no cause but to denude the eye.'"

—Guy Dotremont

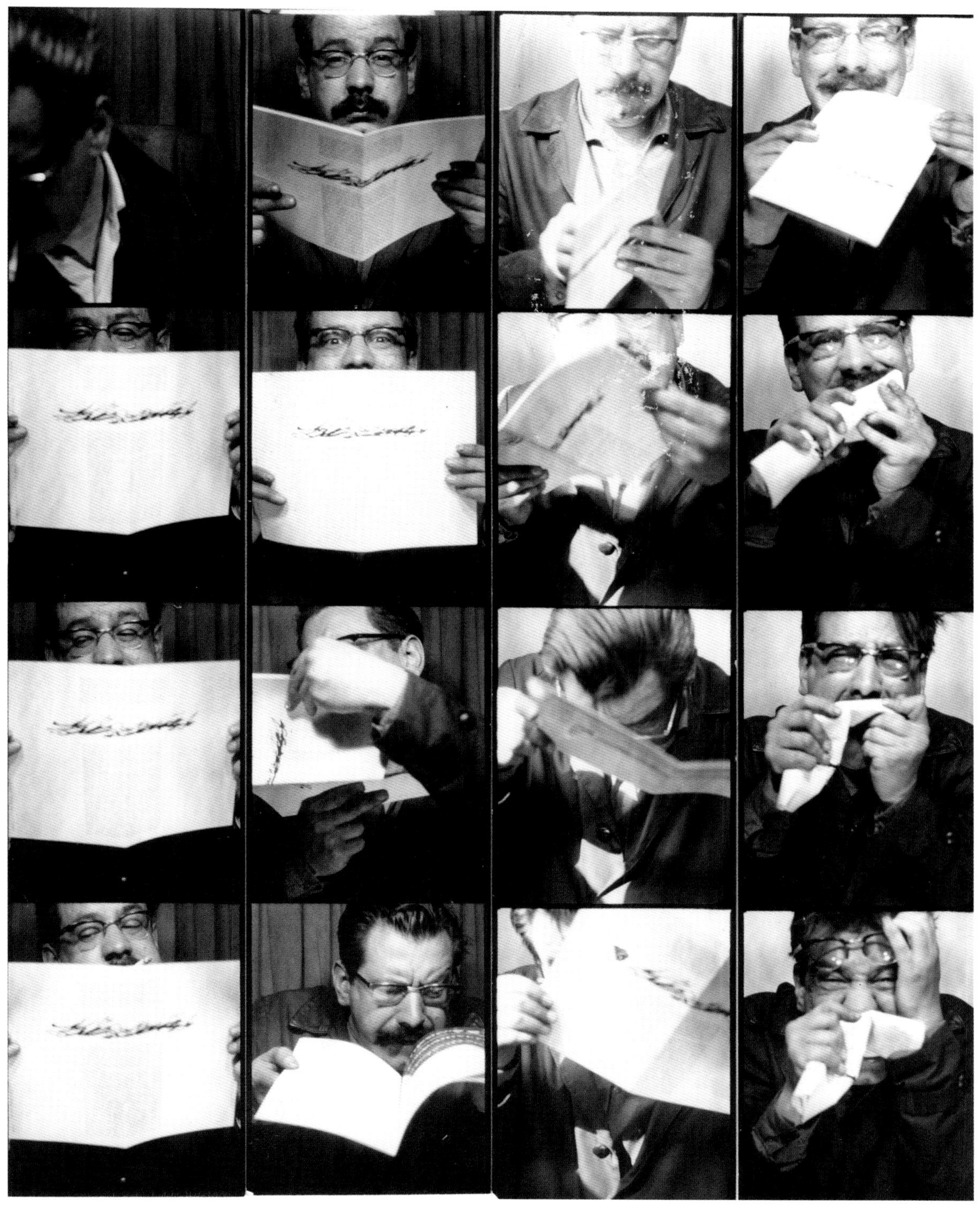

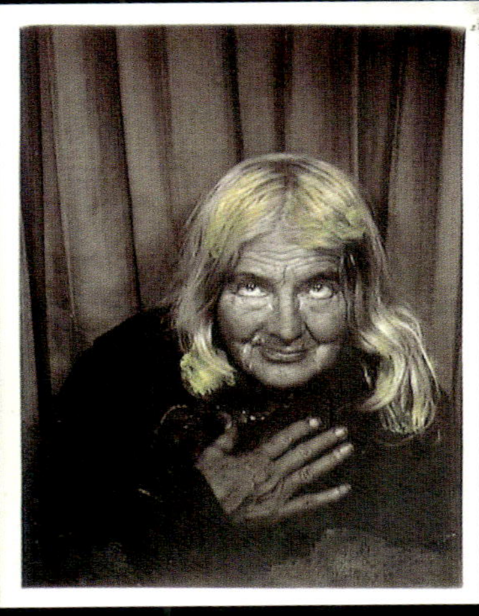

Be My Valentine.

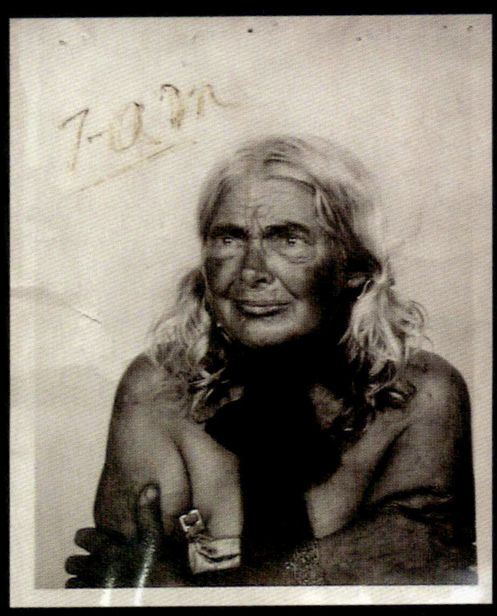

7 A.M.

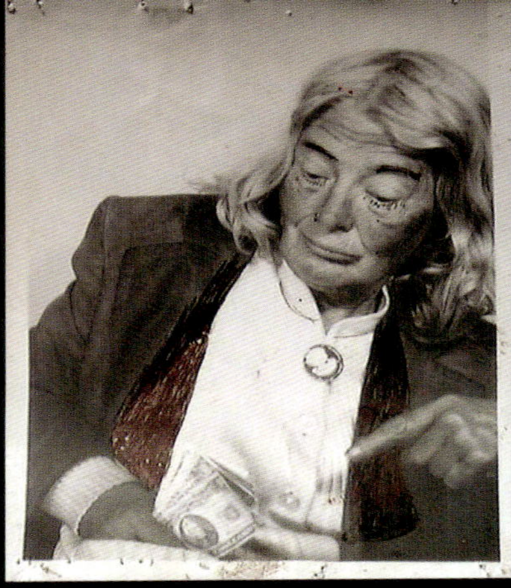

Untitled.

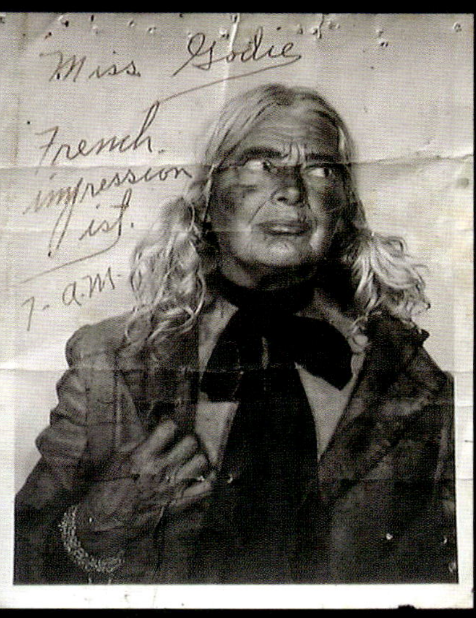

French Impressionist. 7 A.M.

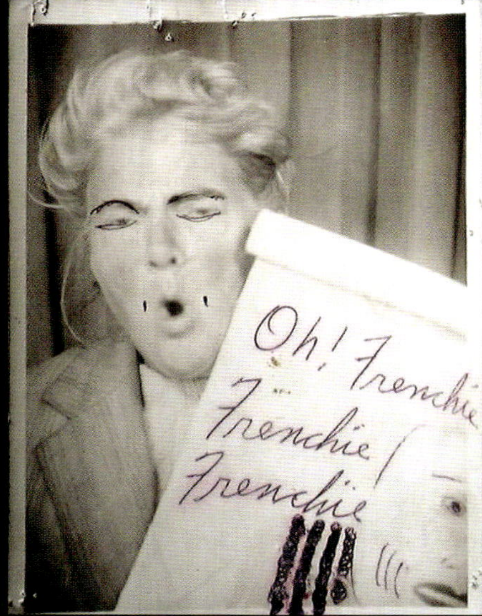

Oh! Frenchie!

LEE GODIE

(1908–1994)

Godie was an American artist, h[...] and living on the streets, who pr[...] herself a "French Impressionist and su[...] Monet, Manet, Degas, and Cézanne." [...] 1968 and 1990, Lee Godie hawked [...] vases to the passersby on the steps o[...] Institute of Chicago. Her work. mai[...] ings and drawings, includes some ph[...] self-portraits she sometimes altered [...] fiti. Godie has had museum shows an[...] exhibitions, particularly at the Carl[...] Gallery in Chicago.

DICK JEWELL

(1951–)
English photographer

"My initial contact with the photobooth was for the purpose of obtaining an image for my passport, and photobooth portraits were promoted as being 'passport approved.' This very premise prompted me to produce *Passport Approved Photo Album* between 1973 and 1974, the remit for which being that none of the pictures in it would be acceptable in a passport. In it I explored the use of disguises, mirrors, altering the lighting even down to entirely blocking the lights and using candles.

"Between 1978 and 1981, I was again drawn to photobooths, which by this time had migrated to a square format with the choice of four poses or one large one. I was interested in the photobooth images that people found unacceptable, especially considering that there was not a photographer's eye involved and that this was part of a public common psyche. This lack of a photographer also meant that the images were 'typical,' leading observers of my 'Found Photographs' to comment 'that reminds me of so and so.' Aside from individual portraits, I also enjoyed discarded slices of life, interactions captured within the photobooth session. This led to my publications of *Found Photos* in 1978 and 1981.

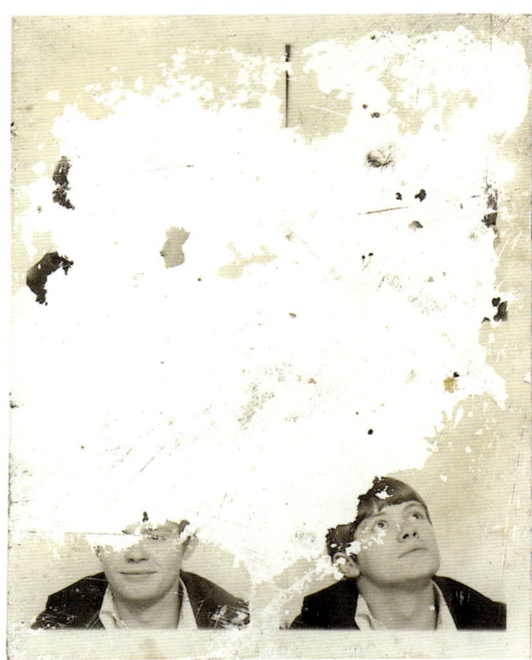

Excerpt from *Found Photos*, Dick Jewell, 1978.

"The time span and enclosed space led me in 2007 to produce five time-based photobooth portraits on DVDs for a gallery. To this end, I produced four DVDs of time-lapsed portraits and arranged monitors in the proportion of a photobooth strip. The speed of the dissolve of each animated portrait was relative to the overall time span that each set of portraits covered. The subjects were Mick Hodgeson in 1971 (a photostrip made each week for a year); Andrew Logan, between 1982 and 2004; John Truelove, between 1982 and 2004; Glo Pringle, between c. 1980 and 2007; and Andre Van Noord, between 1985 and 2006."

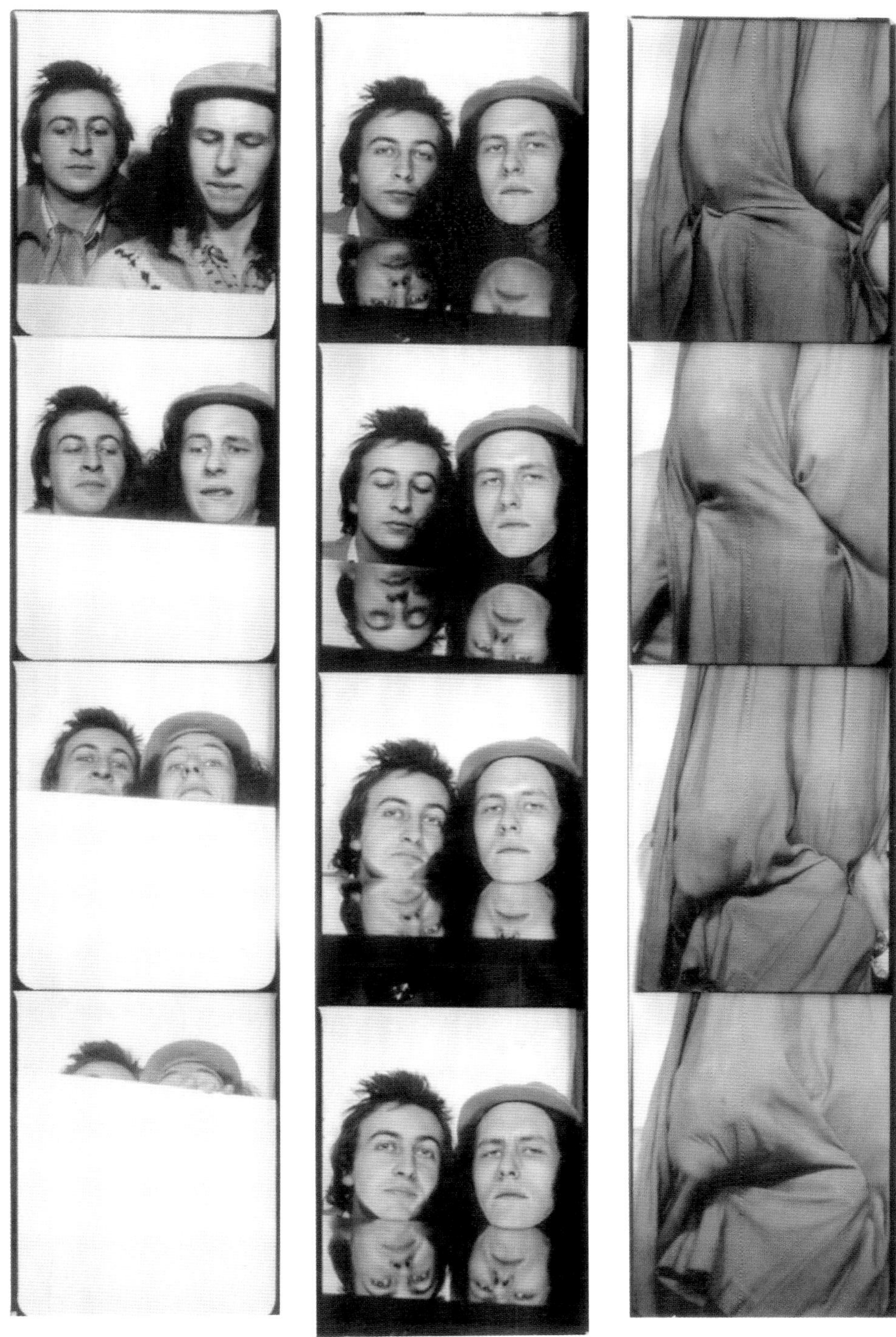

Three photostrips from *Passport Approved Photo Album*, Dick Jewell, 1973–1974.
From left: *White Card Version 1; After Busby Berkeley; After Christo.*

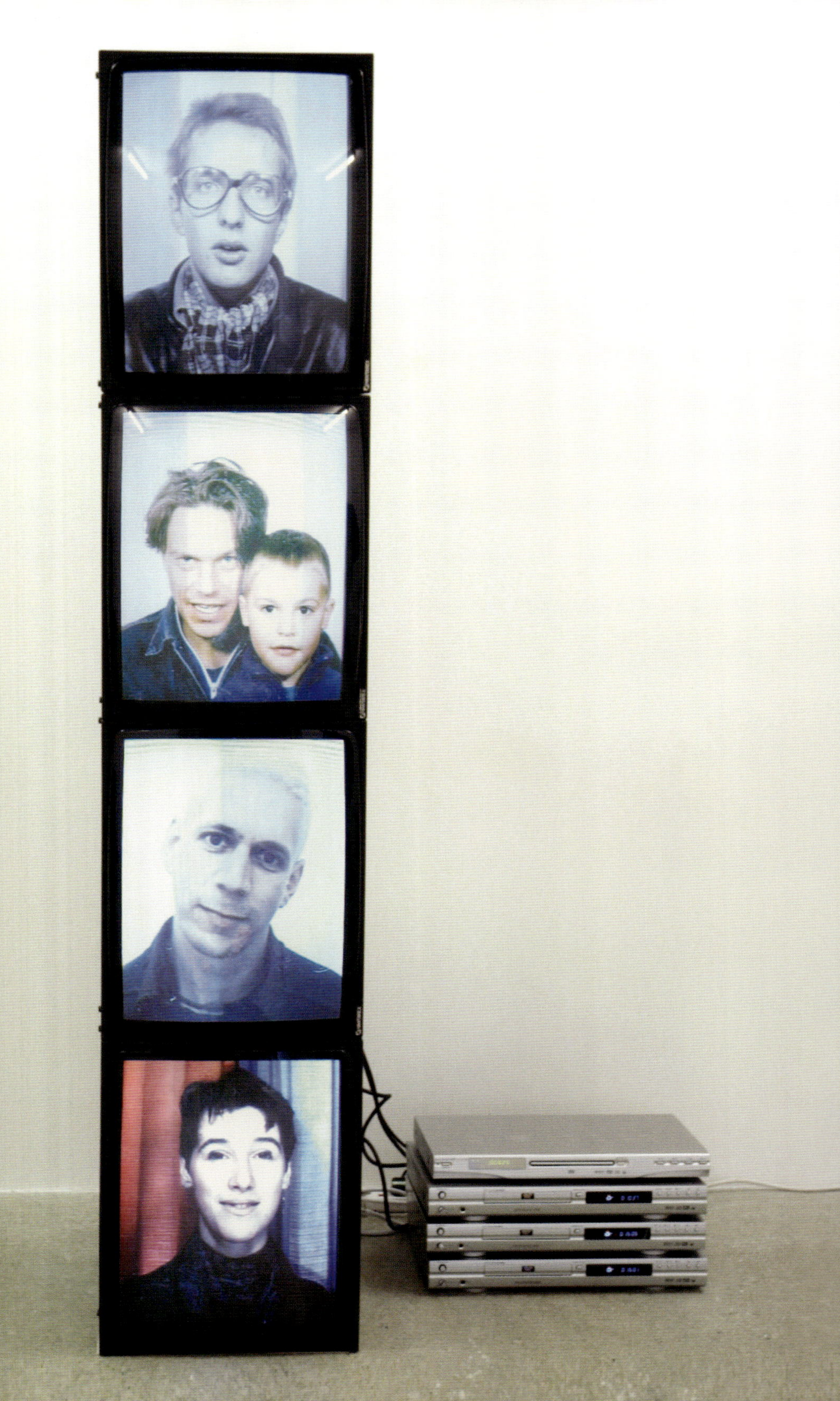

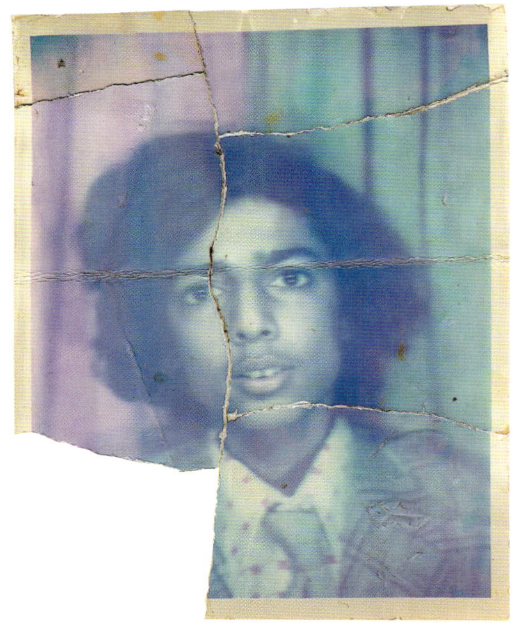

Excerpt from *Found Photos*, Dick Jewell, 1978

Left: *Five Time-Based Photobooth Portraits on DVDs*,
Dick Jewell, 2007

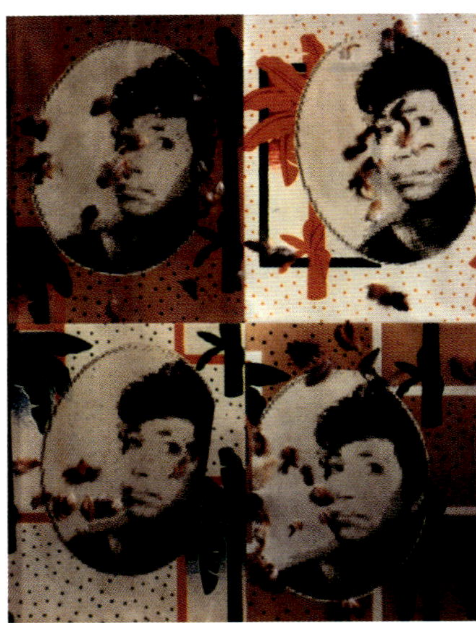

Midnight Boca Raton.
Opposite: *Midnight Waterloo.*

SUSAN HILLER

(1940–)
American artist living in London

"**I** worked on a photomat series of self-portraits for about ten years, and there are a few things—perhaps obvious but maybe not—about why this particular format and this artifact are of such fascination to me.

"The photobooth format is the tail end of the great tradition of portraiture. It's come down to this miniature head-and-shoulders view, complete with draperies in the background, now available for anyone to use as official identification. There's no intervening photographer. You're asked to engage in a private capacity with the automatic camera and to project your own self-image toward that camera as toward a mirror, in order to produce a document that verifies your identity in a public sense. Originally, I was pursuing this in portraits of other people and portraits the machines took of themselves. The departure I made in the self-portrait series is to shift the scale, enlarging the miniature up to the point where the heads become almost life-size, in order to engage viewers collectively by using a more public form of address. The images are made in tube stations, railway stations, and so on, very late at night, hence the 'Midnight' of all the titles.

"The format produced in photobooths says a number of things about the way we identify and document 'self' using these machines. The images produced are episodic, filmic, and multiple. It's a fragmented representation, and I usually maintain that in the final self-portrait.

"I'm also quite interested in the seductive allure created by the texture of paints, emphasized by enlargement while at the same time denied by the flat surface of the photograph. This is my playful reference to photography as a meta-medium, against the claims for the dominance of painting—in other words, my photographs can certainly supply the supposedly exclusive pleasures of painting.

"One has to leave a great deal open, as I'm working blind and have no control over the different focal lengths, lighting, etc. in various photomat booths. So it's a relatively improvised presentation of self.

"Over the surface of these shapes or embodiments are sets of my crypto-linguistic, calligraphic signs or marks. Slips of the pen, they've been called, or automatic writing. These marks are a kind of personal handwriting for me. Automatism has a very long history within modern art going back to Surrealism and continuing in Abstract Expressionism, and so forth. I like the idea of the artist's handwriting and personal mark, the personal touch, which are always contrasted with conventional and coded notational systems."

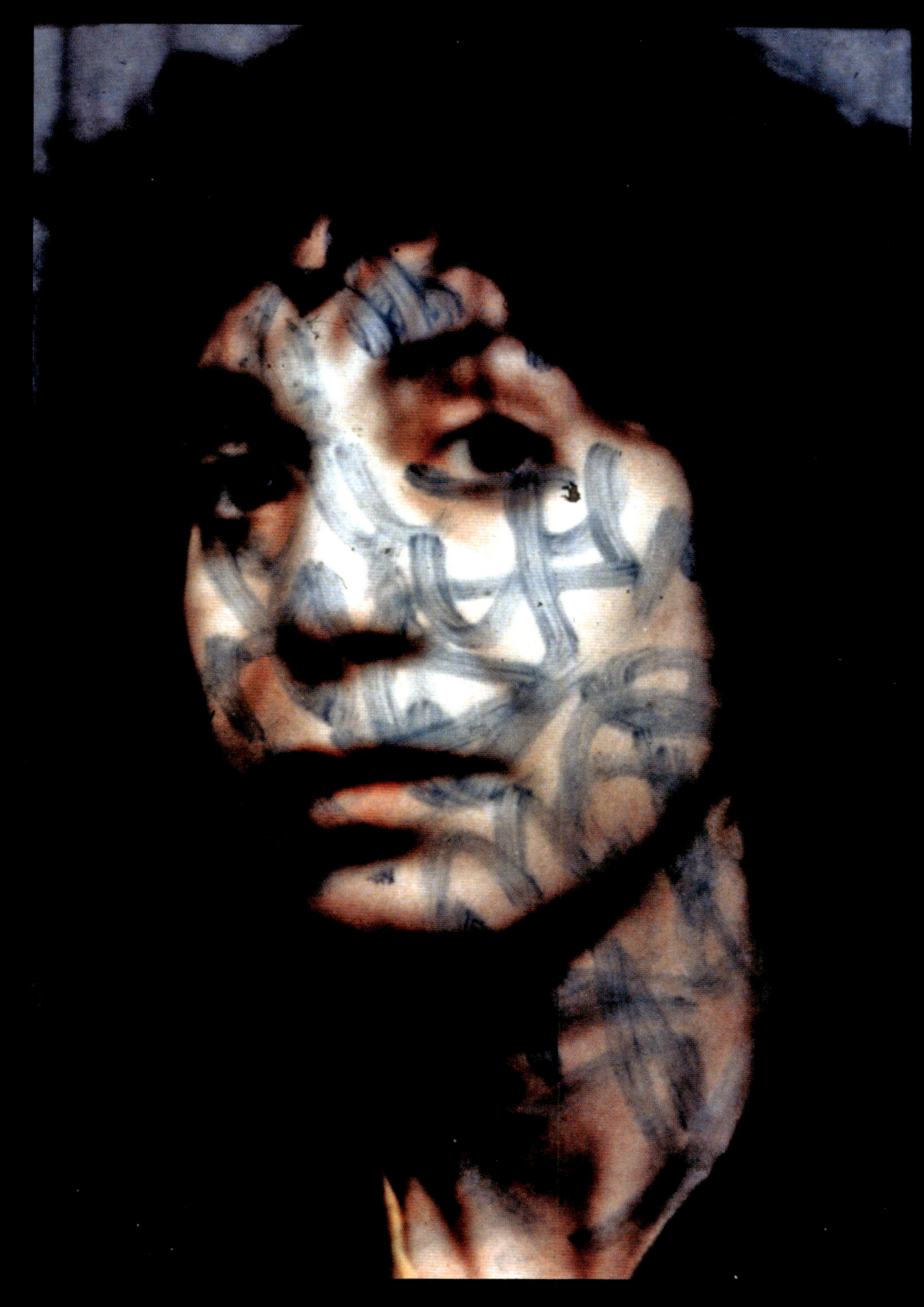

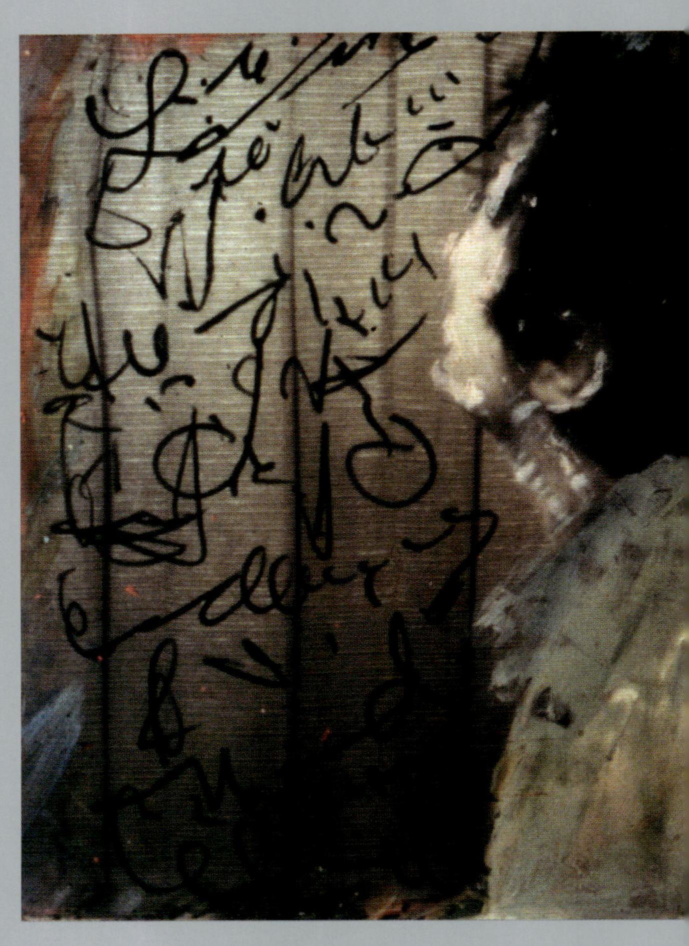

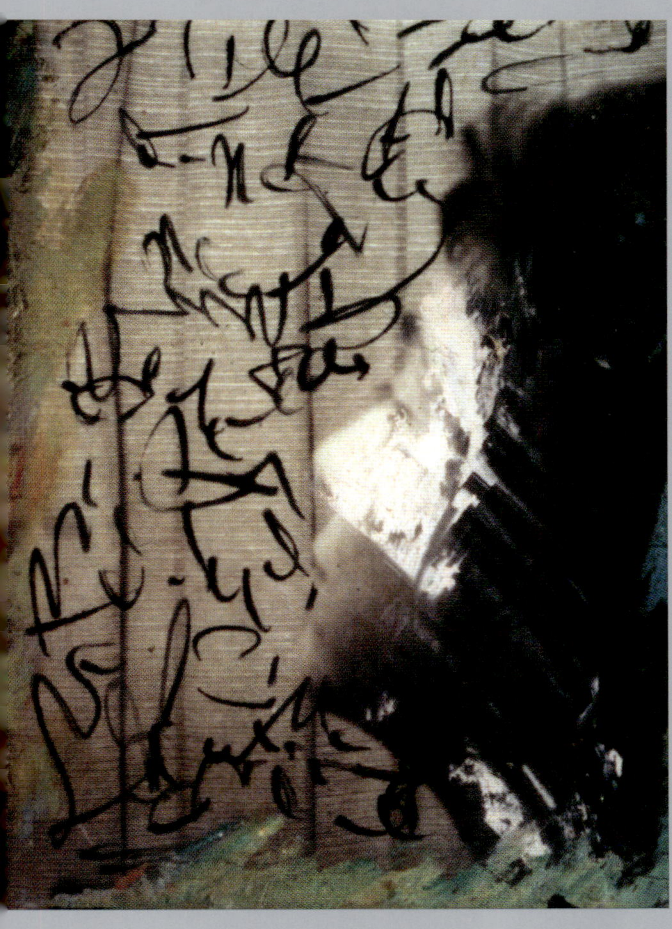

Midnight Notting Hill Gate.

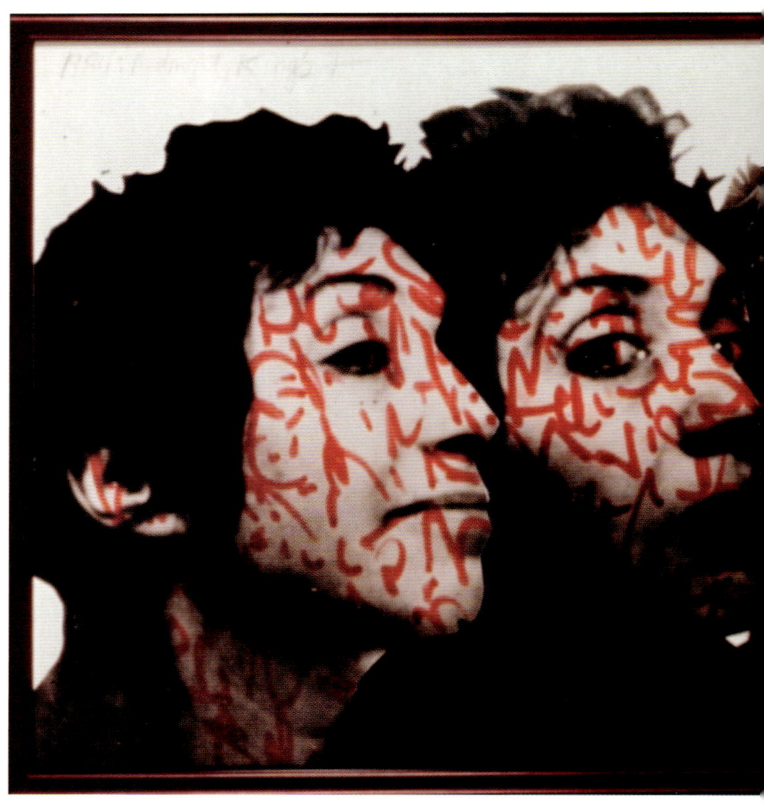

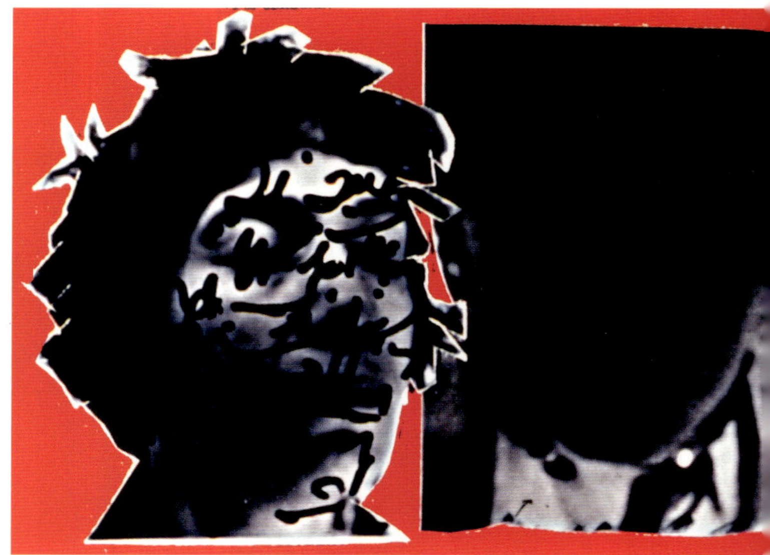

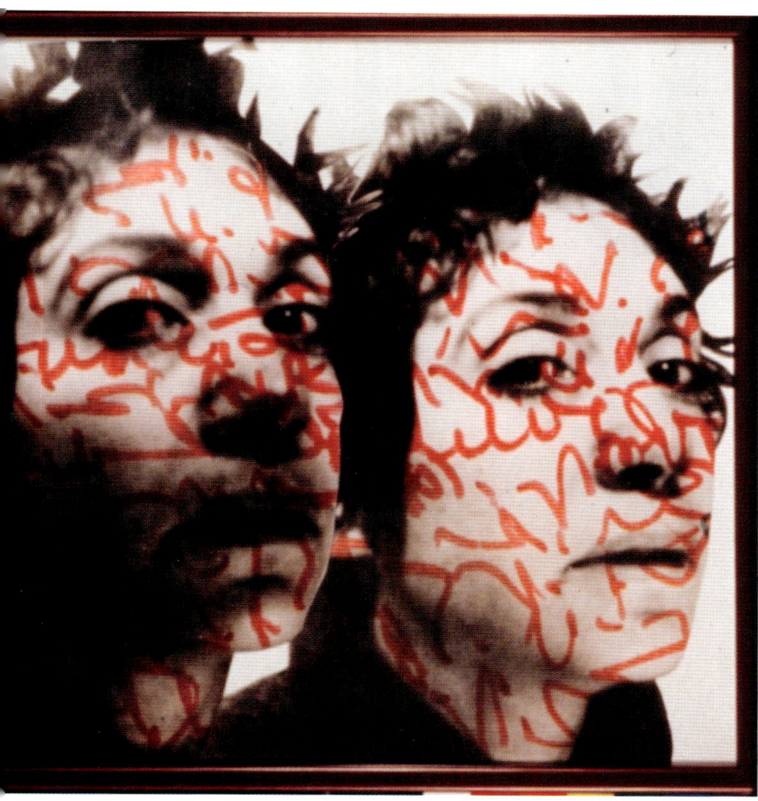

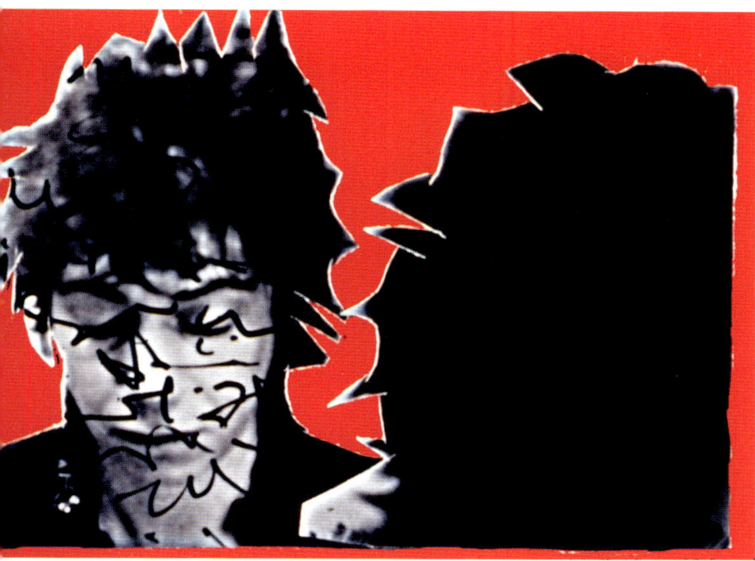

Top: *Midnight Kings Cross.*
Bottom: *Midnight Liverpool Street.*

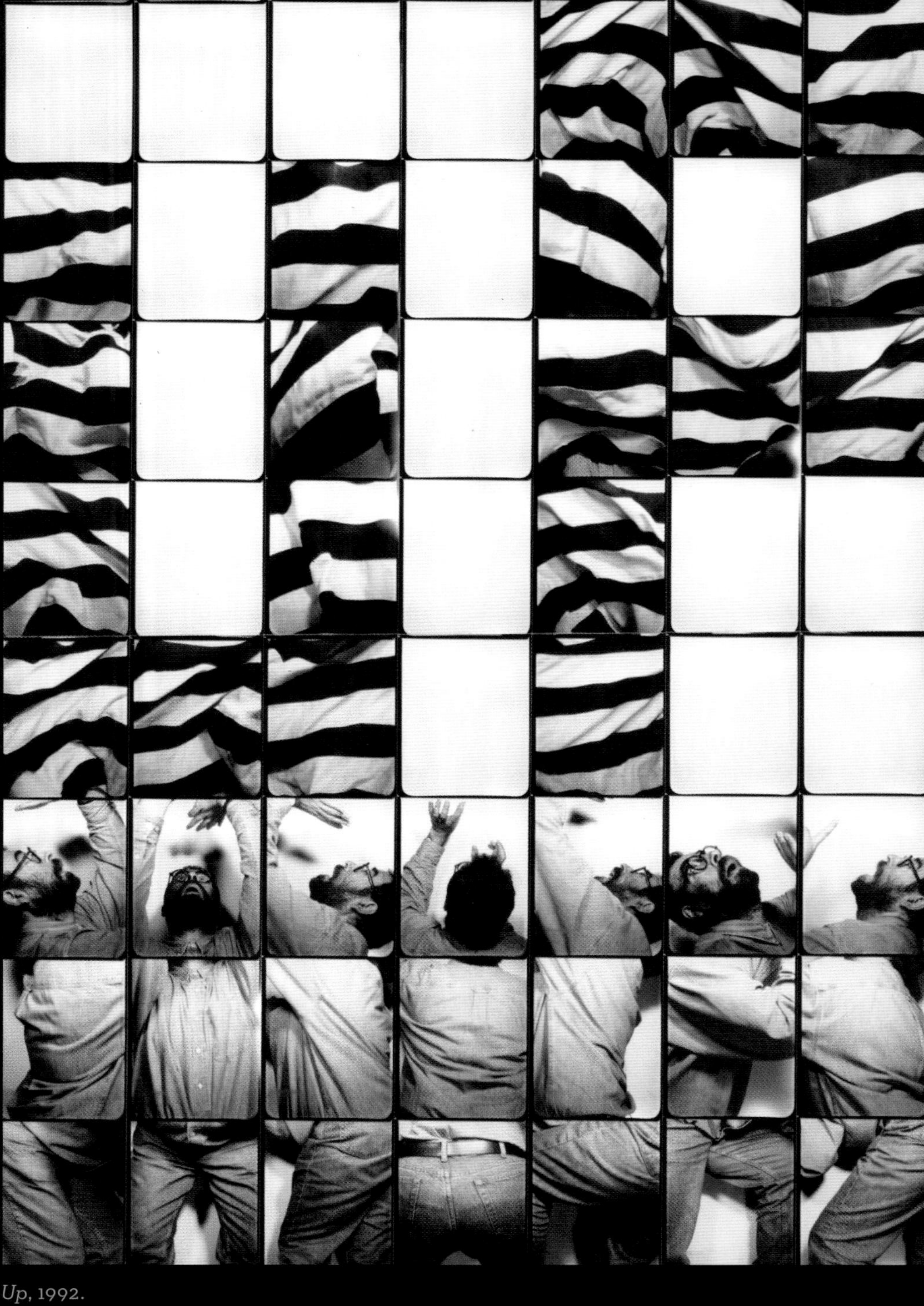

Up, 1992.

HERMAN COSTA

(1944–)
American artist, whose work is in the
permanent collections of the Museum of
Modern Art in New York and the Museet for
Fotokunst in Denmark

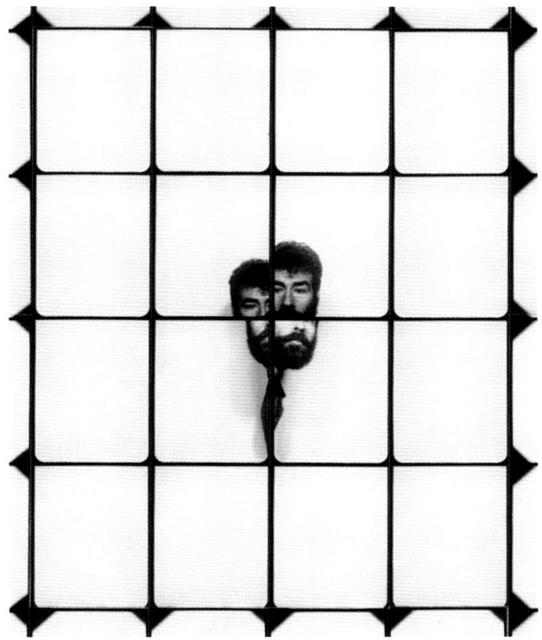

Face, 1986.

"In 1968, I moved to New York City, hoping to find myself. It would be a long, successful odyssey. When I discovered the photobooth in Times Square, a four-frame black-and-white strip was only 25 cents, so I began documenting my life. At first, I obsessively recorded variations on the typical portrait shots we've all taken in the photobooth. Soon, I began to explore. From a dream I had, I created my first head-to-toe portrait in a single strip.

"Over the next thirty years, I generated thousands of strips, which I formed into hundreds of unique art works. During those decades, I worked as a textile designer, made animated films, and went in and out of therapy. As my photobooth work developed—through still life, abstraction, dynamically moving figures—it reflected the growth and change in me. As I became a more whole, connected person, my work expanded, deepened, and became more dynamic.

"I worked on pre-planned constructions, using uncut strips to maintain the integrity of the strip, so the subject had to move around in front of the fixed camera. By placing the strips together, I would build larger, patterned pieces. Along the way there were many exhibits and reviews galore, work published in and collected by major institutions, and the photobooth was always there to record each phase of my journey to self-discovery."

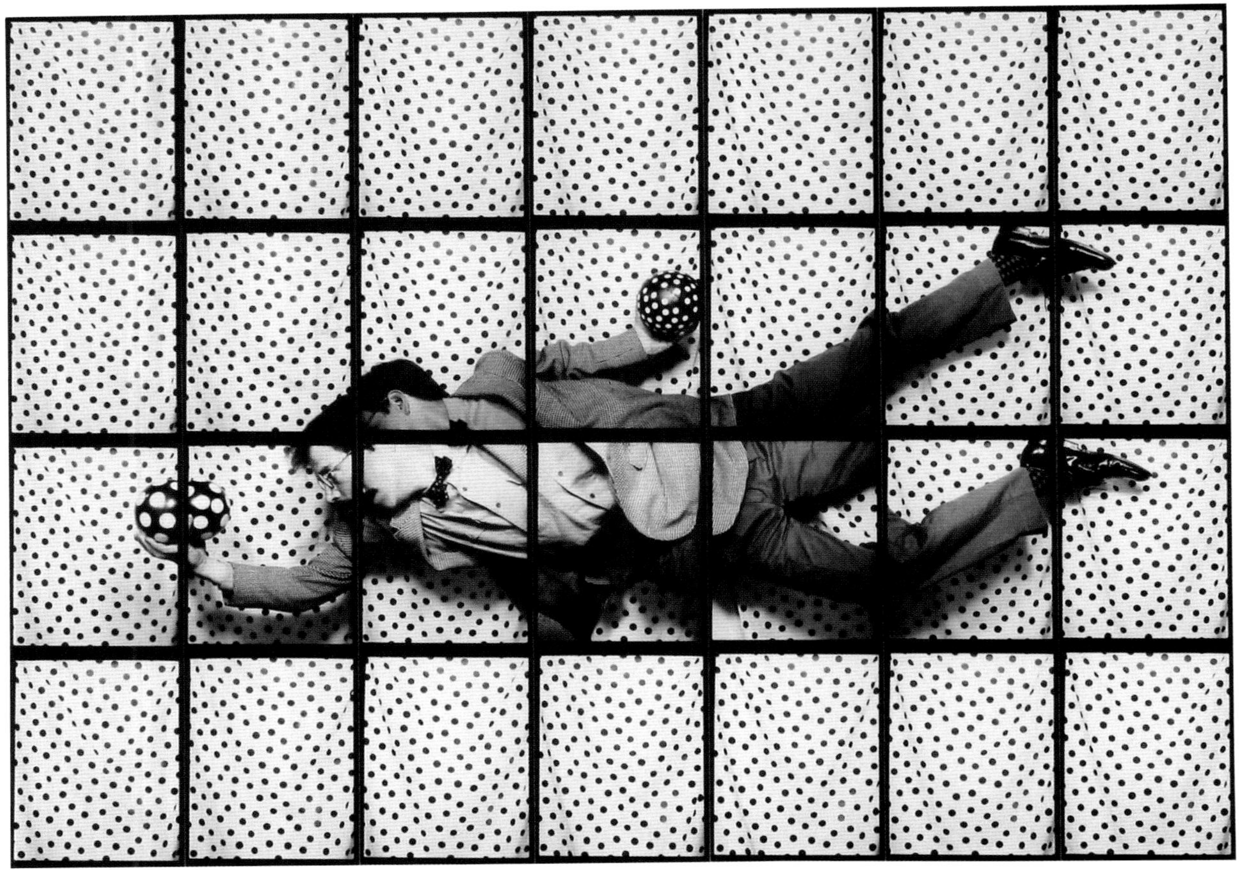

Mark in Heaven, 1991.

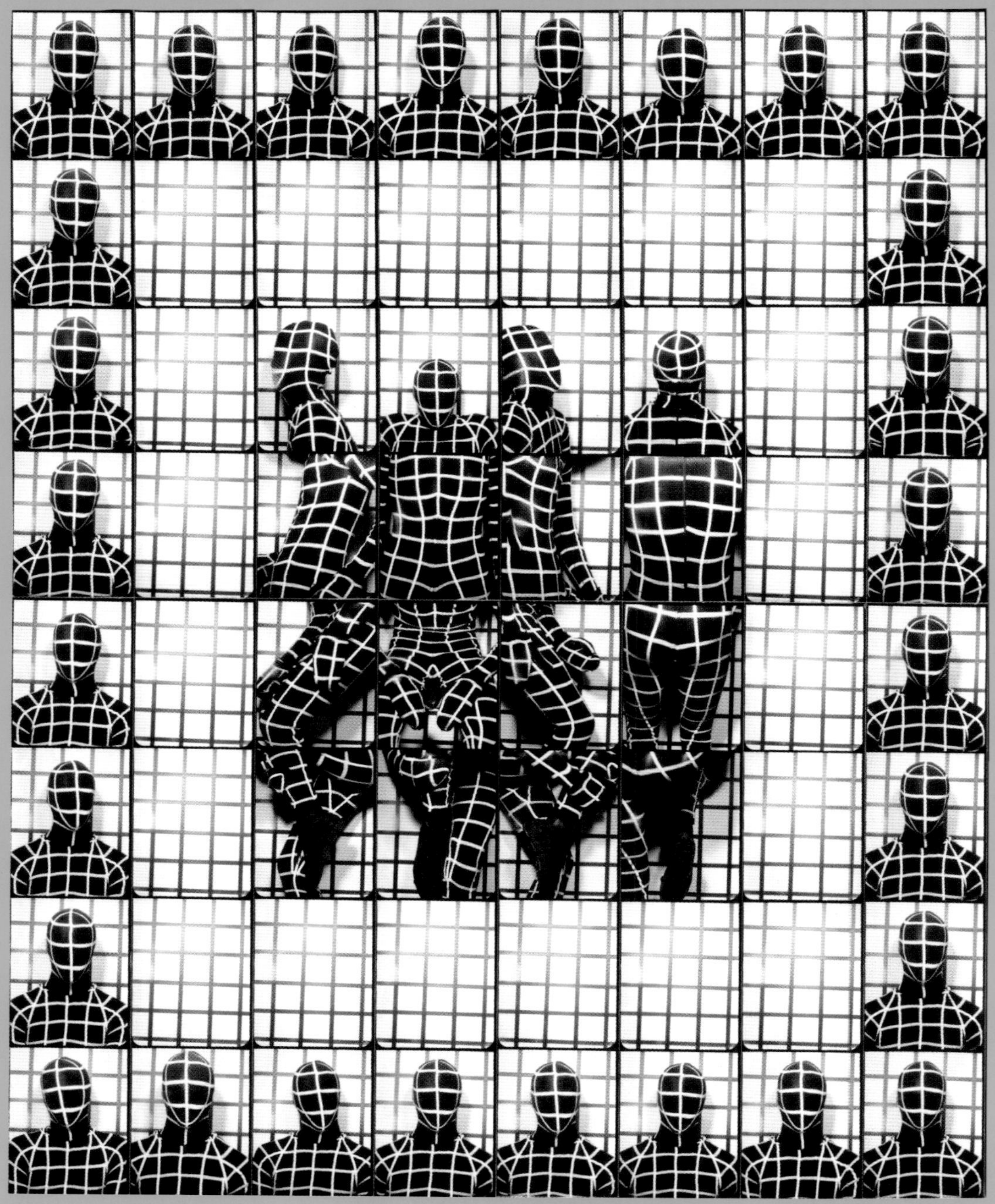

Grid Man (portrait of Neil Gordon), 1989.

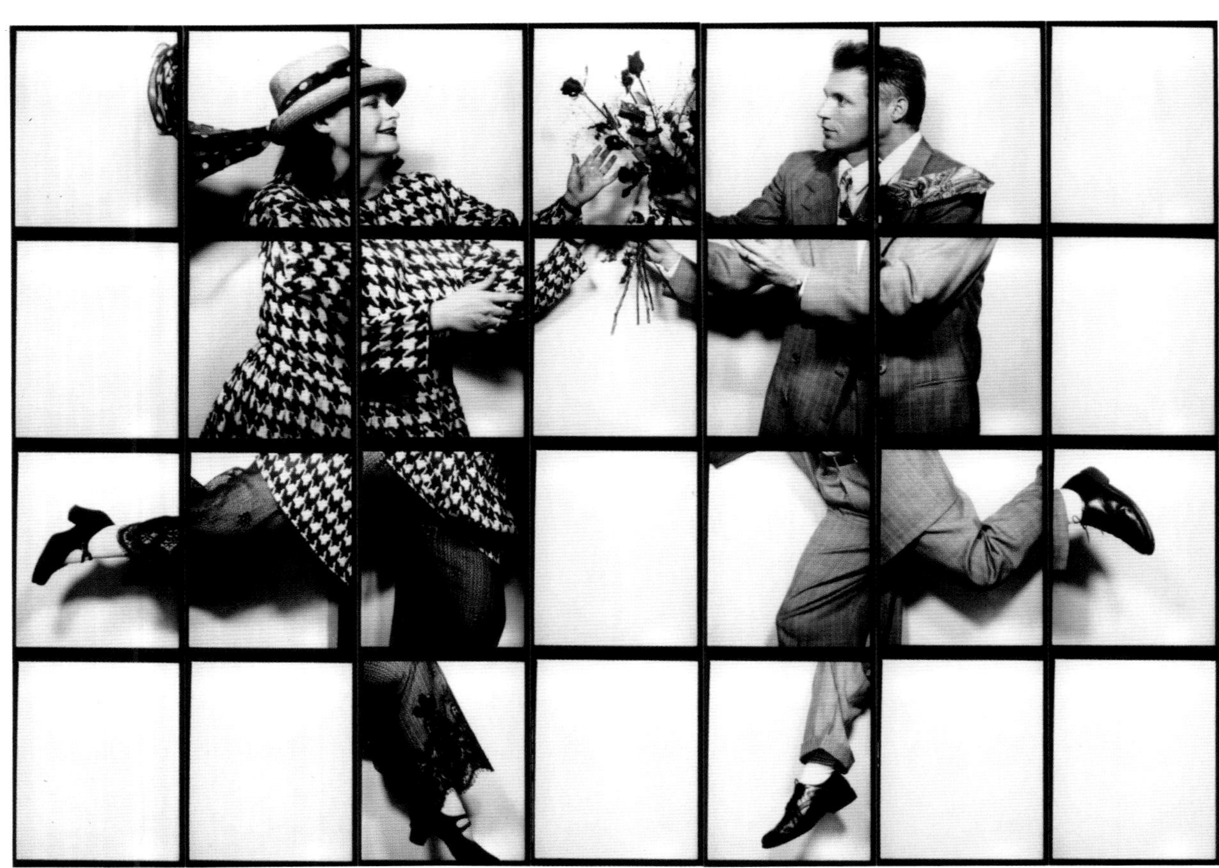

Hope Springs Eternal, 1992.

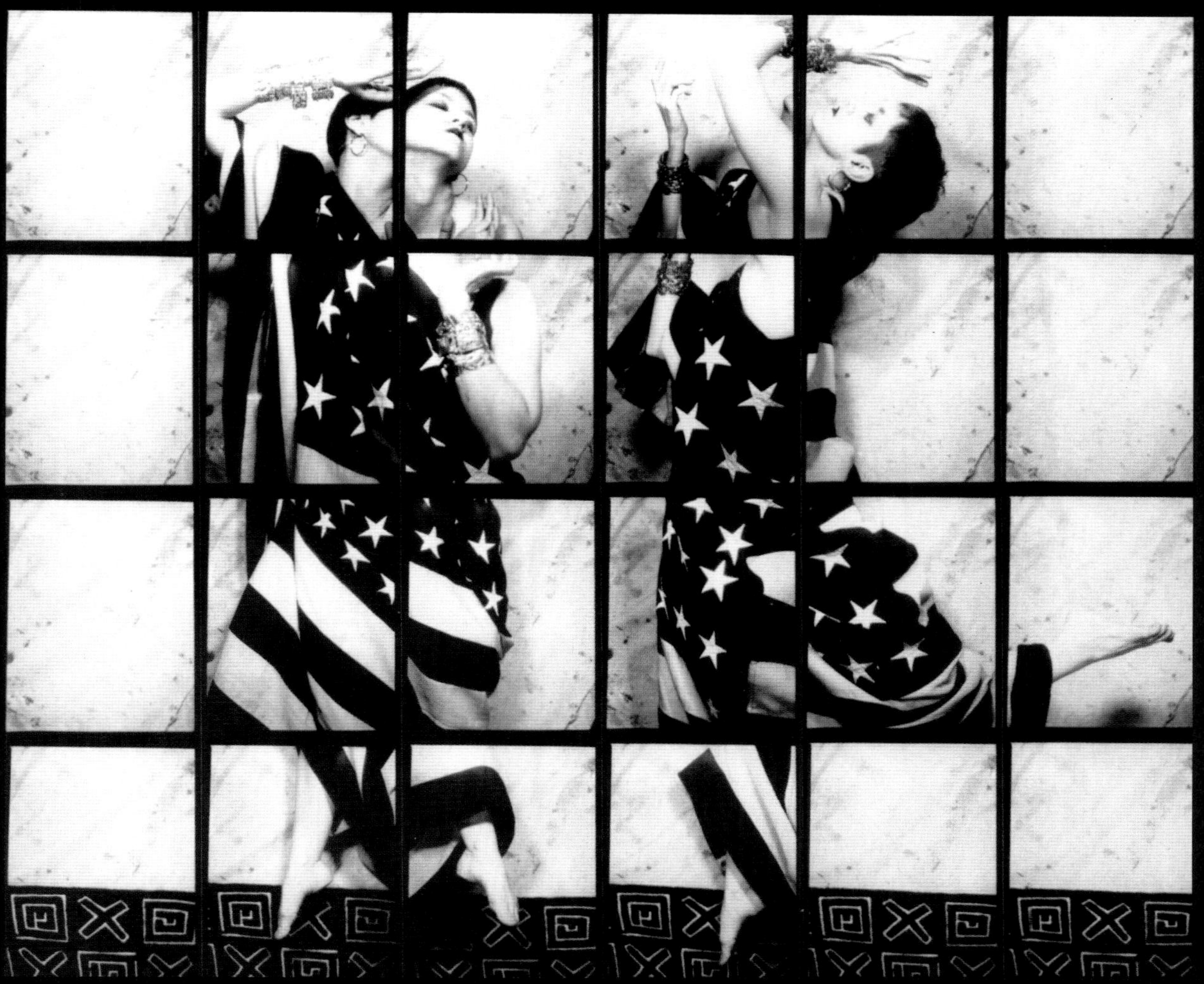

A Dance to the Fourth, 1991.

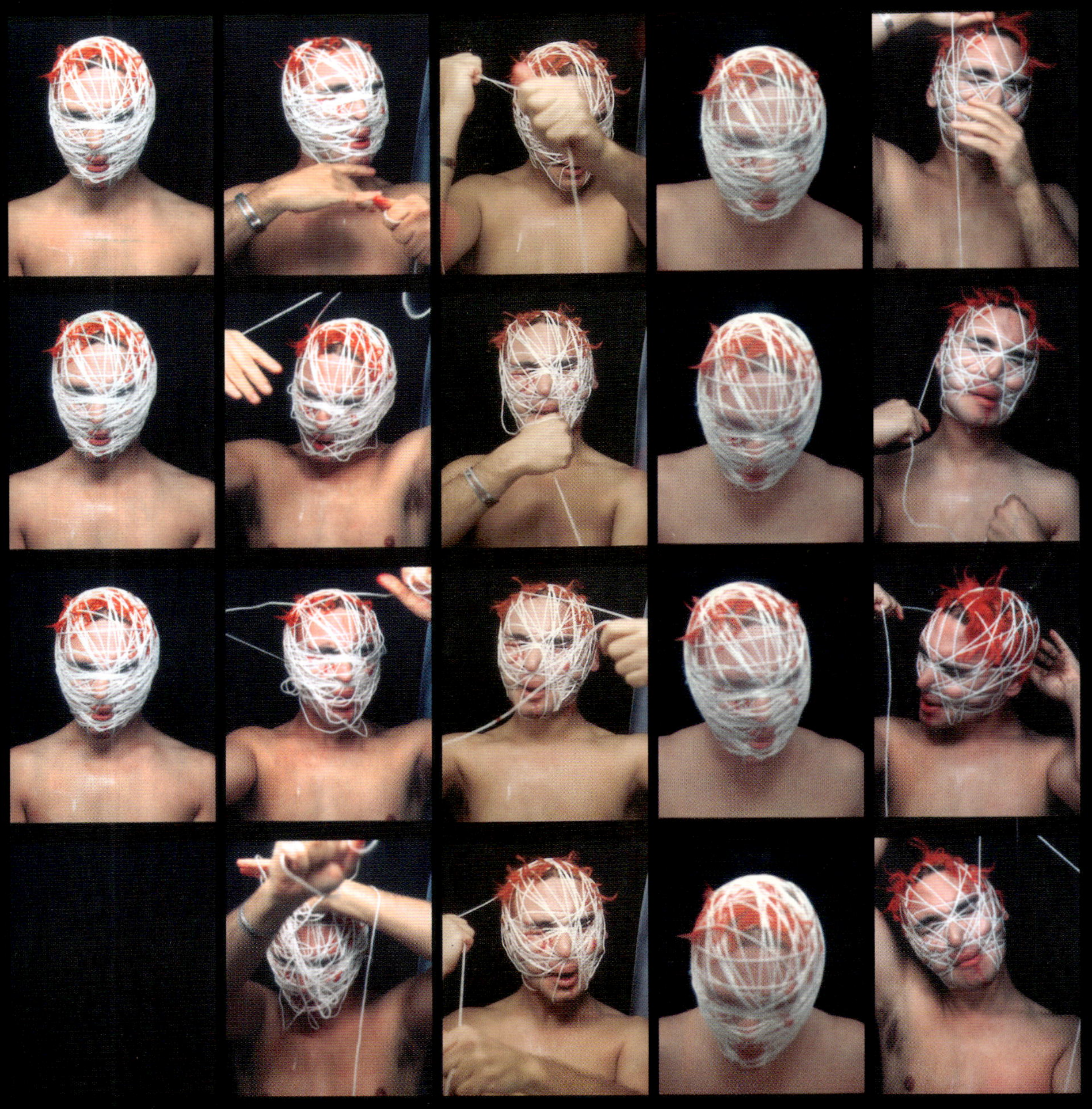

String Theory.

PAUL YATES

American filmmaker, artist

"**P**rivacy is a myth.

"I find it difficult to separate my personal life from my art. In fact, I refuse to separate them. These photobooth photographs, these emotion images reveal my inner affections, passions, humors, beliefs, and moods. Unlike the usual images made in photobooth machines, these images are extremely personal, beautiful, and at times…exquisitely real. I consider them 'Irreal.' Irrealism is the state I find myself in when I have revealed so much personal truth that I no longer know where I end and the canvas begins. In this work I reveal so much about my inner self that my perspective is lost. My reality has become irrelevant—my reality has become Irreal. It is hard to lie about who you are in pictures, and it is remarkably hard to lie in photobooths and I don't wish to. The photobooth acts as the witness, judge, jury, and scribe. Those four quick flashes provide an interesting reality. The machine has a life of its own and takes pictures when it sees fit. No matter what I do, I am never ready for the flash. I am not in control. It is very humbling.

"When I was eight, I was given a camera kit that allowed me to build a camera from 138 pieces. The first picture I took was of myself in the bathroom mirror. It is amazing to me how prescient that was. When I was fifteen, I became homeless. I couldn't risk carrying a camera or even afford to fill it with film. I could afford the one dollar to use in the then ubiquitous photobooth machine. God bless Woolworth's. At first I considered the machine to be the bottle that contained the message. Every time I took a photobooth picture—that picture, along with all of my current thoughts, would be transmitted to those that would understand. I began to photograph everything I could do in a photobooth. I ate, drank, slept, and photoboothed it all. One day when I was changing my clothes in the machine, I put in the dollar. The resultant nude broke open the palette of photobooth photography for me.…Nude self-portraits always leave me with a deep impression of humanity. I am trying to find out who I am. We are all very similar. We just can't see it because of our self-imposed notions of privacy. By over-revealing myself, through Irrealism, I want my pictures to change that.

"Nudity is provocative and dangerous. True ART should be the same. Alone in the photobooth machine, the photobooth opening completely covered, with a friend as a guard to prying eyes, my photobooth pictures have been confiscated and my life threatened by policemen and other guardians of the public moral code.

"We live in a time, perhaps this time has been here for a while, where our thoughts and actions are being monitored more closely than ever. Artistic voices are crying louder than ever with passion, and the sedate society is responding in kind. Making art has become dangerous. Don't be afraid to do anything in a photobooth machine."

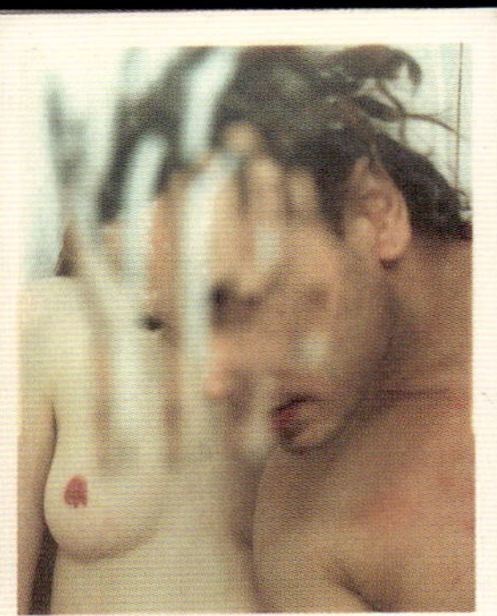

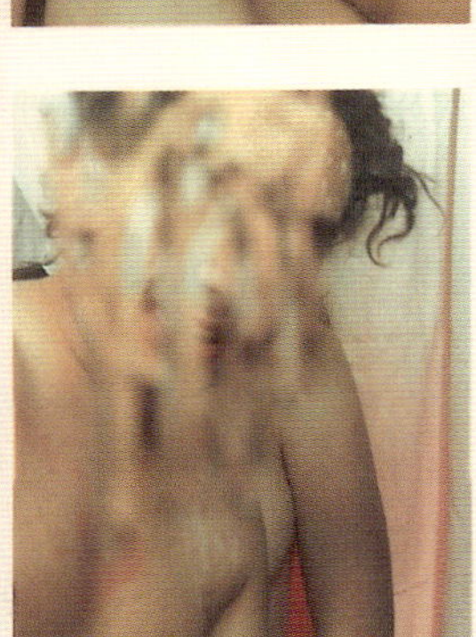

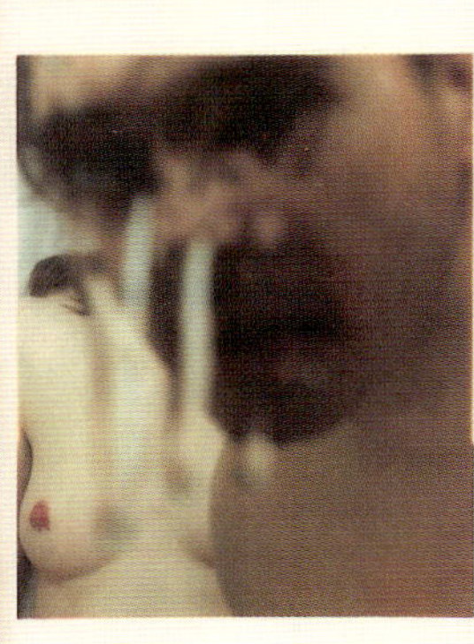

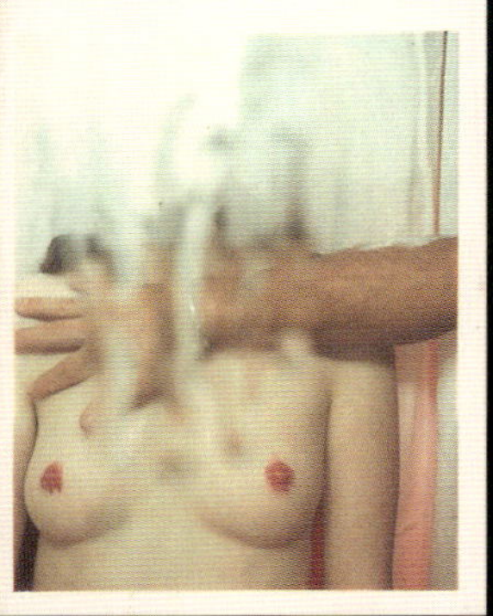

My emotions have become liquid…
and are leaking out of me
(Mes émotions sont devenues liquides
et dégoulinent hors de moi.)

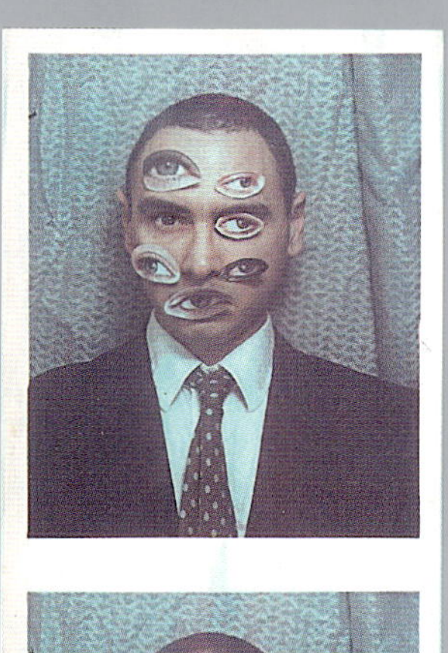
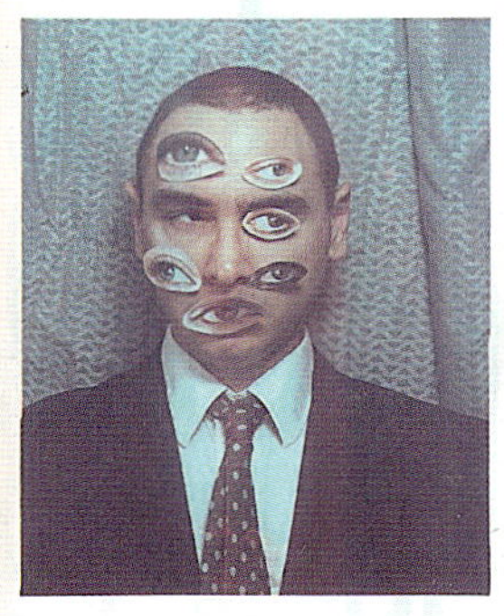
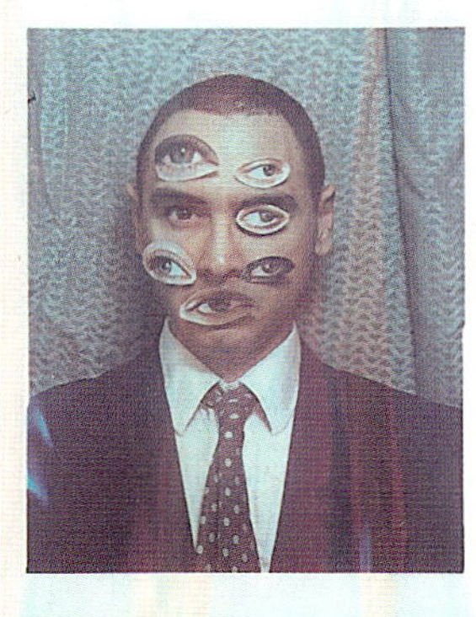
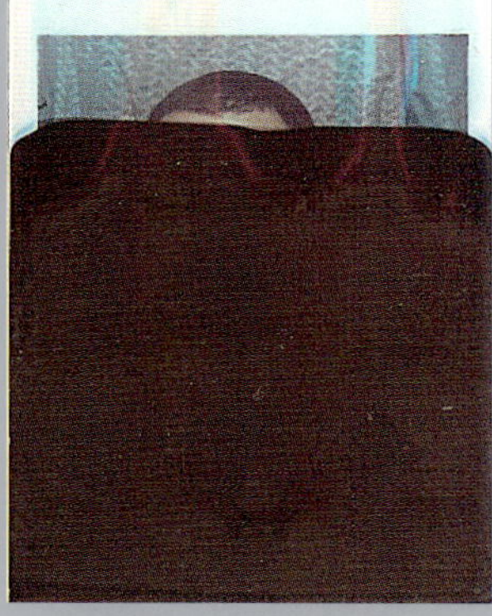

The International Surrealist.

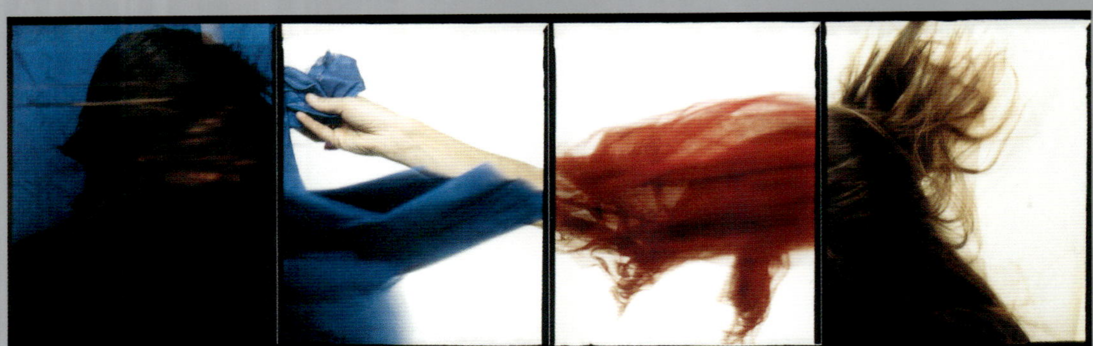

Rush, 1999.
Collection of the artist.

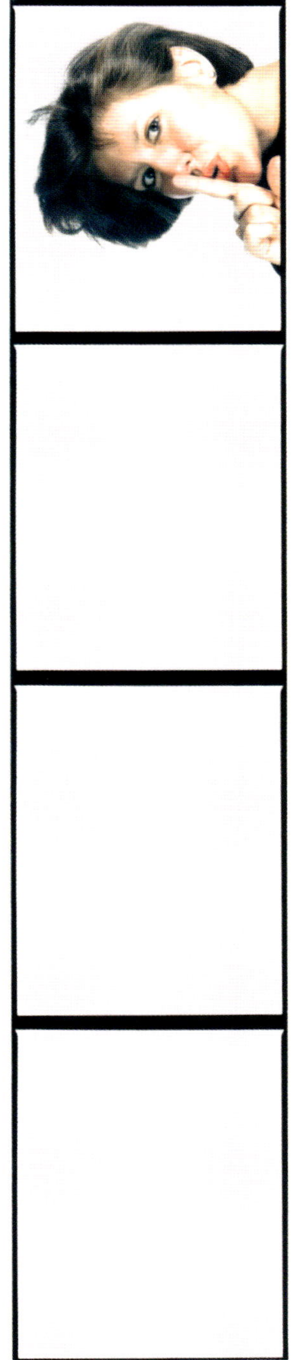

Quiet! (Library!),
1989.
Collection of the artist.

LIZ RIDEAL

(1954–)
British artist

"I started working with the photobooth in 1985. I ran a public participation project at the National Portrait Gallery called Identity, inviting the general public to come and 'disguise or reveal yourself,' in four poses. It was a great success, culminating in an appearance on a popular television program called *Wogan*, watched by ten million viewers and attracting much other media coverage.

"As I had the use of the machine for three months, I could experiment with it, and I invented a way of translating my drawings into photostrips, collaging these together to read as larger composite images.

"I was hooked. It was fascinating and I made artwork with this machine for twenty years. Alongside the public artworks, I made still life work, exhibited in London and New York, and drapery-inspired pieces that became coverings for entire buildings, for example the BBC Broadcasting House. Many of my photobooth pieces are now in public collections, including the Bibliothèque National, Tate, British Museum, and Victoria and Albert Museum. Since the analog booth has been replaced by the digital, I have stopped using the photobooth as my medium of artistic expression."

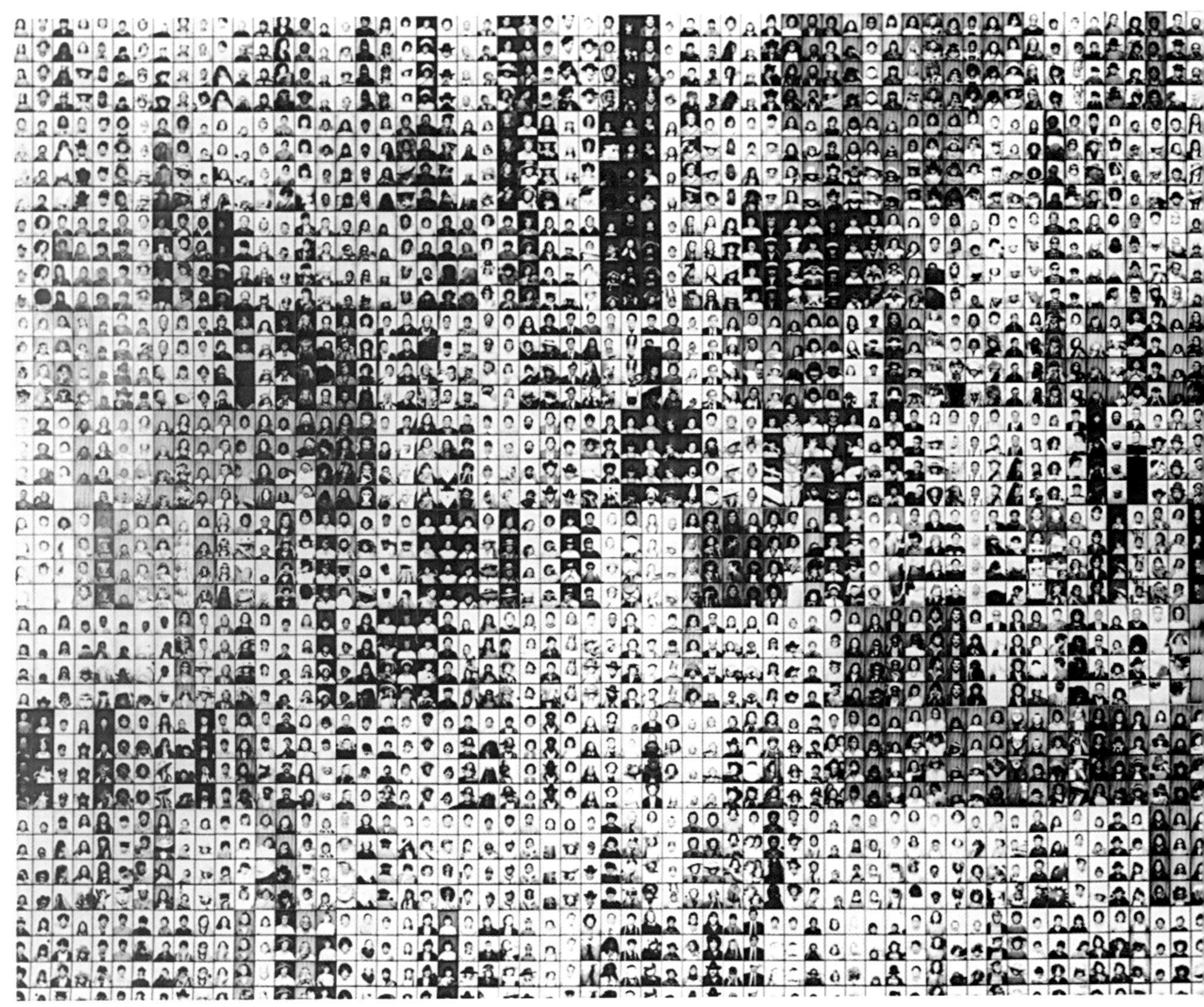

Identity, 1985. Collage of photographs, 6.6 × 16.4 ft. (2 × 5 m).
The National Portrait Gallery, London.

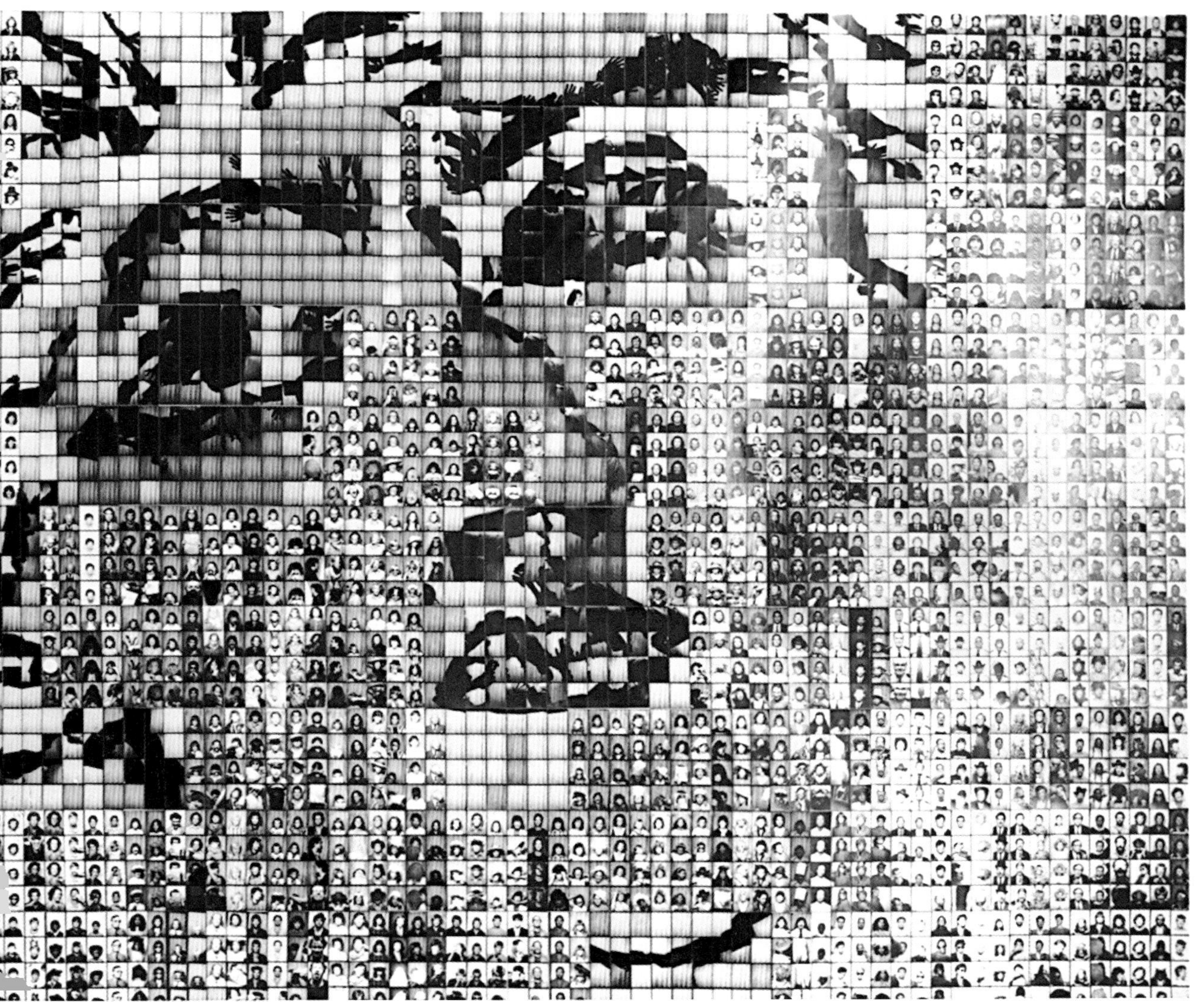

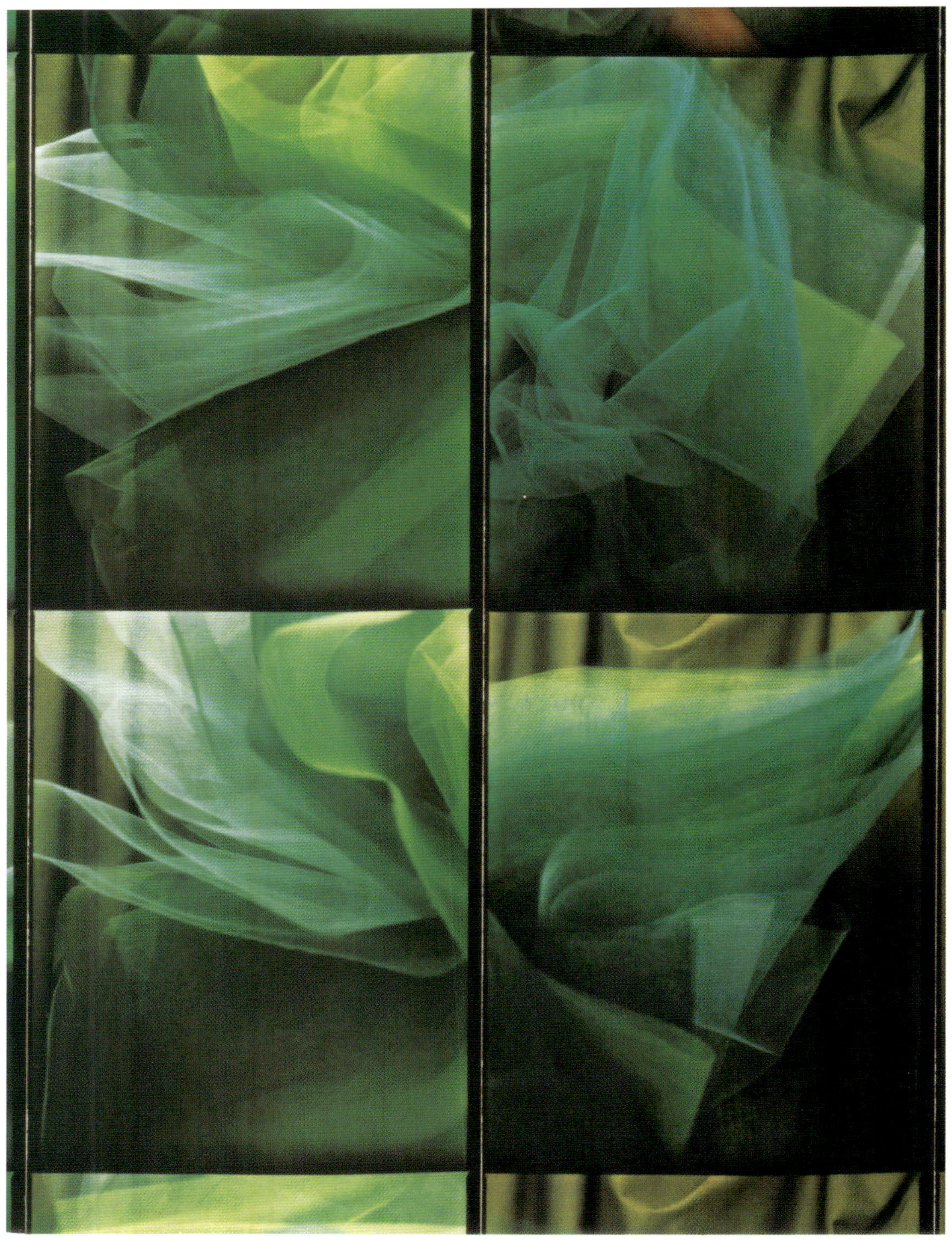

Golden Fern, 1998.
Collection of the artist.

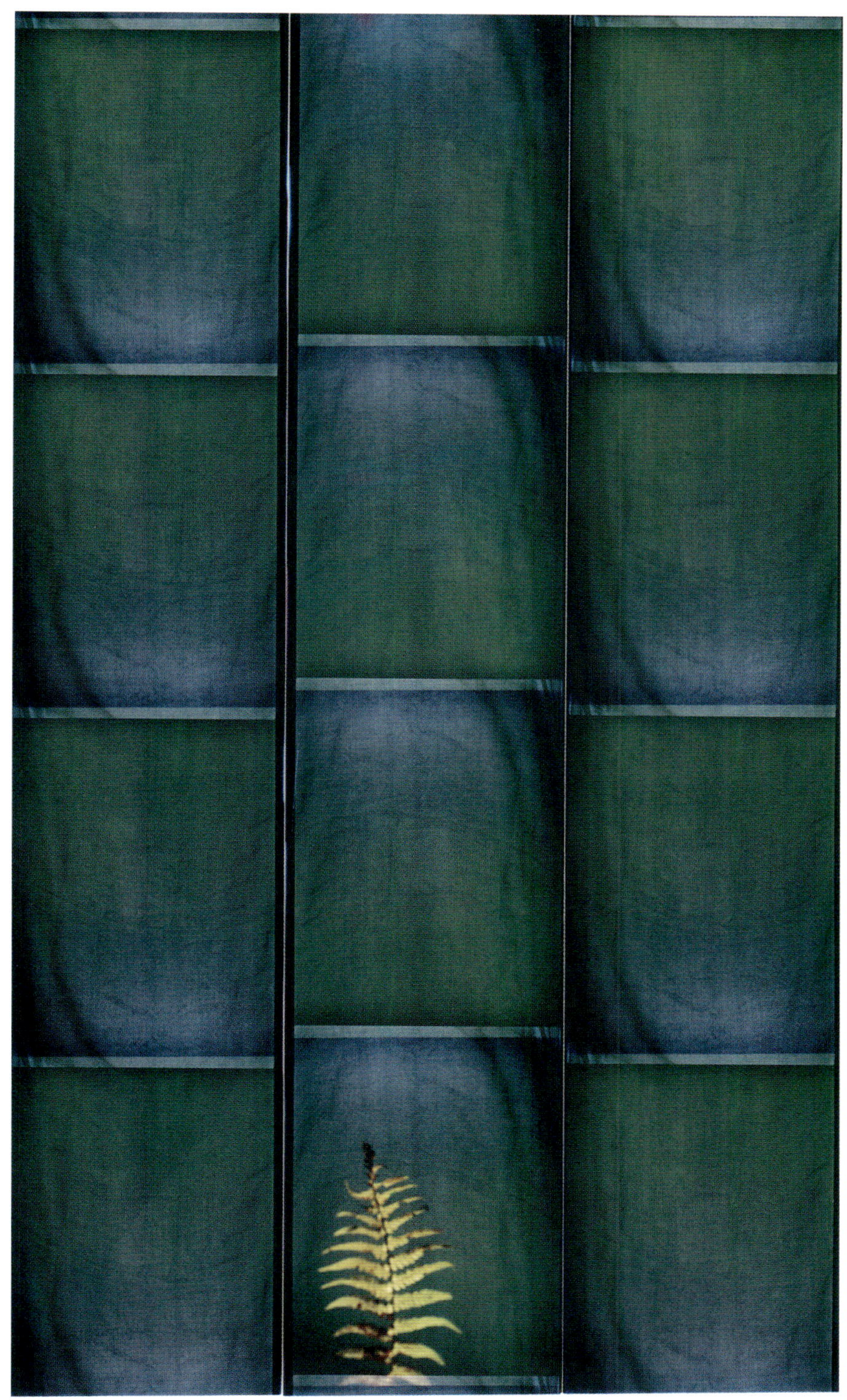

Willow Weep (2), 1999. C-type print from a collage of photostrips.
Ferens Art Gallery, Hull, England

THE SECOND LIFE OF THE PHOTOMATON

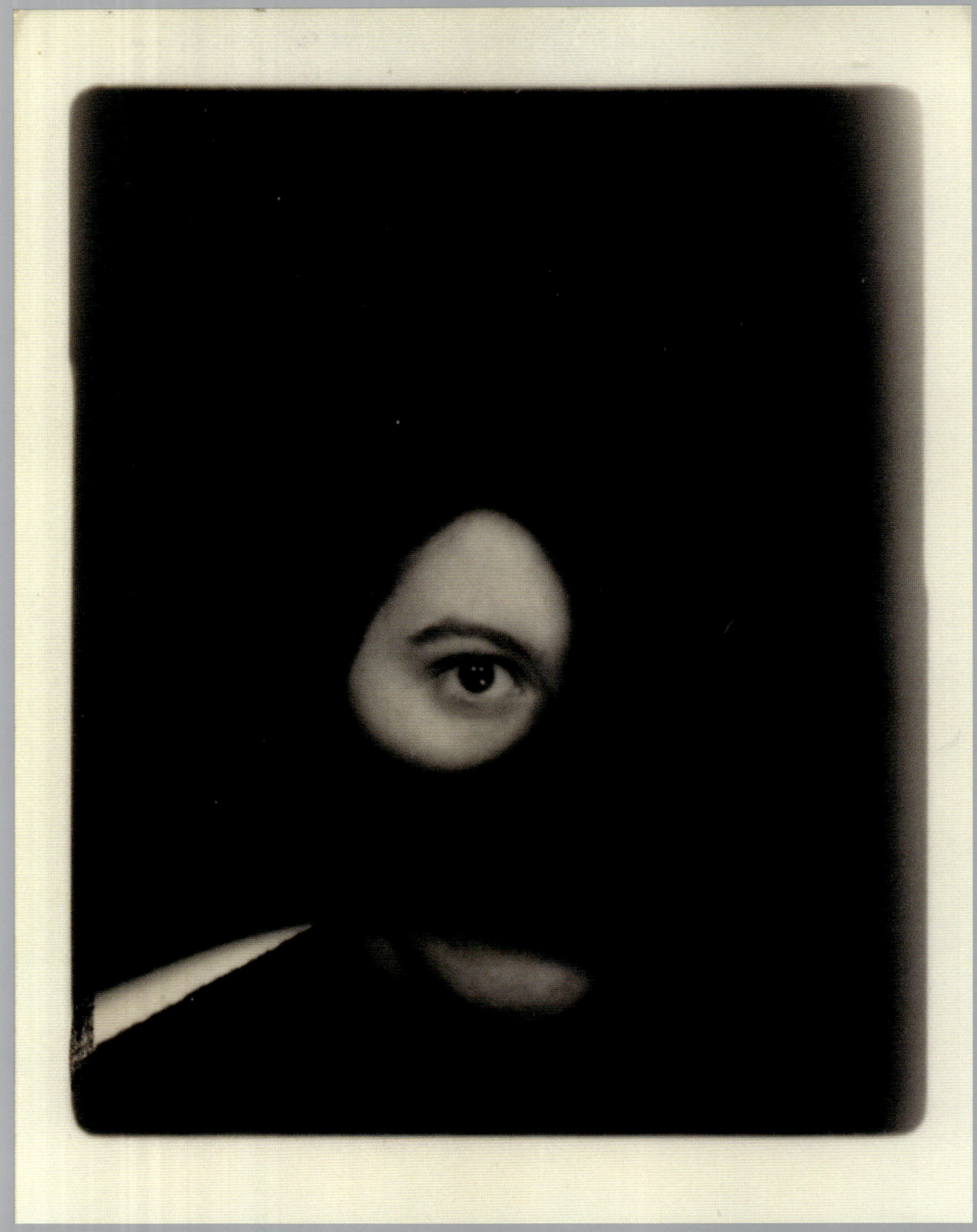

I DELIGHT IN THE CHALLENGE OF "THINKING OUTSIDE THE BOX" WHILE STAYING INSIDE FOUR LITTLE BLACK-AND-WHITE RECTANGLES.

Cori Kindred, American artist

Once condemned to extinction, silver-emulsion Photomaton booths seem to be enjoying a revival of interest. For the past few years, whether in certain art galleries or on the photo-sharing website Flickr, numerous European or American artists, both renowned and amateurs, seem to be resisting the digital wave and considering vintage photobooths as new media for experimentation.

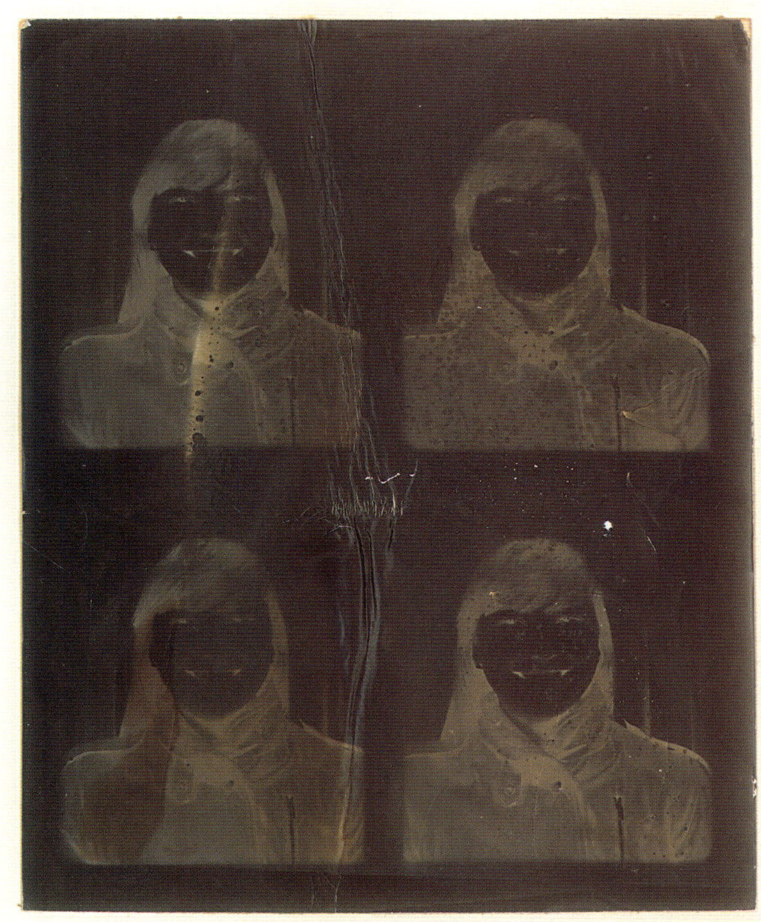

7h 01   GARE de LYON.
le Vendredi 23 Septembre 1983

MICHEL FOLCO

(1943–)
Former press photographer for the Gamma agency, he is now a writer. His collection of Photomatons served as the inspiration for the character of Nino (played by Mathieu Kassovitz) in *Amélie*, the film directed by Jean-Pierre Jeunet.

"As far back as I can remember, I always found photos in the street, but you might say that it all began in the early eighties, the day that I bent over to pick them up.

"The principal stimulus of every collector is frustration, and only the possession of a new collectible can mute that frustration, however briefly. I therefore soon stopped relying upon chance to bring me new photographs, and I set out to search for them. Since I live in Paris, across from the Gare de Lyon, I developed the routine, every morning, of going around to check the five photobooths that are distributed throughout the train station. From two or three portraits a month, I graduated to three or four per week, substantially raising my score when I added to my circuit the three photobooths in the nearby Gare d'Austerlitz.

"One day I bought a Solex moped, so that I could extend my network to include the other train stations of Paris. From three to four photos a week, I raised my score to four or five a day. The authentic maniac moves in a totalitarian universe that he has painstakingly constructed on a set of (strict) laws, (ineluctable) understandings, and (unchanging) values that he holds to be absolute. That is why he cannot accept even the slightest departure from his mania, at the cost of allowing the entire edifice to crumble. My edifice of Photomatons crumbled the day that my watch stopped working, preventing me from making note of the exact time of my latest find. This fissure widened into a full-fledged breach the night when a number of rude individuals stole my Solex and its three antitheft devices, causing a substantial drop in my production. One day I postponed my wash-dry-glue-caption task to the next day. Little by little, the photos accumulated in a shoebox, and I wound up forgetting about them entirely. It wasn't until four years later, when I was moving house, that I exhumed those notebooks filled with "mugs" that had been rejected by their rightful owners. The chronological classification had prevented me at the time from getting an overall view and understanding that this accumulation began to make sense if I arranged them by theme.

"There was the series of people who, seized by doubt, wanted to redo their hair at the very instant when the flash went off…there were those who understood nothing about the operation of the machine and who had been caught unawares by the flash as they fiddled with the buttons…and there were others who shut their eyes, grimaced, adjusted the curtain…

"There was another series, devoted to the smudges and blackouts, in some cases surrealistic, caused by the malfunctioning machine…

"And then there was the guy that I found week after week, always at the Gare de Lyon, always in the same trash can. Who could this eccentric be who regularly had his picture taken and, just as regularly, tore it up into tiny scraps before throwing it away? The mystery lasted months. One December afternoon, I suddenly came practically face-to-face with him: squatting in front of the gaping maw of the machine, both arms plunged into the mechanism, intently working to repair it."

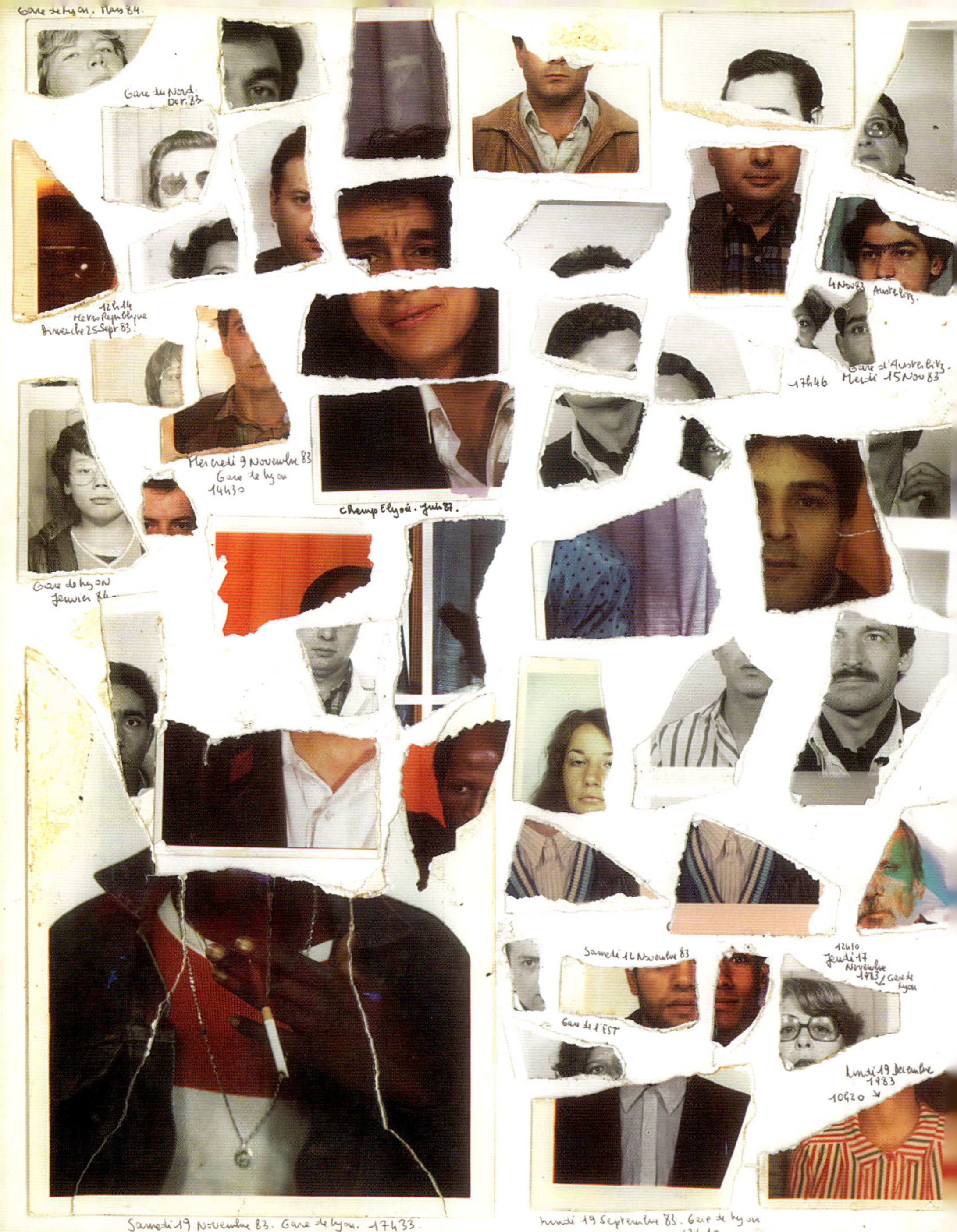

Gare de Lyon. Mars 84.
Gare du Nord. Oct. 83.
12h14
Métro République
Dimanche 25 Sept 83.
Mercredi 9 Novembre 83
Gare de Lyon
14h30
Champ Elysée. Juin 87.
Gare de Lyon
Janvier 84.
4 Nov 83. Austerlitz.
17h46
Gare d'Austerlitz
Mardi 15 Nov 83.
Samedi 12 Novembre 83
Gare de l'EST
12h10
Jeudi 17
Novembre
1983. Gare de
Lyon
Lundi 19 Décembre
1983
10h20
Samedi 19 Novembre 83. Gare de Lyon. 17h33.
lundi 19 septembre 83. Gare de Lyon
12h10

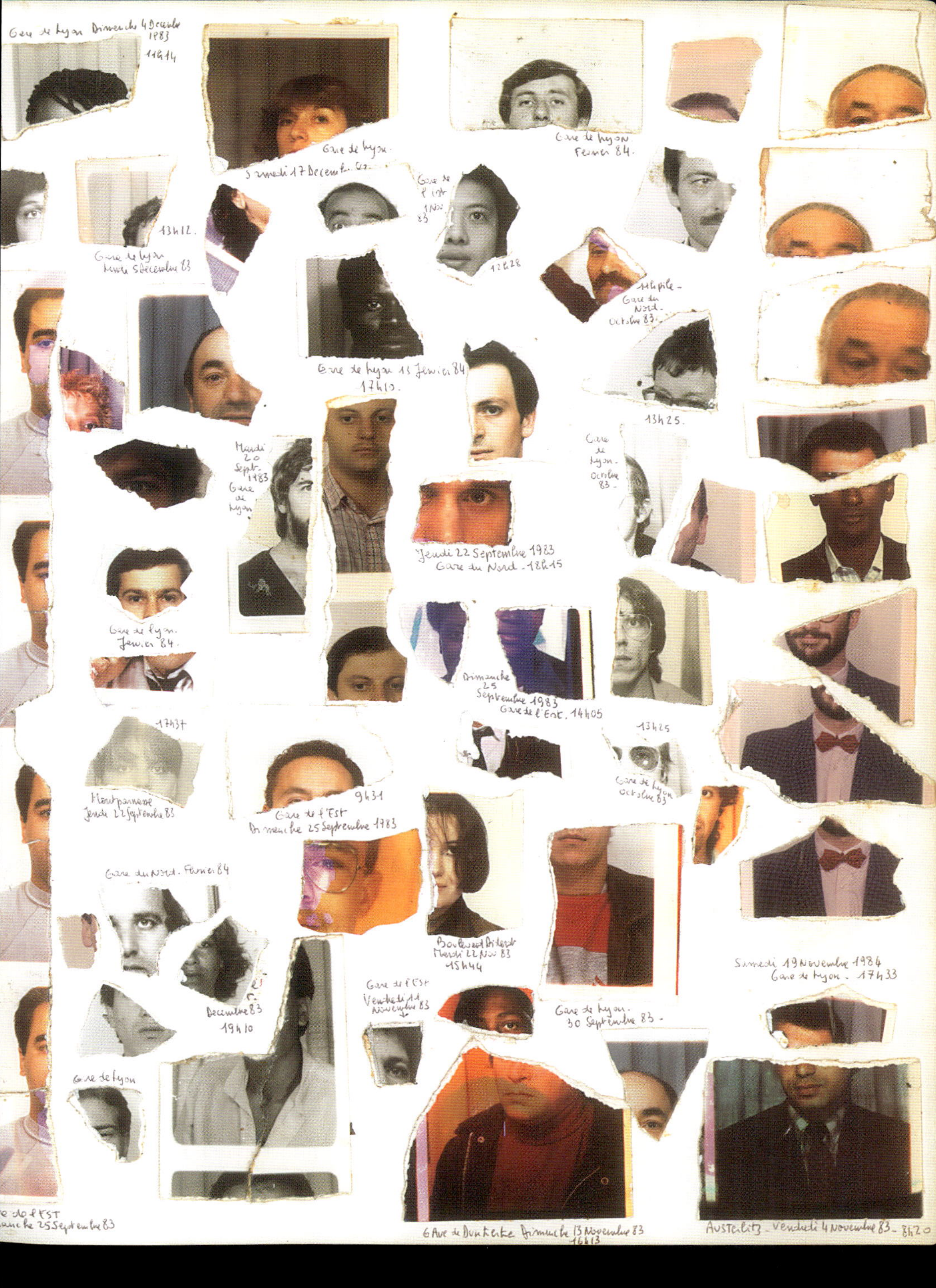

Gare de Lyon Dimanche 4 Décembre 1983 11h14
Samedi 17 Décembre 83
Gare de Lyon Février 84.
Gare de l'Est 1 Nov 83
13h12.
Gare de Lyon Lundi 5 Décembre 83
12h28
Gare du Nord Octobre 83.
Gare de Lyon 13 Janvier 84 17h15.
13h25.
Mardi 20 Sept. 1983 Gare de Lyon
Gare de Lyon Octobre 83.
Jeudi 22 Septembre 1983 Gare du Nord - 18h15
13h25.
Gare de Lyon. Janvier 84.
Dimanche 25 Septembre 1983 Gare de l'Est. 14h05
Gare de Lyon Octobre 83
17h37.
Montparnasse Jeudi 22 Septembre 83
9h31 Gare de l'Est Dimanche 25 Septembre 1983
13h25
Gare du Nord. Février 84
Boulevard Diderot Mardi 22 Nov 83 15h44
Samedi 19 Novembre 1984 Gare de Lyon. 17h33
Décembre 83 19h10
Gare de l'Est Vendredi 11 Novembre 83
Gare de Lyon. 30 Septembre 83 -
Gare de Lyon
Gare de l'Est Dimanche 25 Septembre 83
6 Ave de Dunkerque Dimanche 13 Novembre 83 16h13
Austerlitz - Vendredi 4 Novembre 83 - 8h20

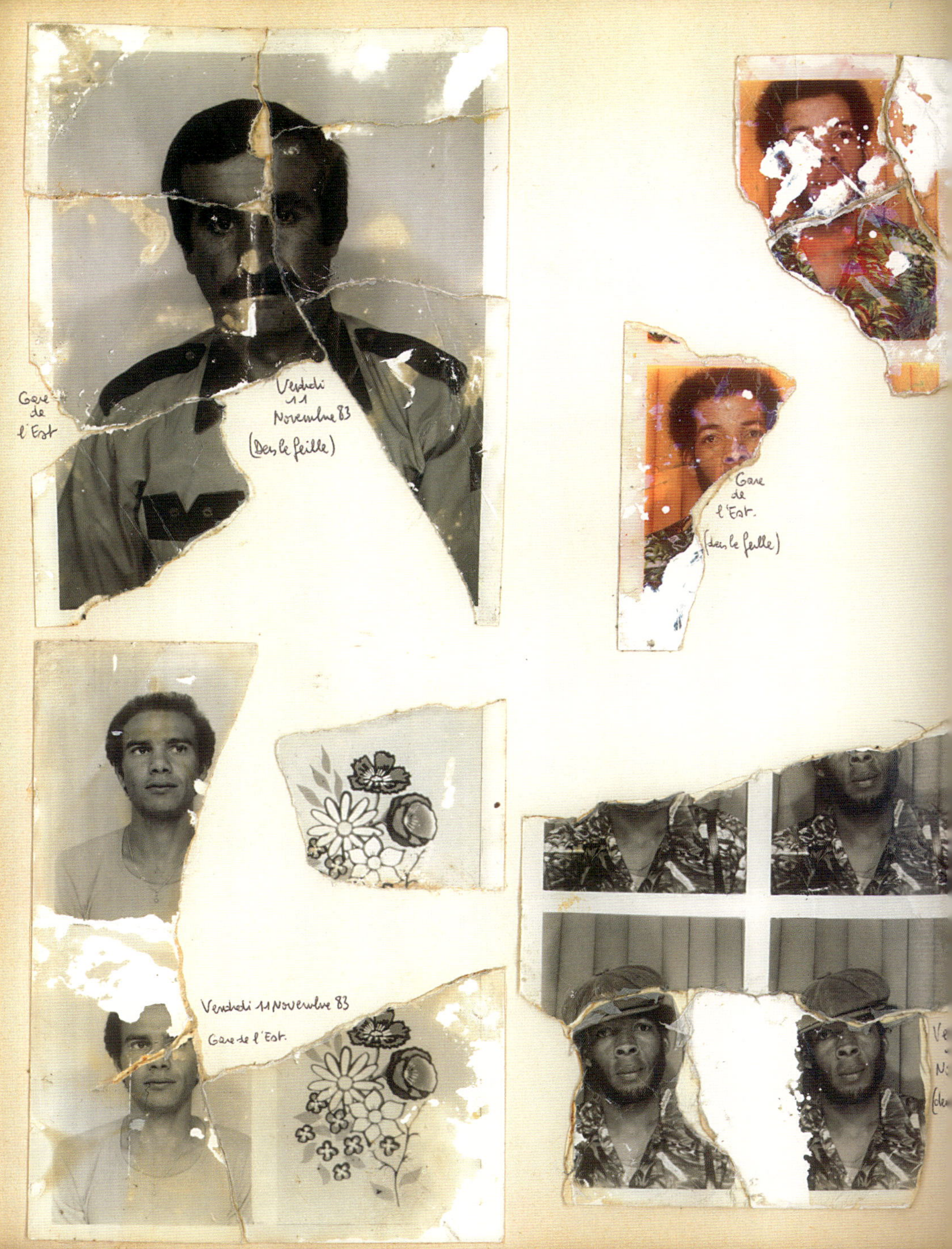
Gare
de
l'Est
Vendredi
11
Novembre 83
(Dans le feuille)
Gare
de
l'Est.
(dans le feuille)
Vendredi 11 Novembre 83
Gare de l'Est.

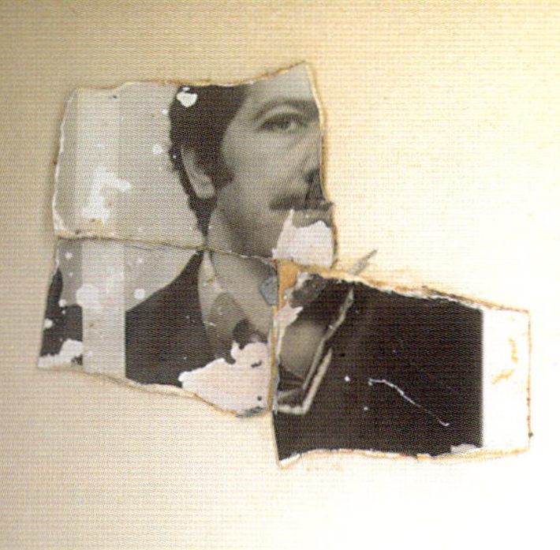

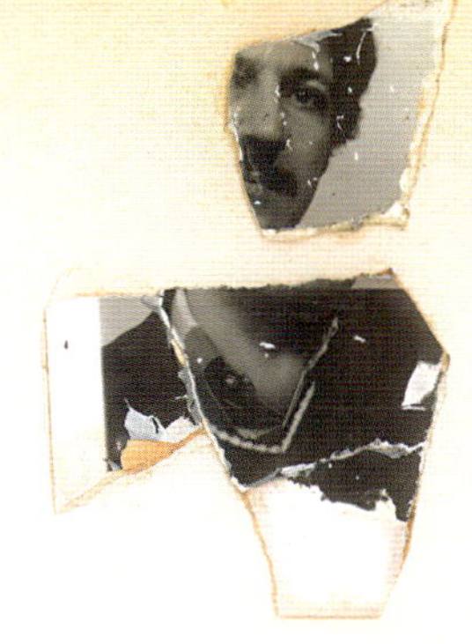

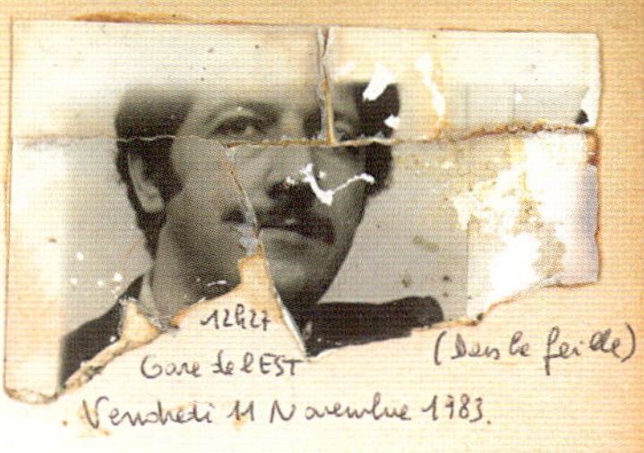

12h27
Gare de l'EST   (Dans le feuille)
Vendredi 11 Novembre 1983.

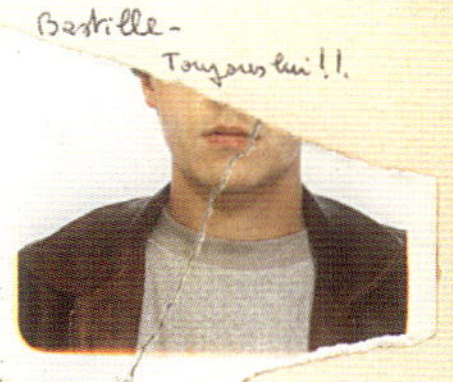

Bastille -
Toujours lui ! !.

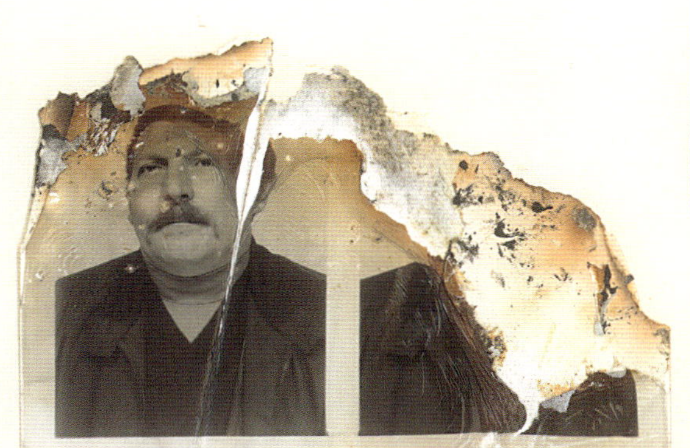

Gare de l'EST . Vendredi 11 Novembre 1983 . (Dans la feuille)

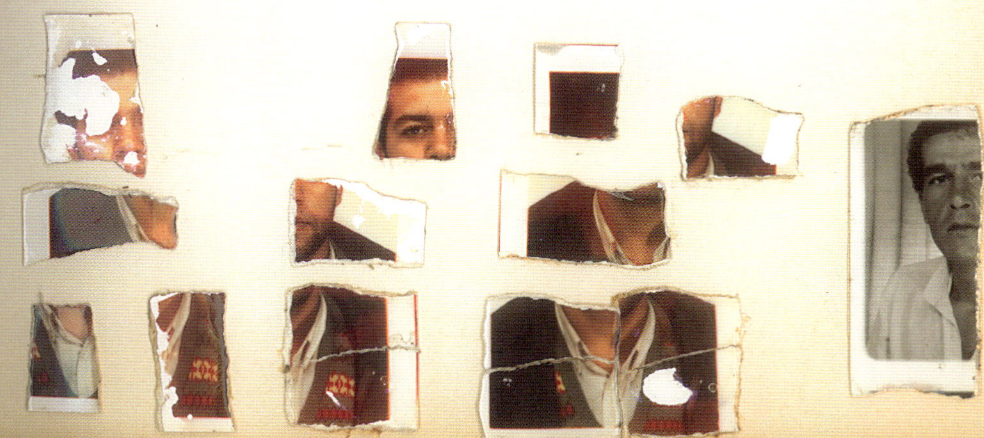

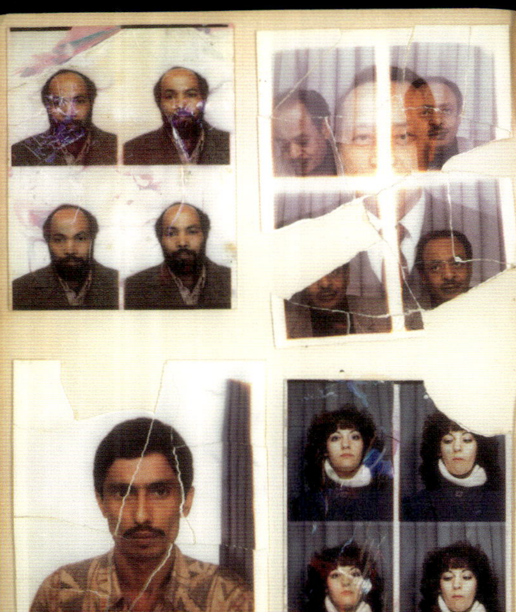
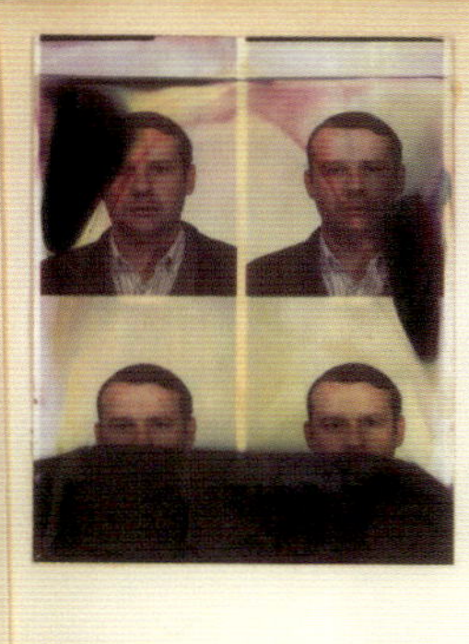
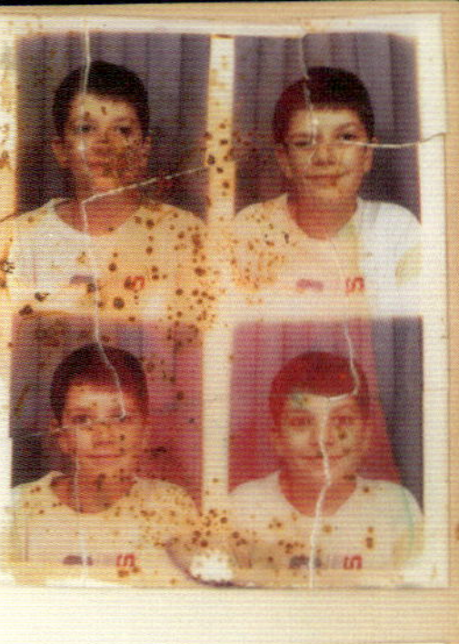
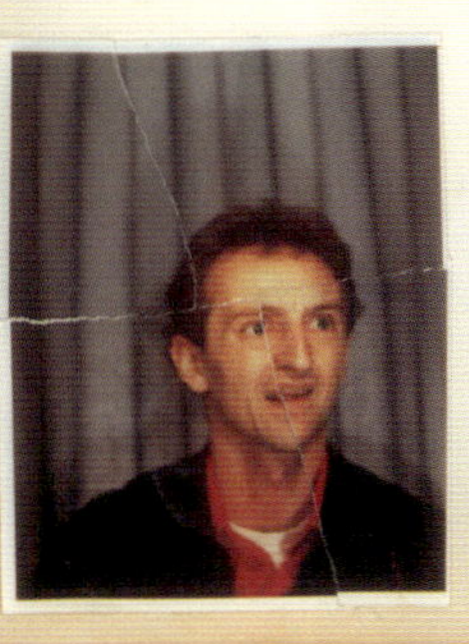
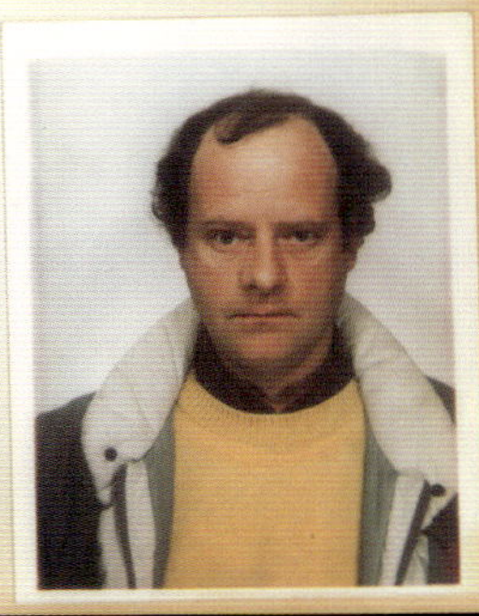
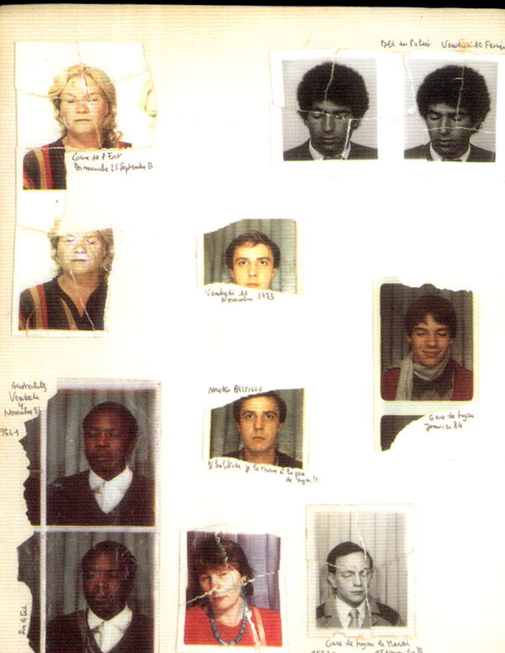
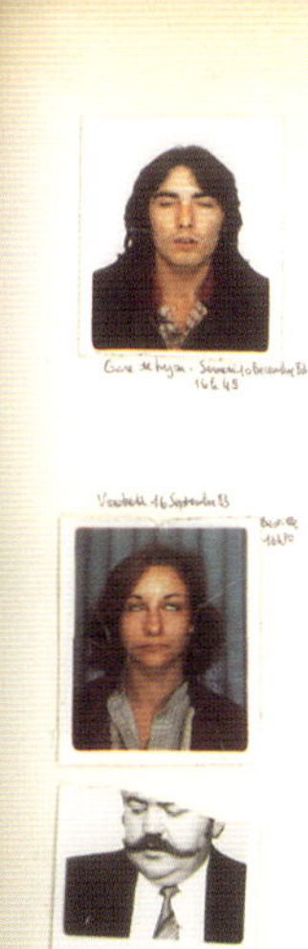
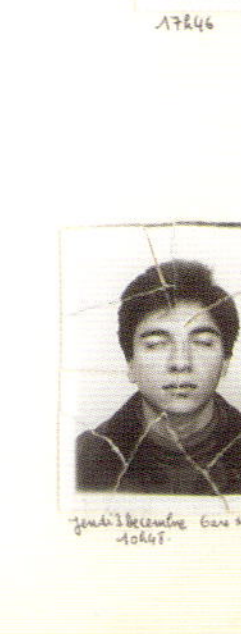
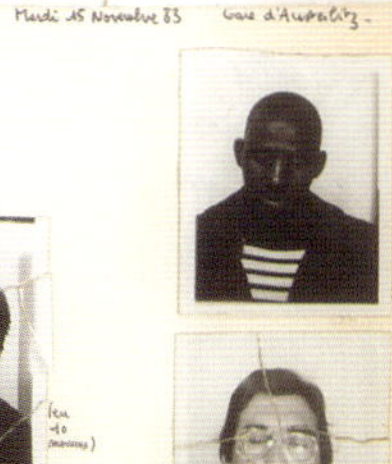

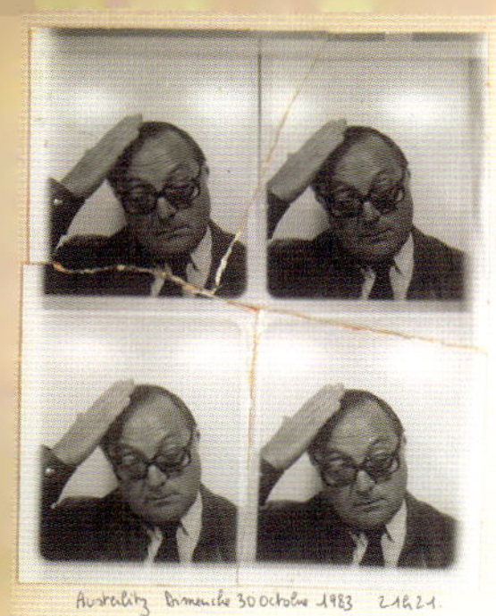
Austerlitz Dimanche 30 Octobre 1983   21h21.

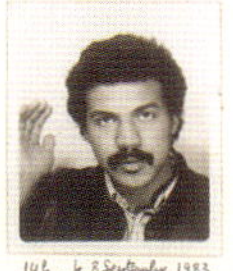
14h. le 8 Septembre 1983
Gare de Lyon.

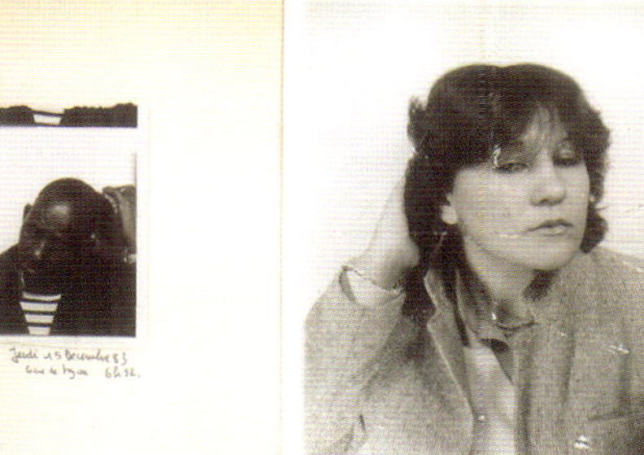

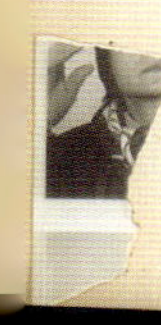

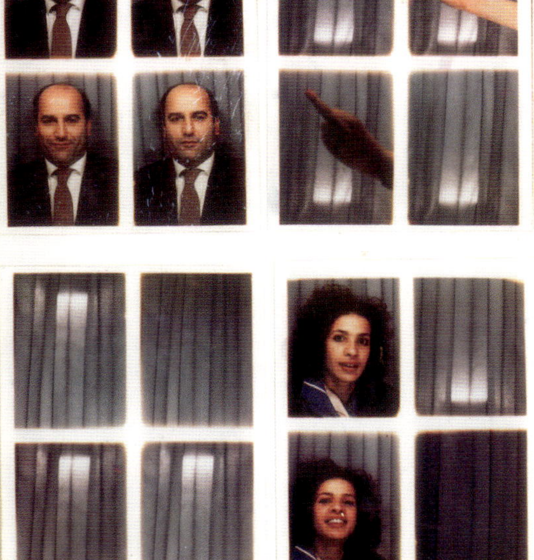
Gare SNCF de Lille
Jeudi 1 Décembre Jumelles
9h11

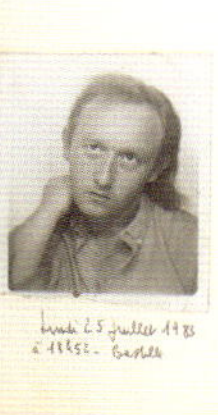
Jeudi 15 Décembre 83
Gare de Lyon   6h52.

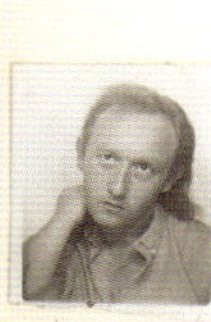
Lundi 25 juillet 1983
à 18h45 - Bastille

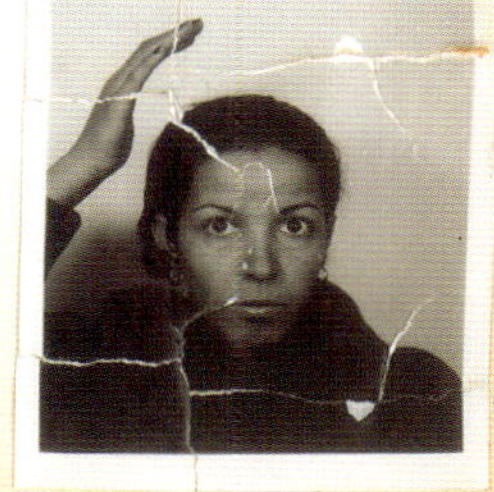
821 Palm Marseille 9 Février 1984

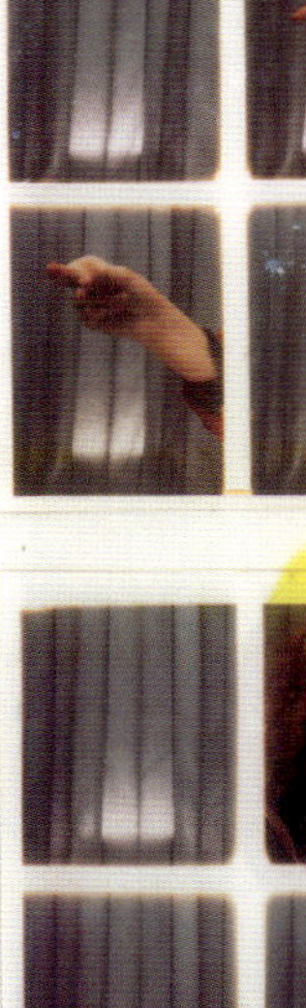

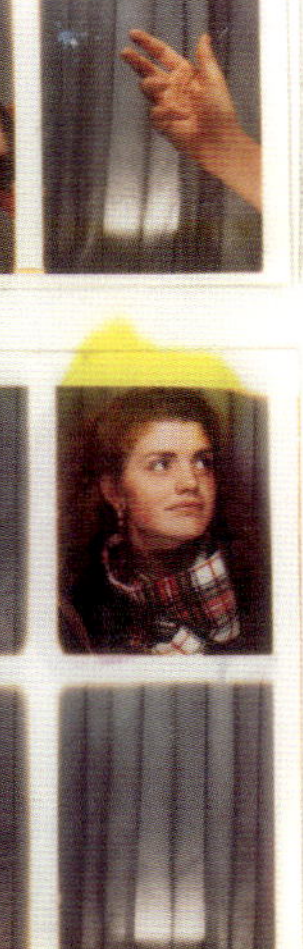

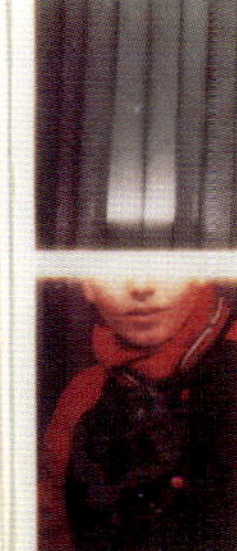

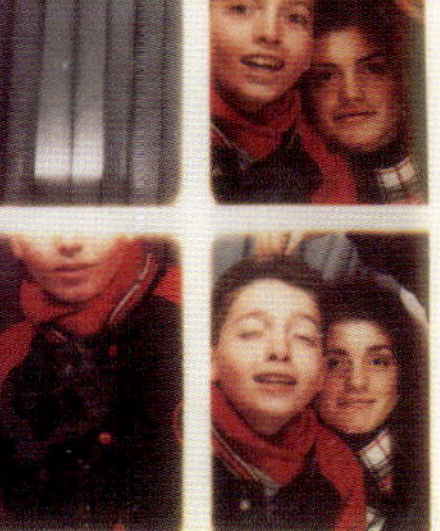

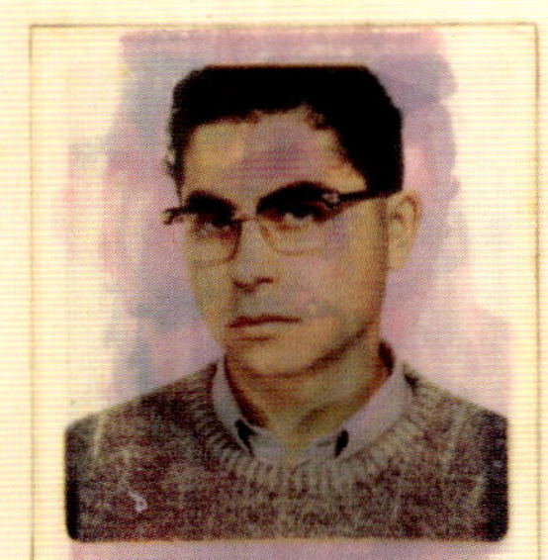
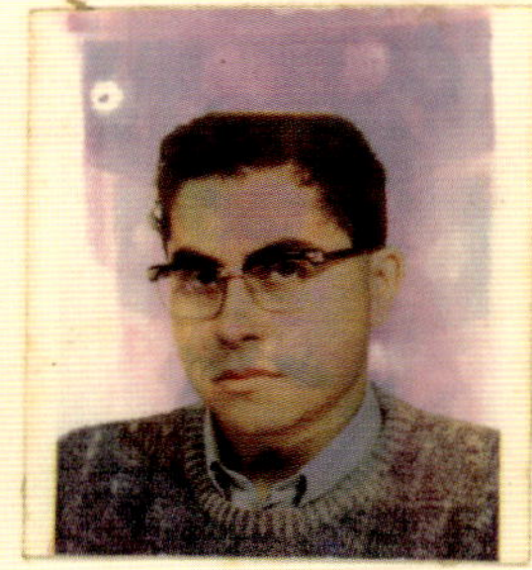
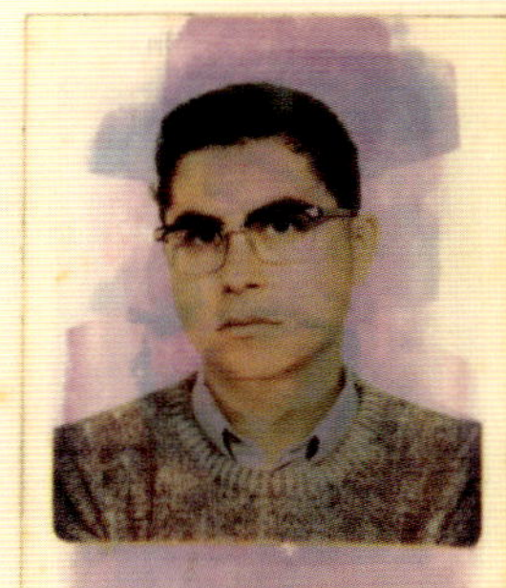

FOTOS
RECOGIDAS
DE LA
BASURA
POR
JOSÉ CARLOS MESA
B   C   N.

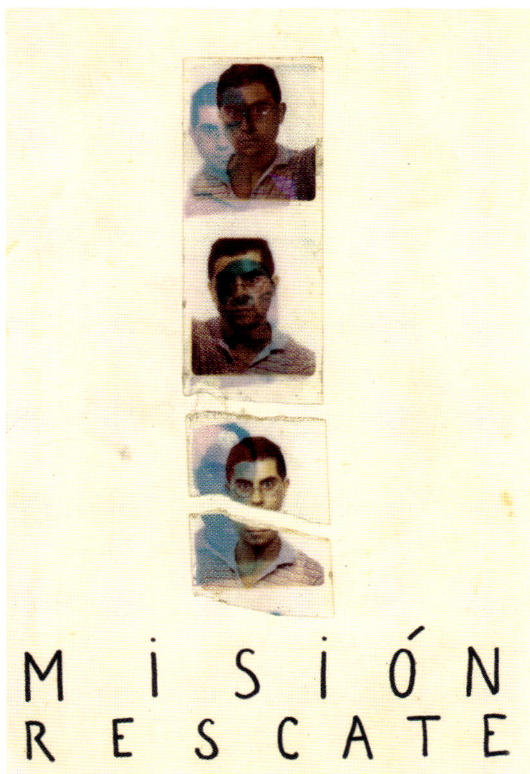

JOSÉ MESA

Spanish photographer

"It all began in 1985, when I was studying at the school of Fine Arts in Barcelona. For a number of months, I prowled the corridors of the metro in search of photobooth snaps abandoned around the booths. I wondered what possible reason a person could have for tearing up his or her photo and throwing it away. At times, the answer seemed obvious, in that it was clearly the result of a technical problem, but more frequently, it was far less easy to understand.

"In that period, you could still find different models of photobooths: color, black-and-white, single-pose, four different poses…. This variety of offerings multiplied to the same degree the possibilities of technical defects and made my research all the more interesting!

"Certain booths were equipped with a clipper to trim the snaps to the standard format of identity cards. For that reason, you would find lots of faces that were partly cut in half…

"To complete my work, I did a number of series of self-portraits that involved the sabotaging of the chemical processing: by making a second series of shots before the first series was dry, and plastering the two series together, face-to-face, the chemical products would be juxtaposed and transferred from one picture to the other, resulting in a double image that was superfluous but very interesting in graphic terms! After each 'harvest,' I selected and glued the pictures on a classic paper. The photos lay forgotten for more than twenty-four years in a shoe box without undergoing any alterations. In 2001, when I saw *Amélie*, let us just say that I got a little something more out of the film than most of the people in the audience."

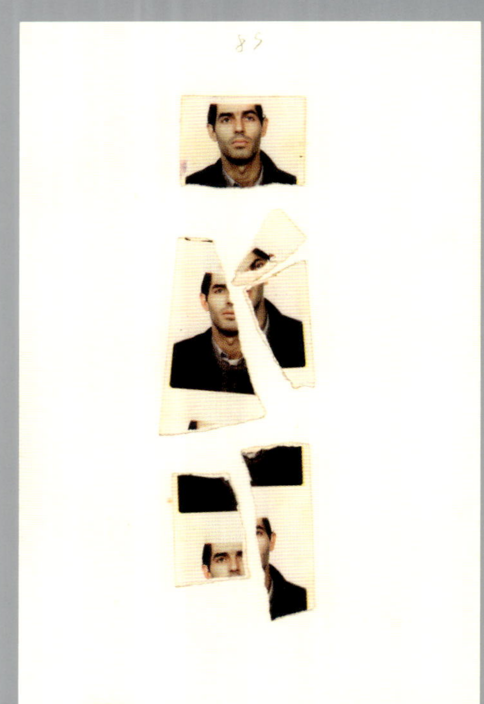
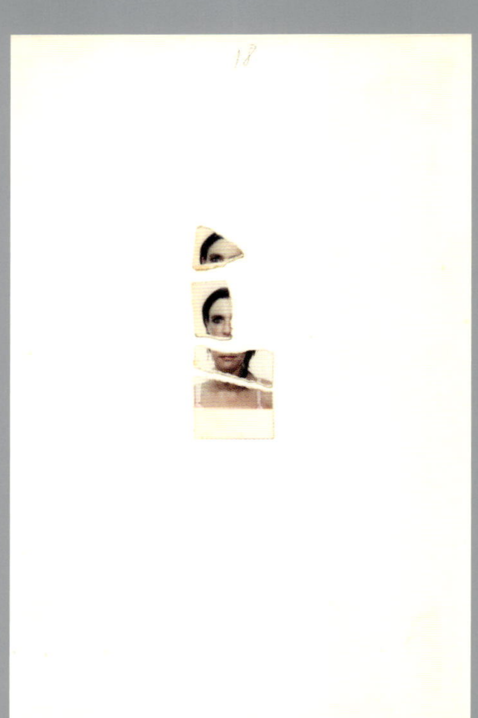
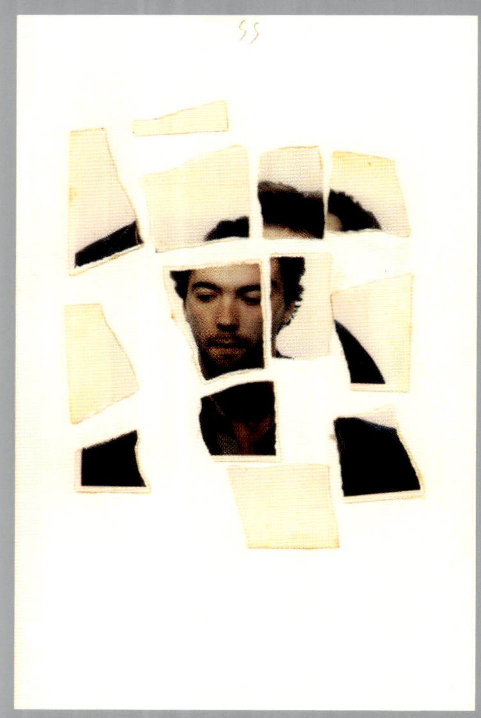
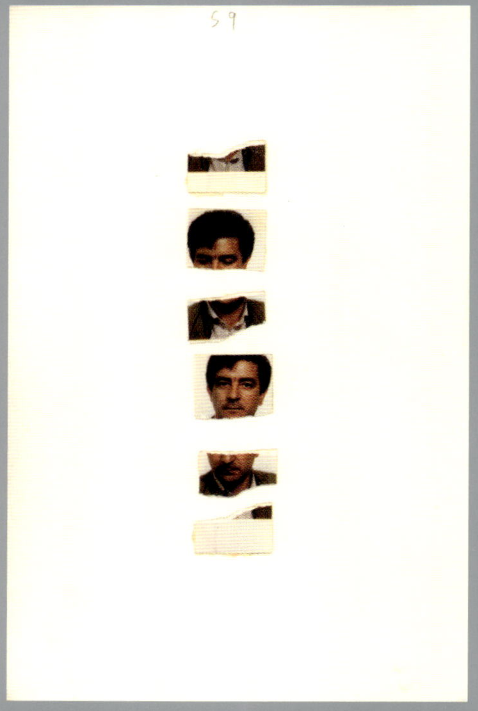

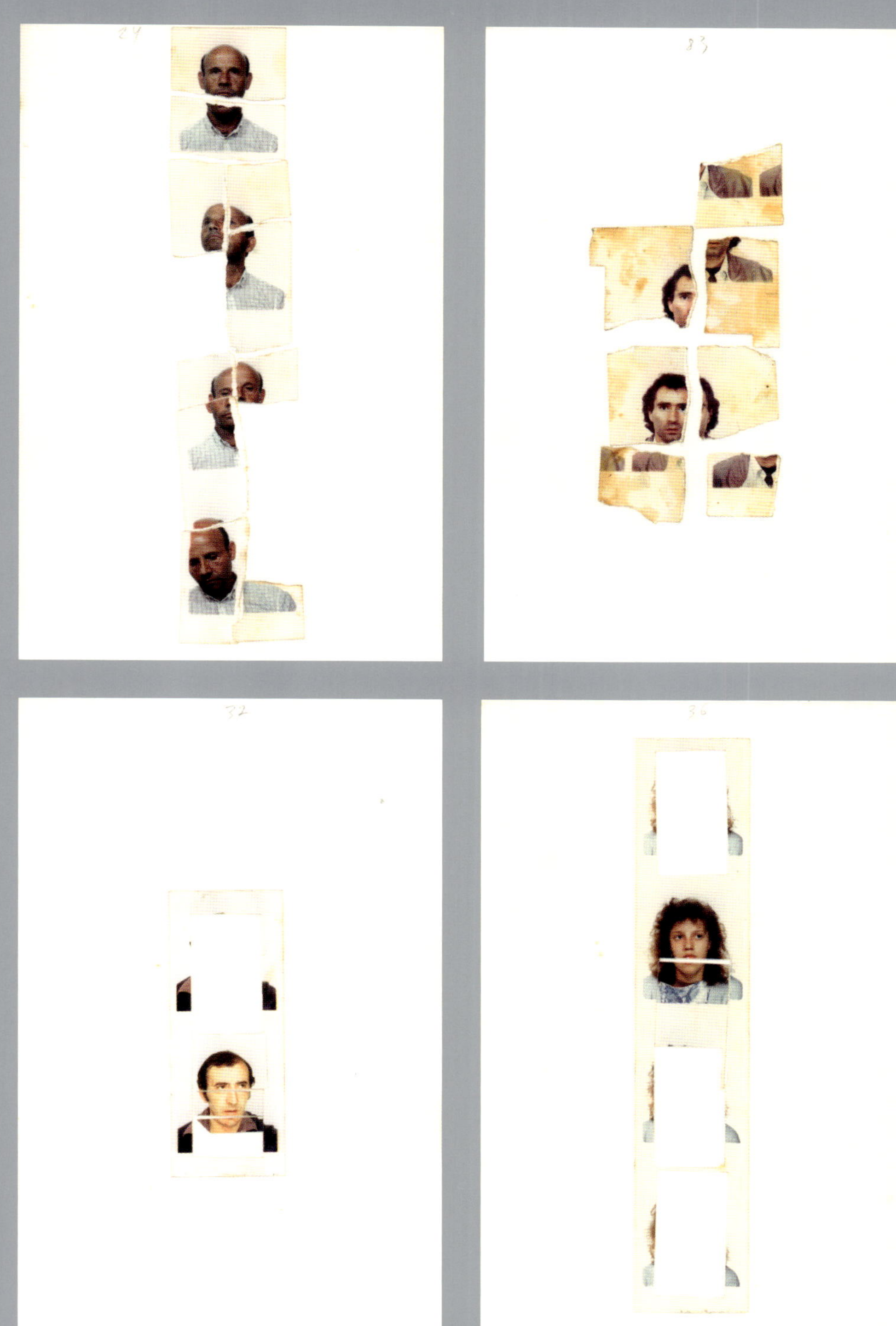

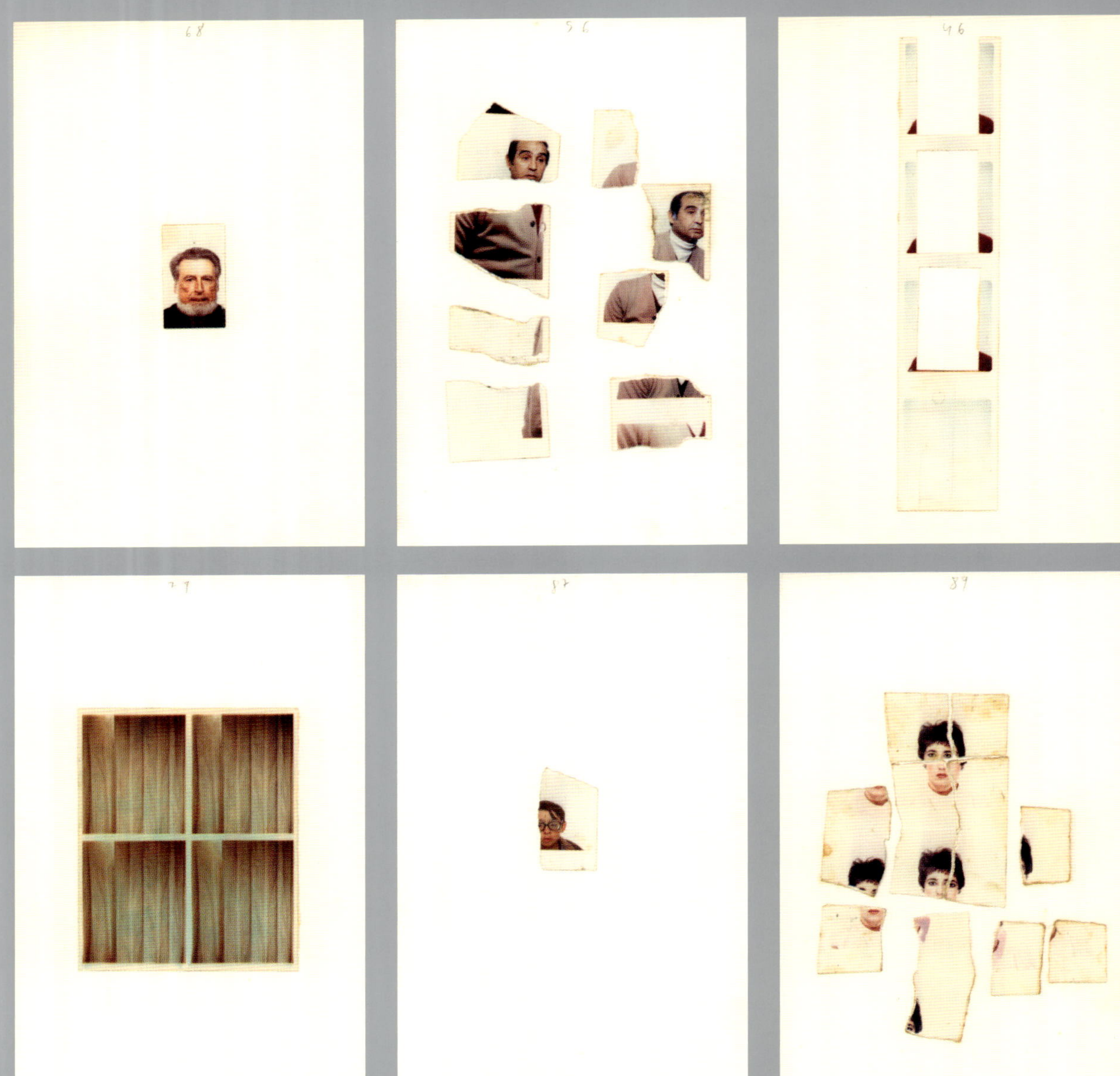

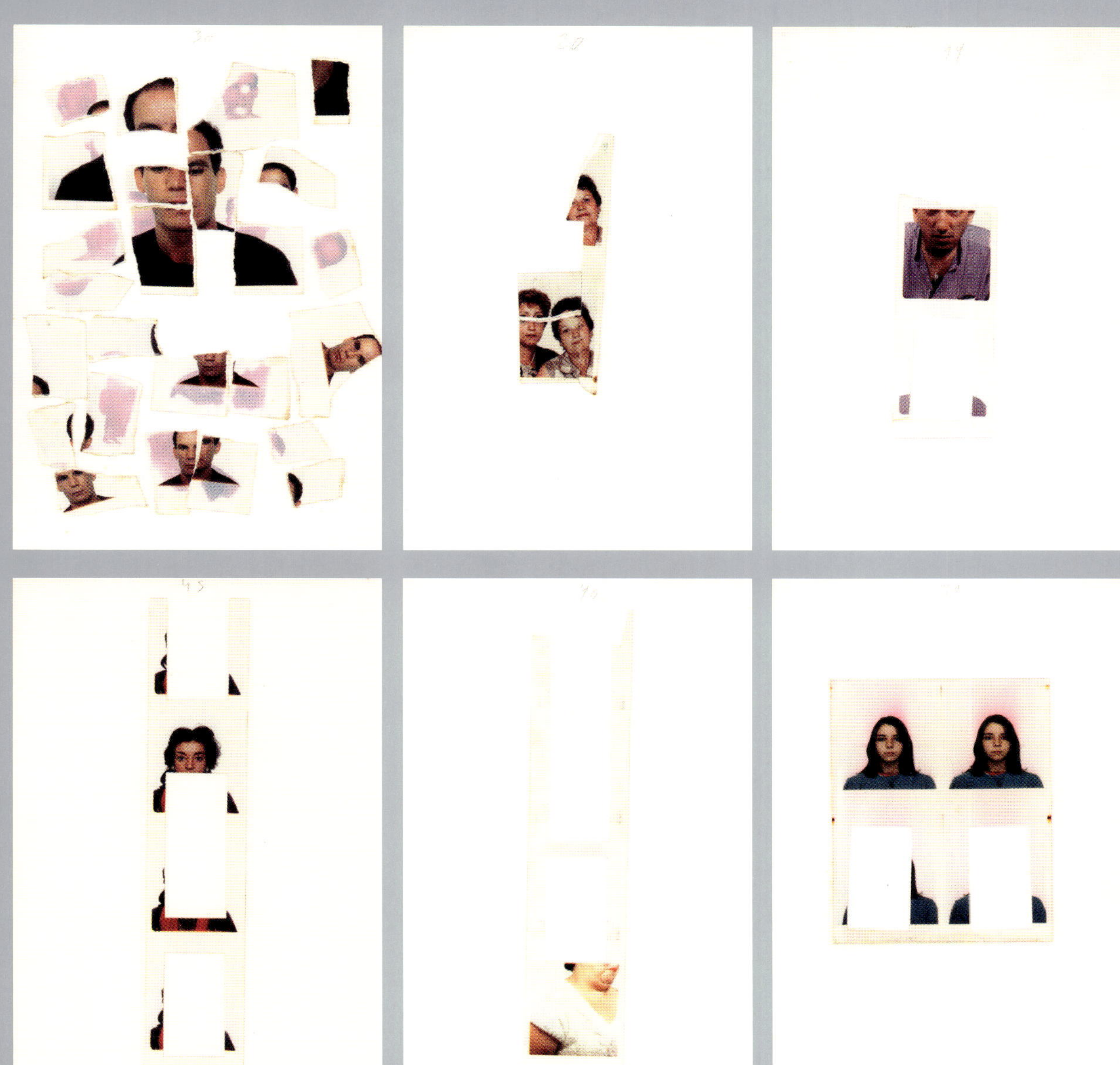

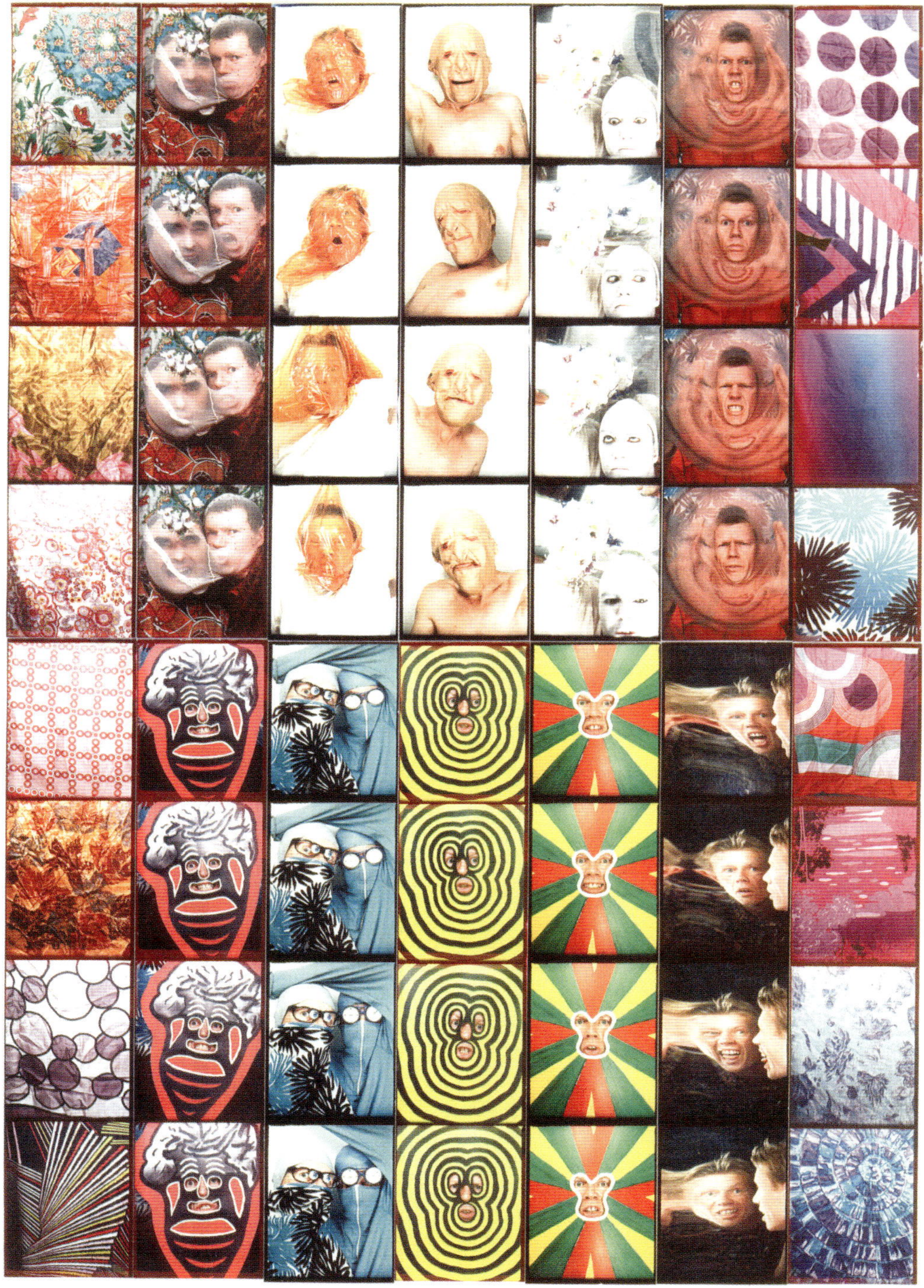

Photobooth Mixup, 2001.

STEPHEN HOWARD

(1957–)
Photobooth artist, founder of the
International Photobooth Convention
in 1999

"Taking influence from popular culture, I use film and music and create images with paint and photography, twisting them to fit my own colorful world without time or place, with faces and eyes my dominant themes. I became known as Mister Mixup when I first used photobooth machines in the late seventies as a tool to produce photobooth art. Using colorful backgrounds and masks, I perfected the craft of quick-change, inventing crazy characters, relishing the opportunity for spontaneity. These machines were present wherever I traveled and soon became a special place where moments of fun could be captured. No negatives, no photographer, the small space and technical limitations make it a unique and instant form of photography, and the styles of 'photoboothing' I've pursued come in many forms: self-portraiture, collage, documentation, figure studies, and surrealistic fantasies. Its location in a public place gives it an air of live performance, and both traditional and digital machines are places of magic. In the course of my own exploits I've met many others who share in my passion and developed the International Photobooth Convention to gather them together and celebrate these machines and the art that can be made from them."

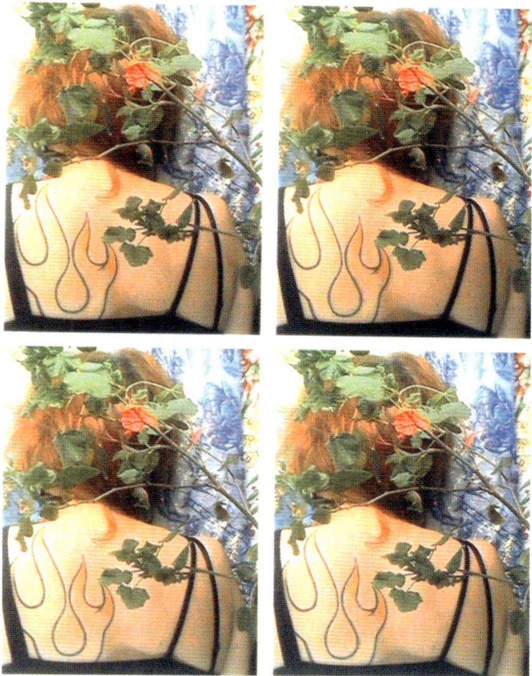

Mel, 1999.

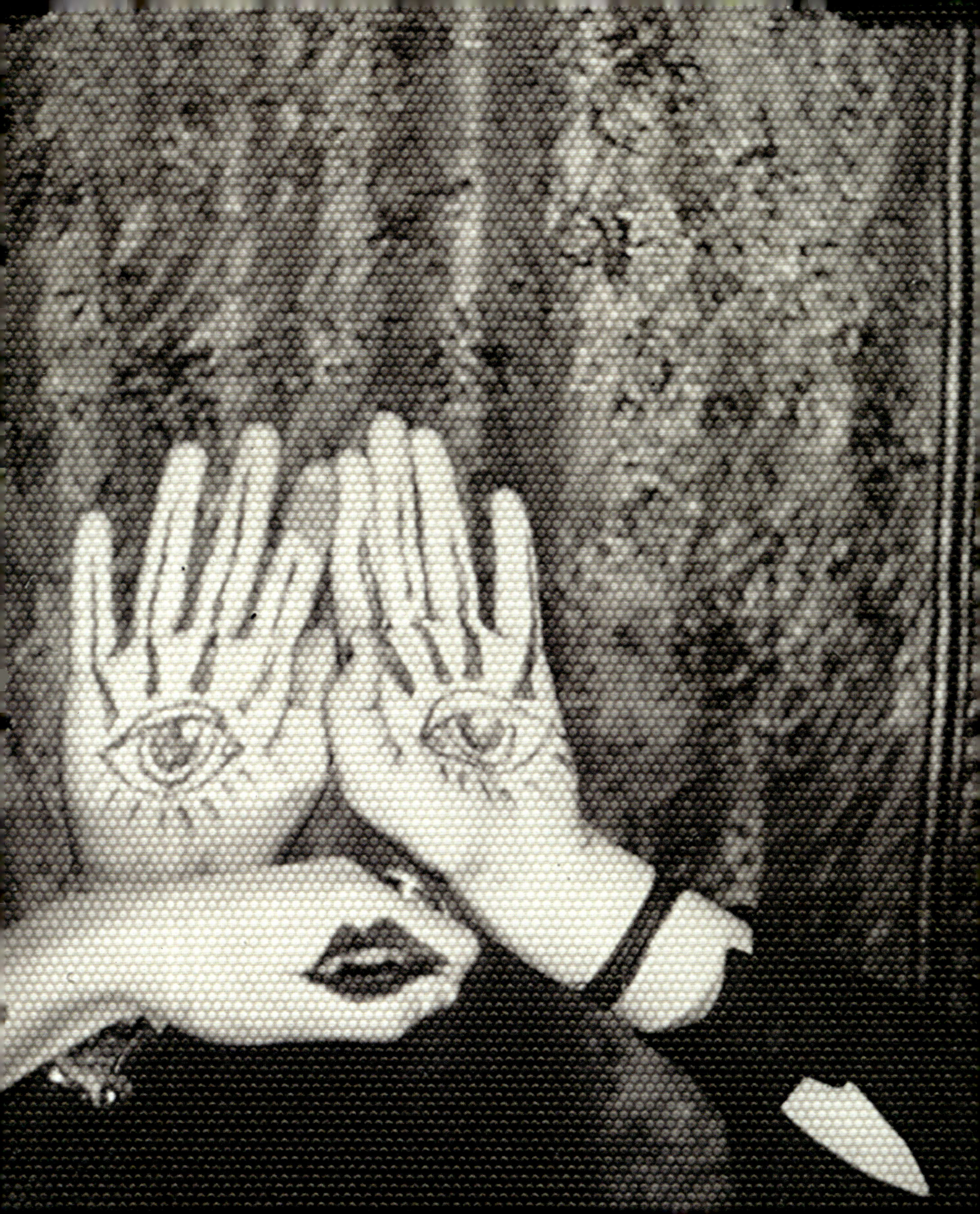

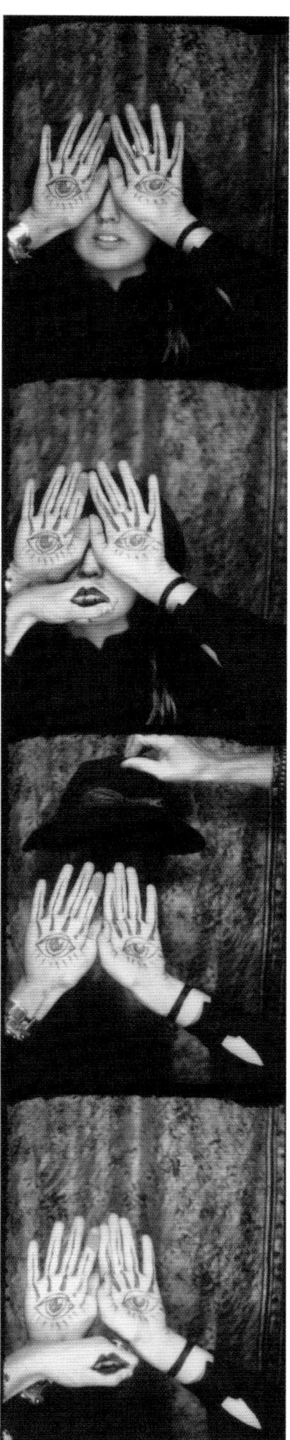

DANIEL MINNICK

American artist

"**I** am not a photographer. For me the process of taking and developing images is secondary to staging and enacting performances within the simulated space of a photograph. My activities don't start or end with an image; the image is simply the by-product of a performance in front of the camera. It is a mechanical and chemical document.

"A photobooth is a machine that primarily records the space inside of itself. This immobile camera photographs and develops four sequential images on one strip of photographic paper. All options such as lighting, lenses, and backgrounds are fixed and not intended to be changed. Its limitations provide me with the ability, through its image, to unfold its interior and create new and otherwise unseen environments in which I perform."

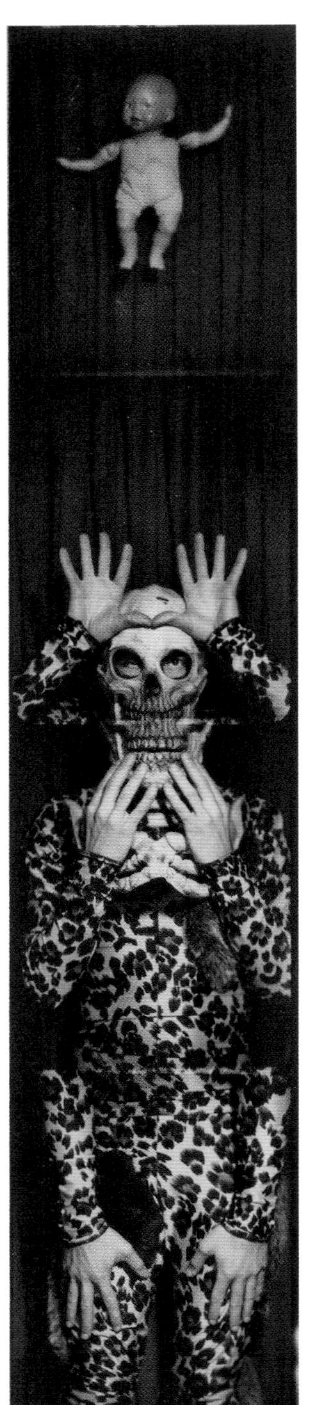

Floating Totem, 2009.

Psychic Zombie, 2009.

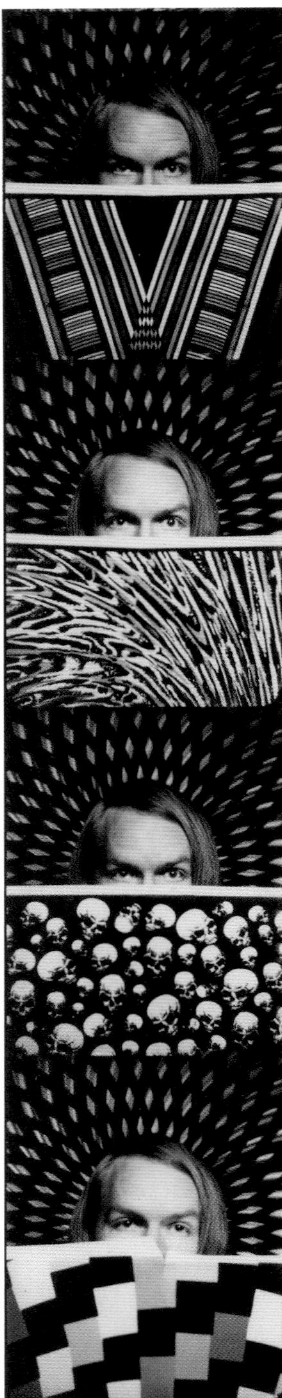

Untitled, 2009.

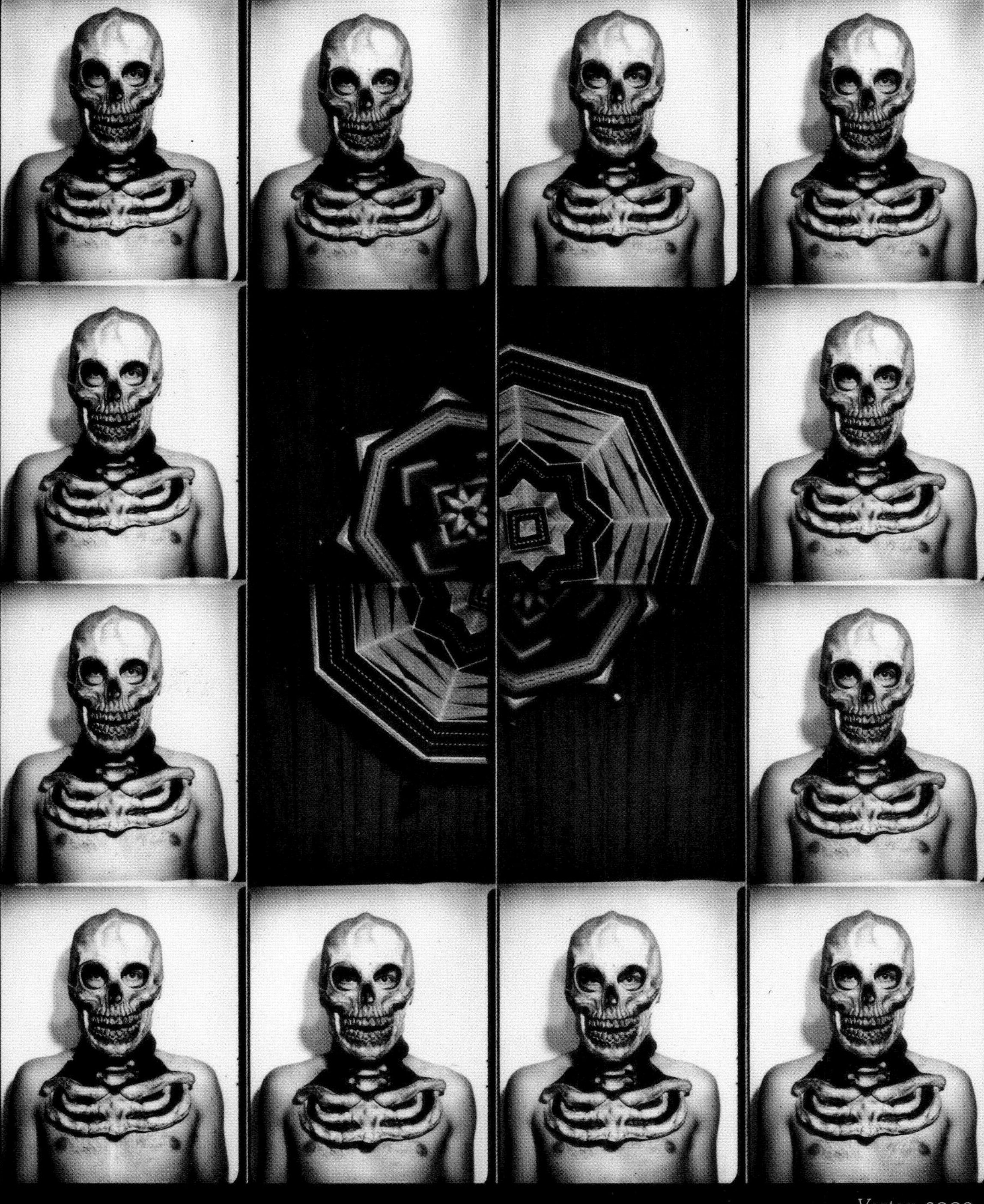

Vortex, 2009.

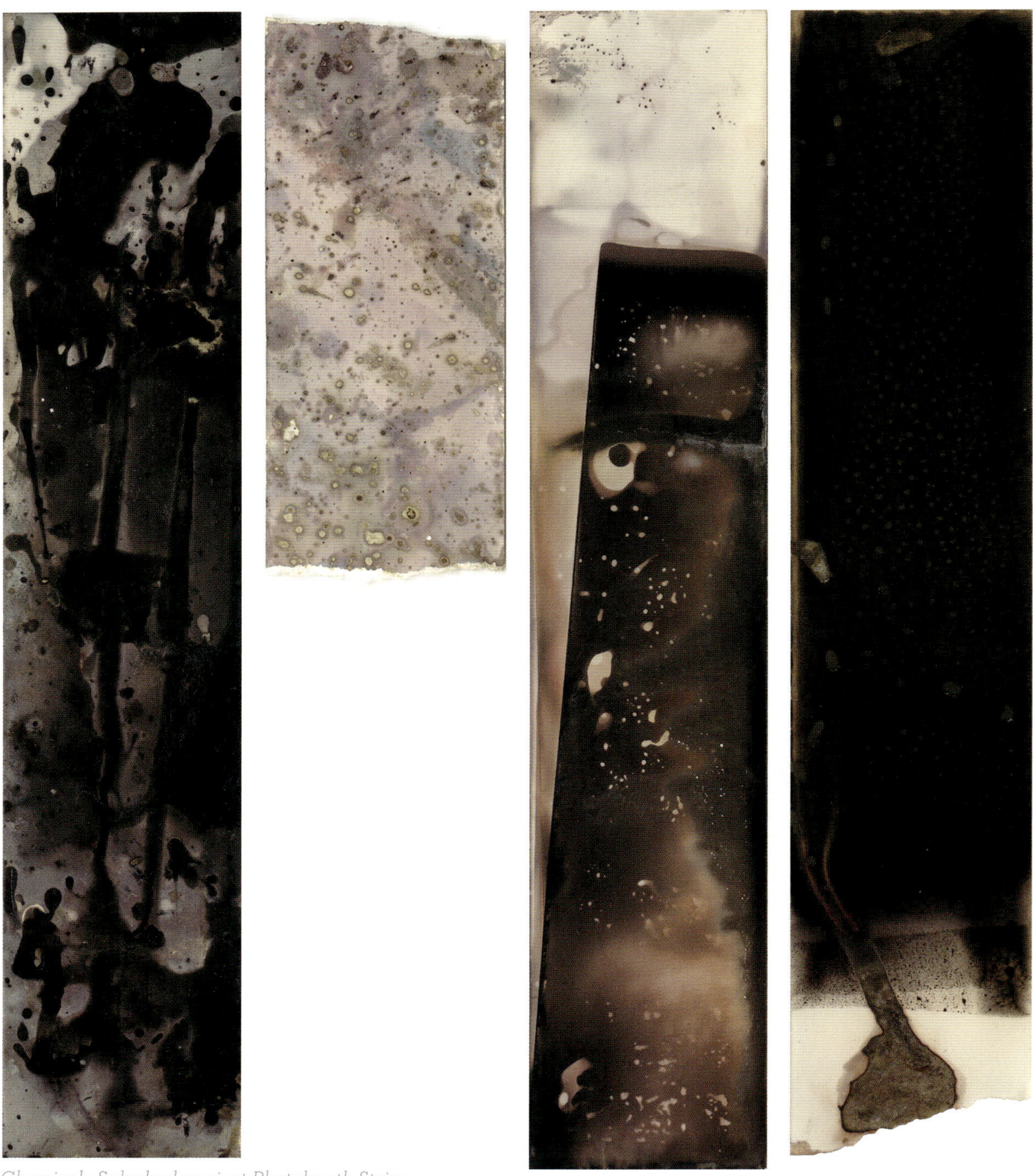

Chemicals Splashed against Photobooth Strips.

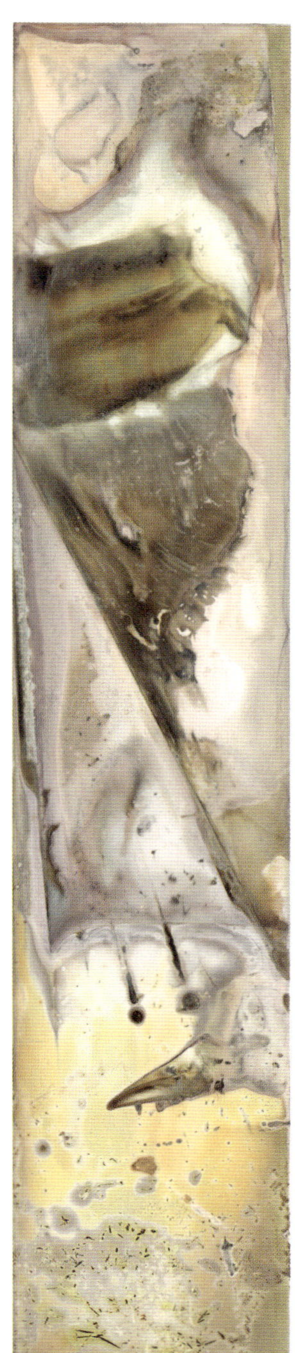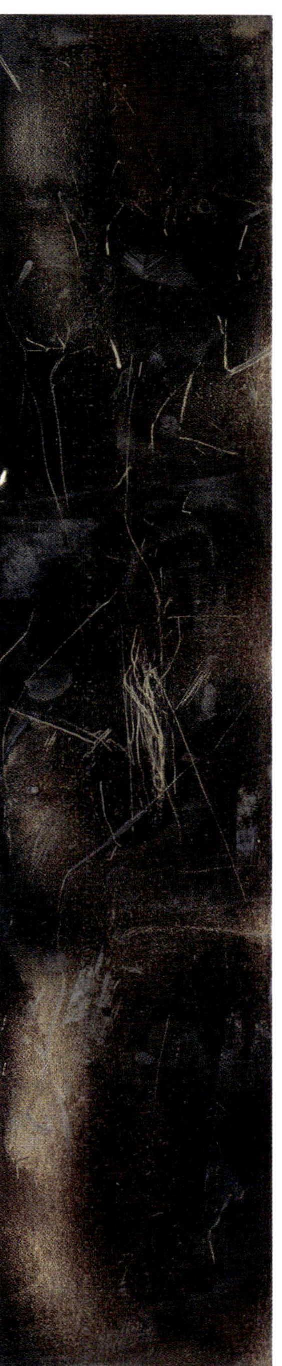

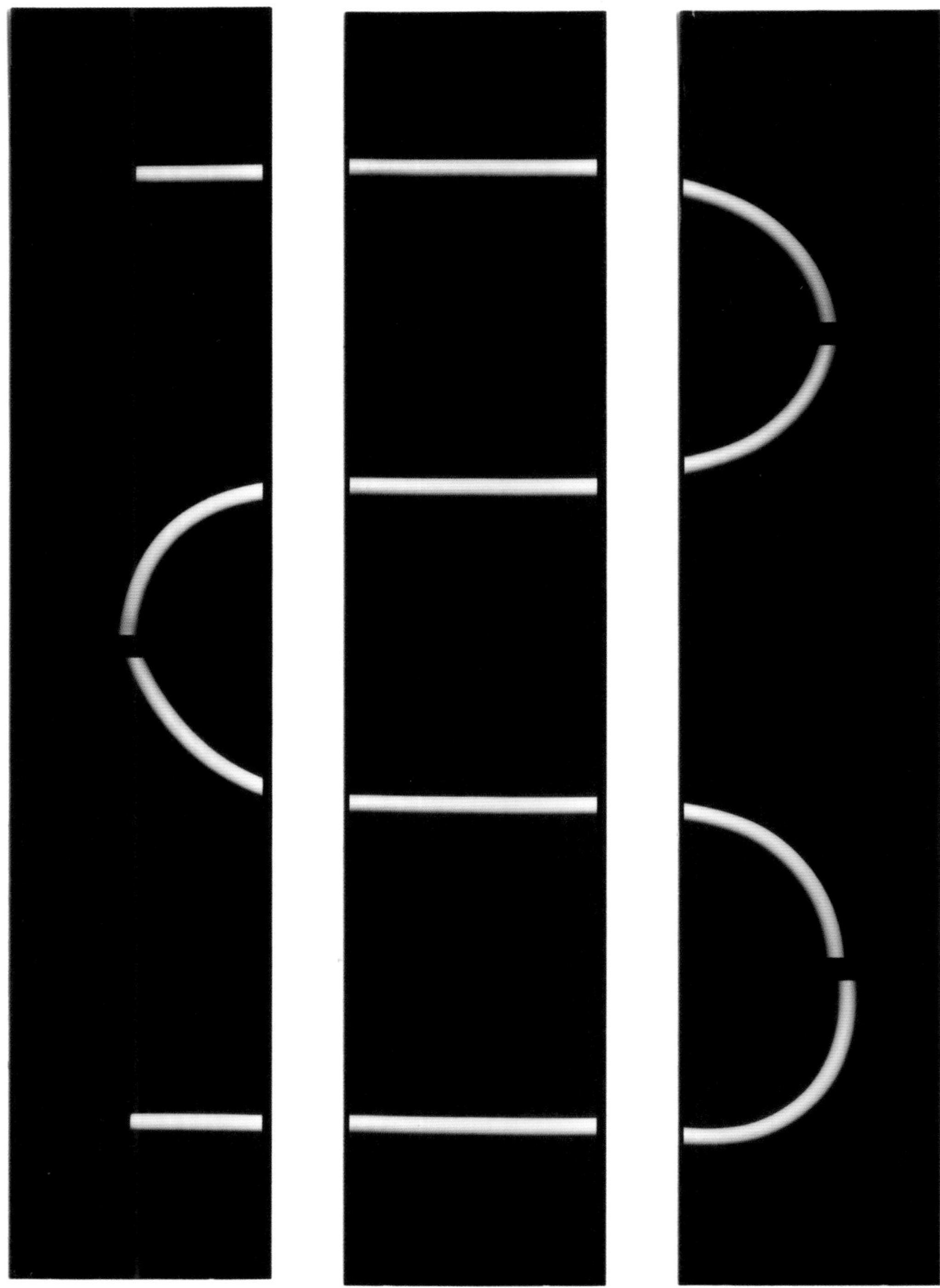

Tube.

TIM GARRETT

American artist

Tim Garrett is one of the cofounders, with Brian Meacham, of the website photo-booth.net. A veritable compendium and reference work for fans of photobooths, this site allows users to locate the rare silver-emulsion booths still functioning around the world, and it provides a considerable body of information on the history and present of the photobooth.

According to Meacham, a film archivist, the quality of the silver-emulsion photobooth strips also contributes to their charm: "The tone and contrast of photos produced by a well-maintained booth can be quite incredible, and since they are made by a direct-positive process using no negative, each is a unique, one-of-a-kind work of art.…People still use them for various projects, some of which we've documented on our site, and will continue to do so as long as they can find one available, but they'll only be around as long as the technology (chemicals, paper, and technical know-how) manages to stay alive.

"I am drawn to the seemingly inflexible constraints the photobooth presents: a fixed focal length, aperture, and camera shutter; the cramped seating area, the mechanical precision and timing of the four shots, and the iconic vertical strip of photos. I enjoy creating photos that play with these constraints and with the expectations of the viewer. I am also interested in the inherent narrative embedded in each strip of images, the four distinct but successive snapshots of time. In recent work, I am beginning to experiment with the photobooth itself as an interactive piece, using the booth's perceived familiarity to create surprising experiences inside."

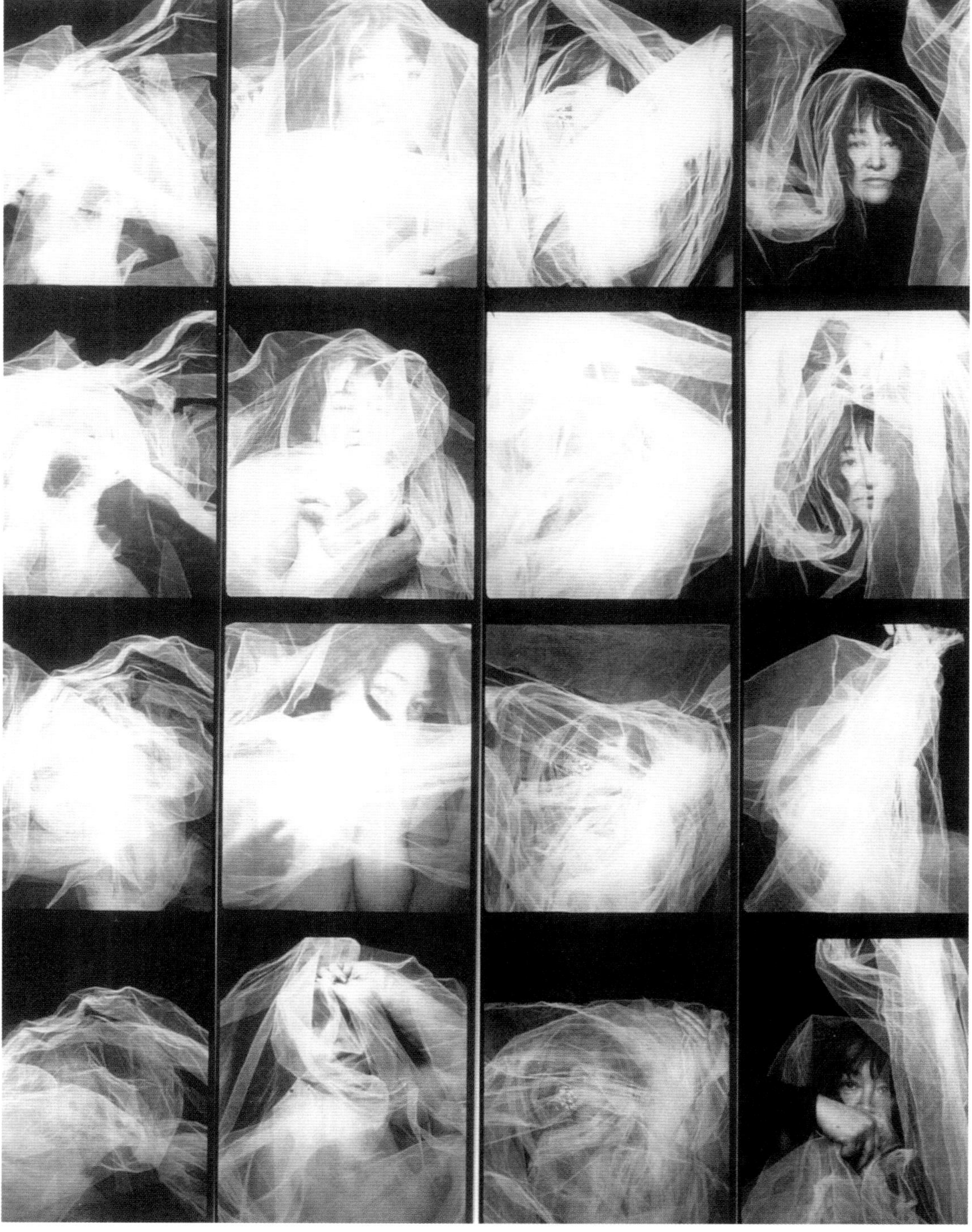

Cosmos.

NAKKI GORANIN

American artist, author of *American Photobooth*

"**I**n my world, the photobooth has always been a little magical house where I can close the curtains and be on my own private stage. A meditation cell, a small theater, I am my own film director. Writing and drawing small, short scripts, I can create static movies. Fear of mistakes or humiliation doesn't exist. I just tear up that evidence. The darkroom in the interior of the booth comforts me. I listen to the whirling mechanical devices, the clicks and hums, and I hear music. The smell of the chemicals is like the perfume of the photo darkroom in my own home. I also am drawn to old photobooth images. There is 'accidental greatness' in the vernacular photos of the past. I've become obsessed with finding vintage photos and equally obsessed with creating new ones. Looking at my photobooth self-portraits from year to year, I see the register of time and age and though sadly, I cannot escape this, I aspire to be reborn in the embracing fantasy of art."

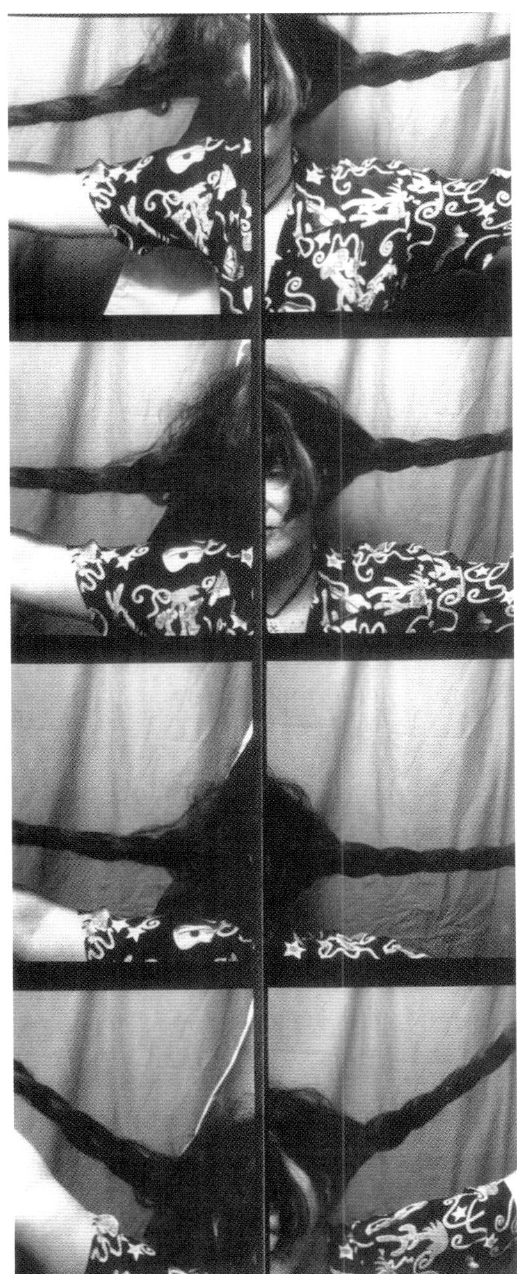

My Hair in Braids.

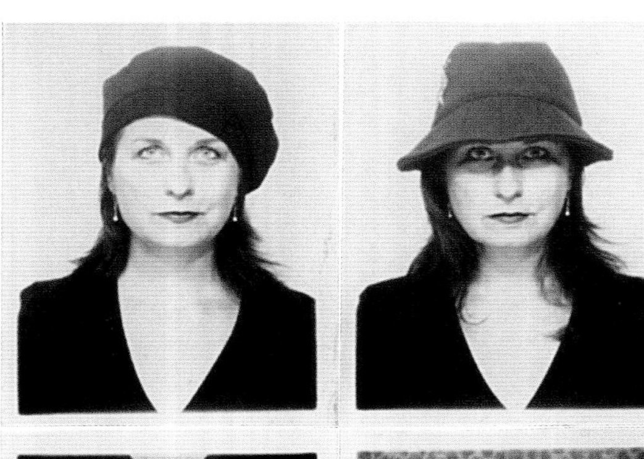

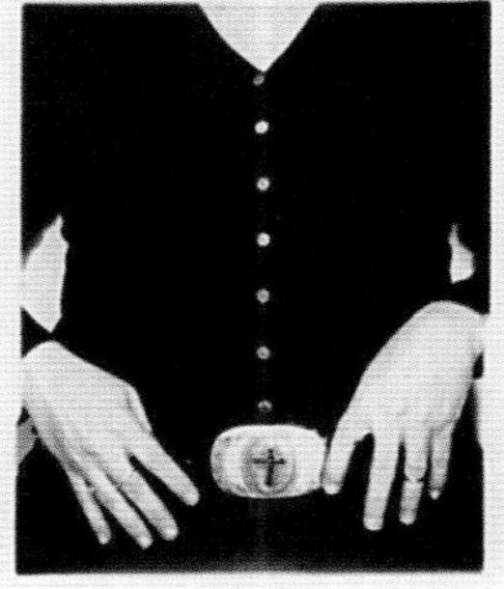
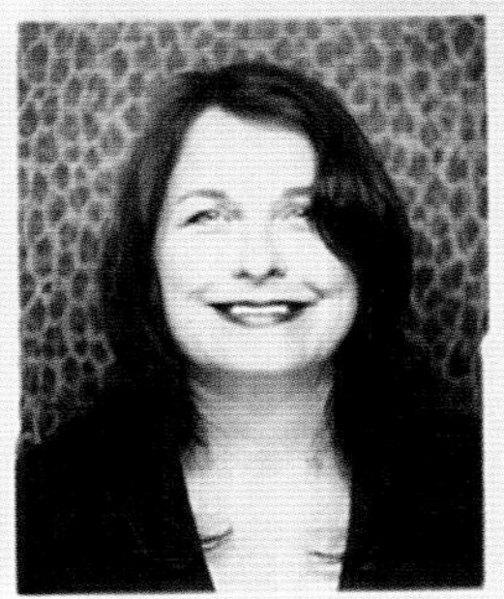

Claire Photobooth.

CLAIRE CONNORS

American artist

"**M**y original photobooth work was more journalistic than artistic. Between the years of 1983 and 1985, I was working for *City Pages*, a local weekly newspaper in Minneapolis. I had a column called 'Public Relations,' and my goal was to introduce the reader to folks in a man-on-the-street style of interview. Lacking a camera, I would hang out by the photobooth machine located in the basement of a Woolworth's department store. I was able to meet different kinds of characters there—from missionaries getting their passport photos to travel to Africa, to young hipsters using the machine for art purposes, to moms and dads wanting to take a quick photo with their kids to commemorate a birthday—and capture them in that brief moment in time.

"After I moved to New York in 1985, I continued to use the photobooth for other endeavors. With my friends Herman Costa and Lisa Lederer, we made a line of jewelry using photobooth images.

"My last piece was done in 2003 during a photobooth convention, organized by Steve Howard, a.k.a. Mister Mixup. It features my friend Abby and me in a sexually tinged religious piece, entitled *The Cross*."

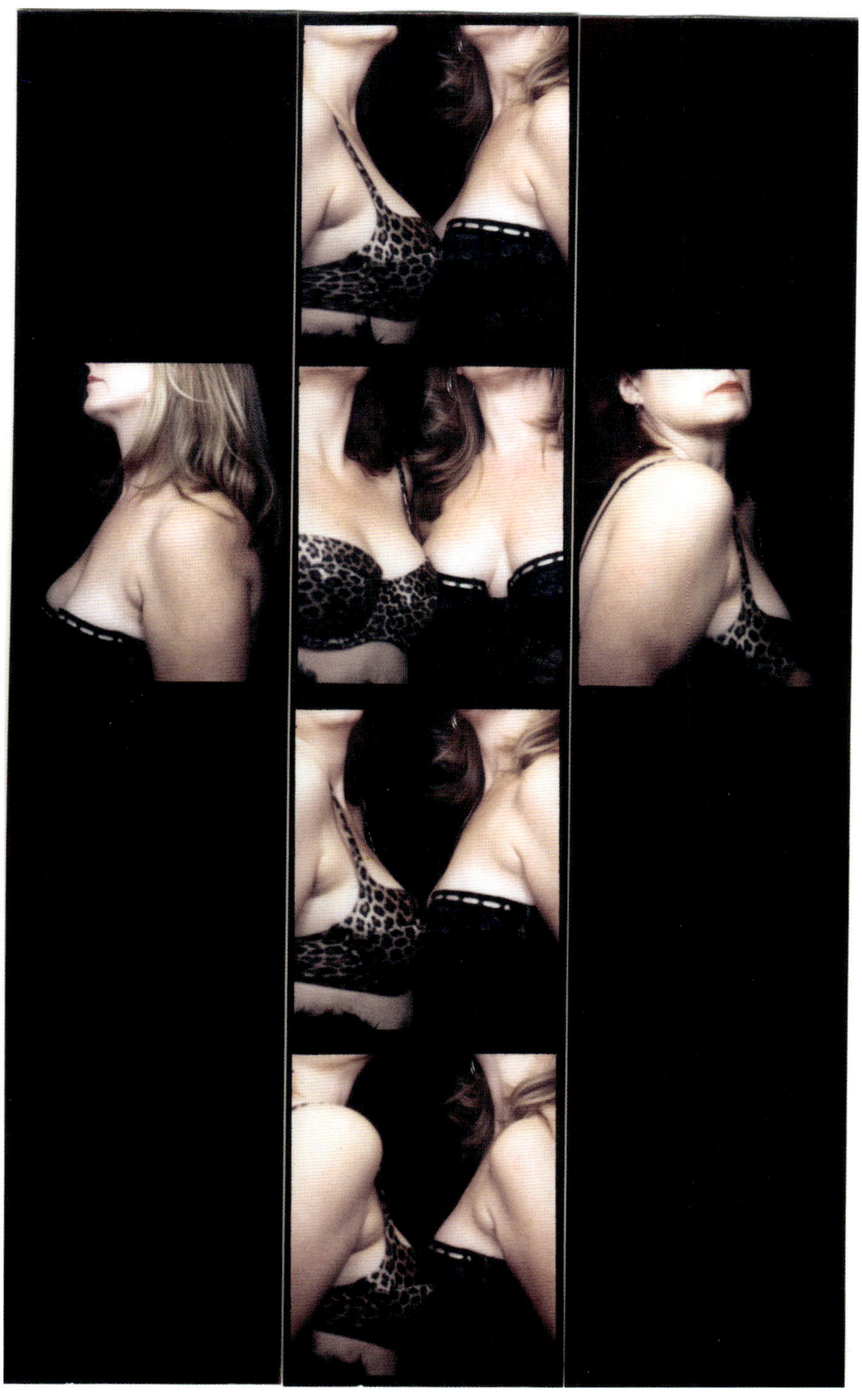

The Cross, 2003.

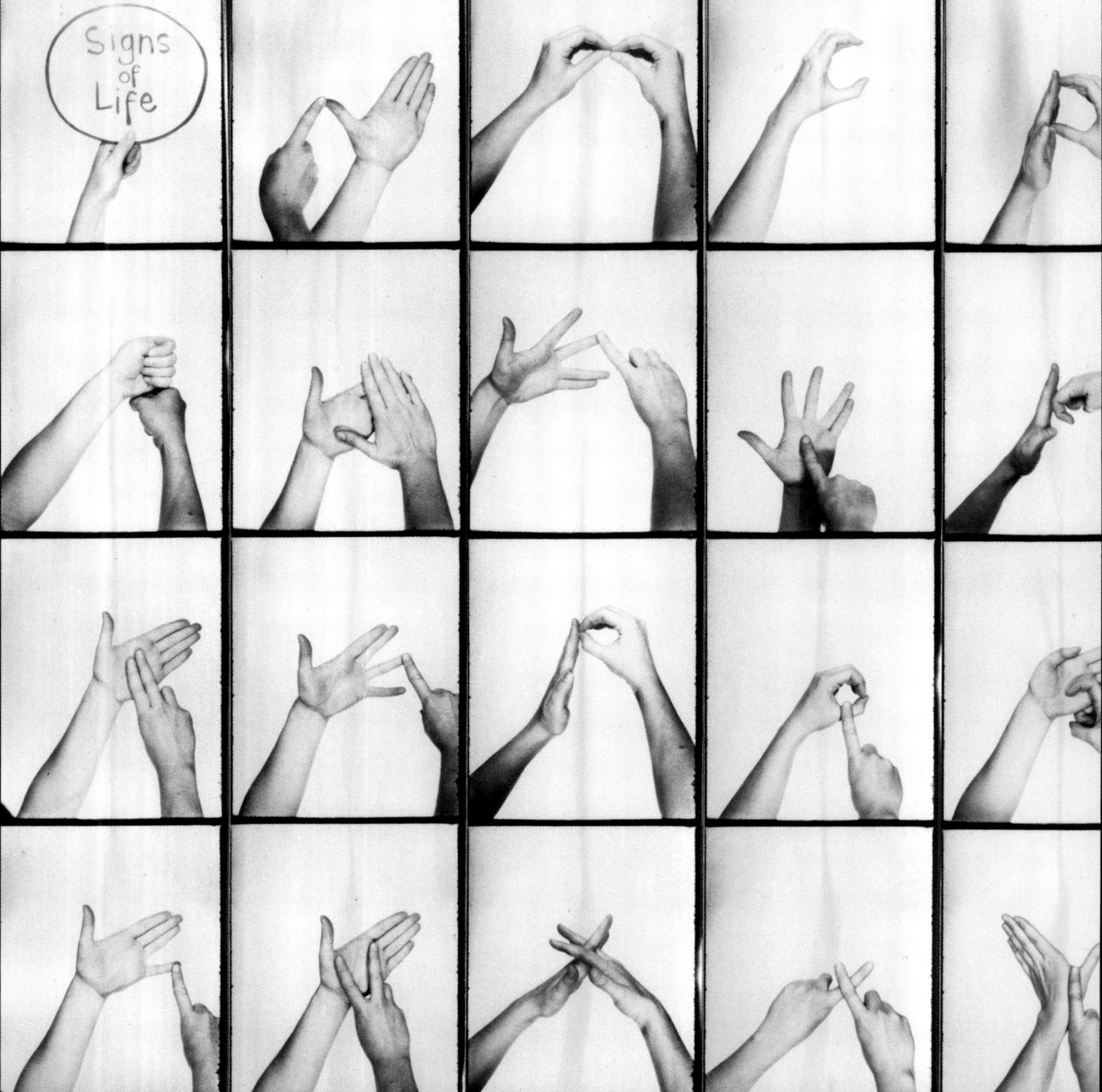

Signs of Life.

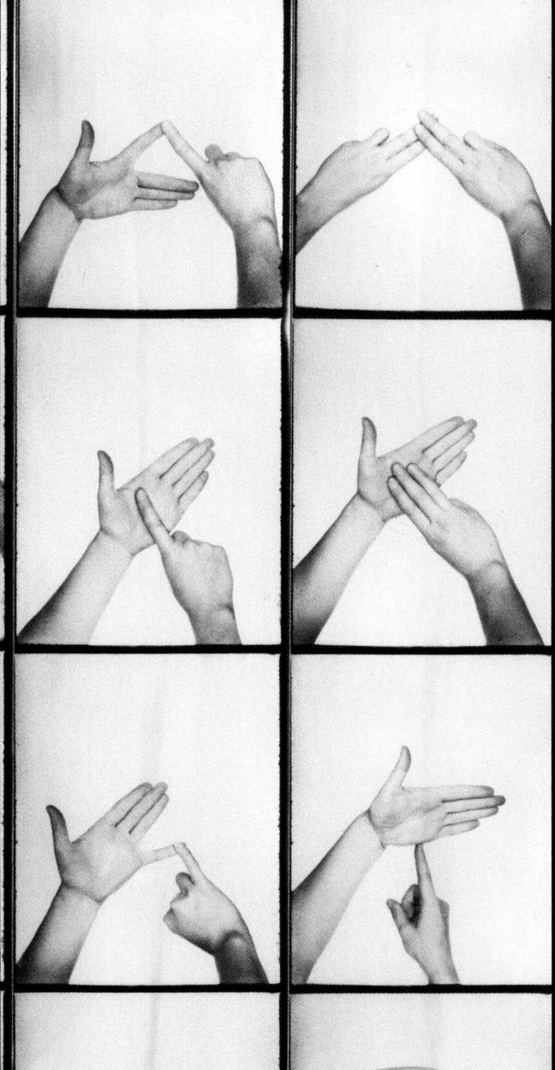

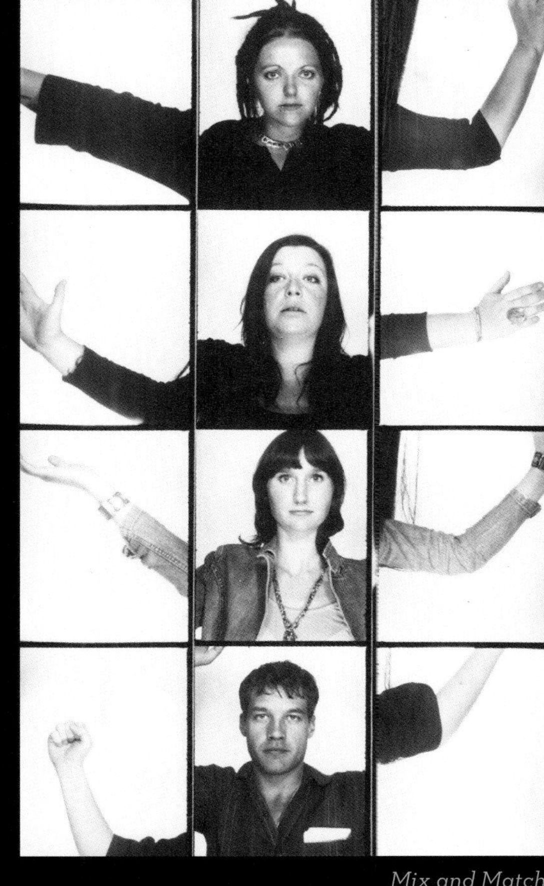

Mix and Match

KATE TYLER

English photographer

"**S**ince 1991, I have been collecting passport photos. I also create my own work,
beginning with photobooths. My artistic development has played with the constraints and
the specifics of photobooths: limited space,
absence of the photographer, and restrictions
imposed by the standard format of four photos

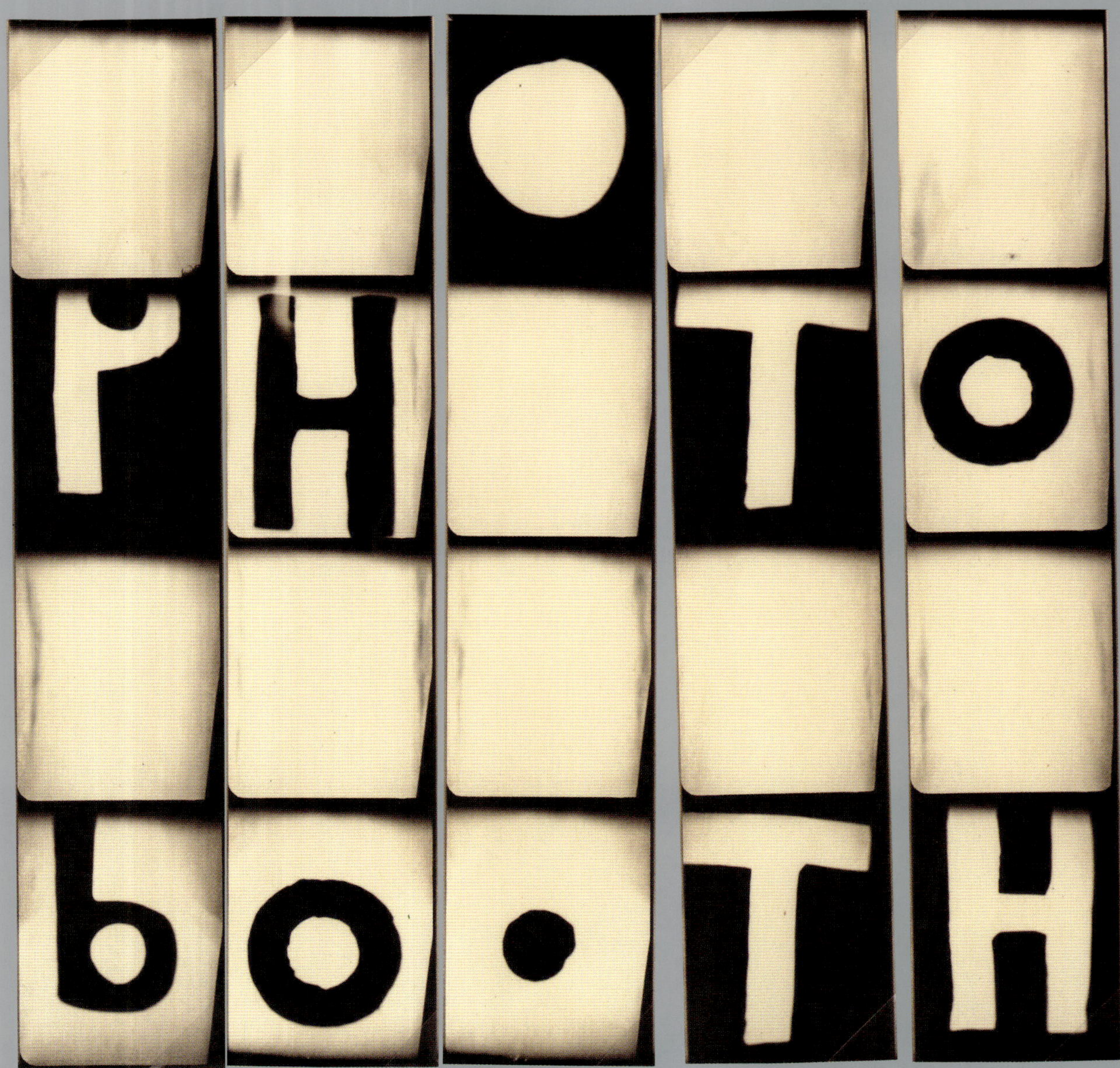

Photobooth, Broadway, Sydney, December 22, 2001.

MISSTER DEAN AND MISS TEEN

Australian artists

In September 1999, Misster Dean and Miss Teen decided to take a photobooth photograph every week. For five years, until October 2004, they crisscrossed Europe, the United States, Central America, New Zealand, and Australia.

"After reuniting in London at Tooting Broadway tube station, we decided on a whim to take a photobooth snap. In the three minutes that it took to develop our picture we made a grand decision: to take a photograph each week for five years using the photobooth machine. We quickly moved beyond traditional portraiture and began to experiment, first with stop-motion animation, which led us to creating comic strips using the four frames. The booth then became a space in which to install our art or create puppet shows, and a medium in which to explore documentary photography. In its completion what we created was a visual diary of our lives!

"Our travels around the world were consumed with visits to bars, airport lounges, train stations, and shopping malls, wherever there was a 'working' photobooth. We encountered many situations that were totally out of our control. When we wanted to work with color all we found were black-and-white machines. Inconsistent lighting led to underexposed images. Poor-quality developing chemicals would cause bleaching. Space was limited to a depth of field of 30 centimeters, and the three seconds between each shot was restrictive—but each problem became a stylized contribution. The most exciting and difficult aspect to manage was working in highly trafficked public spaces (especially when we were naked)."

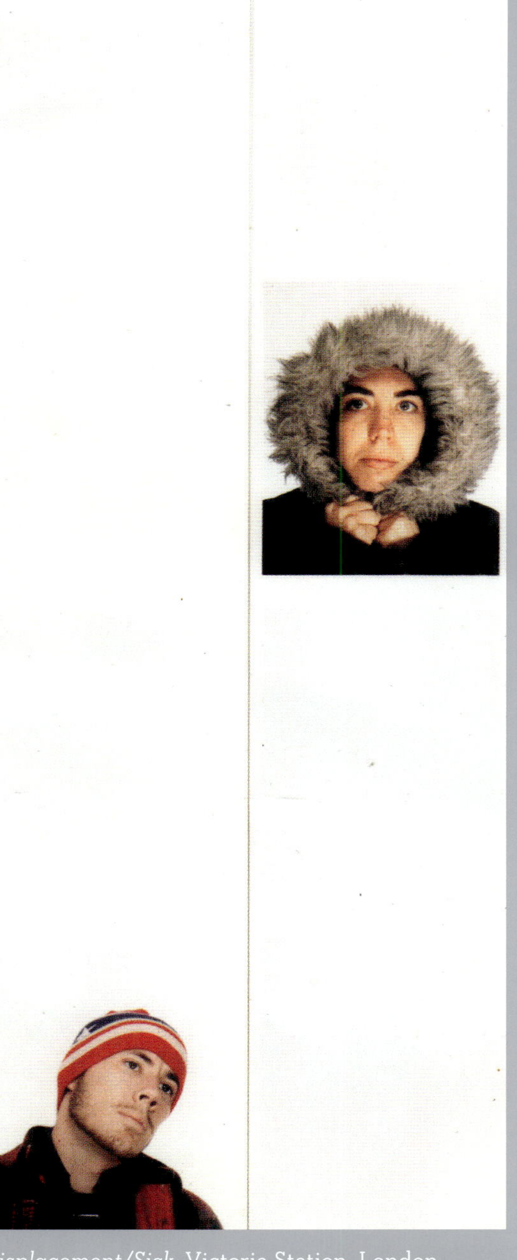

Displacement/Sick, Victoria Station, London, October 19, 1999.

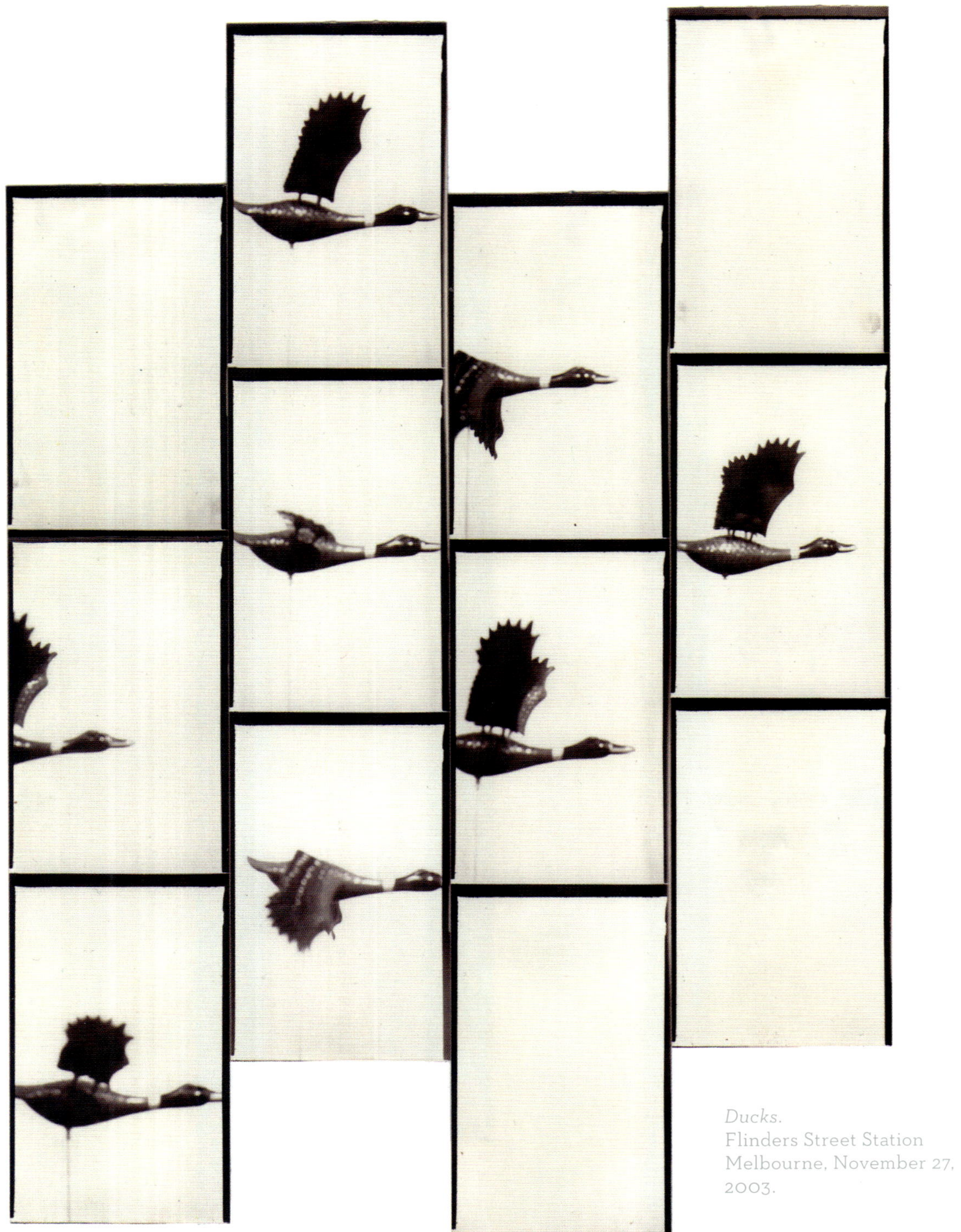

Ducks.
Flinders Street Station
Melbourne, November 27,
2003.

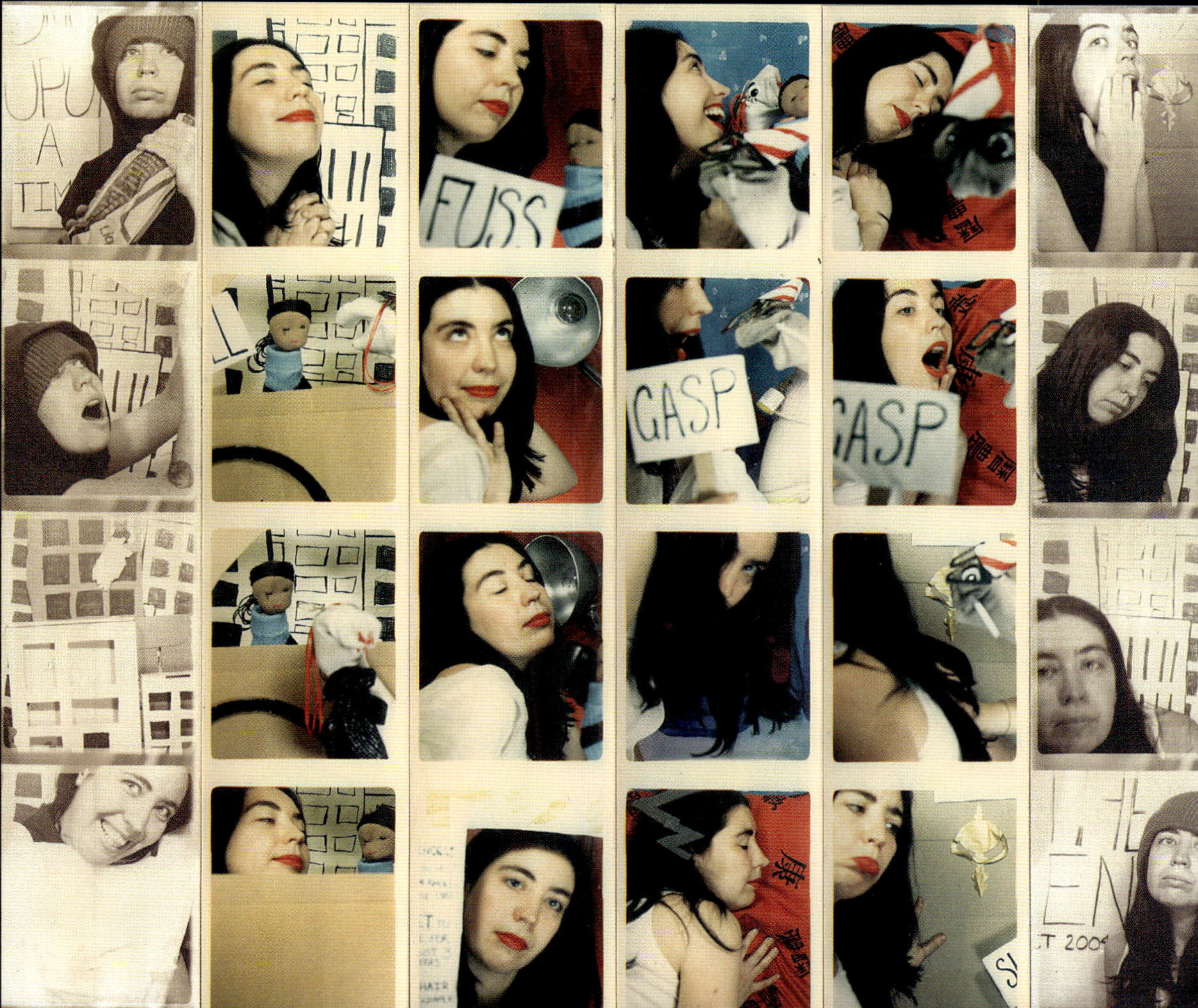

Princess and the P, Broadway, Sydney, October 14, 2004.

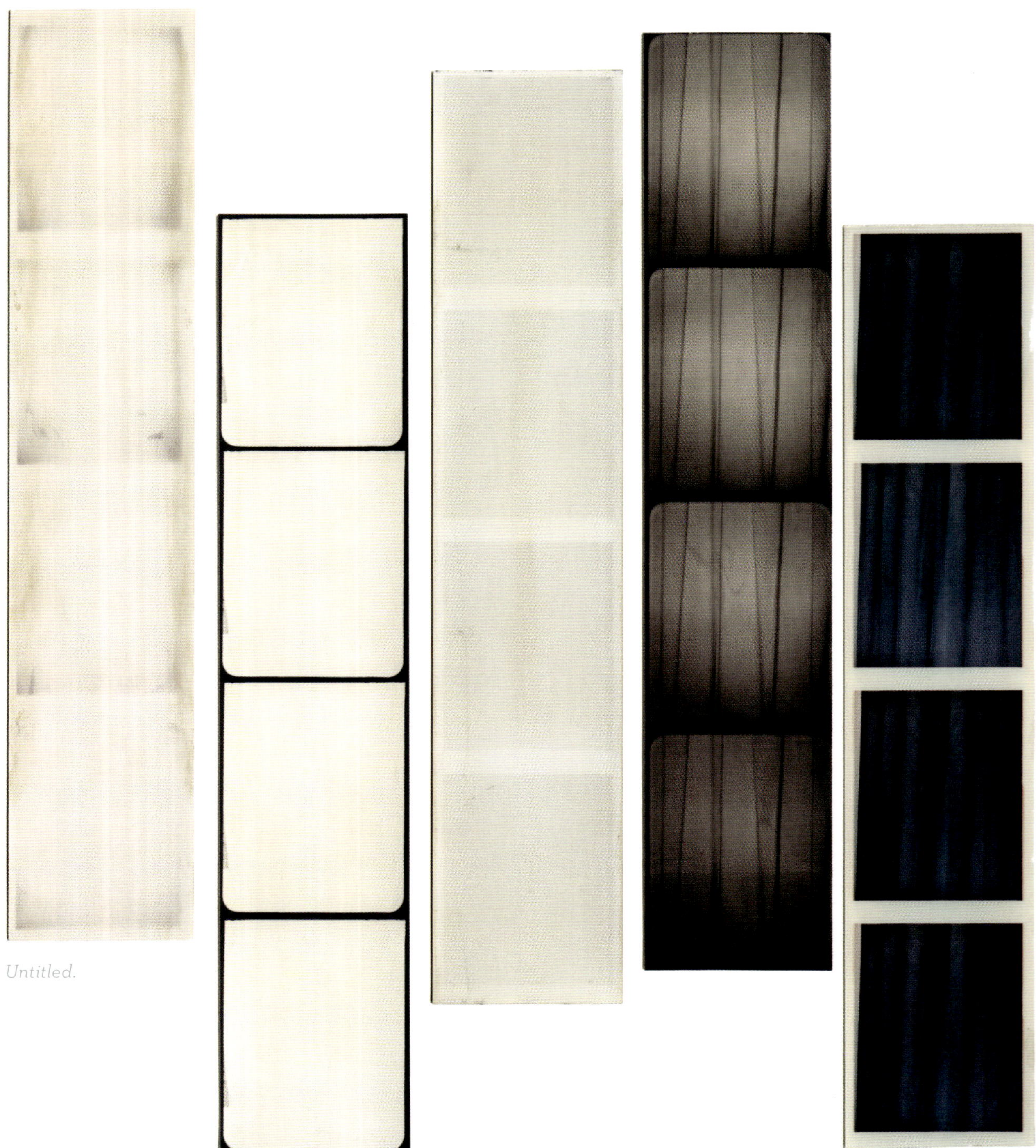

Untitled.

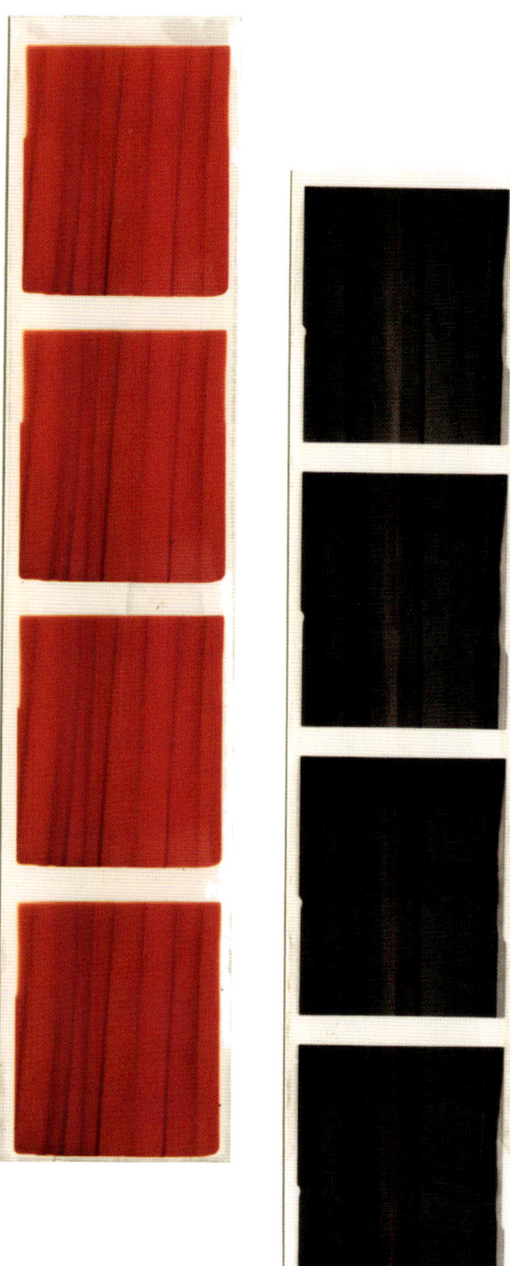

NAOMI LEIBOWITZ

(1983–)
Photographer

"In the present-day world of ubiquitous, low-quality cameras and the widespread unceasing memorialization of every insignificant moment, the photobooth remains an archaic shrine to the formalized capture of ephemeral moments. Its walled and curtained cell should by now have been doomed to obsolescence, but it remains a space of almost religious significance. By removing the human figures who so often purchase memories in these spaces, *Photobooth Interiors* exposes an unacknowledged, barren geography. A format so often romanticized is thus deprived its emotional authority, as the setting takes primacy over its interchangeable, now-absent occupants and customers. Gazing at these abandoned, unprepossessing landscapes, we can discern the perversity of seeking in these impoverished chambers shelter from our actual lives."

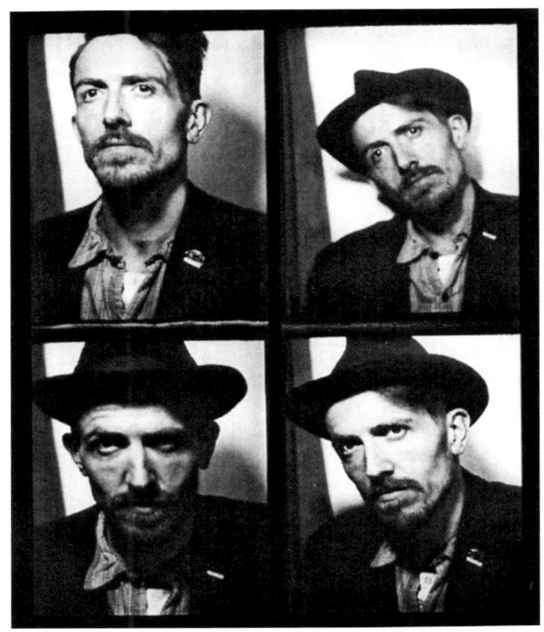
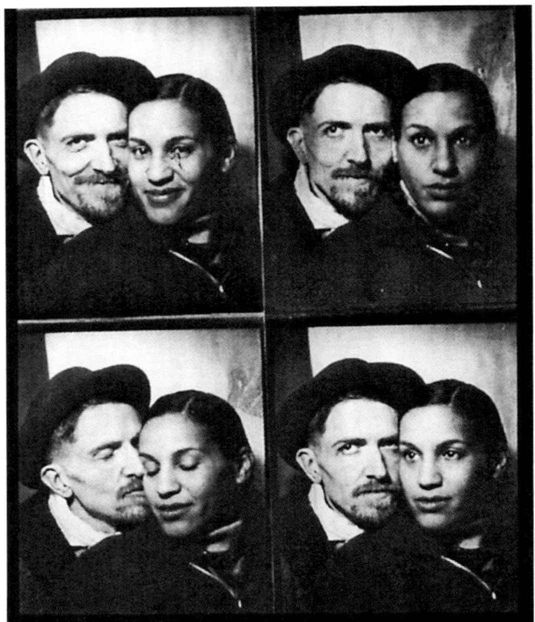
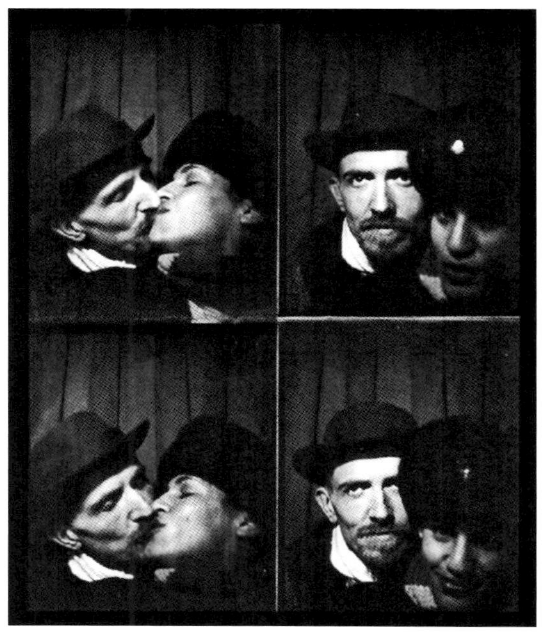
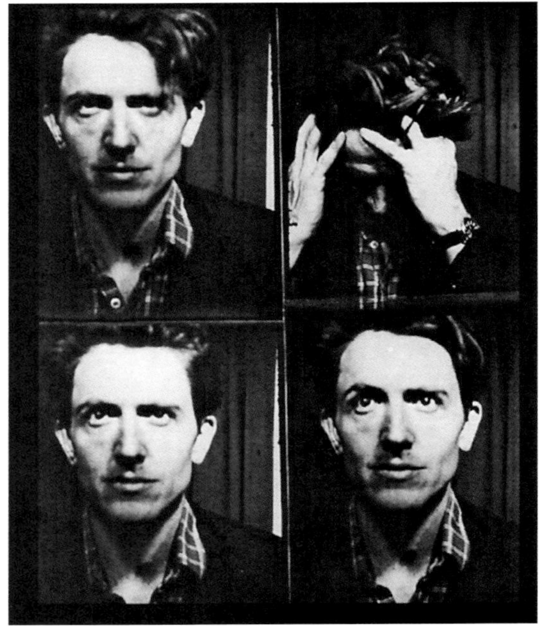

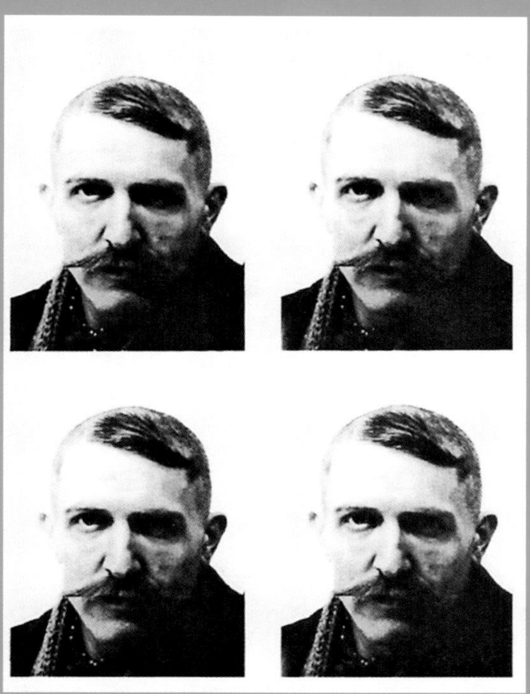 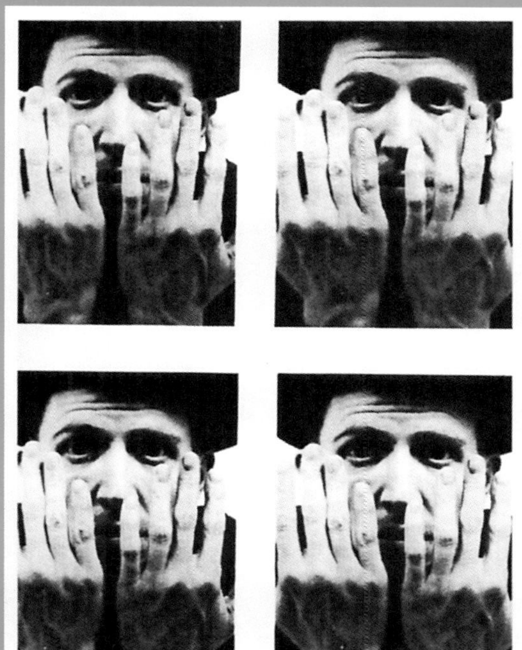

BILLY CHILDISH

(1959–)
British painter, writer, and musician

"I have used photo booths since my early teens. i love the old analog booths. the young me in a few of these photos is drunk and lost.

"in others im in love and found. in all of them im trying to find a face i can show to the world that i can recognise and feel happy in. its like making a charchole drawing and wondering how to be here and be real."

March 2010

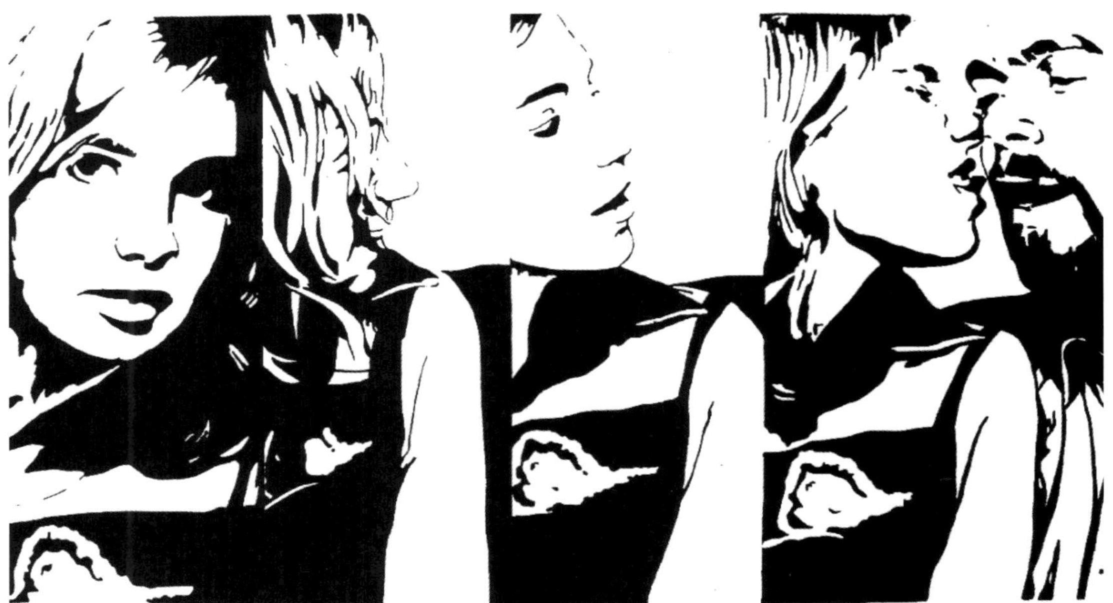

Bancroft Way, Berkeley (Sean & Jaymee No. 3).

JULIE BROWN SMITH

American artist

"**M**y work is about people. What we do in everyday situations, and what goes on around us unnoticed when we go through our lives, as observers and the observed, sometimes aware and often oblivious. The Photobooth Series captures people caught in an artificial environment, changing poses and personalities in a split second between camera flashes.

"The series began with one strip of a couple, taken in the photobooth at San Francisco's Musée Mécanique. This inspired four paintings ten times larger than the actual strip, leading to images laid out like film strips; montages of one image evolving into the next; and individual portraits twenty times the size of the original, larger-than-life, with an intensity of gaze [one is] unable to ignore.

"To me, each of these photos is a self-portrait, spontaneous or premeditated, a mirror of an inner landscape. They are fascinating in their immediacy: people sitting on uncomfortable seats under harsh lighting, reacting to an unseen camera behind a distorted mirror. They are an eternal record of a moment, stripped down to its essence, raw and distilled, a replica of split-second changes captured in the stark black and white of my work."

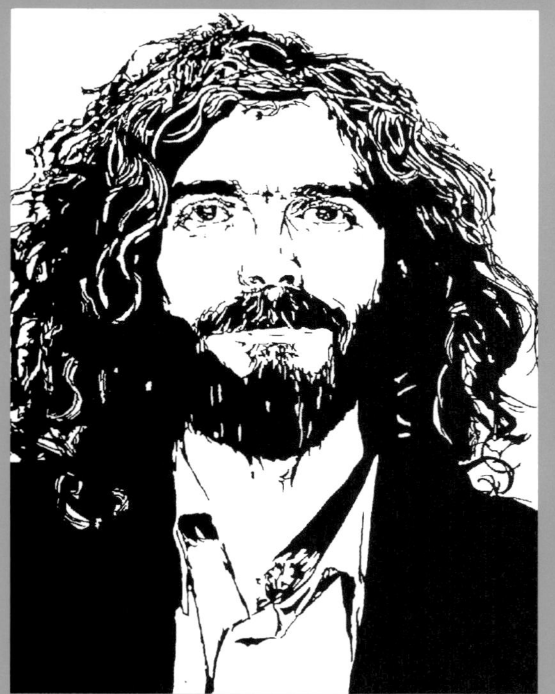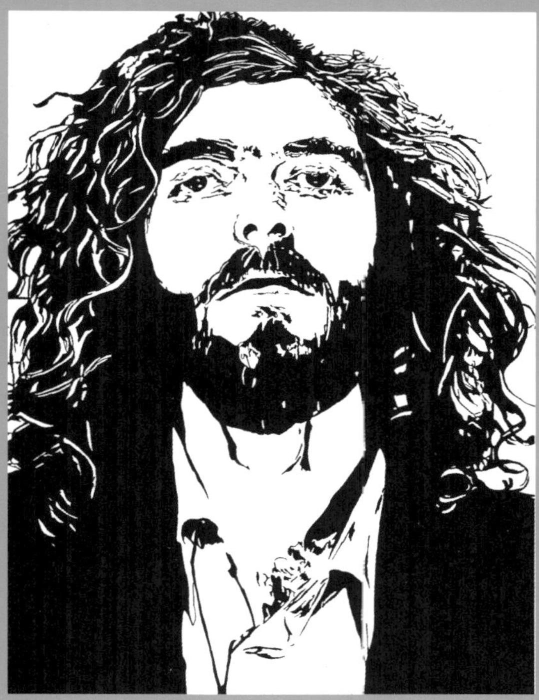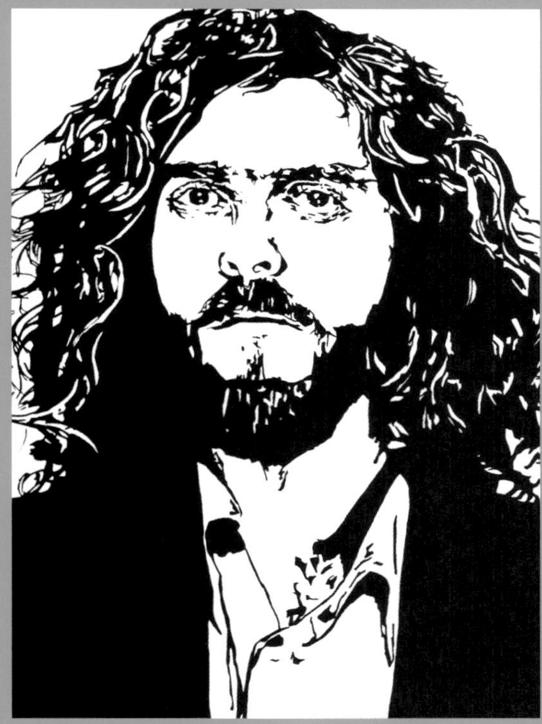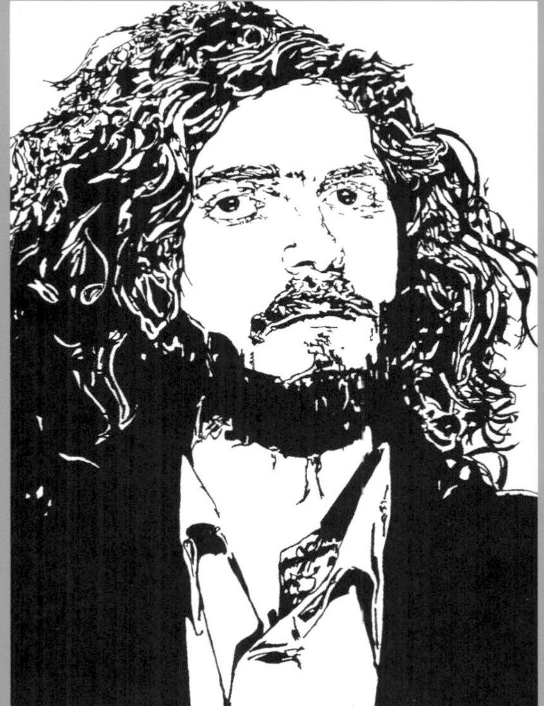

Bancroft Way, Berkeley (Sean No. 1, 2, 3 & 4).

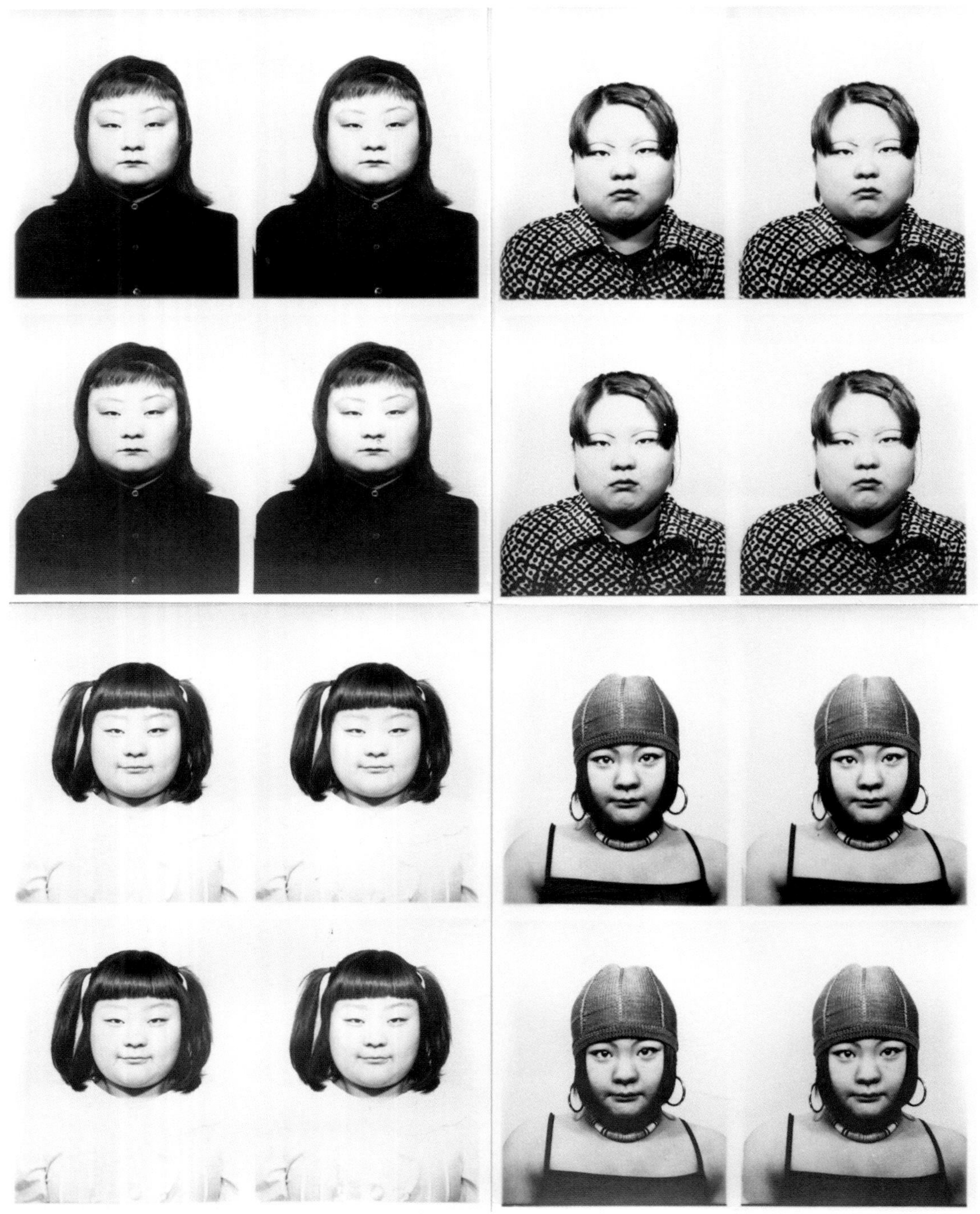

ID 400.

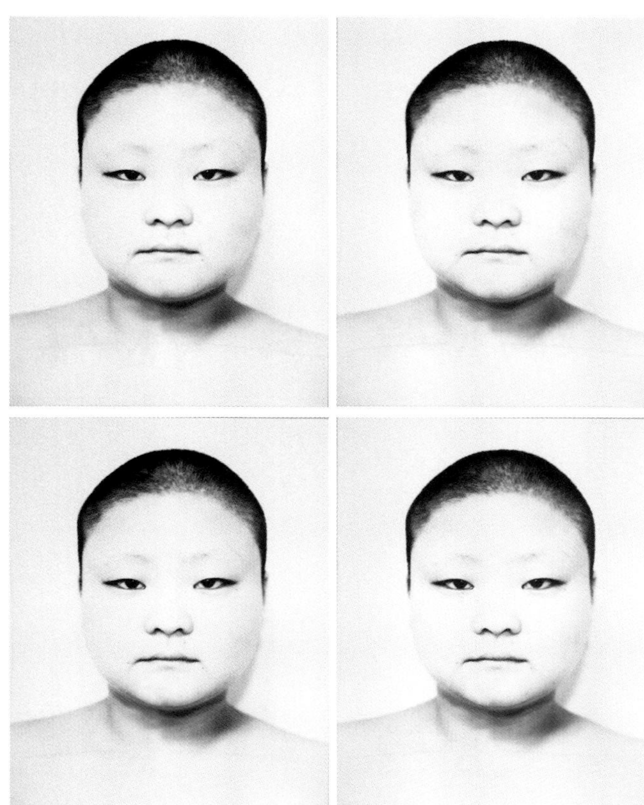

Skinhead.

TOMOKO SAWADA

(1977–)
Japanese photographer and artist

"I did *ID 400* when I was a university student in Kobe, Japan. I always used the same machine and took photo IDs, altogether appropriating 400 different identities. At exhibitions, I arranged and displayed these photos in frames, with each frame holding 100 photo IDs.

"Once I completed these 400 photos, I shaved my head and took a photograph of myself without makeup. When *ID 400* was exhibited, I walked around the exhibition hall with my new look and only a few visitors, maybe about 20 percent of them, identified me as the person they had spent the whole night looking at in those picture frames. Because of this experience, I became fascinated by the relationship between appearance and the inner self.

"Now, I have an intuition that my bald-headed image carries a profound message and might be the key to all my work. Afterward, I worked on the same subject, the relationship between appearance and inner reality, my own and that of others."

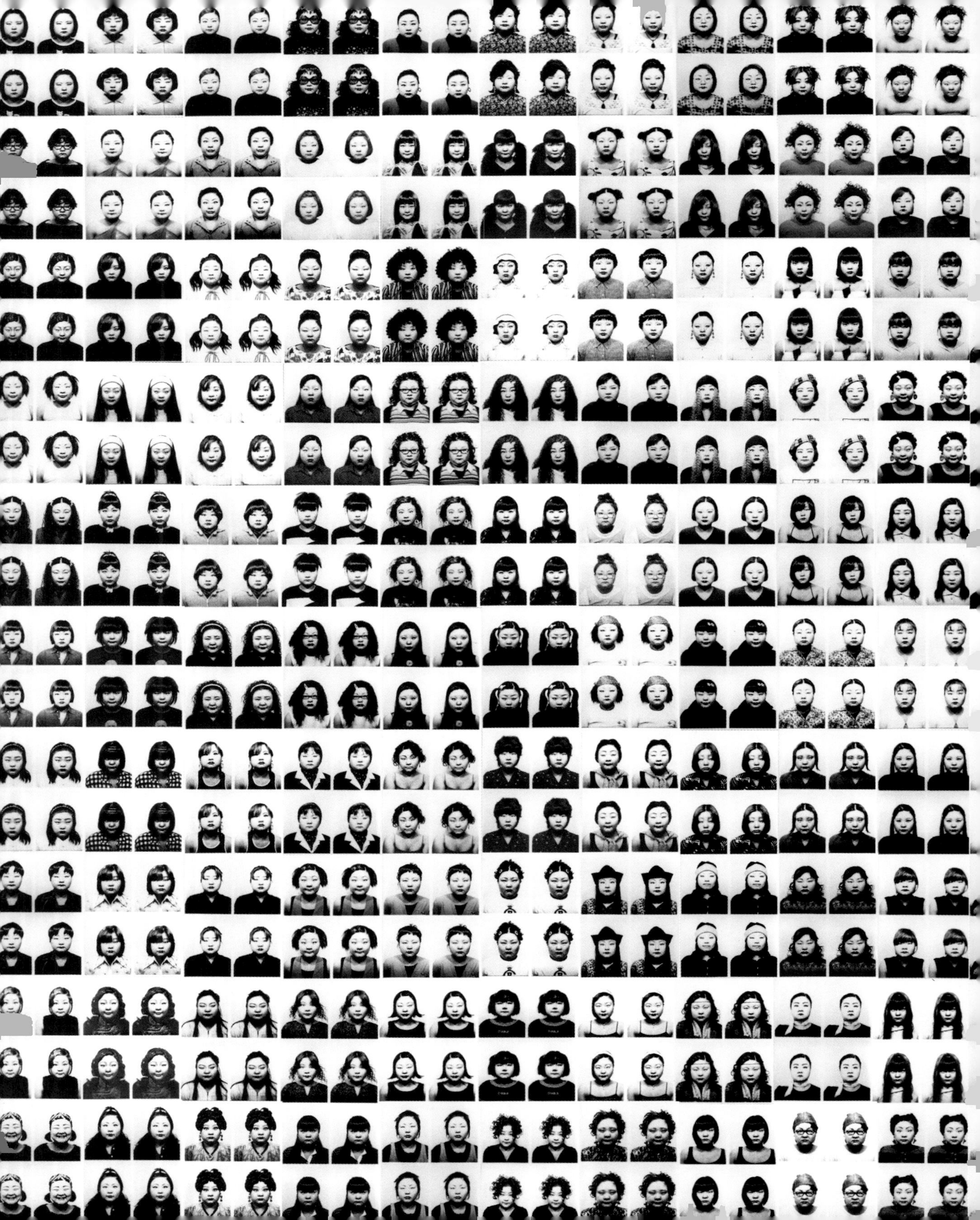

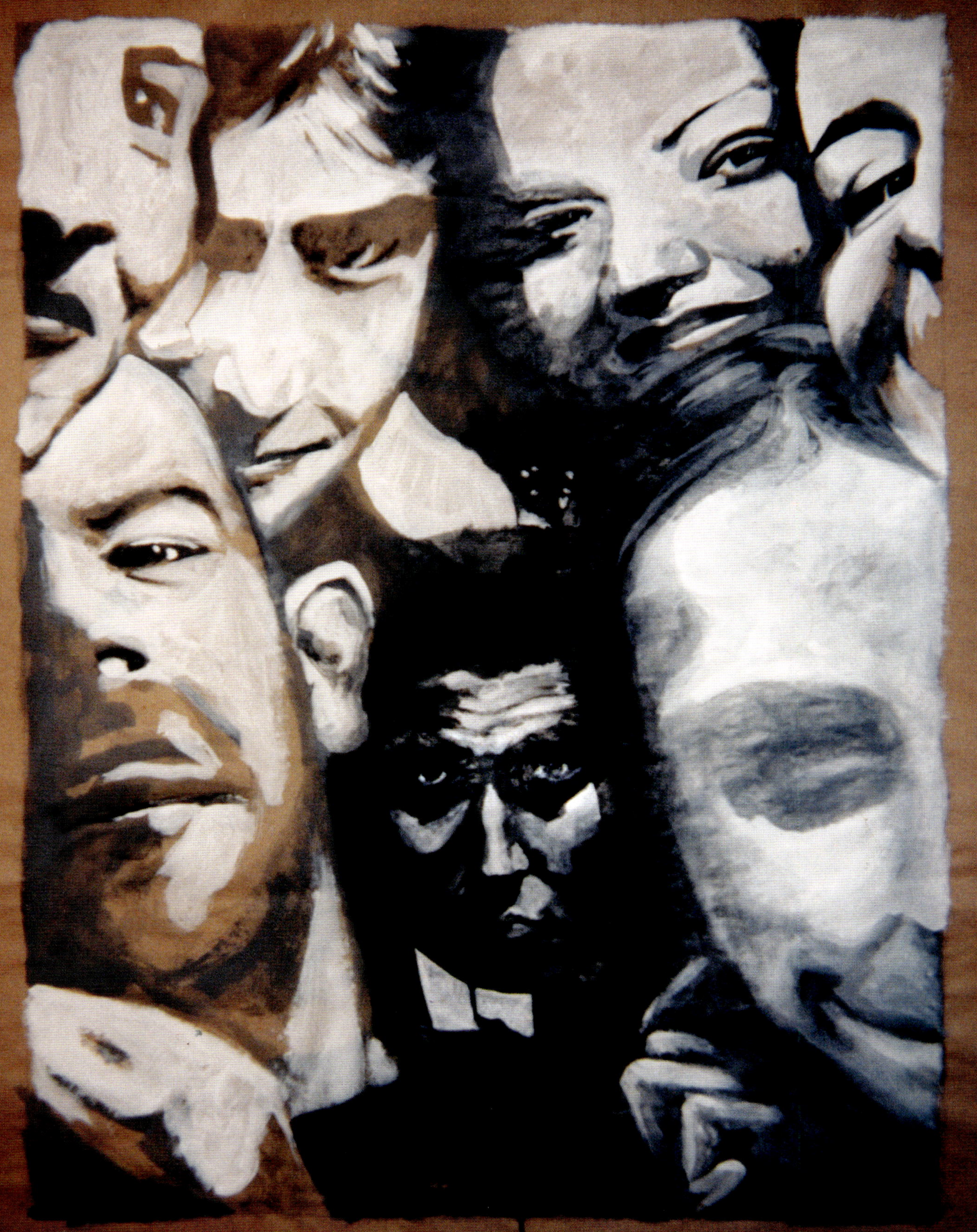

GIUSEPPE "ZELLABY" COLLOVATI

Italian illustrator and graphic designer

"In the sixties, my uncle Daniele played guitar in a group called 'I Satelliti,' here in my hometown of Pordenone (northeastern Italy). Whenever the group practiced, my uncle had to go pick up the bass player at the train station. While he was waiting for the train, to kill time, he would go into the photobooth and take funny photos of himself. Twenty years later, I rediscovered many of those photobooth pictures in a box, and I found them to be truly cool and funny. So I went back, right then, with some friends, to take photos in that train station photobooth. Then I started collecting photobooth snaps, asking my friends and family to do self-portraits. Oddly enough, I found lots of photobooth pictures on the ground, and my collection, which now consists of some three hundred photos, also includes a number of portraits of strangers. I immediately started using those photobooth pictures to make collages in a fanzine called *Plustones*. Years later, the photobooth format again inspired my artwork. In 2008, I decided to do an installation with a number of photobooth snaps from my collection and creating a large patchwork of portraits. That installation was a success. Many of my friends recognized themselves in old or recent photobooth pictures."

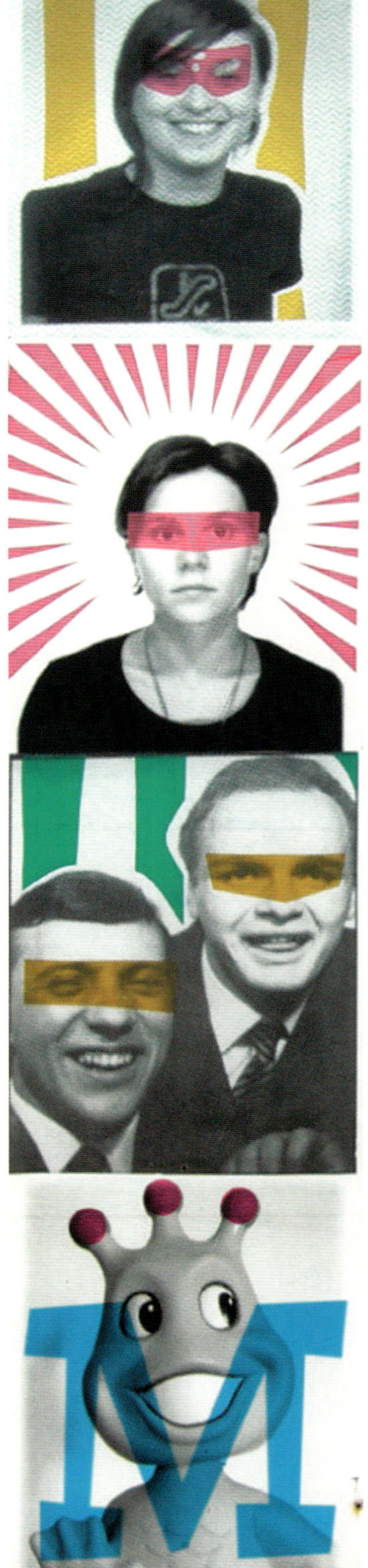

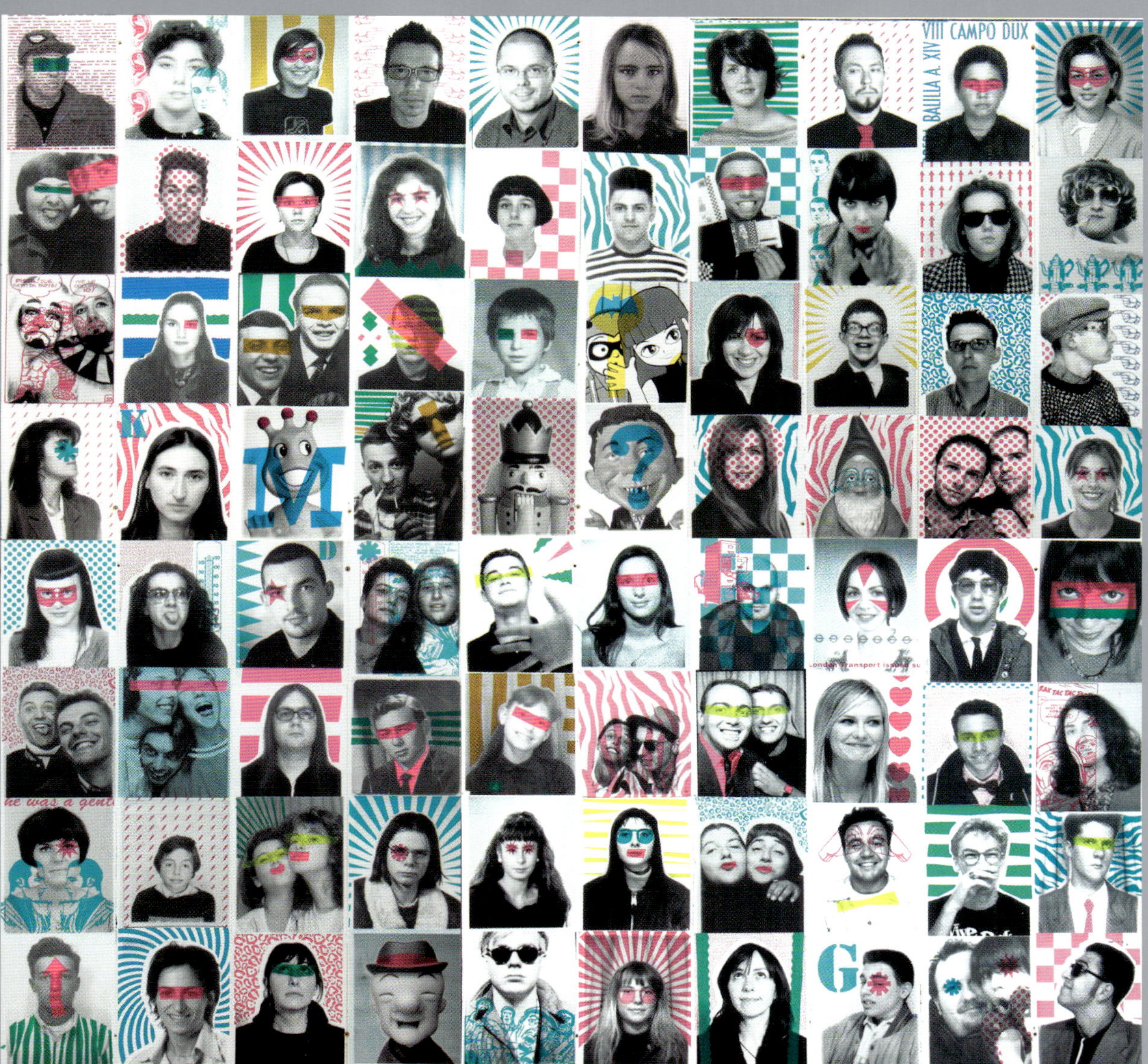

Hall of Fame.

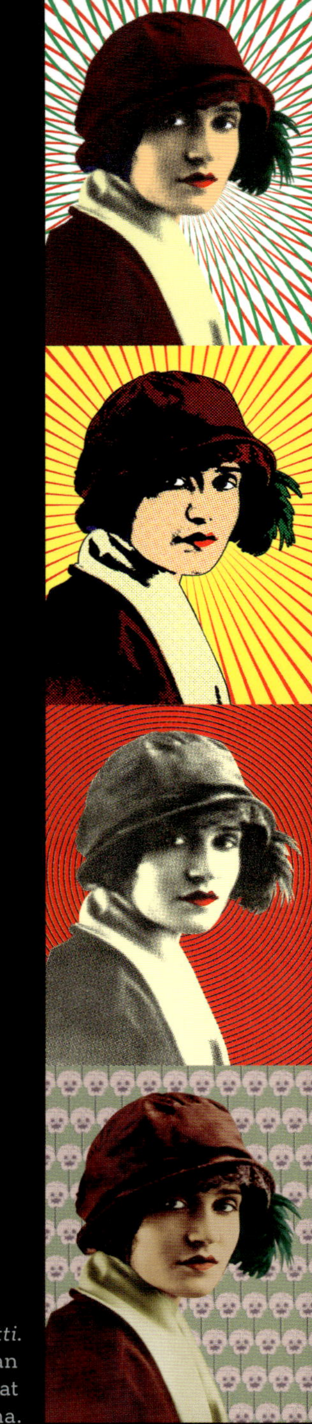

created from an original by Italian
photographer Gianni Pignat, a great
on and admirer of the famous Tina.

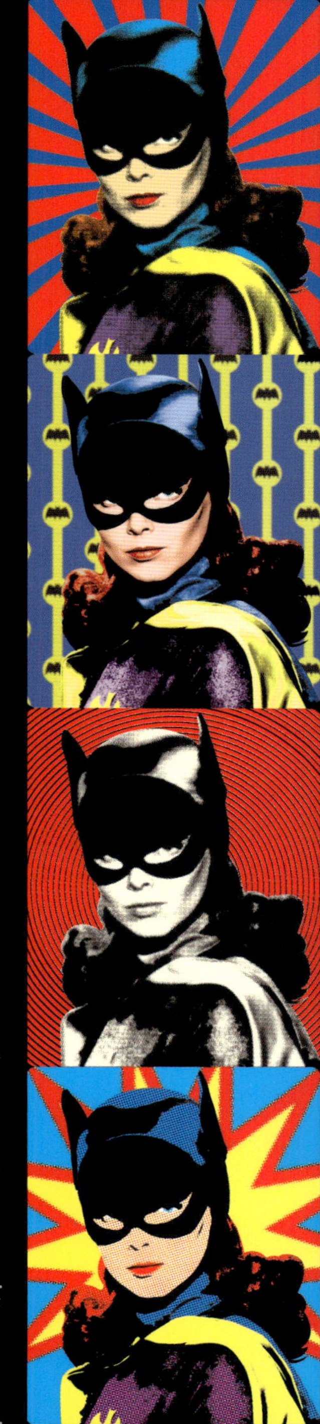

Batgirl.
"I have always loved the world of
Batman and regarded Batgirl as an
ultra-sexy woman! Especially as she
is portrayed by Yvonne Craig in the
Batman television series of the sixties.

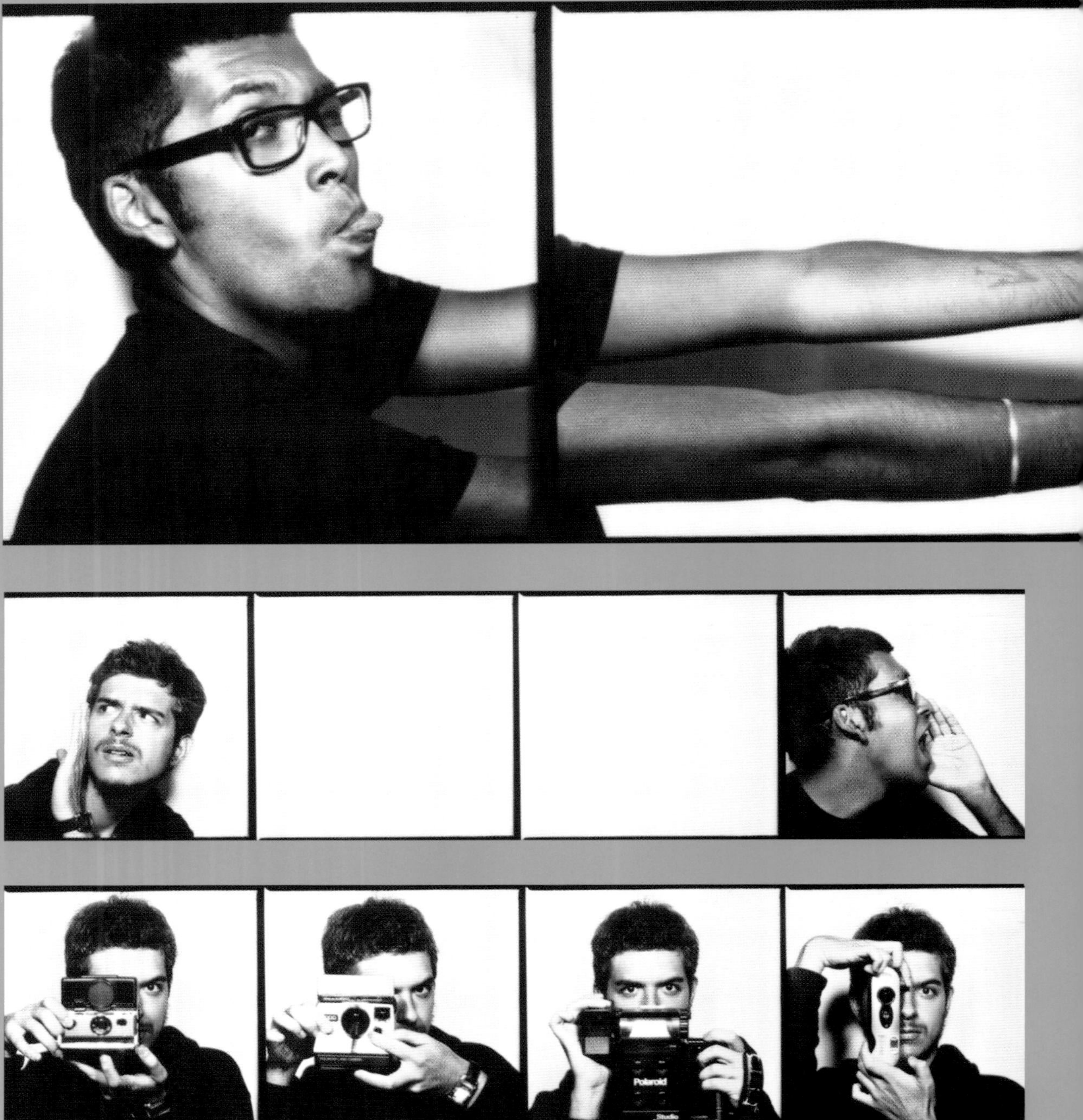

Matteo Jorge Serra.

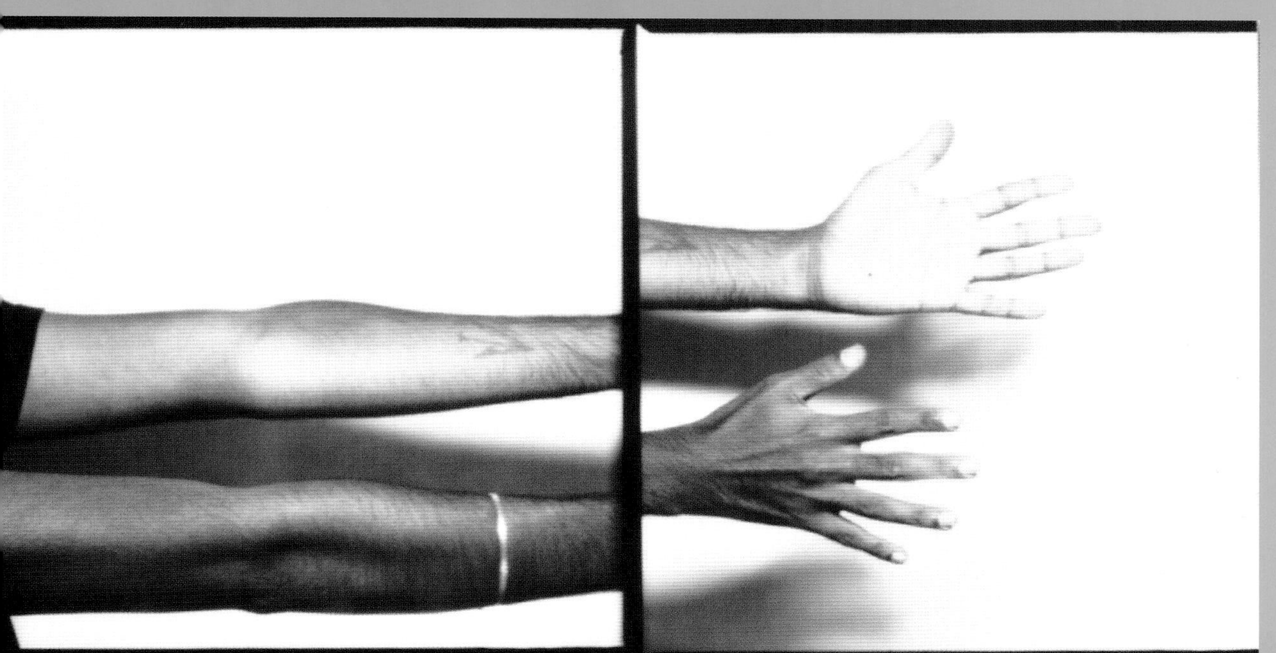

MARCO TAVARNESI

Italian photographer

"I've been in love with instant photos for years. I collect and use all sorts of Polaroids, professional ophthalmological or dental equipment, as well as the cameras used to take passport photos. Without a very clear idea of why, I have the impression that this equipment helps me to create a collection of unique moments. And I consider photobooths to be so many giant Polaroids. I love the vintage silver-emulsion-process booths, the principle of the old curtains that allow you to isolate yourself, the absence of any computerized control, waiting for the film to develop. To take a strip of four photos is an amusing and unpredictable experience that you can share with one friend—or many."

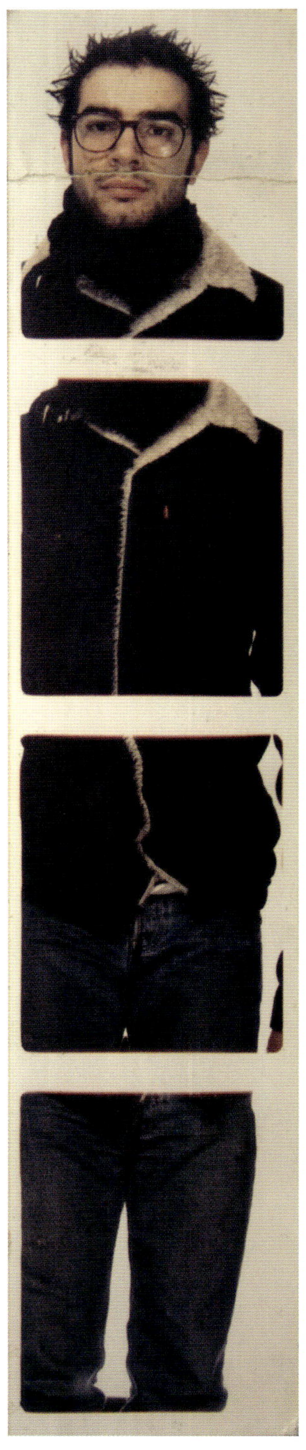

EMILIO CENDÓN

(1977–)
Spanish photographer

"I put together this book of photobooth snaps in December 1999. I was a student at the fine arts school at Bilbao, and I had to do a final project on photographic methodology. After about just two years, from steady use of the photobooth, I had acquired a certain degree of skill in creating 'artworks' in a cramped booth. In order to complete the project, I asked my friends and family to make photobooth snaps, based on the examples that I gave them. The pictures featured in the book, then, were done by members of my family, friends, roommates, and professors. I gave them complete creative freedom, without any intervention on my part. I classified them chronologically, according to when they were shot, and reproduced the notes of each person.

"The cover of the book had to be a photobooth snap! And so I thought of the Russian painter [Kazimir] Malevich and his *Black Square* (1913), which was said to be the sum of all paintings in history superimposed, and then his *White on White* (1918): I deduced that it symbolized the absence of any painting, or else all the paintings that remained to be done. And so this book cover represented, as I understood it, all the photobooth snaps that remain to be taken. There is no authentic photobooth strip, there is no one, the portraits all await completion...."

The first photobooth snap, done in 1997.
"This shot corresponds to a study on the theme of the self-portrait. I hurried over to a photobooth, determined to make a portrait of my body in four parts: the head, the torso, the waist, and the legs. One of the attractions of the photobooth is that it forces me to move, instead of me moving the camera."

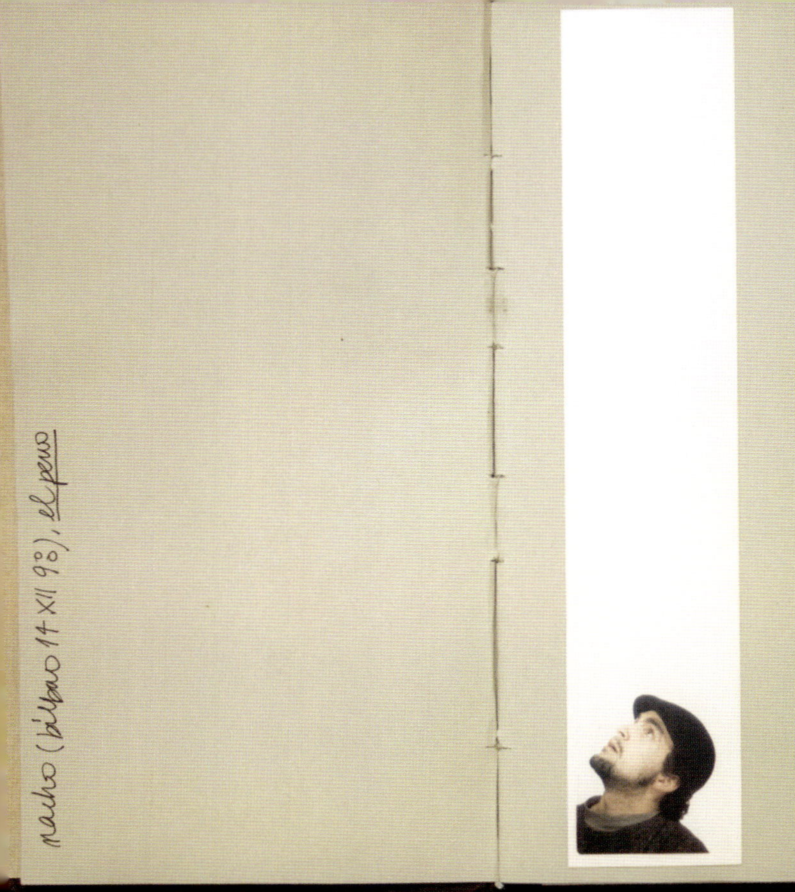

Nacho Vigalondo, filmmaker.
"Nacho was the first to take a photobooth snap for the book. His picture is called *El Perro* (The Dog), with reference to the painting by Goya (one of his famous *Pinturas negras*)."

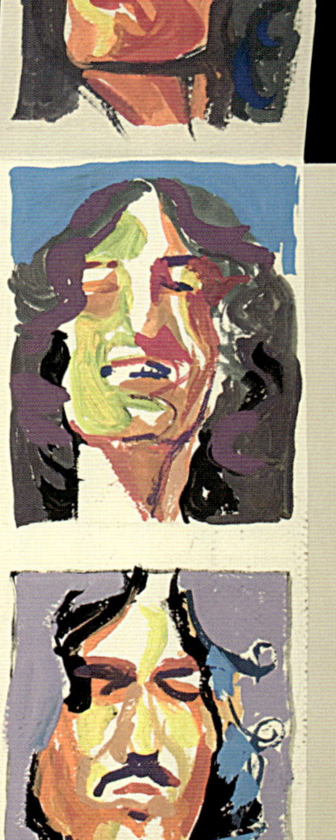

Self-Portrait of Alberto, designer.
"I don't know exactly what happened to him, but something about his vision prevents him from perceiving colors the way the rest of us do. I have to say that he looks the way he does in his sketches. A good resemblance. Since he did not understand the objective of the project, he made large sketches. My good luck…."

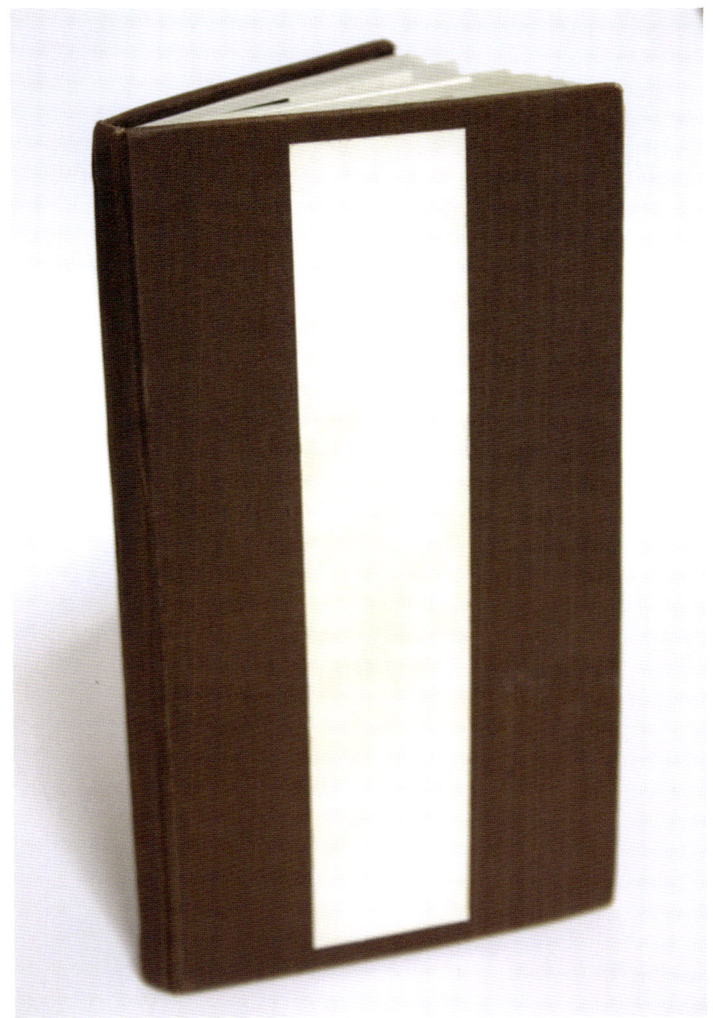

The Cover.

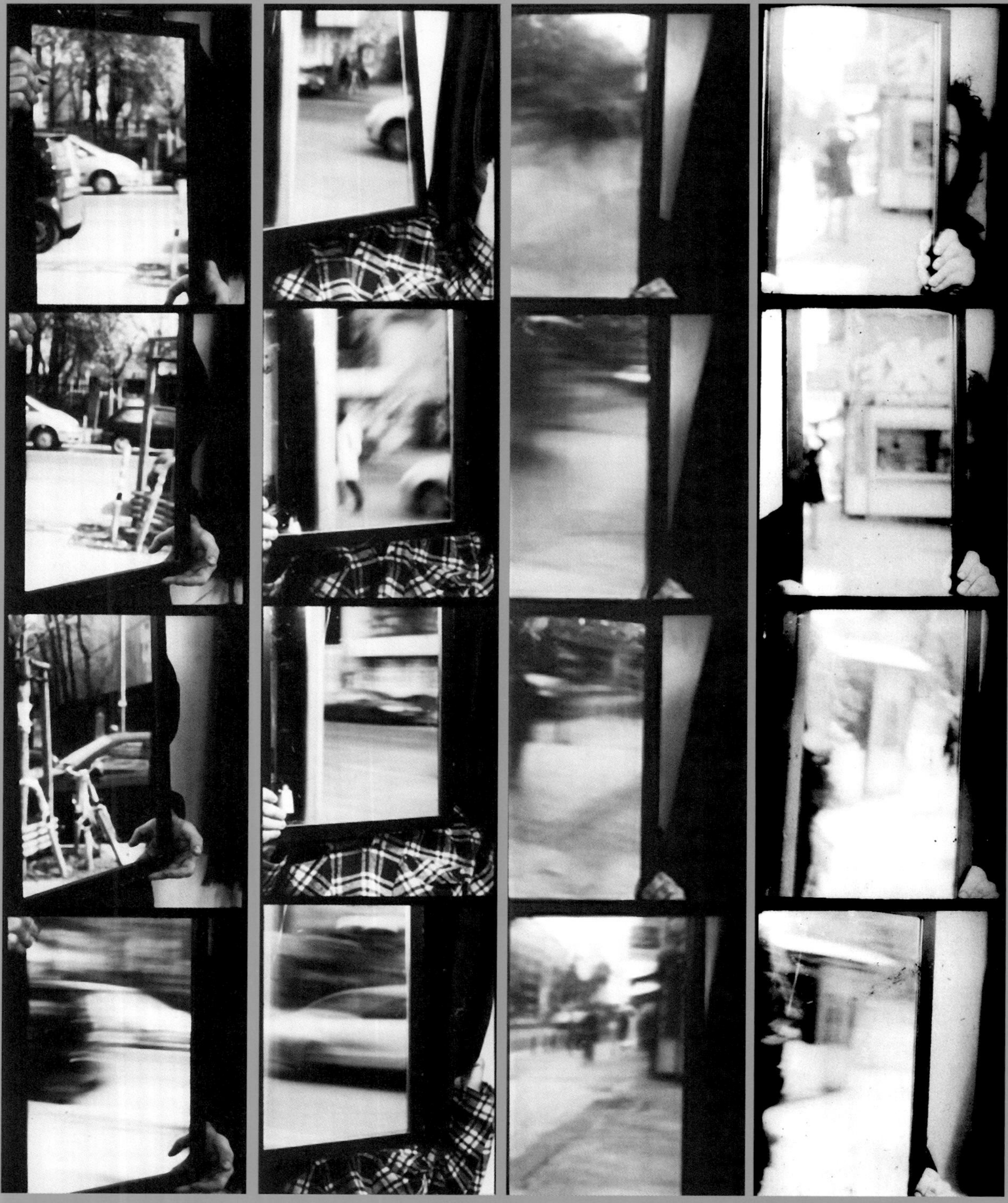

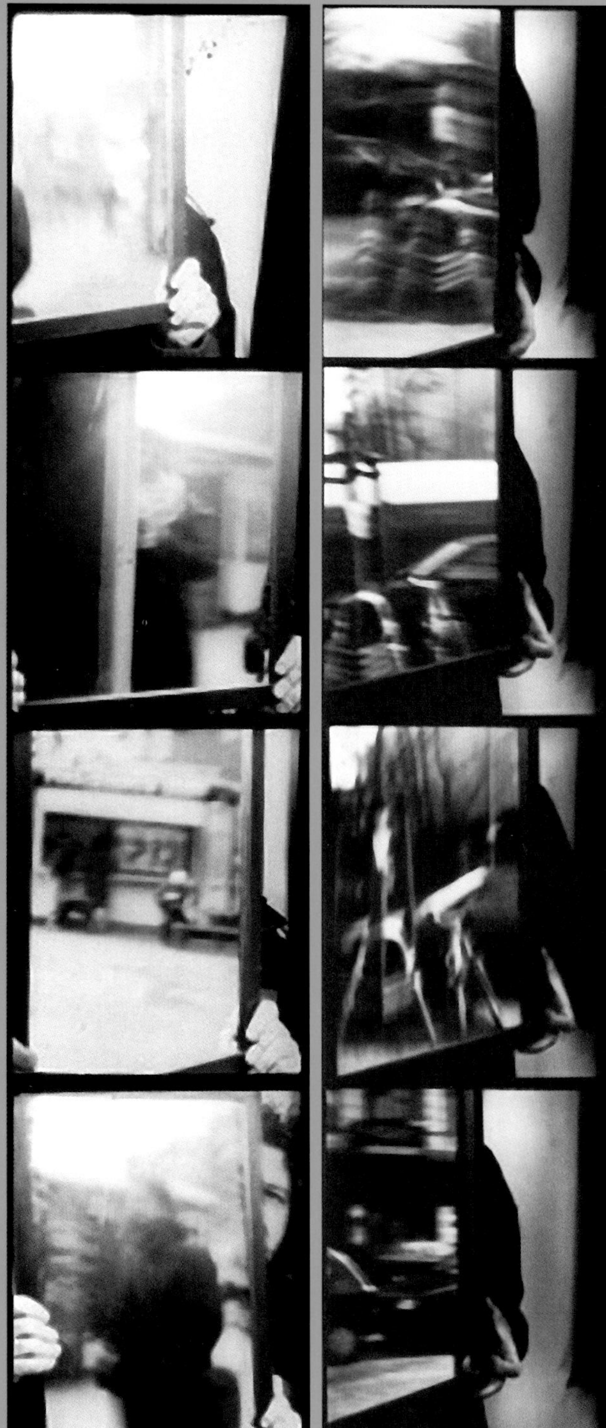

GABRIEL LITWIN

Argentine photographer

"**I**n Berlin, you can still find vintage photobooths. Those silver-emulsion process booths, called Photoautomat in German, produce four different black-and-white shots, in a format of 7.9 × 1.6 in. (20 × 4 cm). They are still pretty popular with the Berliners, who come to get their pictures taken old-style, alone or in a group. For fun or as an experiment.

"Traditional mediums don't particularly interest me. I am far more attracted by alternative technologies applied to the realm of photography. The idea of taking pictures of the landscape or, to be specific, the city, by diverting the photobooth from its primary function, the identity portrait, struck me as so improbable and absurd that the idea seduced me immediately. I love absurd, heroic, and different projects.

"Those photobooths weigh a ton! To move one to take an exterior photograph seemed frankly inconceivable. What's more, since they are designed to take portrait photographs, they are equipped with a single focal length and a fixed diaphragm. I worked around those technical restrictions with the use of mirror and filters and by opening the curtain, which separated me from the intimate space in the street."

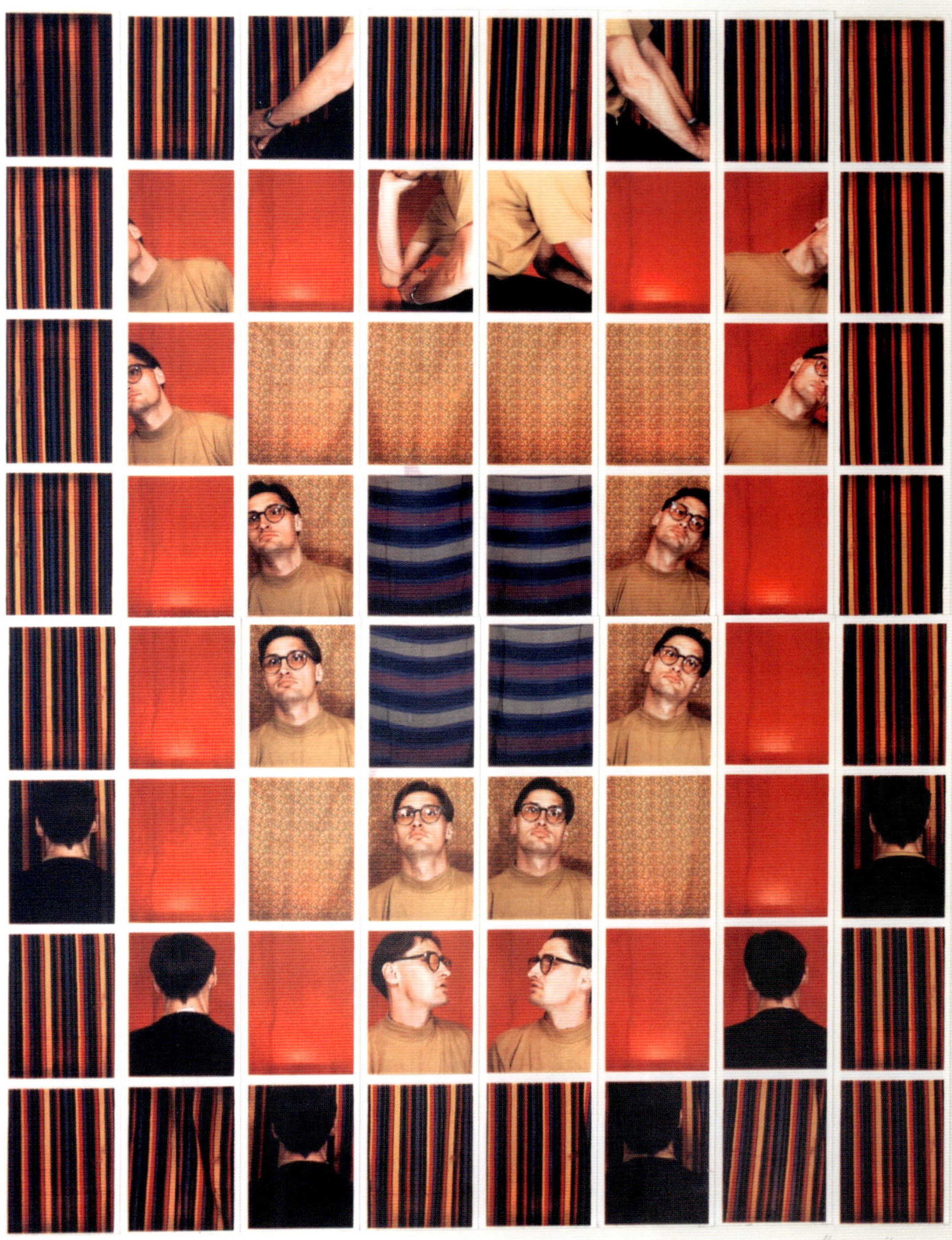

…Oh…, May 1990.

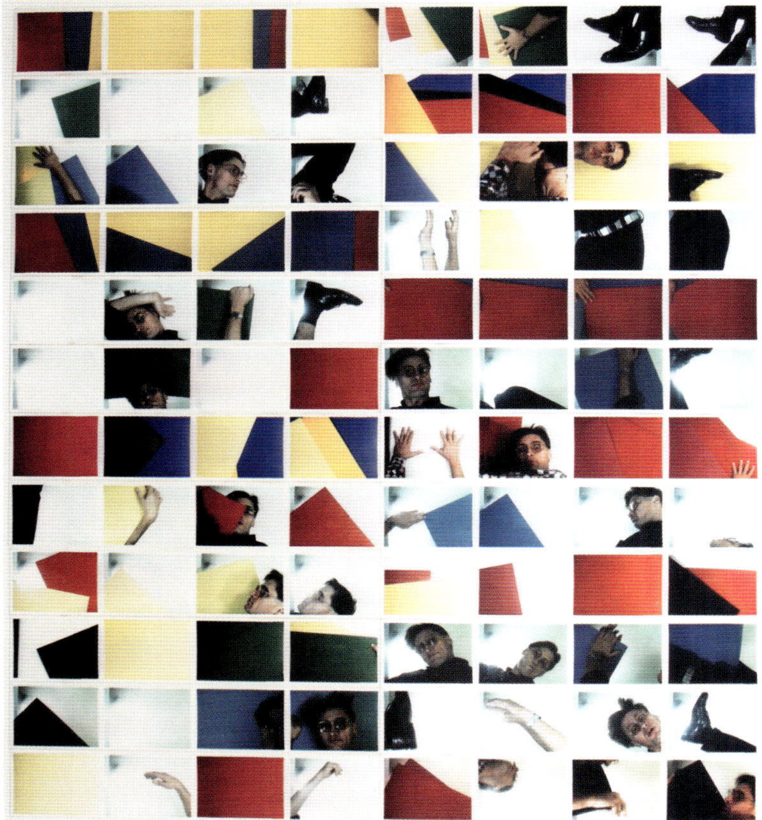

ROLF BEHME

German photographer

"**S**ince 1973, I have focused my artistic work on the blending of photographic techniques. From 1975 until 2000, I created 'fotofix art,' and I worked on it intensely. I love photography in all its forms of expression, but I think that the photobooth snap lost its charm once it went digital.

"At the heart of 'fotofix art' is the concept of self-staged as theater: I recount stories and scenes focused on the fundamental human themes. I never cut a strip, I use them as they came out of the photobooth. In contrast with the standard presentation, my creations follow the course of time, like so many sequences in a movie. I have also created paintings similar to organisms. Moreover, my images are rather fragmented in order to reflect at once the segmentation of human perception and the alienation of the structures of identity."

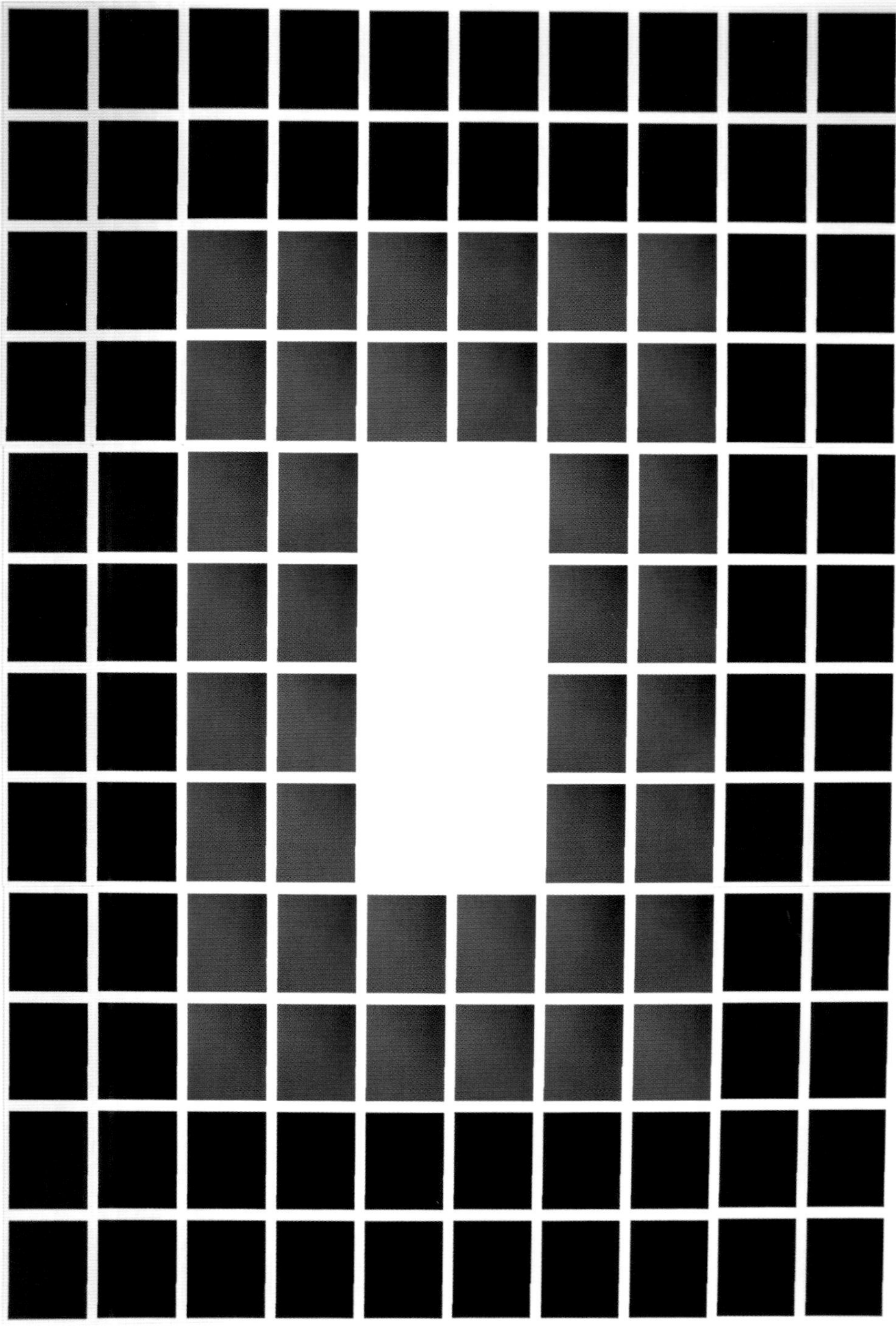

Composition 5, January 1997.

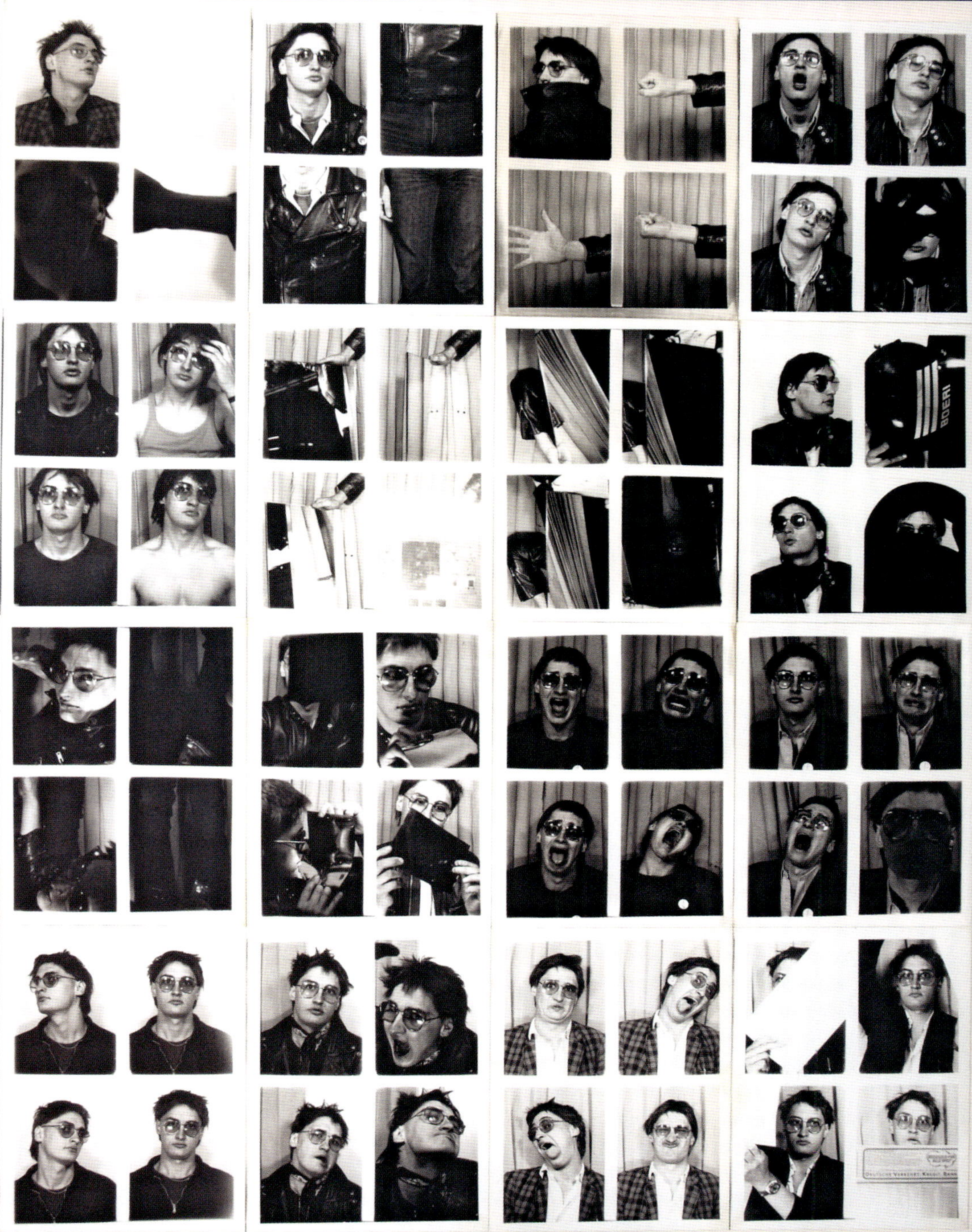

01/1979 - 07/1980, August 1980.

VICTORIA JARVIS

American photobooth artist

"These photobooth photos are simple in concept. I'm just trying to push past conventional uses of the booth. There is a nostalgic draw that keeps people coming back, but the novelty of the photos themselves can wear off, which is what I'm trying to address. By quite literally reaching past the constructed frames, I can manipulate the viewer to see a photo in a different way. I'm very drawn to the uncontrolled variables of the photobooth. I am forced to figure out how to make those elements work for me as they are. This feels less technical and rule-based, and more creative and exciting. I fell in love with photobooths because of their mechanics but also in a desperate attempt to try and do something about their population decline, even if that is simply to take advantage of them while they are still around."

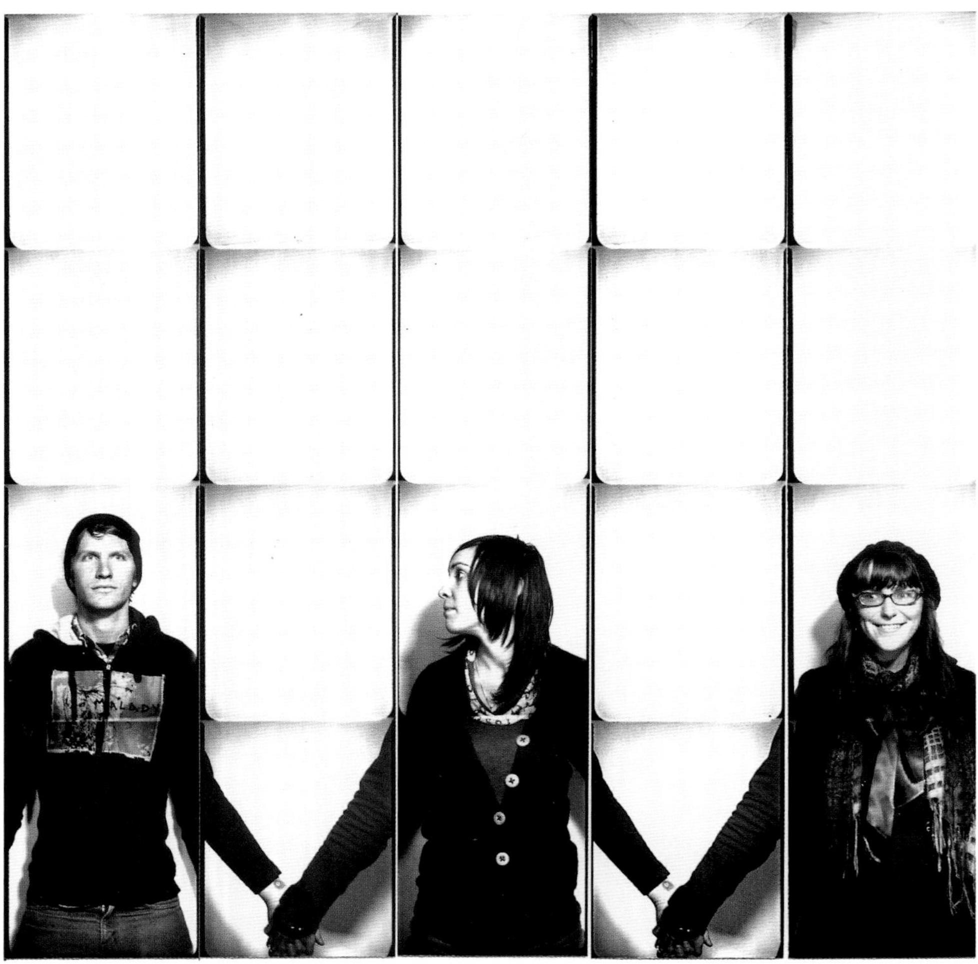

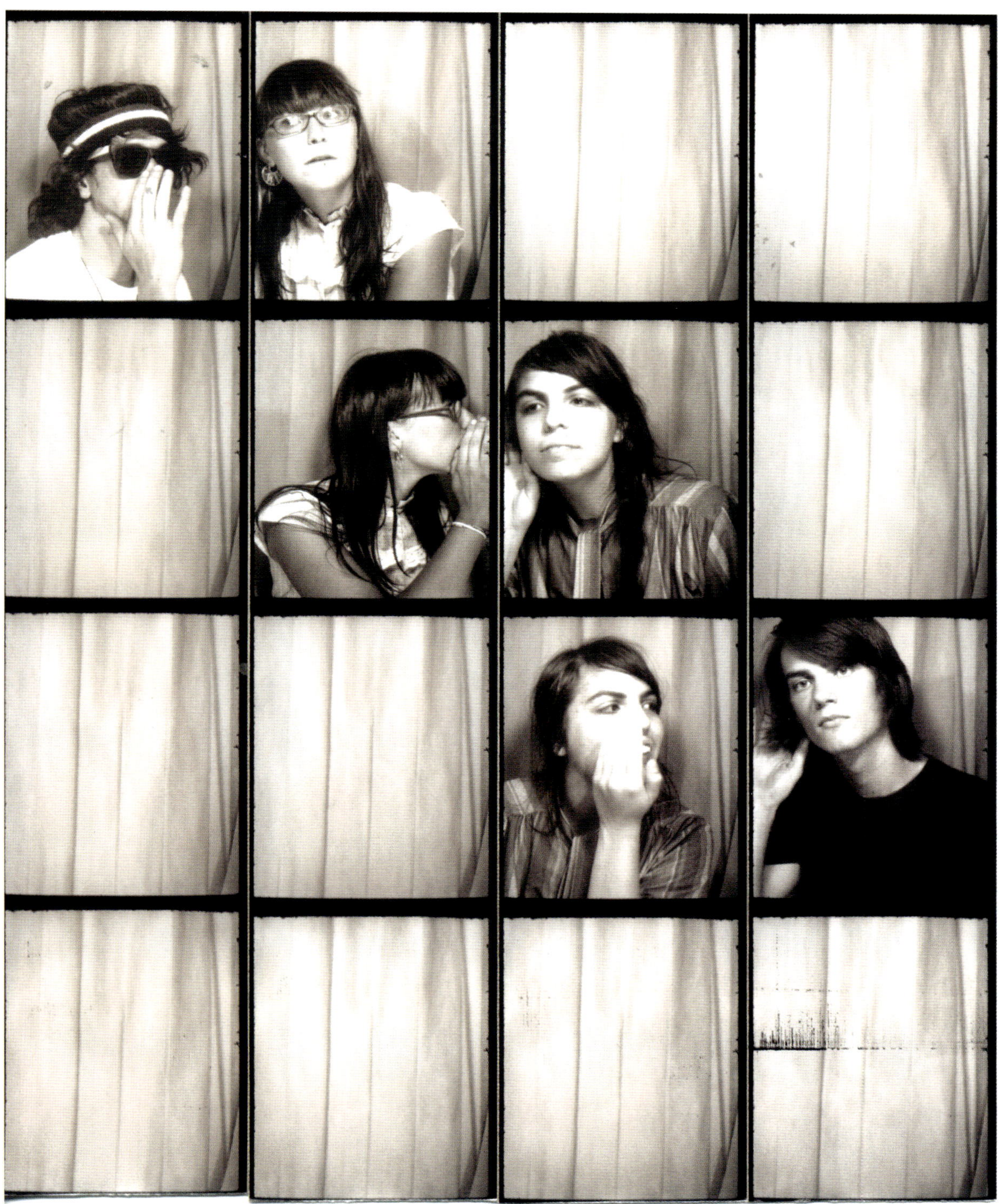

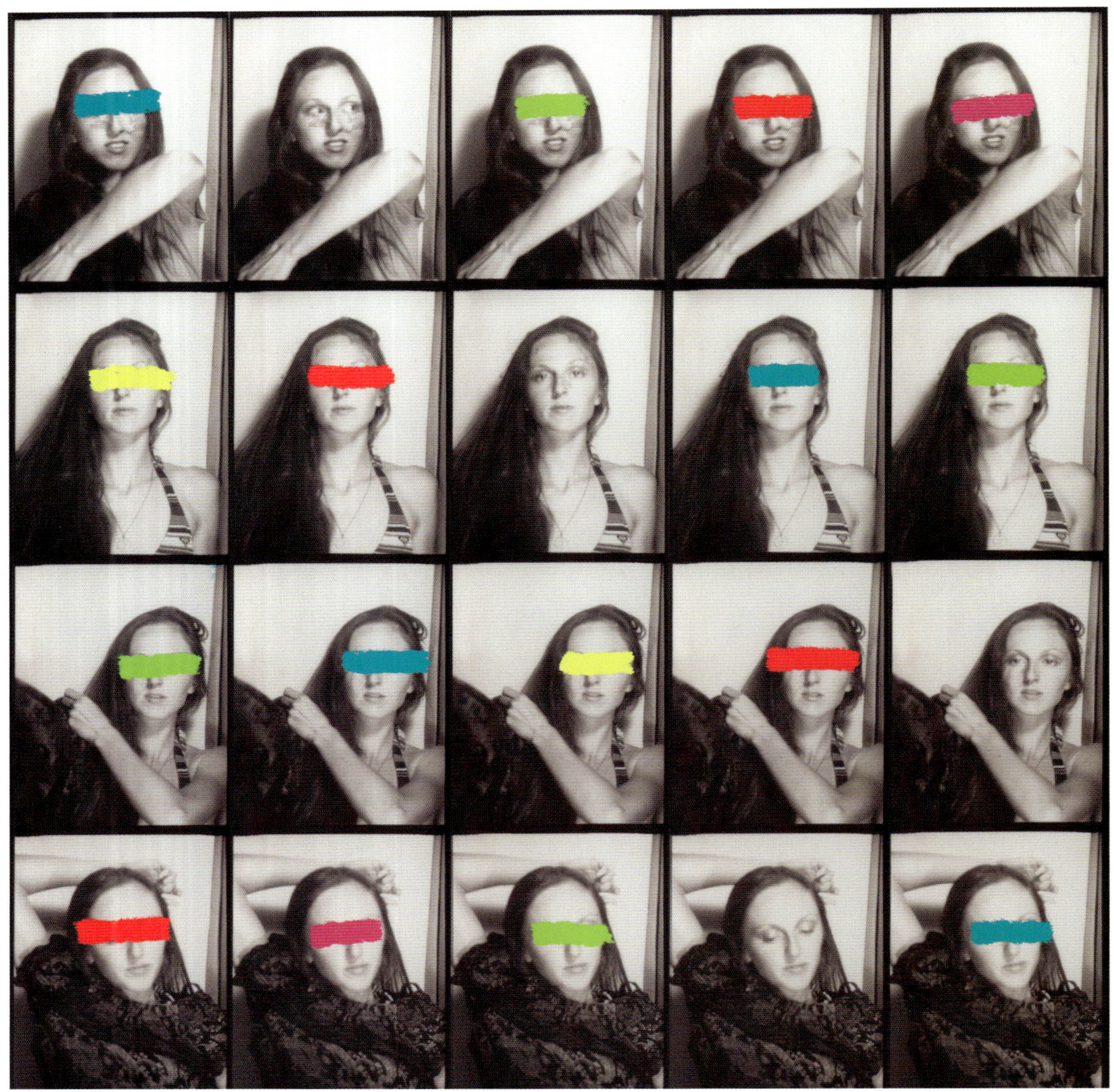

Creature of Habit.

Long Hair.

American photographer

"**M**y [materialistic] goals in life are as follows: 1. Own a beach house. 2. Own a photobooth. Each time I plan a photobooth strip, my goal is to embrace and defy the limitations of my chosen medium. I love the challenge of creating a story in 45 seconds in a small, enclosed space. After enduring the seemingly never-ending three minutes to receive the strip, I have the satisfaction of knowing what I created is one-of-a-kind and original."

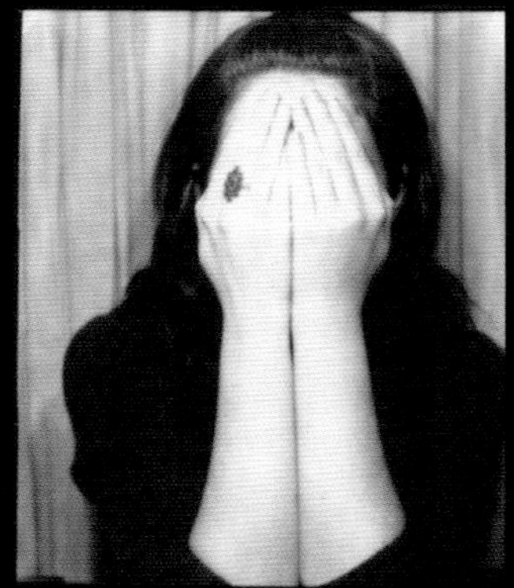
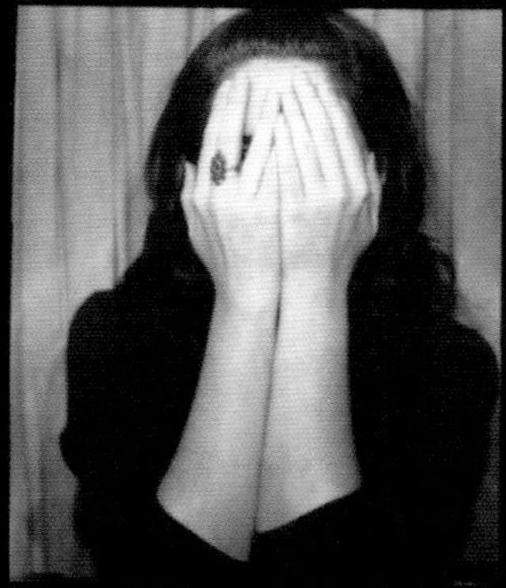

Faceless.

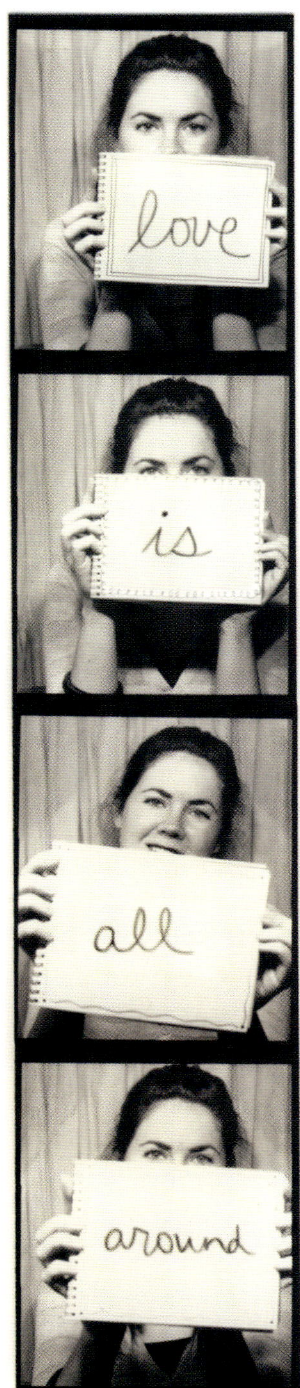

Love.

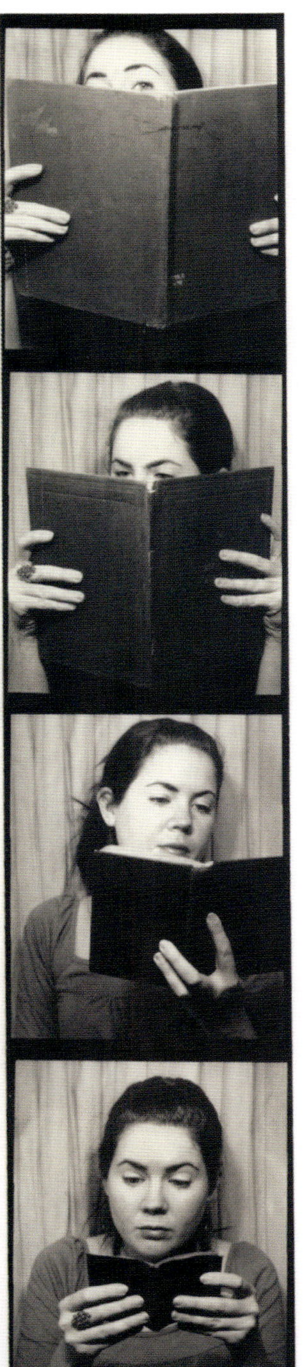

Book.

CORI KINDRED

American artist

"I am intrigued by the sense of nostalgia and a connection with the past.

"I delight in the challenge of 'thinking outside the box' while staying inside four little black-and-white rectangles.

"I admire the contradictions of simplicity and novelty, finding beauty in the imperfections…"

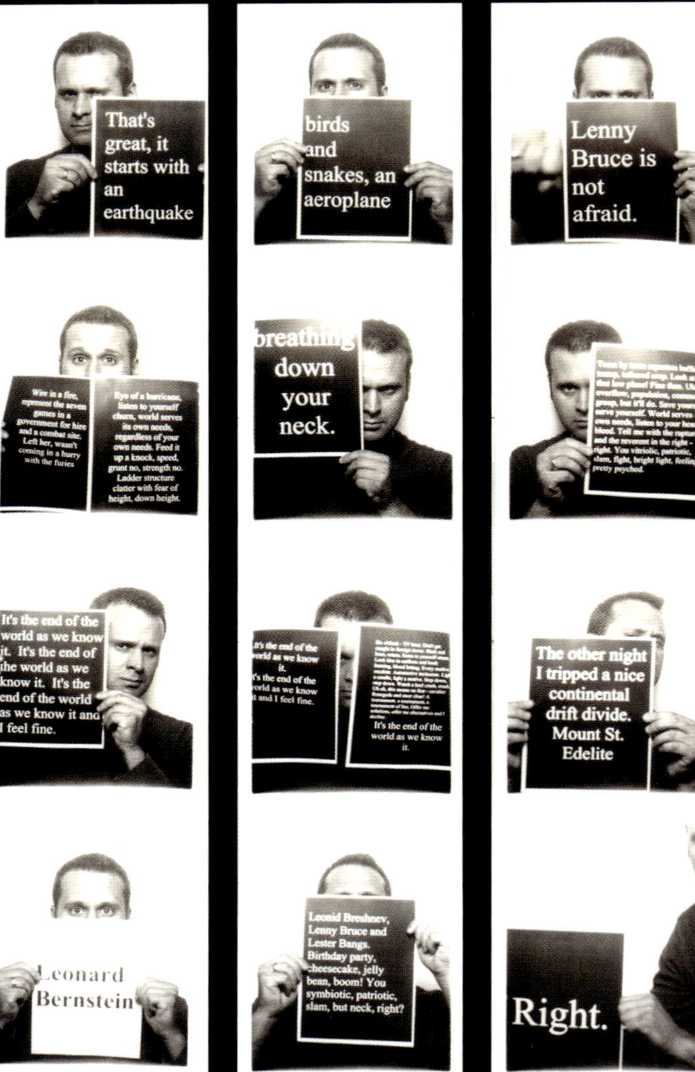

Leonard! Bernstein!

TODD HRYCKOWIAN

Photographer

"**E**very year for my birthday, I go to the Warhol Museum here in Pittsburgh and take a picture of myself in the photobooth. I started doing something simple, different views of my head, but that got boring pretty quickly. So, now I try to challenge myself to come up with something fun each year. I still have no idea if I got all the words right."

KATELL NICOL

Actress

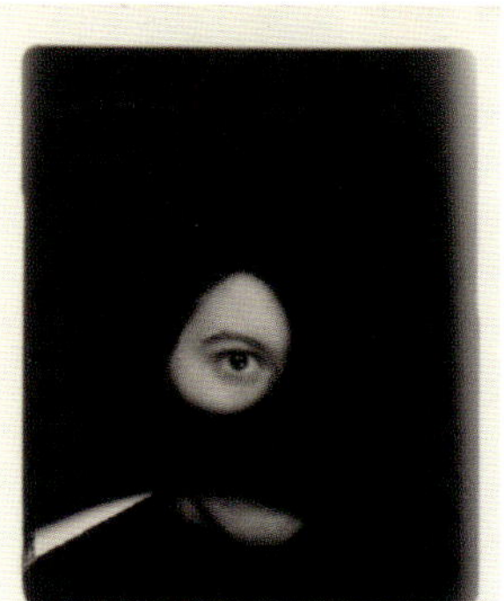

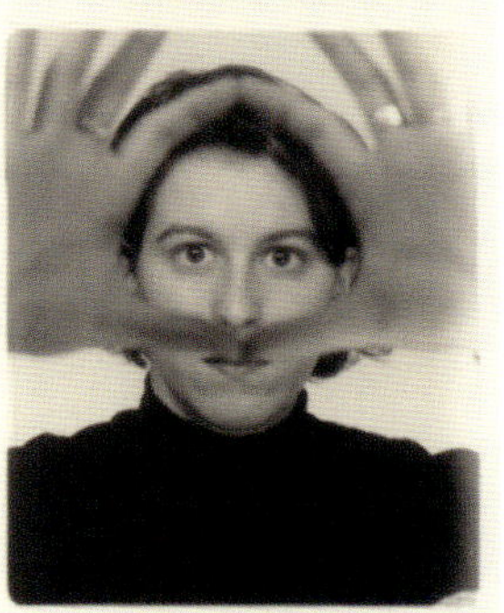

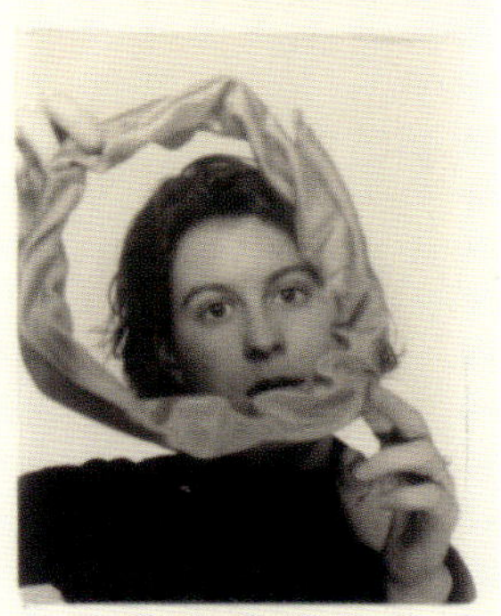

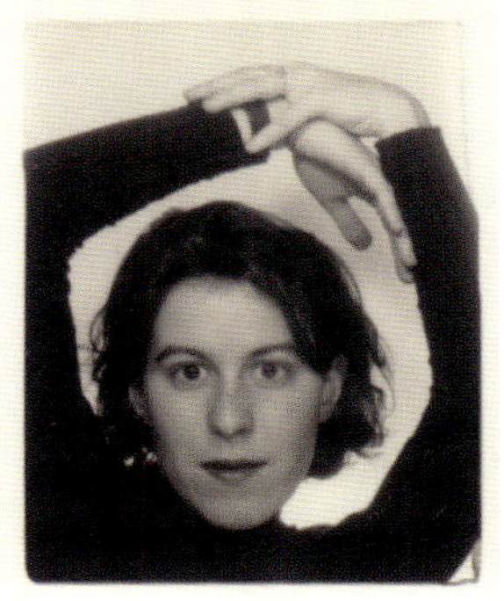

"**I** did these two series of photobooth pictures between 1994 and 1996, when I was a student. I liked playing with this unity of place, to tell a story in four 'panels,' like a comic strip. The very short timing between each flash gave me an adrenalin surge that I really liked. As did the excitement of impatiently waiting to see the result (often defective) as I waited for the photos to develop. More than a formal discourse, a concept, or an 'oeuvre,' it was a game. In that period, I spent a fair amount of time waiting in train stations (places with high concentrations of photo booths). During the week, I would think about the sketch that I was going to stage, a sketch that I would perform while waiting for my train on the weekend. On the back of each photo strip, I noted the date and the place, and you can often read 'Gare de Vannes' or 'Galeries Lafayette' (the department store, my other favorite place)."

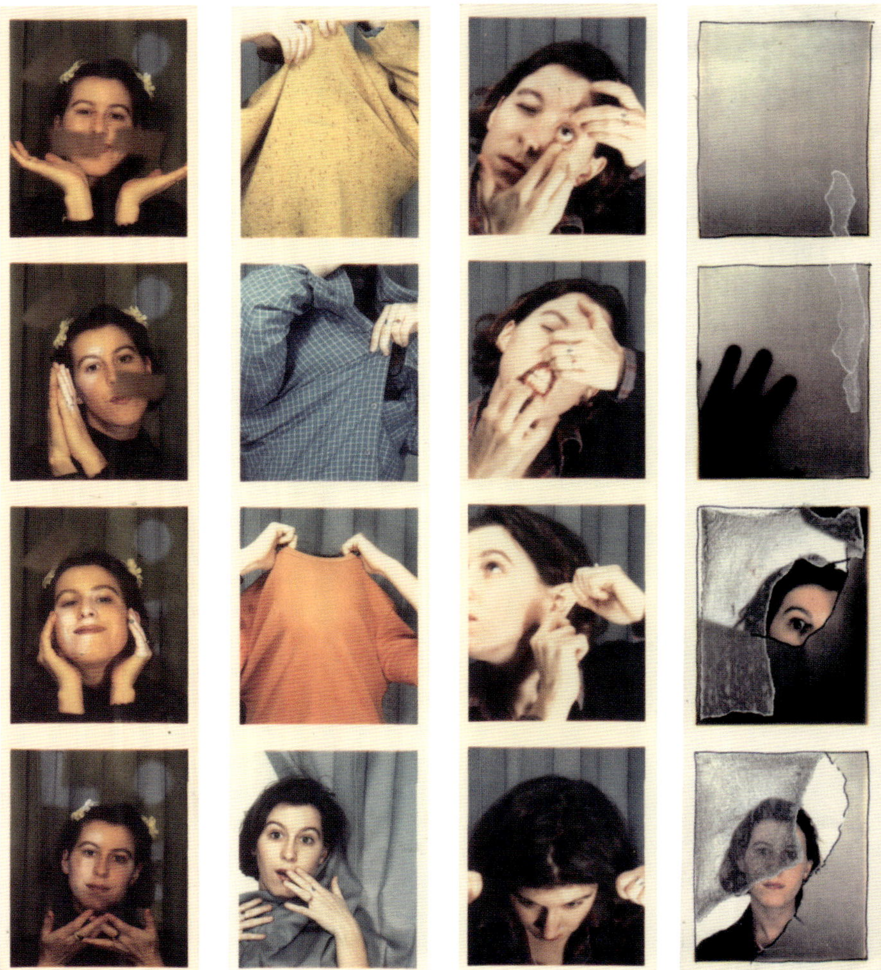

Photo 1: "I had put a yellow strip of celluloid over the glass with the four letters of 'LOVE.' I removed one letter after each flash. The result is not very visible."

Photo 2: "I had put on layers of brightly colored clothing and I took off one article between each photograph."

Photo 3: "Soberly entitled *The Cattle Fair* (because yes, I gave them titles)."

Photo 4: "I had glued a sheet of tracing paper on the glass to play with the transparency, except that the result was extremely opaque!"

Right: "The second series of photos was made in the context of my studies. I had been assigned to do a project on the theme 'habitat/cockpit.' I chose the photobooth as a representation of the living space with archetypal objects or motifs. And so I created an interior decoration, hanging some draperies in the background and sticking some objects on the wall with scotch tape. In one of the photos, you can see my hand holding up a cushion."

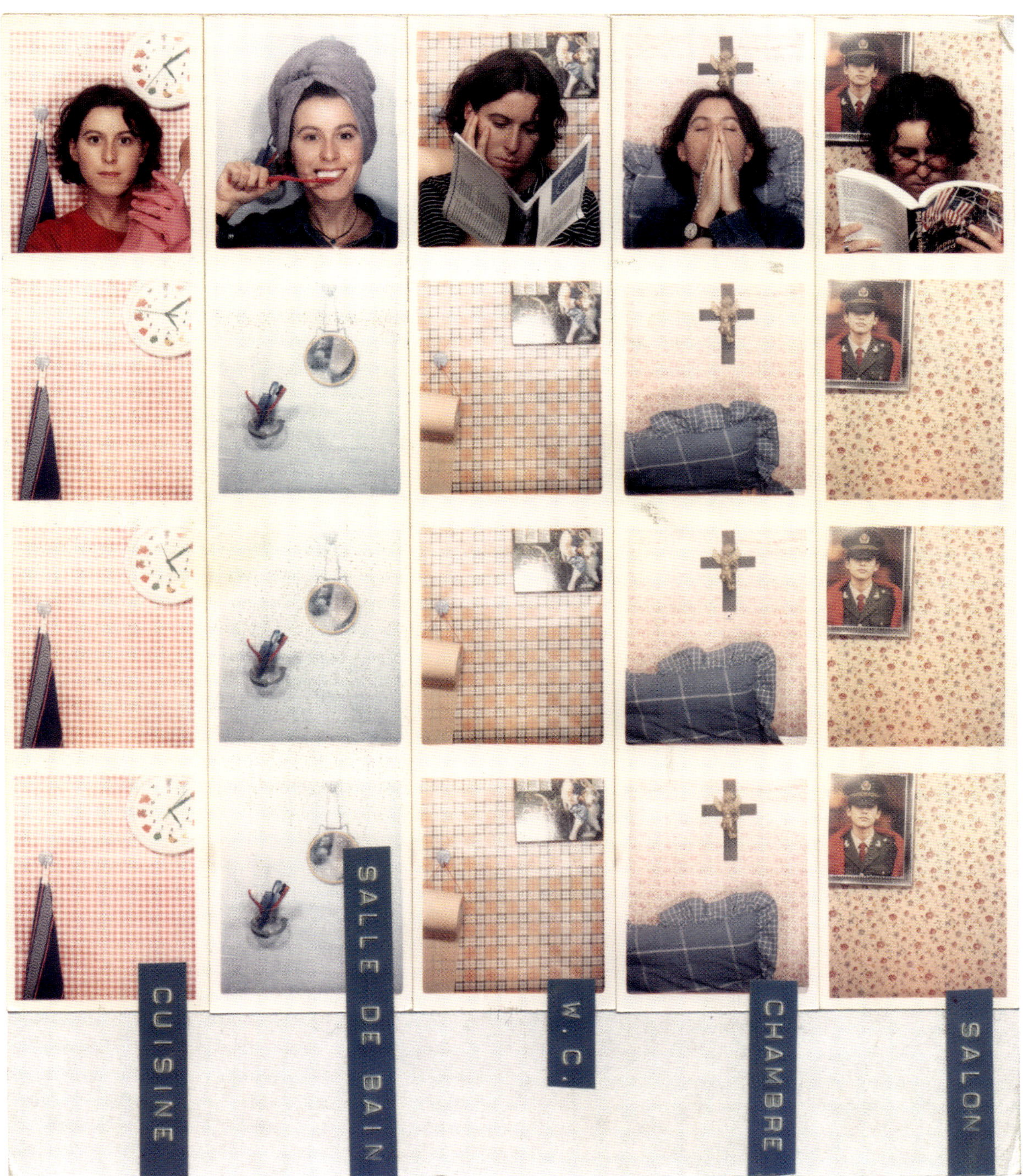

CUISINE
SALLE DE BAIN
W.C.
CHAMBRE
SALON

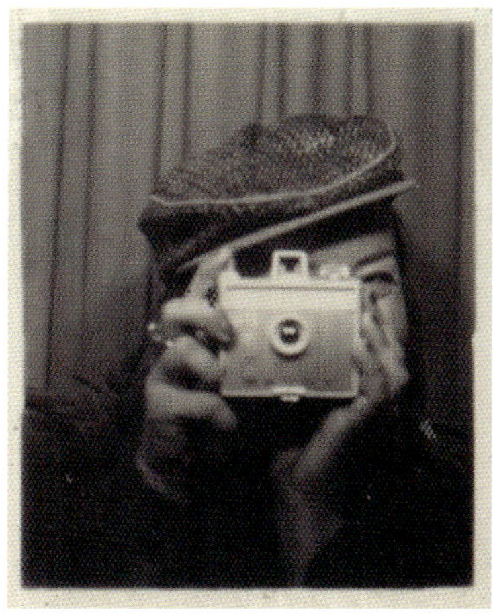

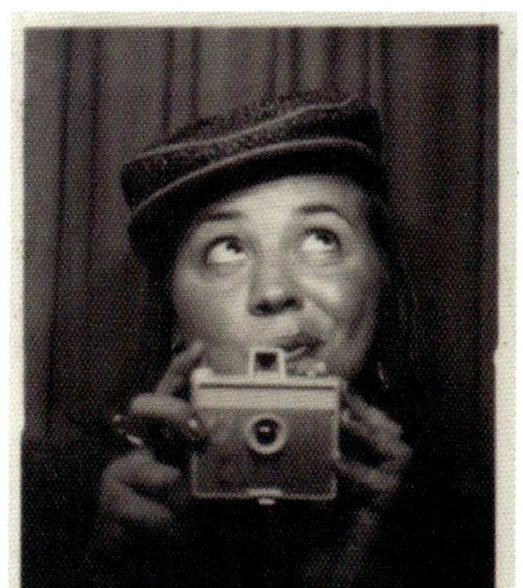

ANDREA CORRONA JENKINS

Photographer

"**E**very once in a while, I get the urge to take out my collection of photobooth strips and arrange them all in chronological order. From 1972 to 2010, they span close to four decades and nearly stretch from one end of the room to the other. I marvel at the fragmented and spectacular way they tell my life story. From dime stores to amusement parks, hotel lobbies to shopping malls, arcades to diners, there always seems to be a photobooth somewhere for me to hop into. I have grown to love the sight of that glowing 'photobooth' sign, that little circular stool that spins around and around, that short pleated curtain. Nothing makes my heart race like the four bright flashes of light that pop and fire as my picture is being taken. In that moment, I can be whoever I want to be. I am both subject and photographer. But perhaps what I love most is what happens afterwards—the moment the photobooth miraculously spits my strip out. There, in four frames or less, is a little bit more of my story, a story that is best told through the anonymous eyes of the beloved photobooth."

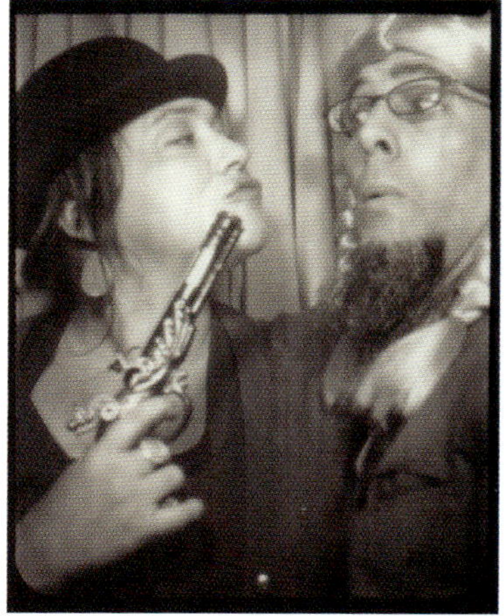

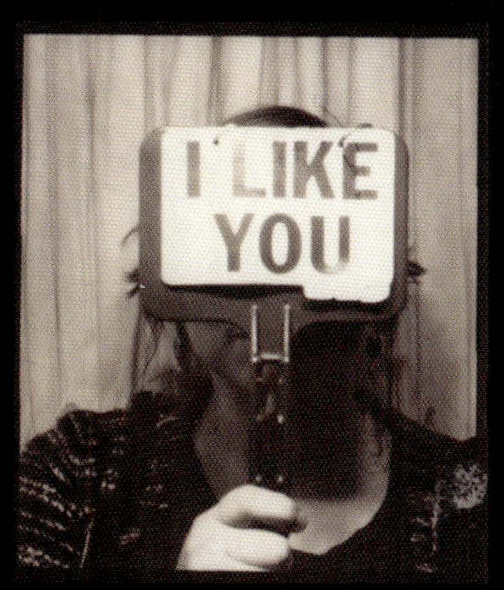
I LIKE
YOU

GALLERY

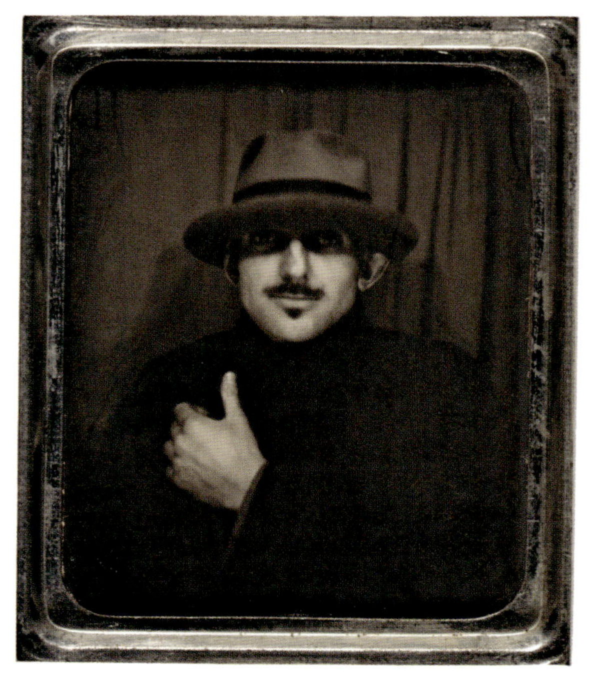

Ansel Adams
(1902–1984)
American photographer
c. 1930

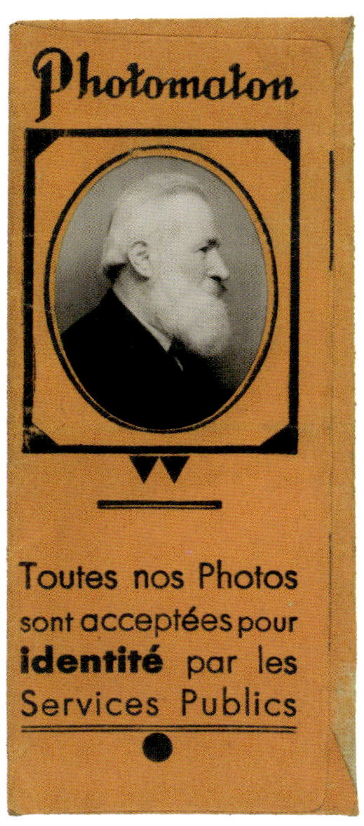

Constantin Brancusi
(1876–1957)
Romanian sculptor
c. 1930

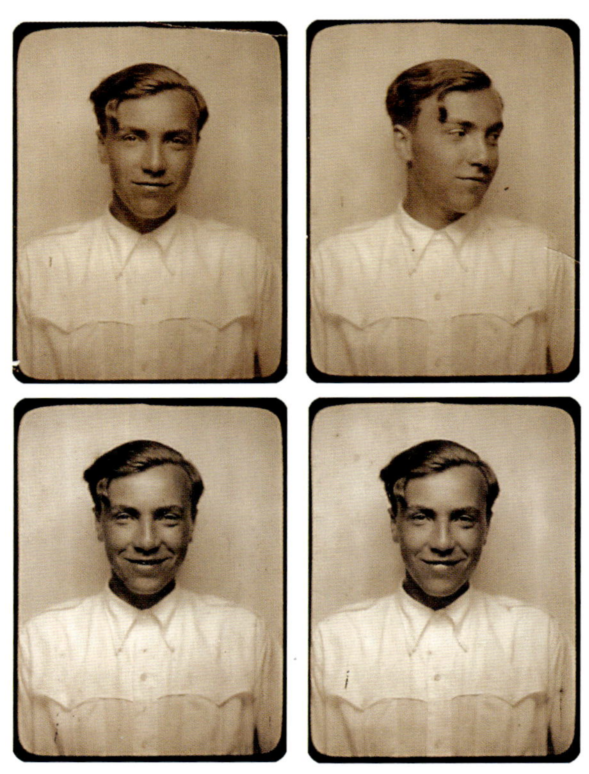

Antonio Delfini
(1907–1963)
Italian author and poet
c. 1930

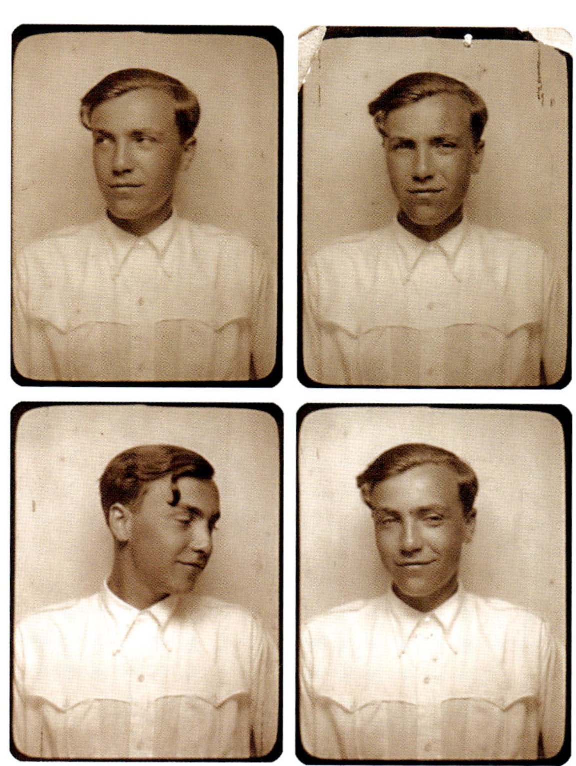

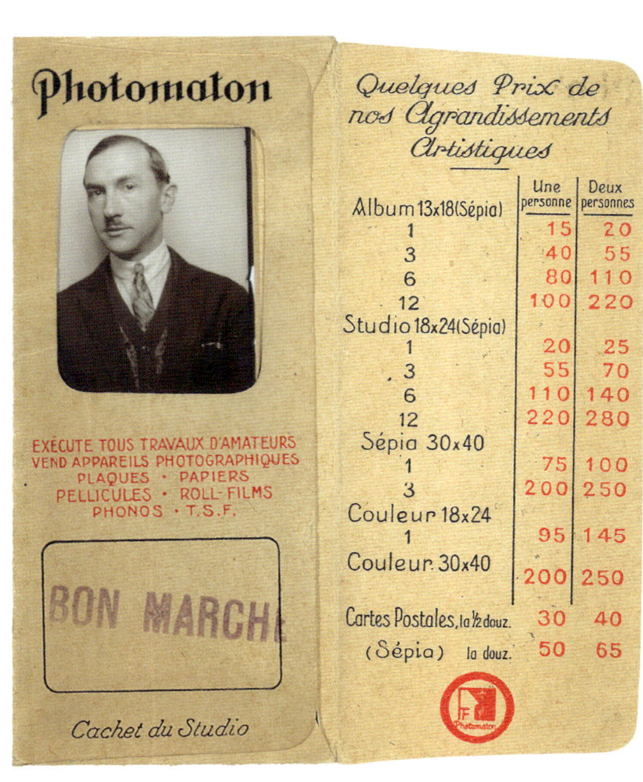

Joseph Delteil
French writer (1894–1978)
c. 1928

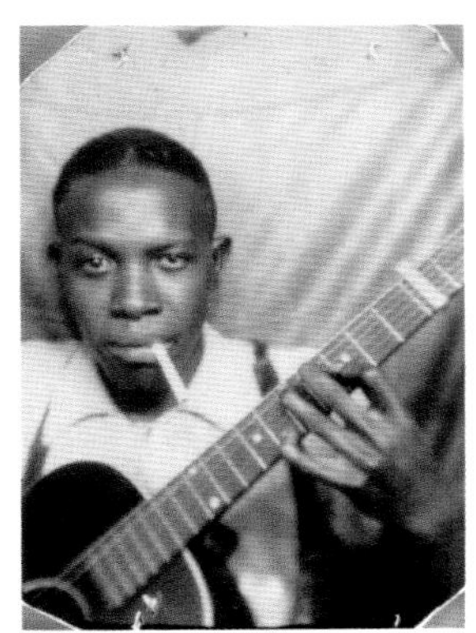

Robert Johnson
(1911-1938)
American blues guitarist and singer born in Mississippi.
There are thought to be only two extant photos of
Johnson, and this photobooth photo probably dates from
1930. The second photo dates from 1938 and was taken
at the Hooks Brothers Photographers studio in Memphis.
The two pictures were discovered by Stephen LaVere
(author of a biography of Robert Johnson and founder of
the Greenwood Blues Heritage Museum and Gallery).

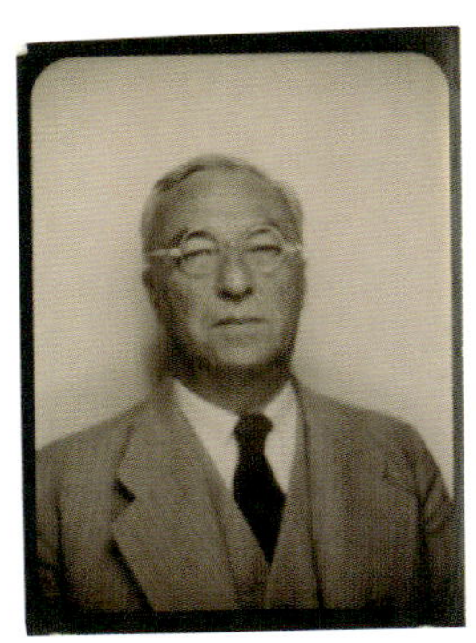

Wassily Kandinsky
(1866–1944)
Russian painter

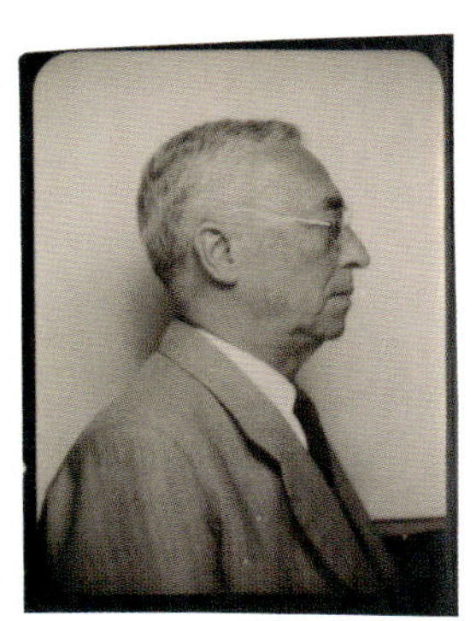

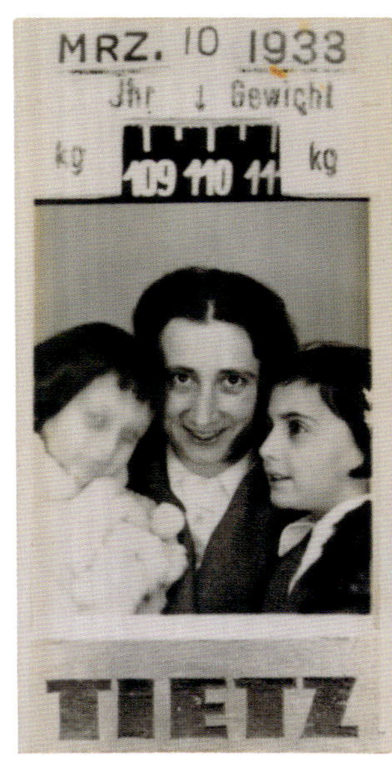

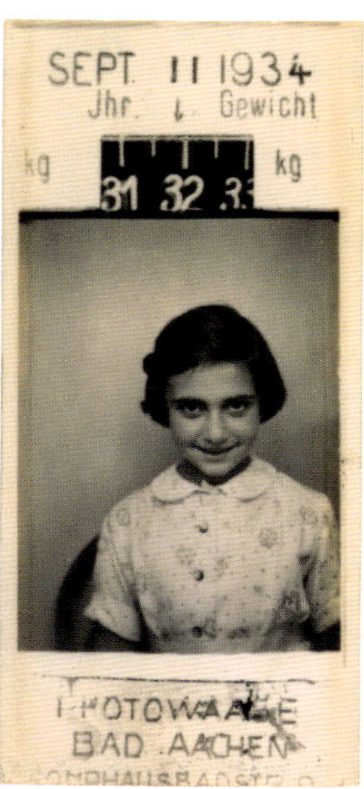

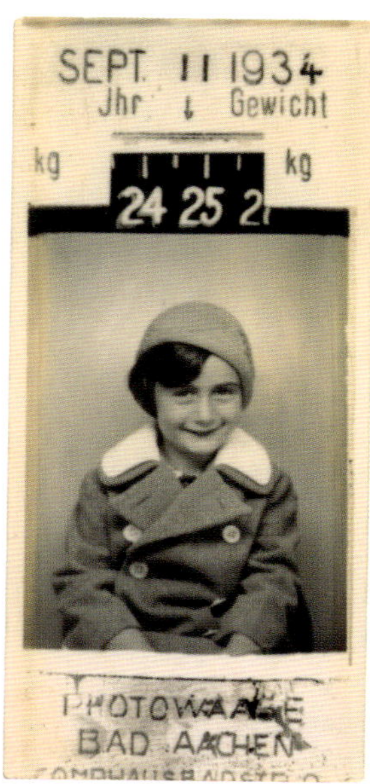

Anne Frank
(1929–1945)
German Jewish adolescent, the author of a personal diary of her
life in hiding from June 12, 1942, to August 1, 1944.

Left: Edith Frank-Holländer and her two daughters, Anne (left) and Margot.
Dated March 11, 1933, this picture was taken in a photobooth in a department
store, Thiez, in Frankfurt, Anne Frank's hometown. In April 1933, two months after
Adolf Hitler came to power, the first anti-Jewish laws were decreed. The Frank
family left Nazi Germany and took refuge in Amsterdam, the Netherlands.

Center and right: Anne and Margot Frank.
These two photos dated March 11, 1934, were probably taken during a
visit to their maternal grandmother in Aachen, near the Dutch border. In
July 1942, the Frank family went into hiding. On August 4, 1944, after being
reported, they were arrested and deported to concentration camps.
Edith Frank died in January 1945 at Auschwitz-Birkenau. Anne and Margot Frank died in
March 1945 at Bergen-Belsen. They were, respectively, fifteen and seventeen years old.

Otto Frank survived Auschwitz and published his daughter's diary in 1947. In 2009,
UNESCO entered the *Diary of Anne Frank* in the registry of the Memory of the World.

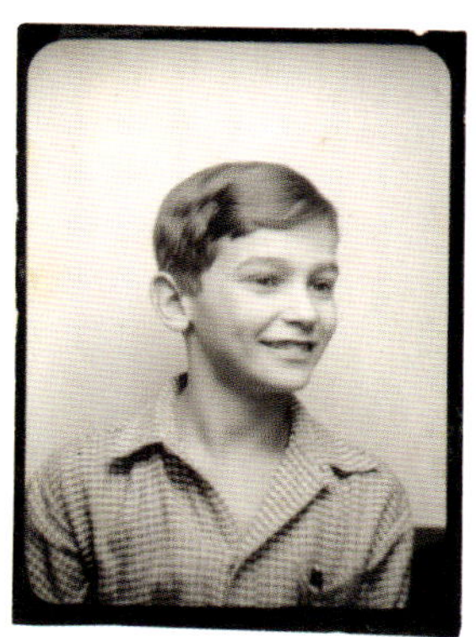

Peter Schiff
The young boy with whom Anne Frank fell in love in Amsterdam during
the summer of 1940. He was thirteen at the time, she was eleven.

"Peter was the ideal boy: tall, good-looking and slender, with a
serious, quiet and intelligent face. He had dark hair, beautiful brown
eyes, ruddy cheeks, and a nicely pointed nose. I was crazy about
his smile, which made him look so boyish and mischievous."
—Extract from *The Diary of Anne Frank*, dated Friday, January 7, 1944

This photograph dates from 1939 and was saved by Ernst Michaelis, a former
classmate of Peter Schiff. It was donated to the Anne Frank House at the
beginning of 2008. Ernst Michaelis and Peter Schiff attended the same Jewish
school in Berlin, the Holdheim Schule, in the late thirties. In 1939, Schiff left
Germany with his family and traveled to Amsterdam. That was when he gave
the picture to his friend: *Zum Freundlichen Andenken an deinen Freund Lutz
Peter Schiff* ("In fond remembrance of your friend Lutz Peter Schiff").

Peter Schiff died on May 31, 1945 at Auschwitz, four months after
the liberation of the camp. He was eighteen years old.

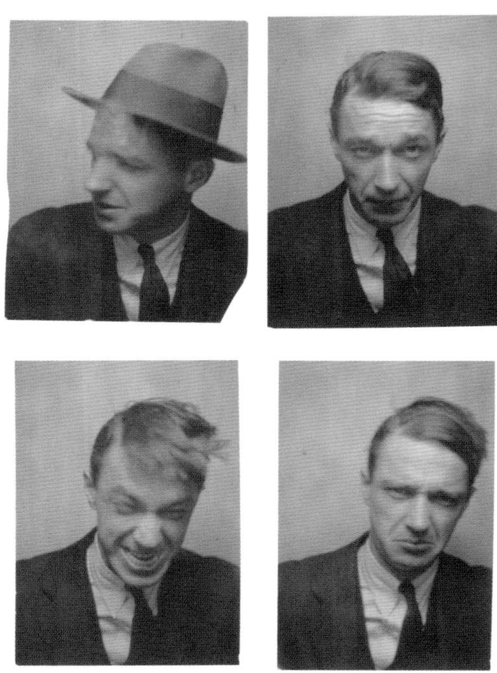

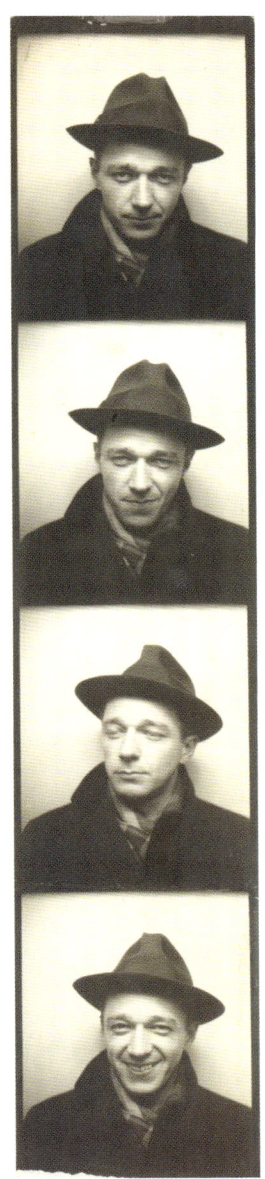

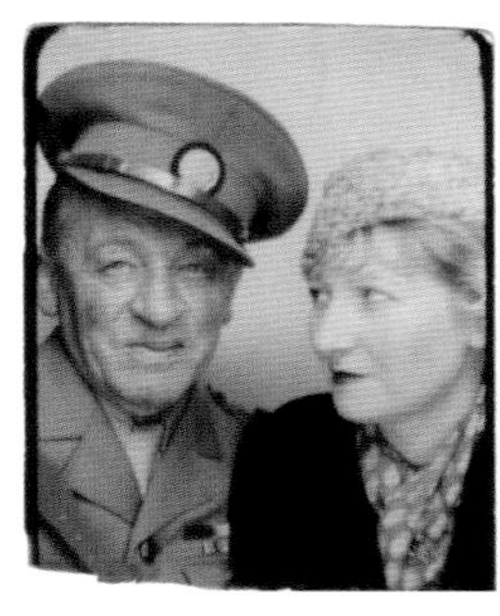
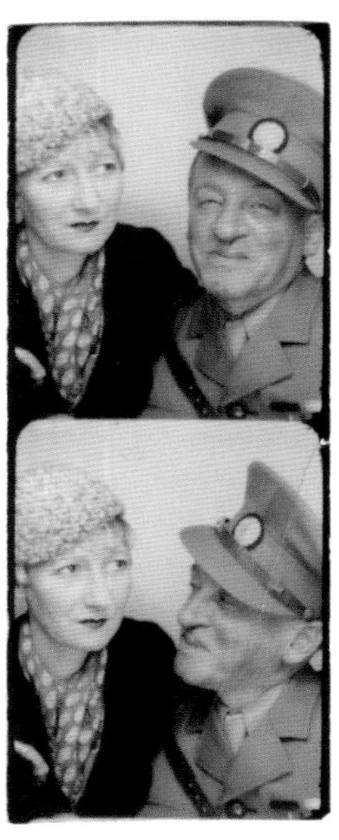
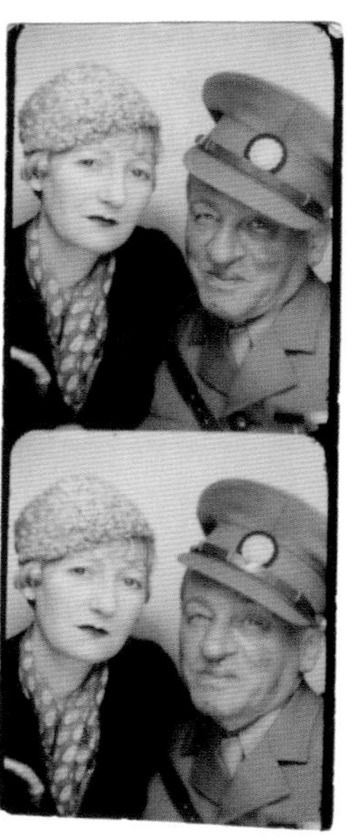

Blaise Cendrars
(1887–1961)
Swiss-born French author
Photos dated September 1939. Blaise Cendrars, in British uniform, was appointed
a "war correspondent" for a number of French publications and attached to
the headquarters of the British Expeditionary Force (BEF) at Arras.
"In Paris, Blaise encountered his friend the actress Raymone Duchâteau, whom
he hadn't seen in two years. They celebrated their reconciliation by posing
together for these photobooth souvenirs." —Miriam Cendrars

Alexander Archipenko
(1887–1964)
Ukrainian-American sculptor
c. 1930

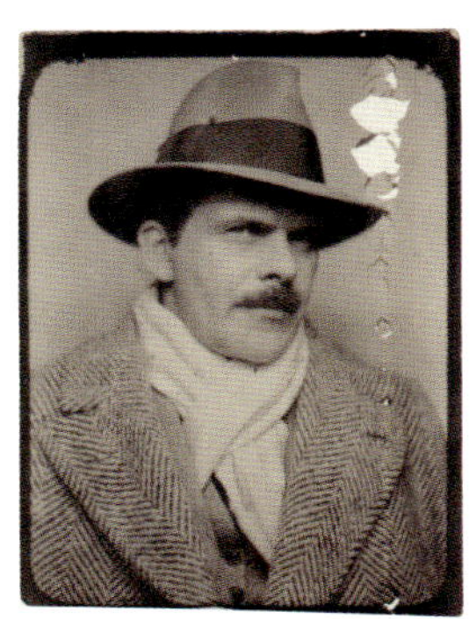

261

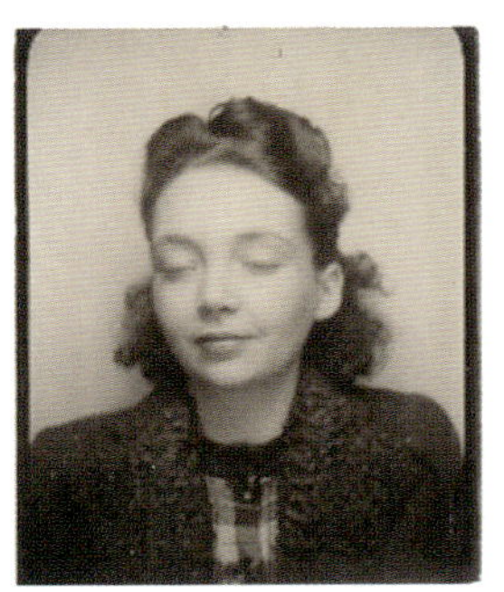

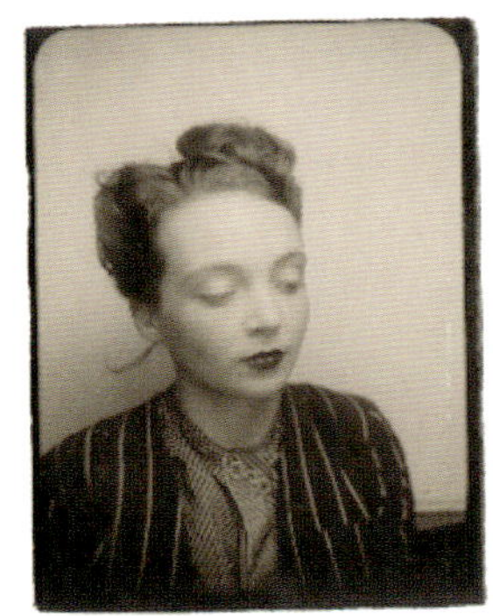

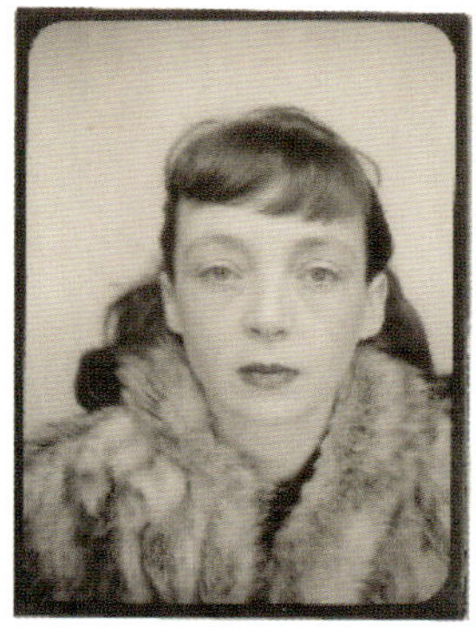

Marguerite Duras
(1914–1996)
Filmmaker and author

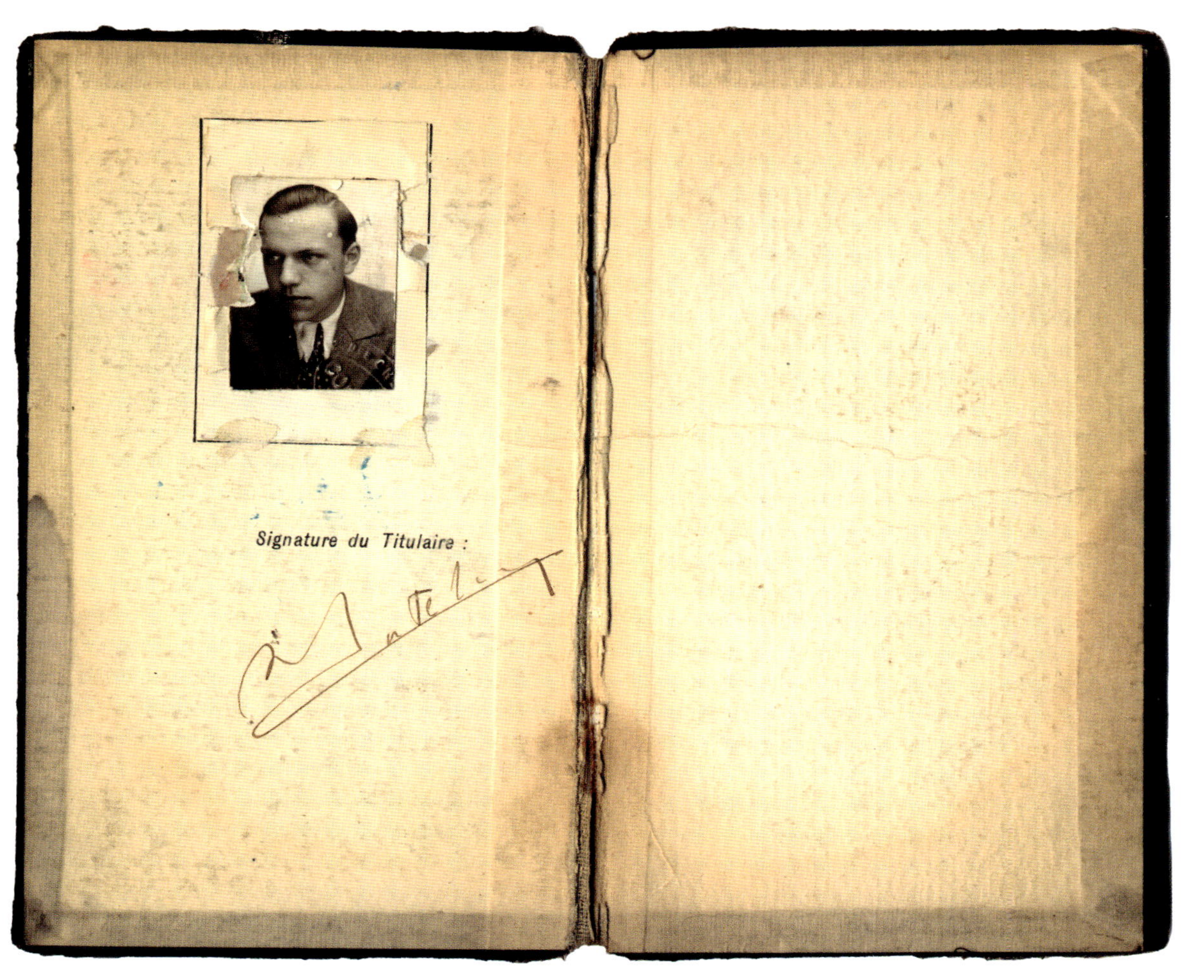

Robert Antelme
(1917–1990)
Poet, married to Marguerite Duras between 1939 and 1946

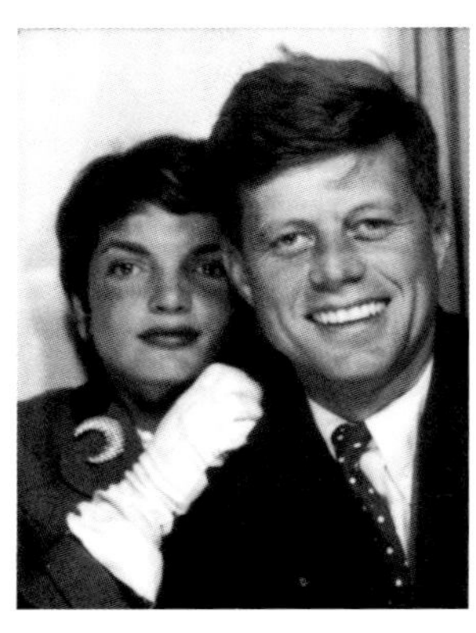

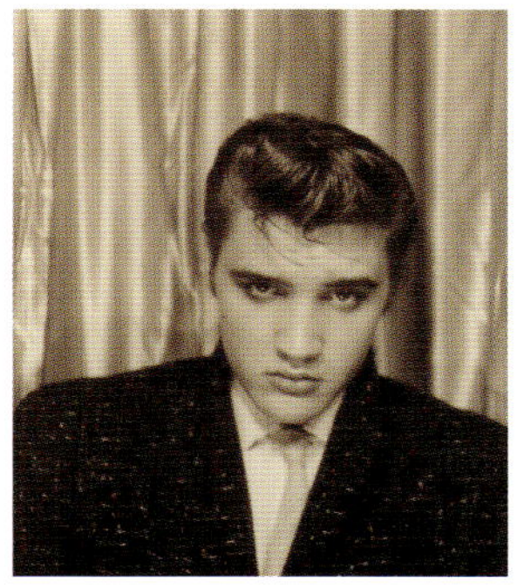

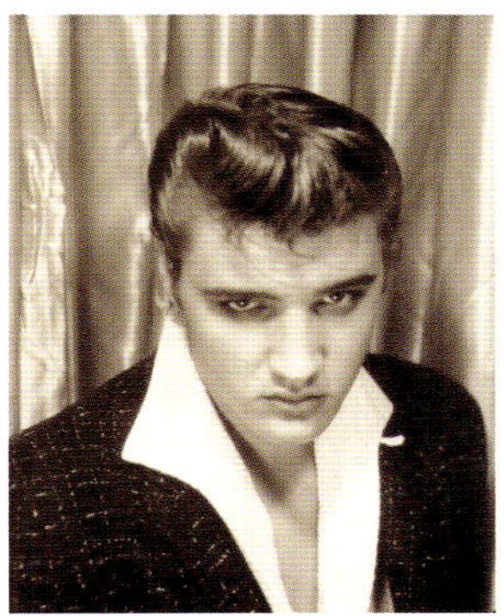

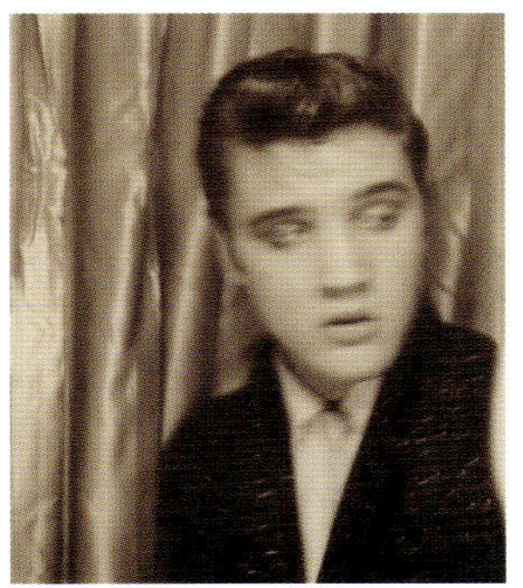

Elvis Presley
(1935–1977)
American singer
Photos taken in the fall of 1954 and the summer of 1955,
while Elvis was living at 2414 Lamar Avenue, Memphis.
Accompanied by the guitarist Scotty Moore and the bass player Bill Black, Elvis performed a concert
for the opening of a Katz drugstore in the Lamar-Airways Shopping Center on September 9, 1954.

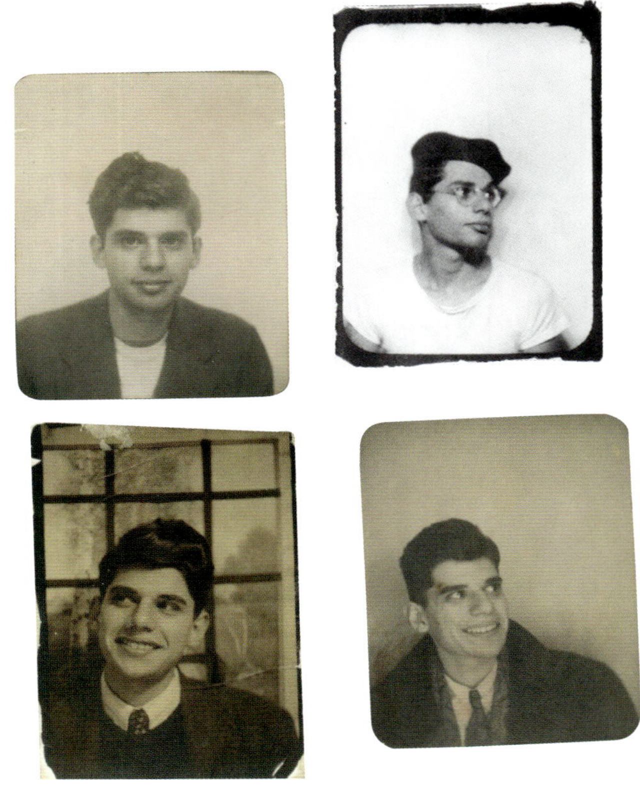

Allen Ginsberg
(1926–1997)
American poet
In 1993, with the publication of *Snapshot Poetics: Allen Ginsberg's Photographic Memoir of the Beat Era*, a little-known aspect of Ginsberg was rediscovered, along with the interest that the author of *Howl* and *Kaddish* felt for photography. Between 1953 and the beginning of the sixties, equipped with a Kodak Retina camera that he bought for thirteen dollars, Ginsberg did a number of black-and-white portraits of the main members of the Beat Generation: Jack Kerouac, William S. Burroughs, Gregory Corso.... After an interruption of more than twenty years, he resumed taking pictures in 1984 and established ties with certain photographers, including Berenice Abbott and Robert Frank.

Photobooth snap done in August 1945, in Sheepshead Bay, Brooklyn. Temporarily suspended from Columbia University, Ginsberg entered a six-week training course for the Merchant Marine.

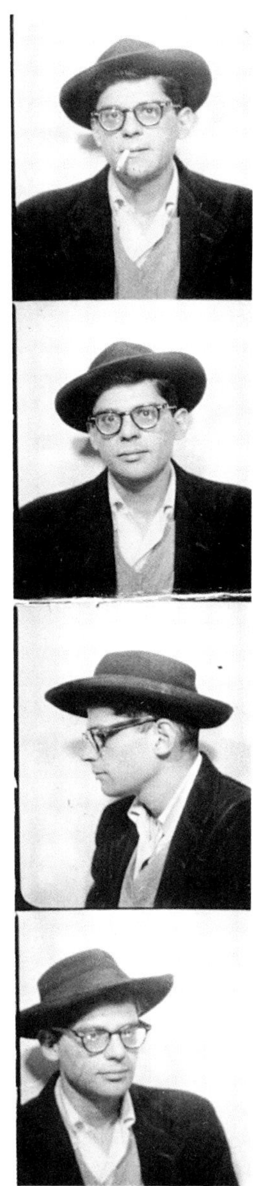

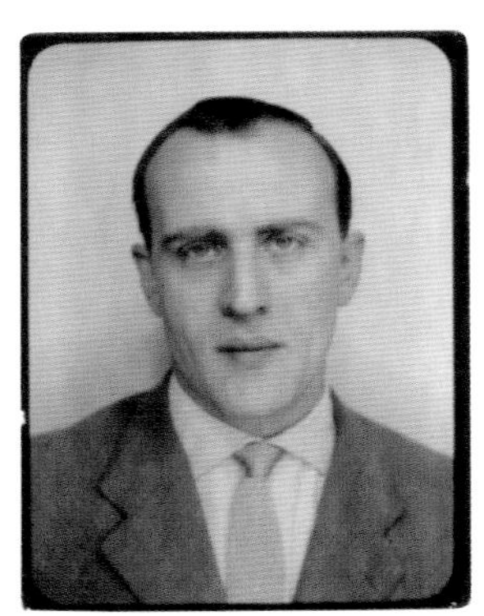

Boris Vian
(1920–1959)
French author

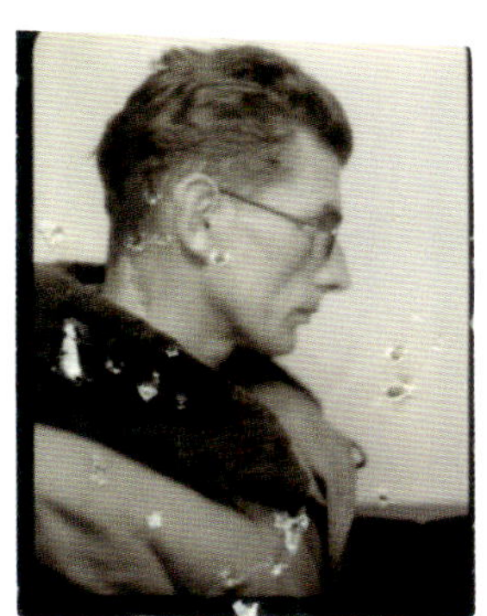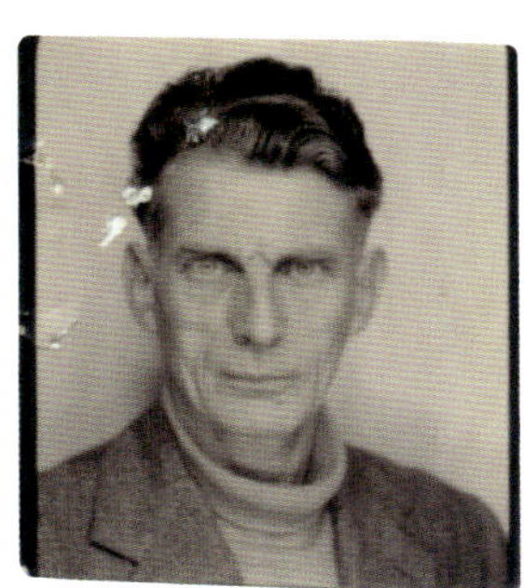

Samuel Beckett
(1906–1989)
Irish author

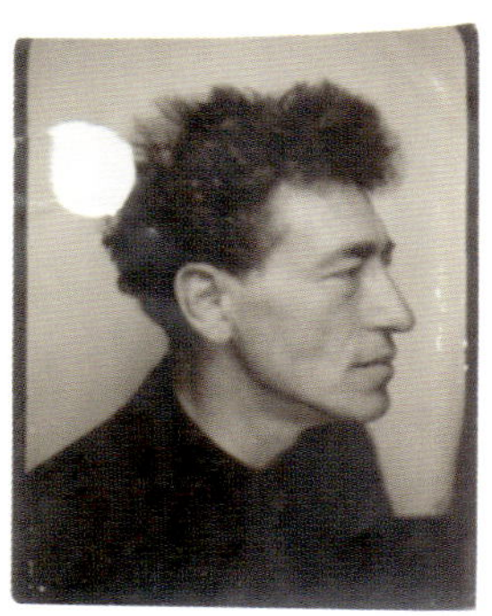

Alberto Giacometti
(1901–1966)
Swiss sculptor and painter

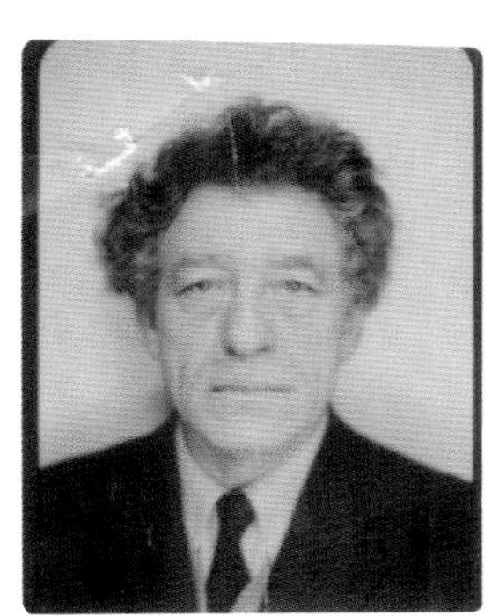

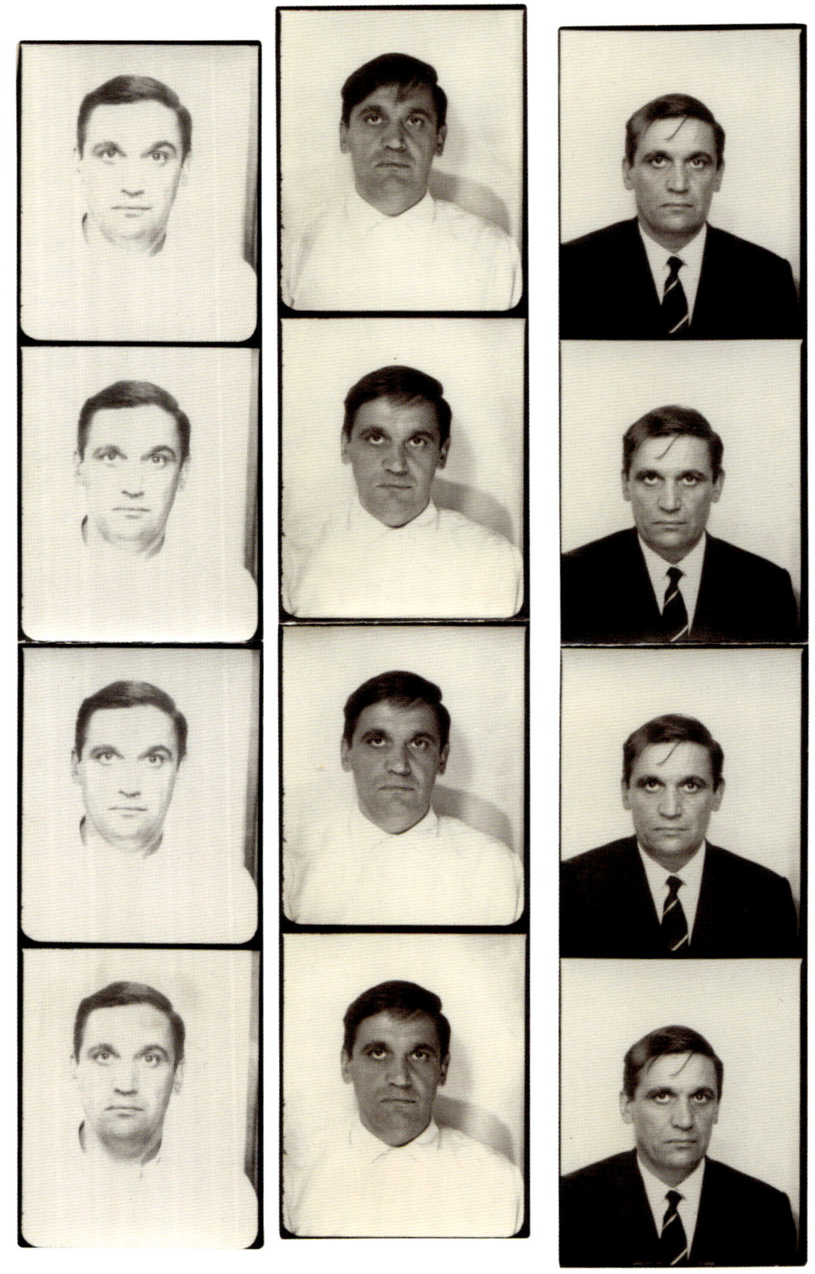

Maurice Pialat
(1925–2003)
French filmmaker, winner of the Palme d'Or in 1987

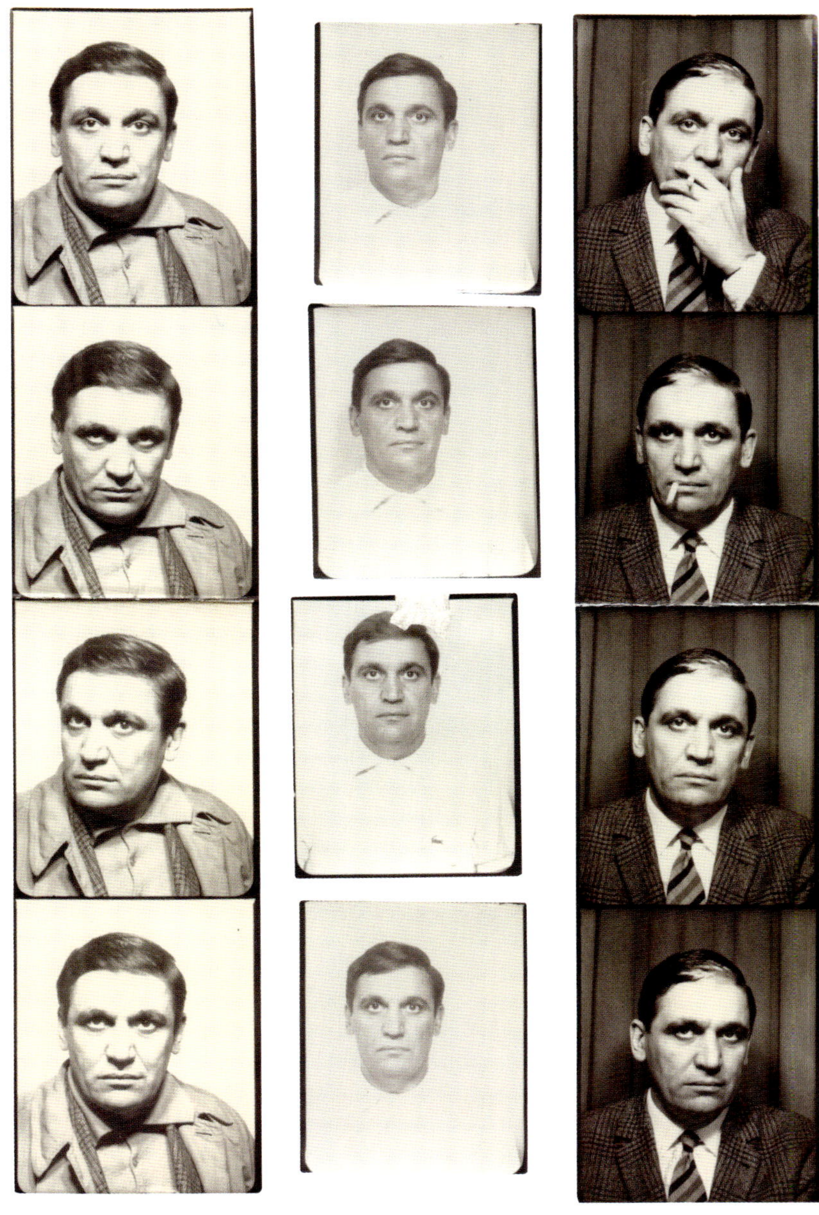

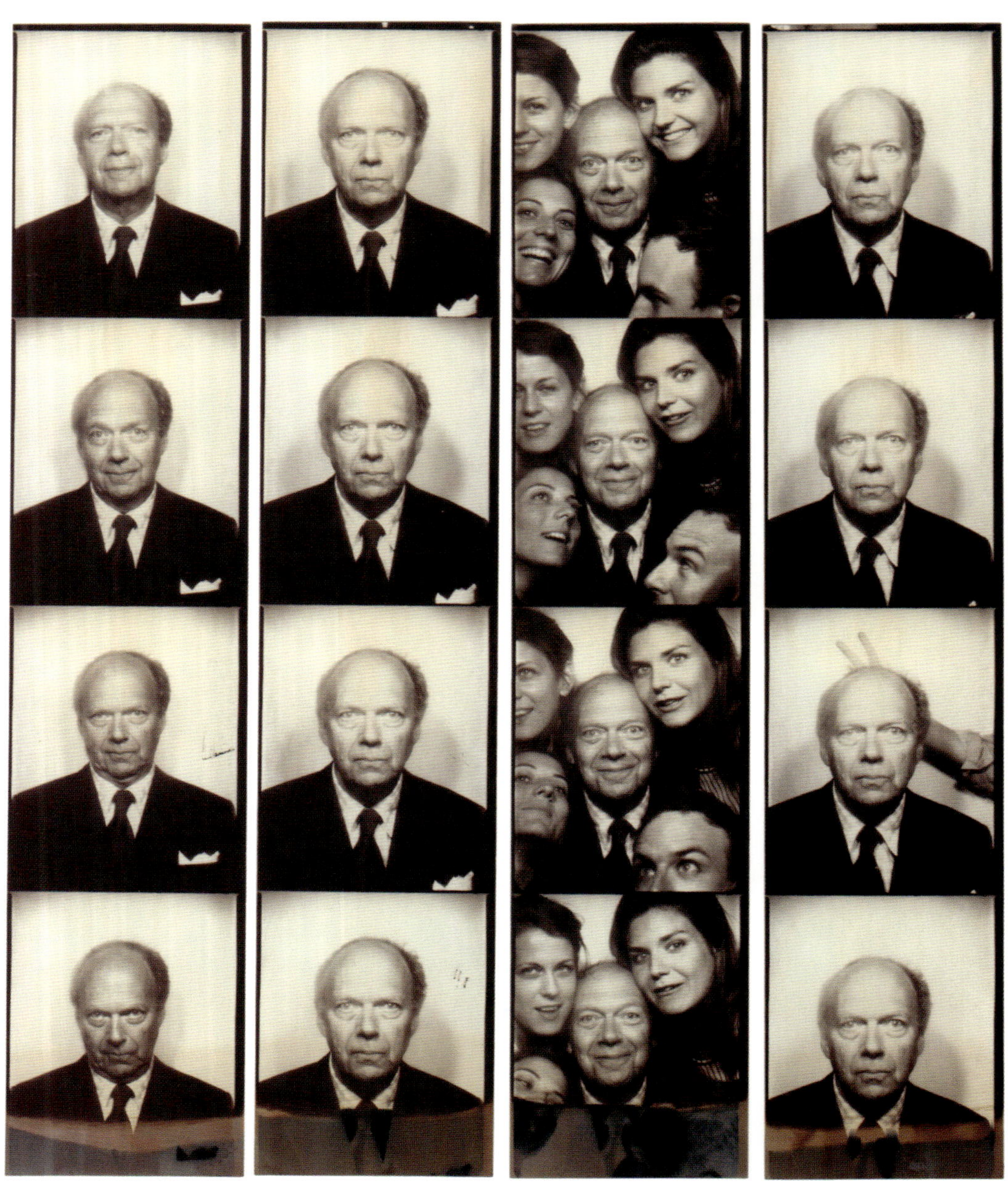

Frederick Seidel
(1936–)
American poet
Photos taken in the summer of 2003 in a photobooth in the
Lakeside Lounge on Avenue B in Manhattan, New York.
The photobooth portrait at the bottom right was used as the cover for a collection
of poems by Frederick Seidel, *Ooga-Booga* (published in 2006).

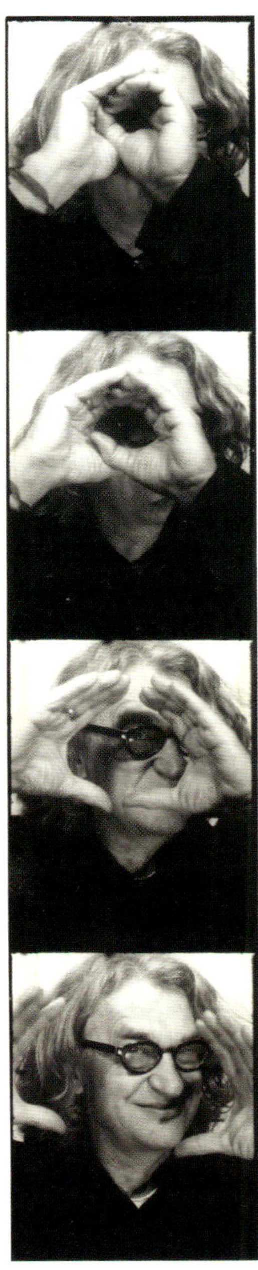

Wim Wenders
(1945–)
German director, producer, and photographer

ACKNOWLEDGMENTS

Sylvie, Léa & Thelma
Nathalie Bec
Carole Fossatti
Emma Giuliani
Francine Ravel
Sophie Postollec
Agnès Poirson
Delphine Piotraut, Bruno Goumi, Société Photomaton
Mrs. Aube Breton
Mrs. Miriam Gilou Cendrars
Mrs. Monique Antelme
Mr. Guy Dotremont
Jean Marie Queneau
Nicolas Topor
Jean-Pierre Godeaut
Patrick Roggiers
Sandrine Mons, galerie d'Art moderne et contemporain, Nice
Galerie Bernard Dudoignon, Paris
Dominique Bert, Fabienne Pejout, Galerie Bert, Paris
Séverine Berti, Drouot, Press Service
Laurence Dussart, Piasa
Pascal Fulacher, Curator, Musée des Lettres et Manuscrits, Paris
Gregory Auda and Malick Ben Miloud, Musée de la Préfecture de Police de Paris
Marie-Dominique Nobécourt-Mutarelli, Bibliothèque Littéraire Jacques Doucet
Mélina Reynaud, Service IMEC Images, Abbaye d'Ardenne
Marjorie Orth and Jean-Pierre Jeunet, Tapioca Films
Jean-Michel Ribes, Virginie Ferrere, Théâtre du Rond Point
Éric Legendre, History Department, Gallimard Picture Library
Sylvie Pialat, Christine Hamon, Les Films du Worso
Aleth Stroebel, Éditions Les Arènes
Michel Folco
Anja Schneider
Elisabeth Stuermer, Münchner Stadtmuseum.
Dr. Ulrich Pohlmann, Münchner Stadtmuseum.
Patricia Sustrac, Association des amis de Max Jacob
Michèle Kastner, Éditions Benoît Jacob
Fabienne Pejout
Virgine Apiou
Nicolas and Françoise Monterrat

CITATIONS AND REFERENCES

American Photobooth, Nakki Goranin, New York: W.W. Norton & Co, 2008.

André Breton, l'amour-folie, Georges Sebbag, ed., Paris: Jean-Michel Place, 2004.

Andy Warhol: Entretiens 1962–1987, Paris: Grasset, 2006.

La Chambre Claire: Note sur la photographie, Roland Barthes, Paris: Gallimard/Seuil/Cahiers du cinéma, 1980. (English edition: *Camera Lucida: Reflections on Photography*, Roland Barthes; translated by Richard Howard, New York: Hill and Wang, 1981.)

Les Conversations Secrètes des Français sous l'Occupation, Antoine Lefébure, Paris: Plon, 1993.

Description des machines et Procédés. Brevets d'invention, Ministère du Commerce et de l'Industrie, Paris: Imprimerie nationale, 1891.

Dictionnaire Mondial de la photographie, Paris: Larousse, 2001.

Identitées: de Desdéri au Photomaton, (exhibition catalog, Paris, Palais de Tokyo, December 18, 1985–February 24, 1986), Michel Frizot, Serge July, Christian Phéline, and Jean Sagne, Paris: Centre nationale de la photographie-Éditions du Chêne, 1985.

Interviews with Francis Bacon, David Sylvester, London: Thames and Hudson, 1975.

An Introspective, Al Hansen, Cologne: Kölnisches Stadtmuseum, 1996.

Je Ne Suis Pas Photographe…, collective, "Photo Poche," Arles: Actes Sud, 2006.

Magritte et la photographie, Patrick Roegiers, Antwerp: Ludion, 2005.

Max Jacob and "Les Feux de Paris," unpublished letters from Max Jacob to Jean Fraysse, correspondence presented by Neal Oxenhaendler, Berkeley/Los Angeles: University of California Press, 1964. *University of California Publications in Modern Philology*, vol. 35 no. 4, pp. 221–308; correspondence in French, p. 259.

Modern Mechanics and Inventions, November 1928.

La Photographie et L'Inconscient Technologique, Franco Vaccari, Chamalieres (France): Créatis, 1981.

La Subversion des Images, exhibition catalog, Paris: Centre Pompidou, 2009.

Sites

www.photobooth.net

www.peopleinphotobooth.it

Art Direction and Layout: S A J E
Photo Research: Francine Ravel
Proofreading: Renaud Bezombes

ENGLISH-LANGUAGE EDITION
Project Manager: Aiah Rachel Wieder
Designer: Shawn Dahl
Production Managers: Jacquie Poirier and Erin Vandeveer

Cataloging-in-Publication Data has been applied for and may be
obtained from the Library of Congress.
ISBN: 978-0-8109-9611-3

© 2010 Éditions de La Martinière, an imprint of La Martinière
Groupe, Paris
English translation copyright © 2010 ABRAMS

Simultaneously published in French under the title
Photomaton in 2010 by Éditions de La Martinière, an imprint
of La Martinière Groupe, Paris
Published in 2010 by Abrams, an imprint of ABRAMS. All rights
reserved. No portion of this book may be reproduced, stored in
a retrieval system, or transmitted in any form or by any means,
mechanical, electronic, photocopying, recording, or otherwise,
without written permission from the publisher.

Printed and bound in China
10 9 8 7 6 5 4 3 2 1

Abrams books are available at special discounts when
purchased in quantity for premiums and promotions as well
as fundraising or educational use. Special editions can also be
created to specification. For details, contact specialmarkets@
abramsbooks.com or the address below.

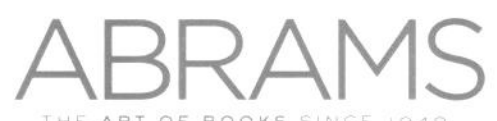

115 West 18th Street
New York, NY 10011
www.abramsbooks.com